M000006934

STILL STA...

How I Overcame Guilt, Shame, Hopelessness,
Devastating Loss & Paralyzing Fear

Valerie Silveira

STILL STANDING

How I Overcame Guilt, Shame, Hopelessness, Devastating Loss, and Paralyzing Fear

Published by: The Still Standing Group

ISBN 978-1-7341675-2-8

Cover Art by: Svetlana Dragicevic

Cover Design by: Raphi Eisenberg

For the 3 Loves of My Life

Rich, not one word would have been shared with the world had it not been for your unconditional love and support. When you said, "for better or for worse," you really meant it. Thank you for believing in me and for being the best husband and friend.

Sean, you were my first reason for standing, and I will keep standing for you. Thank you for never doubting me or my mission. Witnessing you work to become a better man, to find your way to forgiveness, is the best gift I could ever receive.

Jamie, we are doing it, girl! It may look far different from the vantage point of an angel, and certainly not what either one of us imagined, but I feel you standing with me every day. Without your journey, this mission would not exist. If I had to do it all over again knowing how it all would go, I would do it in a heartbeat. Being your mom is one of my life's highest honors.

I am blessed to call you my family, and I love each of you more than I could put into words.

Acknowledgements

A heart full of gratitude goes out to you, Sarah Earle, for hanging with me through several iterations of this book. I am grateful for your attention to detail, and valuable perspectives. I cannot thank you enough for your time, and your heart for this message.

Thank you, Svetlana Dragicevic. Once again, you have taken my vision, and somehow put it onto paper. The wings are stunning.

Raphi Eisenberg, I am grateful for your support and belief in me and my mission over the years. For this book, your expertise brought the book cover, and journal covers, to life.

As always, a huge thank you to you, Rich Silveira, for your support, through the long process of putting pen to paper, and winding up with a published book.

To the courageous women and men who have allowed me to join them on their journey – thank you. Your stories inspire me to keep standing and fill me with hope that anything is possible. I am honored and humbled to be standing with you.

Valerie is an outstanding inspirational leader and teacher, who uses her pain to bring hope to others. She is relatable, and draws people in with her honesty, humor, and transparency. I am impressed by Valerie's comprehensive program, and how she uses her story, and The 9 Actions to help people develop hope, and commence rebuilding the lives they desire and deserve!

~ Dr. Simone Ravicz, PhD, Licensed Clinical Psychologist
Certified Clinical Trauma Professional

Valerie's newest book, "Still Standing," her most versatile to date, contains the tools and resources to make overcoming any challenge both practical and possible! Are you faced with a difficult diagnosis, broken relationship, harrowing addiction, or financial hardship? Are you struggling with the stress of compounding frustrations that seem hopeless to overcome? Join thousands who are making meaning from the madness and enjoying triumph over tribulations; I did, and you can too!

Sarah Earle, Secondary Assistant Principal, Charleston, S.C.

From the moment I met Valerie, I knew she was different, not just because she is a fiery redhead with a fun personality, but because when you meet her, you can't see or feel the pain she has walked through. During our time working together, she helped me to work through some past pain that I fully ignored. She helped me put current day stress in perspective, with deeper insight as to why I may be stuck in certain areas. The greatest blessing about Valerie giving me advice and insight, is her zero-tolerance stance on living with a victim mindset. So many people are not living their best lives because they feel like they are victims of their circumstances, including me. I realized that I was holding onto anger and other feelings that really weren't serving me. I'm in the process of forgiving and setting some clear boundaries in my world that have never existed before. I feel like I can survive anything with the right tools and a sisterhood of support if any other challenges come my way.

Kalen Arreola, Veteran, CPT, US ARMY,
CEO of Kalen Marie Consulting, Brand Strategist
Deputy Public Affairs Officer, US Navy

The 9 Actions That Saved My Life

Life is tough. You may not expect a statement such as that from a motivational speaker and courage coach. However, it is the truth. Life is tough, but it's also beautiful, magical, and filled with possibilities.

We all have stories, and they are essential to share, or at least parts of them. If we hide the pain, it keeps us trapped in victimhood, or covered in shame. Having the courage to share your story helps people not to feel alone. Overcoming hardship or heartbreak, gives them hope they can do the same.

During my journey through life, with all of its ups and downs, I have learned a great deal. After all hell broke loose, I had two choices. Either I would continue down the path of self-destruction, or I would stand up and fight. I chose to fight.

As I look back on my journey thus far, the experiences that come together as my life story, I realize **The 9 Actions** were in the process of being developed long before I put them together and gave them a name. In one way or another, I have used the actions at various points in my life. Had I used them all at the same time, and consistently, I can only imagine where I would be today, but I didn't. No matter, I am Still Standing.

The 9 Actions are not linear, nor do they come with a simple, step by step process. Life is complicated, and each person's experiences, personality, and realities are unique. What will work well for one person might need to be slightly different for the next.

The goal is for you to learn about the actions, and then begin applying them to *your* journey. You have experiences that give you a unique viewpoint, allowing you to use the actions in ways that work best for you.

A few things can be remedied with a quick fix, but not many. It is doubtful whatever brought you to this book could be fixed in a hurry. If you are looking for a quick fix, I am not your girl. Whatever you are wanting, or needing - will take time. The journey to courage is a marathon, not a sprint.

The saying goes, "it all starts with our thinking." I agree wholeheartedly with this fact. However, if you don't turn positive thoughts into decisive action, nothing will change.

The 9 Actions were not developed after a moment of clarity in which I figured out the meaning of life. They were created out of desperation. Initially, it was simply about survival. Next, the hope that I could be happy, even on occasion. It turned out; these actions gave me my life back. Not the life I had known, but a new one, where I found unwavering courage, more faith than I had thought possible, and collateral beauty amongst the collateral damage.

If they could work for me in overcoming my many challenges and losses, then I knew they could work for anyone. Some aspects of **The 9 Actions** will be familiar. No doubt, you have heard the concept of changing your attitude, wearing spiritual armor, or making a difference. What is *unique* is the combining of these specific actions, the synergy between them, and the perspectives presented. **The 9 Actions** are relatable and approachable. They are practical actions with spiritual principles. Use them to take down a Beast you are wrestling with, to be happier, or to move your life to a whole new level. (More about Beasts later).

They are the very same actions countless people are using to reclaim their lives, overcome grief, step away from chaos, build confidence, stand up to fear, find their faith, rebuild relationships, and embrace their purpose.

Become familiar with **The 9 Actions** and start using them. It is possible you are already utilizing one or more of the actions, without realizing it, so you may have a head start. There will be times, you will use one or two for a particular situation, but the most valuable approach is to work on implementing all of them into your daily life, so they become second nature.

I chose to represent **The 9 Actions** with a puzzle heart and wings, for three specific purposes – first, a puzzle which is a powerful visual, representing the synergistic nature of the actions. Next, the heart holds the actions, since most of the situations that are the most challenging involve the heart, and it is the heart that helps to put the pieces back together. Lastly, wings are a reminder that life is full of possibilities, but the only way you will know how high you can soar is if you find the courage to spread your wings and fly.

The 9 Actions

1. **Decide to Stand Up & Fight.** Decide that you are all in and that you will stay in the ring until the final round. Make an initial decision, then continue making choices in support of your initial decision. Each time you get knocked down, decide to stand again.

2. **Get On Your Spiritual Armor.** Whatever your spiritual armor looks like, get it on. Don't just pray, and then wait for God to act; take consistent actions that align with your prayers.

3. **Put On Your Oxygen Mask.** Give yourself permission to matter. There is only one You, and you get only once chance at this thing we call "life." To be there for someone else, you first have to be there for yourself.

4. **Build Your Circle of Strength.** The Circle of Strength is all about your relationships. Spend time analyzing and understanding the different sections that make up the Circle of Strength, and then consider where people belong. Find the courage to strengthen certain relationships, make some changes, and possibly to remove some people altogether.

5. **Change Your Attitude.** Your attitude developed over time and experience, and it has become a habit. Habits are hard to break,

but you can do it with consistent effort. Attitude is one of the few things you can control 24/7, so take control of your attitude.

6. **Adjust Your Focus.** It's easy to get out of focus when life is going sideways. In this day of social media and *reality* television, we find ourselves obsessing over other people's lives, or at least, our perception of them. As with your attitude, focus is a habit you can kick. The wrong focus keeps us trapped as victims, while the right focus can change our perspective in a heartbeat.

7. **Stop Being a Control Freak.** Focusing on what you can control (basically, what you think, say, or do), will put you in a position to let go of what you cannot control. Learn to use the "F" word every chance you get, and let go of judgment. When you stop trying to control so many things, your life will be more *in control* than ever.

8. **Stand <u>On</u> Your Story.** Shed the shame and guilt, and use your experiences as stepping stones to climb higher. Be committed to being the best version of yourself, standing with humble confidence, knowing you are valuable.

9. **Make Meaning From the Madness**. You don't have to be Mother Teresa to make a difference, so don't hold back. No matter where you stand today, someone needs what you have

to offer. You are creating a legacy right now, your imprint on the world, so be mindful of the one you are leaving behind.

Had I not decided to stand, a decision that altered the course of my life, I cringe to think where I would be today. I stumbled around, grasping at anything that might help me, but you don't have to do that. Use **The 9 Actions** to stand up in the middle of the storm, keep standing after it subsides, and to remain standing, no matter what the future holds.

Download a copy of **The 9 Actions** at www.the9actions.com

About Beasts

You will hear me refer to Beasts quite often. They show up in many forms, including guilt, shame, low self-worth, chaos, heartbreak, constant grief, and fear. Some arrive as the result of an alcoholic or addict in the family, abuse, betrayal, abandonment, an accident or illness, death, loss of self-worth, or something else. A Beast is a situation, person, attitude, or circumstance that has left you lost, defeated, frustrated, depressed, angry, hopeless, guilty, ashamed, cynical, negative, helpless or living in paralyzing fear. Many Beasts are a combination of two or more of life's challenges.

Our Beasts remind us of the past, keep us from living in the present, and fearful of the future. Lots of things are Beasts, and most people are living with at least one. They will do whatever it takes to keep us living in these various states, or regrettably, in all of them.

While our Beasts only have a few tricks up their sleeves, they are all carefully chosen for each of us. What we value most will be threatened. Our gifts and talents questioned. The more we try to accomplish something, the harder our Beasts work to derail us.

I have had many Beasts to deal with, but the one that had me down on the mat, flat on my back, was my Codependent Enabler Beast. He whispered in my ear and screamed in my face what a terrible mother I was, convincing me my best days were behind me and that I no longer had a purpose. While he merely made the suggestions, I came into full agreement with my Beast.

That was until a pivotal moment. It was my lowest point, and yet it was the catalyst for my decision to reclaim my life. It was a decision to stop believing the lies of the Beast. The day you stop agreeing with *your* Beast, is the day your life will start to change for the better.

My Journey to Courage

It's Not How You Start

My life didn't start on a high note, but I have learned that no matter how it started, I could decide how I finished. Some events occurred without my choice, and others had much to do with my decisions. Life is messy, and I have chosen to reveal some of the messiness of mine to help you find hope. I want you to believe that you can overcome anything. If not for my journey, as painful as some of it has been, I would not be the warrior I am today.

Like many people, my childhood was full of challenges. My mom had her first child at seventeen, and by the time she was twenty, she had three children. A couple of years later, she was a single mother, and my father was not super interested in parenthood, nor paying regular child support.

I can only imagine how disappointed my mom was in those early years, realizing she made a huge mistake, and now she had three kids to raise, with little financial or emotional support. Gone were the straight 'A' student's dreams of college scholarships, or much else a little girl might dream about for her future.

She was sad much of my early years, and I was worried. I worried about a lot of things in my young life. I could read the newspaper when I was five years old, but my only recollection was a headline about China threatening to bomb the United States. I spent many nights alone in my room worried, and scared.

I grew up in the Seattle area of the Pacific Northwest, where Boeing was pretty much the only game in town. It was before Microsoft changed the world and made its mark on the Seattle area (which we fondly refer to as The Puget Sound area since that's the body of water where Seattle and surrounding areas reside). The entire Puget Sound area felt every Boeing upswing and downturn. During one recession, I recall a billboard that read, "Will the last person leaving Seattle – turn out the lights."

Times were tough, but mom did her best. She worked many jobs, including a night shift on the kill floor of a meatpacking plant several miles away from where we lived. I have a hard time picturing my neat-freak mom standing in blood that came up to the tops of her shoes, but she did what she could to take care of her children.

During her meatpacking plant stint, mom brought her ex-sister-in-law to live with us, along with her daughter, my young cousin. It wasn't easy to find trustworthy care for three children, at night, so it was a workable solution. It also allowed my aunt to get away from an abusive husband.

The problem was – the husband knew where we lived. One time he put sugar in the gas tank of our car, which was barely limping along as it were. Other times he would come to our house drunk and mad. One night while mom was at work, he broke into our home and abused my aunt, while four terrified kids hid in my brothers' bedroom closet. Another time, he made the mistake of showing up while my mom was at home, and she chased him down the road with a butcher knife until the police arrived. That may seem crazy, and it was, but I always admired my mom for being brave enough to do something crazy to protect her family.

****

Mom established rules and led by example. We had chores at an early age, and we were expected to make good grades in school. In the fifth grade, my brother, Darryl, came home with a 'D' in a class, and after that, I knew I would never bring home a report card with that letter on it!

We were expected to be polite, respectful, and clean. Sometimes while mom was doing chores, I would be reminded,

"Just because you're poor doesn't mean you have to be dirty. How much does a can of Comet cost?"

I believe the answer was *ninety-nine cents.*

She was a strict disciplinarian, but I would come to appreciate how difficult it was for mom to fill both parenting roles. So many vital qualities were instilled in my brothers and me in our young lives, that I wouldn't trade for any amount of leniency.

****

Money was very tight, so my mom went without much to care for us. She had significant dental problems but chose to put our needs first, leaving her with lifelong dental issues.

The only snacks in our house were big tubs of vanilla ice cream and popcorn. I longed for real snacks like chips, or Ding Dongs. One time I was at a friend's and spotted a bag of potato chips in her cupboard. After about an eternity, she finally offered me some. I tried not to drool as she opened the bag, and then carefully placed three, count 'em, three chips on a paper towel! I stared down at my three chips, and while I appreciated them, I could have eaten the entire bag. The lack of snacks explains my willingness to skip junior high school, to sneak over to my friend Laura's with her, and enjoy the coveted Twinkies her mom kept in a cookie jar.

One winter night, we had run out of heating oil. Mom received her paycheck that day, and oil was going to be delivered the next, but it was cold in the house. So, she chopped up our coffee table and burned

14

it in the fireplace, only to discover the cheap partial wood table provided more smoke than heat.

While between jobs, my mom received one welfare check. As soon as she got her first paycheck, she marched directly to the welfare office and tried to repay the assistance. Of course, they looked at her as if she had lost her mind. Who attempts to pay back government assistance? Mom was just trying to do the right thing, but I was watching; and learning.

****

In those days, we had a few play clothes and even fewer school clothes, which doubled as dress clothes. When we were to go with our dad, we eagerly changed into our school clothes and sat on the couch, looking out the window in anticipation of his arrival. Many times, he didn't show up, and the disappointment was overwhelming. My dad was handsome, fun, and told tall tales. I loved him and hung on his every word, wishing I was daddy's little girl, like my friend Kathy was to her father.

Dad came from a family of thirteen children. They were from Arkansas, and my grandfather, whom everyone called "Big D" was a big man (at least he seemed big to me, and had "Big" in his name). He wore a Stetson cowboy hat and a belt buckle the size of a salad plate.

Everything seemed big about Grandpa Big D, including his smile and the twinkle in his eye. I never knew my grandmother on my dad's side as she died before I was born. Grandpa Big D worked hard and tried to finish raising the younger children and deal with some of the older ones still living at home. He was a loving and gentle soul who played the fiddle. It was hit and miss seeing my dad, so spending time with my Grandpa Big D was rare. The few times I did, I loved hearing his stories, and listening to him play the fiddle. While he was somewhat of a stranger, I knew he loved me.

****

My grandparents on my mom's side were a saving grace in my childhood. Grandpa was hilarious and fun, and Nana made bubble baths and gave the best back scratches.

I remember more than once, Grandpa taking me to the bakery to buy the six maple bars (my favorite) Nana had requested. She was a small woman without an ounce of fat on her, but to her credit, she was very disciplined. Grandpa, on the other hand, not so much. Plus, he was big-boned, like me. When we returned from the bakery, Nana would set one donut on each of two plates for Grandpa and me. Since neither one of us tore into those maple bars, I wonder if she ever suspected that Grandpa had purchased a dozen of those tasty treats, and we each ate three of them on the way home.

Grandpa was a surrogate father in many ways, driving my brothers to hockey practice at the crack of dawn, or before. His face is the one I remember seeing first after my tonsillectomy. He taught us to play dominoes and throw darts. Since we couldn't afford gymnastics class, he made me a floor exercise mat, and balance beam.

Grandpa had a special place in the hearts of all three of his grandchildren. He was the best man at my brother, Darryl's wedding, and Brad was lucky enough to be named after Grandpa - Bradley Harold. I was a bit envious, but I doubt Valerie Harold was ever in the running.

He worked at the meatpacking plant as well, but Grandpa was in purchasing, so his benefits included free hotdogs, and we ate a ton of them in those days. Too bad Grandpa didn't have a job at the *filet mignon* meatpacking plant. I am not a fan of hotdogs to this day, or the macaroni and cheese in the blue box that were a life-saver at three for a dollar.

At the beginning of each school year, Grandpa took us to buy shoes and a winter coat. He never used a credit card in favor of peeling off twenty-dollar bills from his money clip. I thought my Grandpa was rich, and one time I told him so. He laughed and told me the real story of the fat money clip. Grandpa had grown up poor in a large family in

Winnipeg, Manitoba, Canada, and he vowed that when he finally had some money, he would keep it in his pocket.

****

I am the middle child and am twenty months younger than Darryl and seventeen months older than Brad. I was particularly close to Brad growing up. So close were we that he didn't speak until he was around two and a half. I always knew what he needed, and would talk for him. It could have been he was secretly speaking to me, but more likely, we didn't need words to communicate. When Brad finally spoke, it was a full sentence.

When I was nine, and Brad only eight, he went to live with our Dad in Yakima. That is in Eastern Washington, on the other side of the Cascade mountains from the Puget Sound area, which back then, was like moving to Mars. At the end of the school year, we loaded Brad and his belongings, me, Darryl, and our German Shephard, Czar, into my dad's car and headed to Yakima for the summer. My mom stood on the porch sobbing as we left. It helped that I spent the summer with Brad, but my life was never the same after he moved. My dad took good care of Brad, for which I am grateful, but back then, I was merely sad.

****

We had a brown, leather photo album, which was one of our most treasured possessions. It had a big cutout on the front cover, where you could prominently display a picture. The one in our album was a professional shot of an adorable little boy, wearing chinos and a sweater. Although the photo was black and white, I knew his hair was jet-black, because he was my dad's son from his first wife, and he looked just like him. While he is a few years older than I am, as the years went by, Donny remained frozen in time – a four-year-old in the family photo album, a brother I had never met. At age twelve, I finally met my eighteen-year-old brother, and I thought he was the coolest guy ever. I felt bad for Donny, spending years without his father, assuming the three kids who replaced him were living it up with the *father of the year*.

Spending time with my dad was sporadic at best, but when he moved to Yakima, we only saw him once or twice a year, over school breaks or some summer vacations. We would make the trip via Greyhound bus, across the mountains. Back in those days, there was no freeway from the interstate into the Yakima Valley, so we traveled that stretch on a narrow, winding, two-lane highway, with a steep drop on one side of the road. I held my breath as we went around each turn, praying the bus didn't careen off the road, plummeting us to certain death.

****

To say my brother Darryl and I didn't get along well, was an understatement. Two fiery redheads were not a great mix. One day, we were fighting about something, and we had just taken chicken pot pies out of the oven. He stuck a fork into his pie, until it was nice and hot, and *branded* my arm with it. I retaliated by chucking mine at him, but he was too quick. The pie hit the wall and left a streak of chicken, carrot, and pea filling, as the container slid to the ground. I left the whole mess there, counting down the time until mom would be home, and my brother would be in big trouble. Of course, she didn't see it my way when she walked in to find chicken pot pie all over the wall and the floor.

Part of our relationship issues probably had to do with the fact that Darryl had to grow up fast; to be the man of the house at an early age. On more than one occasion, I remember Darryl being ready to fend off danger, as he came flying into a room, hockey stick in hand. Thankfully, we are great friends now.

****

Mom vowed we would never live in an apartment because she wanted us to have a yard to play in. She delivered on that promise, but it came at the cost of moving every couple of years to the next safe place she could afford. I made friends quickly, but it seemed I finally fit in when we had to move again. Each time I got the news, I would cry myself to sleep.

The last house we lived in before my mom was remarried, backed up to a cemetery. It was worn down and filthy, but with the help of my Grandparents, and my soon to be stepdad, we scrubbed, tore up carpeting, painted, and made it home for the next two years. A chain-link fence was the only thing separating our yard from the cemetery. I had a few nightmares about that cemetery but mainly tried to pretend it wasn't there.

The one good thing about the cemetery house was that I had a good-sized room. I hung up sheets in one corner, simulating a separate room that I turned into a library. I even had a book checkout system, although I don't recall one book ever being loaned out from my *library*.

I would also have my friends play "school" with me, and of course, I was the teacher. I am sure they were thrilled to be playing school on the weekends, but I loved it. I wanted to be a teacher when I grew up. I did not become one in the traditional sense, but a teacher nonetheless.

****

Karen and her family lived across the street from me, and she was a year older, which to an eleven-year-old elementary schooler, hanging out with a junior high kid is pretty cool. Karen's parents spent most of their time at a local tavern, and their house was very different from mine. It was filthy and filled with cigarette smoke. I was at Karen's one night when her mom fell asleep on the couch, with a lit cigarette burning in the ashtray on the coffee table. I was a bit shocked when Karen picked up the cigarette and took a puff. She handed it to me, and I, nervously, did the same. Considering the amount of coughing I did, her mom, who never opened her eyes, was more likely passed out than sleeping. That began my secret life of smoking, which didn't last long.

While I thought it was cool to be smoking (the cigarettes Karen stole from her mom), I didn't care for the smoke in my lungs. What sealed the smoking deal was the day I asked my Grandpa when he was going to quit smoking cigars, to which he replied,

"When you stop smoking cigarettes."

By the time I stopped cigarettes, Karen's older brother had introduced me to marijuana, something I wish my Grandpa had known about, because I probably would have quit that for him, too.

****

The first decade or so of my life was full of uncertainty and fear. It was also chock-full of opportunities to use my courage muscles. I recall longing for a home with two loving parents. I couldn't get enough of television shows that depicted near-perfect families. I vowed one day, I would have a family, like those I had been watching. Somehow, someway, my life would matter. I was going to do something significant with my life. What that big something would be – I had no idea.

From Hot Dogs to "Near-Stardom"

My mom married Chips when I was twelve years old. He was the junior hockey coach in our area, and that was a big deal. Chips was the nickname he acquired when he was a professional hockey player, and it stuck. Mom's relationship with Chips propelled us to near-stardom in our little hockey world.

At the time we met him, Chips was a linesman (like a referee for you non-hockey fans) for the Seattle Totems WHL hockey team, the last team he played on before retiring from professional hockey. Mom, Darryl, and I attended a few games, and we cheered when they announced Chips' name, resulting in some strange looks from the other fans since NOBODY cheers for the officials in hockey.

With my new dad came an additional brother, Rod, and finally, what I had always hoped for, a sister, Karen. They were a few years older, so it took some time to get to know one another, but we bonded like blood, and have been standing as a family ever since. I give my mom credit for working hard to make us into a real family.

Life was on the upswing after mom married Chips. His professional hockey career preceded the NHL expansion where the real money was, so he worked at Rainier Brewery for decades after his retirement from hockey. The brewery had a big red R on the top of the building, which stood very close to Interstate 5 in Seattle. He wasn't exactly raking in the bucks, but since the brewery had much to do with our improved financial situation, my mom taught us to put a hand over our hearts when we drove past the Big Red R.

We were definitely in better shape than we were pre-Chips, but funds were still minimal. Since Chips was the infamous junior hockey coach and Darryl played, we spent a great deal of time at the ice rink. I so wanted to be a gymnast, but there wasn't enough money for hockey *and* gymnastics. I was very disappointed, but hanging out at the rink with a bunch of boys was a close second to gymnastics.

****

As soon as I had my driver's license, I worked after school and full-time on school breaks and over the summers. My mom finally had enough money to have a little help around the house, so she hired me to do the weekly cleaning and grocery shopping. With my extra money, I bought my clothing, cars, insurance, and personal items. I also bought pot.

I drank beer, smoked pot, and had a great time partying, but I kept my act together. I was a responsible partier, I told myself. I was even in the honor society in high school, sitting in the photo with all the *good* kids.

I made a lot of mistakes as a teenager and probably shouldn't have lived through some of them. I drove my car into a tree in my neighborhood, but thankfully, the tree took the worst of it. I wrecked another car in Eastern Washington, leaving that one in a junkyard.

Two other accidents were as a passenger. At fifteen, my friend, Diane, and I took a ride back from the beach with our friend Mark and his girlfriend. We were on a windy four-lane road in his parents' car, and all was well until our friend swerved and hit the curb, then over-corrected, speeding across all four lanes, and launching us over the embankment, air born, until we came to rest in the parking lot of an apartment complex. The car we were in flattened the top of another vehicle, on our descent into the parking lot. All four of us walked away without as much as a scratch. I guess God wasn't quite finished with me yet.

The other time was in an open Jeep, four-wheeling in the woods when the driver hit a tree root, and the Jeep rolled down a steep hill, spilling everyone that wasn't buckled in, onto the forest floor, in amongst trees, roots, and rocks. Nobody, including yours truly, who had been tossed out, had more than a bump or a scratch.

Believe it or not, those years were some of my best, and I have many treasured memories. I may have made some foolish choices in those growing years, but I also learned a great deal about responsibility, friendship, and family. I learned to get back up every time I was down. I created an ability to focus on the positive and use humor to lighten the load. I was learning to overcome adversity. I was building courage.

Marriage, Motherhood & Other Stuff

When I was twenty years old, I made the brilliant decision to get married. I know – I should have known better! I could try to come up with a compelling reason, but I still have no idea. I knew it was a bad idea because my soon-to-be husband was far from ready for marriage. He had proven so during the months of our engagement. Unfortunately, the wedding train had left the station, and I allowed my ego to keep me from putting a stop to it. It would have served me well to listen to Chips. He was a quiet man, but he is the only one who tried to talk me out of getting married. With every step down the aisle, I had a sinking feeling in the pit of my stomach. I believe God was trying to warn me, but I kept putting one foot in front of the other, rather than risking the embarrassment of being a runaway bride. I was far from ready for marriage, too.

Only two months into my marriage, my husband cheated on me. It was a couple of weeks before Christmas, and I was heart-broken, staring at the carefully wrapped packages under our tree. I was embarrassed and humiliated, but didn't want to be a divorce statistic. Plus, I had become a Catholic like his family, and they frowned upon divorce in a big way. I stayed, but never fully trusted him after that, and he gave me plenty of reason not to trust him. There would be many instances of my husband not coming home for hours at night, or not at all. He is a good person but struggled with alcohol and drug addiction, something I would not fully understand until after our seven-year marriage ended.

One day I just stopped smoking pot, and any other crazy drug I had tried. It was easy for me to make decisions like that. When I decided to stop anything, I stopped. It was hard for me to understand how others couldn't do the same.

We bought our first house and worked hard to fix it up. Every inch of the place needed work, including the yard, which took two dumpsters full of yard waste, to clean up and landscape. We were both very hard-working, but our marriage was not stable. Still, we stuck it out and planned for our first child.

Jamie was my firstborn, and she was strong-willed, brilliant, and strong-willed. Wait, I already mentioned strong-willed, but it bears repeating. After all, I was reading Dr. Dobson's book, "The Strong-Willed Child," when Jamie was a one-year-old.

At the age of eleven months, Jamie started to walk. I worked part-time, and on my workdays, Jamie stayed with a close family friend, Teresa. Knowing Jamie was about to start walking, I jokingly told Teresa,

"If she walks at your house, push her down."

I got a call one day from Teresa informing me that it had happened - Jamie was walking. Thankfully, Teresa didn't push her down, but I was sad I had missed the big moment.

I arrived at Teresa's to discover she had not taken one or two steps, but that Jamie was walking. We tested her on linoleum, hardwood, carpeting, and with or without shoes. No matter what, Jamie could walk.

That night we attended a holiday party, and by the time we arrived, my parents and Teresa had delivered the big news. Everyone stopped and turned as we came in, waiting in anticipation of the Jamie walking show. Excitedly, I placed her on the ground and removed her coat and hat. She immediately plopped onto her bottom. I pulled her back up, and down she went again. After a few repeats and raised eyebrows, we let it go. Jamie didn't take another step for two weeks. From that moment forward, she did life her way.

I loved being a mom more than anything. The day Jamie was born was the best day of my life (until Sean was born two years later). It was the day I understood unconditional love. It was the day I first strapped on my Supermom Cape, one I figured would come in handy for life's bumps and bruises. I had no idea then, how worn out the cape would become.

My husband and I went through the motions of building a life together, but I knew something was not right. I loved Jamie and Sean in a way that could not be duplicated, but there should have been stronger feelings for my husband. I had forgiven him long ago for cheating, but I had never really forgotten. My trust level was very low, and we were drifting apart.

So, I gave him the news and bought a do-it-yourself divorce kit. I played junior lawyer, creating all of the documents, including the parenting plan.

We sat together, in a courtroom full of couples, duking it out over money or children, and vowed never to do that to our kids. When it was our turn, we stood in front of the judge. He flipped through the documents, looked up at me with a surprised look on his face, and asked,

"Did you do this yourself?"

"Yes, I did," I answered, not sure if I should have admitted it.

"Great job," he said, as he stamped our packet.

Much to the disapproval of my in-laws, and the Catholic church, at the age of twenty-seven, I was divorced. I was now a single mom of a three-year-old (Jamie) and a one-year-old (Sean).

Single Motherhood

The three of us set about creating our new life together. I did feel lonely at times, but for the most part, I loved my single-mom years. I worked very hard and was able to provide a safe, happy home for Jamie and Sean. My mom and Chips were terrific grandparents, and we spent a great deal of time together, and with extended family.

Shortly after my divorce, I started as an accountant for a public company (without a degree or much experience). After only a few months, the Controller was let go, and I accepted the Controller position. I was excited for the opportunity, and it meant a pay raise, but that night, as I sat looking at the Securities and Exchange Commission (SEC) manuals I brought home with me, I wondered what in the heck I was doing. Very quickly, I taught myself how to keep the accounting records to the strict SEC standards, file the required public company forms, and oversee an annual audit.

Because of that experience, one of the major accounting firms recommended me for another position with a new company that was going to be taken public. With a staff of three and a securities attorney, we did just that. It was an incredible experience that no college degree could have prepared me to go through.

After the company went public, we started to build our staff and decided to implement a psychological testing policy for new employees. The psychologist agreed to administer the test for me, gratis, and to go over it in detail.

I was impressed; the test nailed even the most complex parts of my personality. As the psychologist explained specific results, I would recall particular questions from the test that would have led to those conclusions.

When the psychologist came to one area on the graph, he made a statement I will never forget.

"You think people are a lot more honest than they are."

My mind was racing, recalling questions that may have led to that conclusion. One particular question popped into my head - a scenario was presented in which a person could gain access to a large sum of money with a guarantee that nobody would ever find out. The question went something like this, "would *most* people do it?" To my logical brain, *most people* translated to fifty-one percent. I was sure most people would not take the money. I explained my logic to him,

"It can't be true. Most people wouldn't take the money."

He told me I was wrong. He said most people would indeed take the money, and reiterated that people were not as honest as I had believed.

When I learned that there was no Santa Claus, I knew in an instant that if Santa was fiction, then so were the Easter Bunny and the Tooth Fairy. Not a good day for an eight-year-old girl.

The day with the psychologist was much worse.

Jamie had the same experience when she was eight. She spent the first couple of hours of Easter morning, enjoying her Easter basket when suddenly she looked up at me and said,

"I saw you in my room last night."

She appeared to be fast asleep as I placed the basket next to her bed; I had no idea she was lying in the dark with one eye open.

Once Jamie had seen the elusive Easter Bunny, she demanded the whole truth and nothing but the truth, so I had no choice but to come clean about all of the lies I had told in the name of childhood fun. When her grandparents arrived later that afternoon, and I told them what Jamie had learned, she denied the whole thing and stomped off with her basket in hand, not wanting to believe what she knew to be true.

I don't know if the psychologist's statement is true, or if there is any way to know for sure. What I did know is that I didn't want to accept that I was living in a world where *most* people are dishonest. I wanted to grab my Easter basket and stomp out of the office.

****

During a routine physical, my doctor discovered what turned out to be a tumor on my thyroid gland. My first biopsy was in my doctor's office, performed by a specialist. I was feeling a bit nervous while this stranger numbed my neck, but when she came at me with a needle that looked to be about a foot long, I nearly passed out. She was having trouble isolating the tumor as it was moving while she tried to take the samples. That meant repeated punctures with that long needle, which seemed to grow with every jab. I was becoming nauseated, so the doctor stopped and told me I would need to schedule a needle-assisted biopsy at the hospital. What she was able to remove, was mainly liquid, so my doctor assured me it was likely nothing more than a cyst.

At the hospital, I laid in a room, waiting for the next doctor to come at my throat with another foot-long needle. As promised, the procedure was much more comfortable than the previous neck-stabbing session. However, this doctor must have skipped his bedside-manner class. When he finished, he said,

"I can tell you one thing; that is *not* a cyst. It's a hard lump."

With concern in my voice, I asked,

"What does that mean?"

"It means you need to go back to your doctor right away."

With that, he turned and walked out of the room, leaving a twenty-nine-year-old single mother lying there, terrified. I got dressed and drove straight to my mom's office. In the forty-five minutes it had taken me to get dressed, make my way out of the hospital, and to my mom's office, I convinced myself that I was dying. We didn't have Dr. Google back then, but I didn't need search results to convince myself of a cancer diagnosis. I headed straight to the worst-case scenario on my own. I had visions of my kids growing up without me, and with a father who was not reliable. They needed me! Maybe I could last another four or five years, and I would teach them everything I possibly could in the time I had left. I would record cassette tapes for after I was gone, giving them advice, and reminding them how much I loved them. I held back the tears and decided to be brave.

The moment I saw my mom, I burst into tears. So much for brave. I called my doctor and said, whimpering,

"You said it was a cyst."

When my doctor heard about the lack of bedside manner from the doctor performing the biopsy, he arranged for my next biopsy with a different doctor, and I would have a pathologist present to give me immediate results (something they rarely did in those days). All samples were benign. It looked as if I could put away my cassette recorder.

My doctor was pushing hard for me to have the tumor removed in case a portion of the nodule not biopsied contained cancer cells. Also, it was a hot nodule, meaning it was causing my thyroid to be overactive, so it couldn't stay in there forever.

I asked him what the odds were that it was benign, and he said eighty-five percent. I told him I would head to Vegas with those odds.

He kept pressing, but I told him,

"Nobody's cutting into my throat."

I wasn't particularly vain, but I didn't want a scar on my neck. The doctor claimed the surgeon could place the incision where there was already a line in my neck. Hello! I was twenty-nine – there were no lines on my neck. His rebuttal was that I could wear turtlenecks. I lived in the Seattle area, so that was a viable option for most of the year, but I feel like I am suffocating when I wear a turtleneck, so that was not happening.

Finally, I told him,

"I'm leaving that thing in there until it becomes a grapefruit hanging off my neck."

It didn't become a grapefruit, but before long, I did have to do something about it when my tumor became so overactive that my heart was racing and hands were shaking.

I found myself in a lead room drinking radioactive iodine from a lead container. The goal was for the radioactive material, attached to iodine, to be taken up into the thyroid gland, and destroy the tumor, but leave the parts of my gland intact, and functioning.

I was crossing my fingers it worked since the thyroid is a vital hormone gland that plays a significant role in metabolism, heart and digestive function, muscle control, brain development, mood, and bone maintenance. And I did not want to spend the rest of my life dependent on pharmaceuticals.

All was well, until a couple of years after that, when I was extremely sluggish and gained ten pounds while working out daily. Thus, began my dependence on thyroid replacement medication and the eventual issues that come from the thyroid not functioning naturally.

****

I had a sneaking suspicion I was not my dad's favorite child, but one Christmas shortly after I was married, it became very apparent. Brad, who was nineteen still lived at my dad's. It had always been the tradition that he could open just ONE of his many gifts on Christmas Eve, while Darryl and I opened ours. He would open the rest on Christmas morning. Brad tore into his first gift of the holiday – a leather jacket. Darryl started ripping through his – wheels for his car, a fishing reel and rod, and more. There was one lone gift under the tree for my husband and me. It was a cheap, plastic meat slicer. Grandpa had gotten my dad a job at the meatpacking plant, in sales, so the slicer was probably something he had received for free. What in the heck would we do with a meat slicer? We sat there looking at each other, trying not to burst out laughing. It wasn't about the gift or the monetary value of it, but the realization that my dad had so overtly played favorites. I was clearly at the bottom of his favorite kid list. Years later, my half-brother, Donny, would tell me he always assumed his name was below our dad's dog.

Each June, I made the dreaded trip to the card shop to search for an appropriate father's day card for my dad. I agonized because there appeared to be two types of greeting cards. Some had messages to the tune of "To the Best Dad." Others said, "For a Fine Man on Father's

Day," or something to that effect. The first wasn't true, and the second sounded like something one would give to the mailman.

I never knew what to buy my dad for a gift either, since we didn't know each other very well. He never acknowledged my kids' birthdays, and he was somewhat of a stranger to them. He didn't even know about my thyroid tumor. One time, he announced that Darryl and I were not in his will; he would take care of Brad, and my mom should take care of Darryl and me. Now, I don't expect to be in anybody's will, but that was another nail in the father-daughter coffin.

No sooner would the stress of Father's Day be over, when his birthday would roll around, then the holidays. My little family would show up at his place on Christmas Eve and go through the motions of pretending we were family. It was uncomfortable for me, as I only wanted real relationships in my life, and this was not one of them. The cycle continued until I decided to get off the roller coaster. I wrote him an honest letter letting him out of his obligation of being my *dad*. It must have been a relief for him since I never heard a word back. It should have hurt my feelings that he could let his only daughter go so easily, but the truth was, he had let me go years before.

****

Nana was born with club feet, a condition where the feet are rotated inwardly toward the ankles. My great-grandmother, Fannie May, was a nurse and rode horseback. I have an image in my mind of Great-Grandma riding a horse through the prairies of central Canada, her long red hair, blowing in the wind. I'm sure her single-mom life after her husband died, was far less glamorous than that, but I love the visual. Nana would recall arriving at home from school to find a patient sprawled out on the kitchen table, her mother standing over them, knife in hand.

Fannie May was a brave and strong woman, who knew how to take matters into her own hands, so she would massage my Nana's feet several times a day until they began to straighten out, at which point Nana wore steel braces until she was twelve years old.

Nana's life began with health issues. She had exceptionally thin, delicate skin, was born with a couple of extra ribs, and spent her life with bronchial problems. She was a smoker in her younger hears but quit back in 1964 when the Surgeon General announced that smoking was harmful. Years later, she was diagnosed with emphysema. Nana was on oxygen for many years, lugging around a small tank wherever she went, but she never complained. Not once.

Nana was a big Seattle Supersonics basketball fan and watched the NBA games religiously. Nobody in my family was a basketball fan, including Grandpa, so she would sit by herself and cheer for the Sonics, or even yell at the opposing team. No swear words, though; that wasn't Nana. I must have gotten that gene from someone else.

She was an artist who could have easily sold her beautiful paintings. It impressed me that Nana could take an image in her mind and put it on paper or canvas. I can only draw stick people – really bad ones. Nana recovered furniture and was an amazing seamstress. She made clothes for me when I was little and even into junior high, when she made me the coolest faux suede jacket with faux fur sleeves. (It was the 70s).Nana showed me how she used the resistance of only her muscles to build strength, and exercised right up to the last trip she made to the hospital. Nana cooked with herbs and made delicious meals without salt. She never let her hair go gray and was always put-together. She was a quiet, five-foot-tall redhead, with the softest lips I have ever felt.

Nana's heart finally failed, as a result of her emphysema. She died while I was going through my divorce. Shortly after, I got Chickenpox. I had them as a kid, but getting them as an adult was unbelievable. There must have been thousands of blisters all over my body and in every orifice. I counted at least fifty in my mouth and had them down my throat. My organs ached, and I had to take Novocain so I could swallow. That was a low point in my life, but remembering Nana's courage helped me through.

She refused to be a victim, no matter how much she suffered. Nana had a positive outlook up to the moment she died. She was not one that most people would consider a hero; Nana never went out and changed the world. But, she changed mine, and she was my hero.

****

Grandpa died a few years later. He had been diagnosed with Parkinson's Disease about six years before. It was sad to watch my Grandpa, who always had a big belly and a quick wit, wither away and lose his happiness. My parents cared for him for most of those years, but toward the end, he was in a nursing home, a short distance from my house. I visited Grandpa a great deal, but often, he didn't even know who I was. Still, I would go, and often brought homemade cookies for the staff, treating them the way I hoped they were treating my Grandpa.

He was declining rapidly, having trouble swallowing, and he no longer communicated with or recognized us. Grandpa got pneumonia, and the doctor explained what his quality of life would be like if he recovered, so we chose not to treat it, in favor of allowing the incredible Hospice workers to manage his care until his body had enough.

I saw Grandpa each of the ten days he laid there on morphine, with the rattling in his chest getting louder and louder. I wanted to be with him when his soul left his body and was waiting for the call, day or night. Unfortunately, I got the call that he died. I rushed over and spent a few minutes with the man I loved and appreciated more than words can express.

Grandpa was Scottish and had a great sense of humor. He used to say that one day he would "shuffle off to Panama." I smiled through the tears, as I removed the family photos and drawings his great-grandchildren had given him, from the bulletin board above his bed. I boxed up the very few possessions he had left, gave my Grandpa one last kiss goodbye, and thought to myself,

"Enjoy Panama, Grandpa."

****

One of the most challenging things I have ever done was to deliver my Grandpa's eulogy, but someone who loved him as much as I did, had to speak for the family. My brother, Darryl, showed up at my house a day before the service. It was December, but he was wearing sunglasses. He handed me a piece of paper and said,

"This is what I would say if I could."

As he turned to leave, I saw the tears dripping onto his cheeks from under the sunglasses.

I gave it my all that day, speaking on behalf of my brothers, and the rest of the family, not knowing how important those few minutes of bravery would be to my future mission.

****

My kids were my everything, and our lives were going well. Jamie and Sean were safe and protected. I set about keeping things in order and doing everything I could to make their lives happy and peaceful. They attended Montessori school for the first few years of their schooling. We read books, watched movies, did homework together, baked cookies, played games, went rollerblading, bike riding, hiking, and went on a few fun vacations. Sure, I made parenting mistakes and would do some things differently if given a chance, but all in all, I was a good mom. My Supermom Cape was even in good shape since I hadn't needed to use it much.

****

I learned to be fearful of even low heights at a young age. Standing at the edge of a cliff, or next to a window in a skyscraper made me physically ill. I didn't like being unreasonably scared of heights, so I decided to do something about it. My friend was helping me with this mission, and while in Phoenix, at the tail end of a business trip, we went on an early morning hot air balloon ride. Next, we headed to Scottsdale for a ride in a private airplane that took us to the Grand Canyon. He also secured a helicopter ride into the canyon upon our arrival, but it was so windy that day that by the time we arrived (with me sicker than a dog), all flights were canceled.

I didn't let that setback stop me, though. When I returned home, I went on another hot air balloon ride, this one taking me up much higher than the first one.

Next, I went hiking to the top of Mt. Pilchuck and stood out on a rock outside of the lookout building. I had been up the same mountain before, but that time, it was quite a different story.

At the 5,327-foot summit of the mountain, there is a small lookout tower, which is a tiny building, cabled to large boulders. In the past, it was a fire lookout, but now it's a fantastic opportunity for a three-hundred-sixty-degree view of Central Washington and the Puget Sound area. The lookout building has decking all around it, but to get there, you first have to climb up a short ladder. The first time I was there, I got to the landing at the top of the ladder and immediately climbed right back down to solid ground.

This time, I climbed right up the ladder and walked around the outside deck of the tiny lookout building. I stepped through a break in the railing and walked across a plank that led to a huge boulder. I stood with my arms in the air, on top of the world, and unafraid.

I wanted to hike Mt. Rainier, but my mom convinced my kids I was going to fall into a crevasse and die, so they begged me not to do it. It is amazing how much fear drives our decisions, and I didn't want my kids to be fearful, which is one reason, I tried to be brave. But, I didn't want them to worry that their mom was going to die on Mt. Rainier.

****

While I would have preferred to be married, my single mom years were good. I swore I would stay single forever, rather than to be in an unhealthy marriage.

With no college degree, I had to work my tail off to climb the business ladder and earn enough to allow Jamie and Sean to be safe and to enjoy some life experiences, but I would live with the guilt of being a single mother on and off for years. When my daughter went off the rails a few years later, I would flat-out blame myself.

Until then, my life was full of hope and possibilities. My confidence was high, and I was feeling brave. I believed amazing things were in our future.

A Man Named Rich

I dated a couple of guys during my single mom days, but it was tough trying to balance a romantic relationship with protecting the best interests of my children.

In early 1997, I was working as Director of Operations for a small company in startup mode. We had recently hired three new people for a particular project, that was more of a test project. I was leaving the office one evening when one of the new employees, Terri, asked me if I would like to meet a friend of her fiancé, Randy. She went on to tell me all of the wonderful qualities this guy named Rich possessed, and then proceeded to explain he was going through a divorce. I placed the appointment book I was holding onto her desk and made the cross symbol with my two index fingers.

"No, thanks. I have been single for eight years; I don't need to deal with that," I said.

She was persistent and argued that worst case, I would meet a new friend, so I reluctantly agreed.

I learned later that Rich had a similar reaction when he heard my first name, which was the same as his soon-to-be ex-wife, and my last name, which was eerily similar to her maiden name.

We met on neutral ground, joining Randy and Terri at The Bellevue Club, where both Rich and I were members. We enjoyed sushi and lively conversation and were having a good time when suddenly, I looked at my watch and let out a small gasp. It was nearly 10 p.m. My children were at my friend, Maria's house, and our kids were best friends, so Jamie and Sean couldn't have cared less about going home, but it was a school night.

I ran out of the club and down the stairs like Cinderella, leaving the ball. We would realize early on just how different perspectives can be, when I teased Rich, saying,

"You never even walked me to my car."

To which he replied,

"I didn't have a chance; you just got up and ran out the door."

Such was the life of a single mother.

The next morning, the President called a couple of us into his office to inform us the test project was a bust, and we were going to let the employees go. I had the unfortunate duty of delivering the news to Terri.

I felt very badly, since she had only been employed for three weeks, and had done nothing wrong. Terri's response was unexpected. She said it was okay with her because she believed the reason she found the job was so that Rich and I could meet. I wasn't so sure I was meant to meet Rich since he was still going through a divorce.

Over the next week or so, Rich called me at my office to invite me to lunch three times. The first two times, I had eaten early that day, something I rarely did. The third time, I didn't call him back because I took Sean to the doctor that afternoon, and then to have dinner with my parents. We had cell phones, but they were not attached to our bodies like they are these days. Rich informed his friend that he was done trying to ask me out.

The next morning, I retrieved his message, and we made another plan. I got over the fact that he was going through a divorce, and in fact, helped him through it. He realized dating a single mother wasn't so bad. A year after we met, we were married. Jamie was twelve, and Sean was ten. We moved to Rich's beautiful home in the Lakemont area of east Bellevue, across Lake Washington from Seattle. Life was going in the right direction.

****

I didn't need Rich for parenting; I had that one down. Remember, I had a Supermom Cape. He was more for *me*, but it was nice to feel as if my family would finally be complete. Life was pretty good before I married Rich, but the new chapter promised to be amazing, just like I imagined.

Jamie and Rich clashed early on. He wasn't taking her newfound attitude, and she didn't want to be bossed around. I should have purchased a referee shirt and whistle since I seemed to be in the middle of their confrontations.

There were some growing pains for all of us. My kids suddenly had a stepfather, and Rich had no children of his own. He wasn't used to lights left on or socks on the floor. Jamie and Sean were not used to having another adult to answer to; one they didn't know all that well.

The kids had the bottom floor of the house to themselves most of the time, with three bedrooms, two bathrooms, and a huge family room with a pool table. So, socks on the floor on occasion, or a light left on downstairs, should not have been a big deal, but they were for Rich. One time he asked me,

"How many times do I have to tell them to turn off the lights?"

I grabbed my imaginary parenting manual and replied,

"I don't know; let me look."

I turned the imaginary pages, and moved my finger down the non-existent page, and stopped in mid-air, exclaiming,

"Let's see...lights...here we go...5,362."

Rich became good friends with my brothers, and all of my family loved him right away, so he settled in well with the extended family, but the four of us struggled to create a family unit. I felt pulled between the man I was planning to spend the rest of *my* life with, and the children I had already spent all of *their* lives with.

****

Pre-Rich, Sean brought home a little library book, which would be the basis for his first book report. It was about Jerry Rice, the San Francisco 49er football player. He announced that he was a San Francisco 49er fan, although he lived in Seattle Seahawk land. No amount of poking or prodding deterred Sean; he was a Niner for life.

Rich comes from the San Francisco Bay area, and he's a long-time San Francisco 49er fan, so he and Sean had that instant bond. The San Francisco 49ers would wind up being the glue that held Sean and Rich's relationship together through the first few years of our married life.

****

It was eight years since I sent the fateful letter to my dad. Sean, who was around eleven or twelve, was home "sick." I had a feeling he wasn't sick, but my usual tactic had not worked. When he would say he was too ill to go to school, I would let him know he could stay home, but that meant no television, video games, or toys. He would need to stay in bed and read or sleep. It usually turned into what I called an "MR" – a miraculous recovery – and off to school, he would go. But no MR that day, which would turn out to be a blessing.

I received a call from my brother, Brad, telling me our dad had suffered a heart attack and was in the hospital. I hung up the phone and cried. Then, I tried to figure out what to do. It was an awkward situation, not knowing what kind of response I would get if I showed up at the hospital, or if one of his twelve siblings might throw me out the door.

I prayed and asked God not to *go with me* to the hospital, but to *take me there*. I was sure glad Sean didn't have an MR that day, because I was grateful he was going with me, and God, to the hospital.

I was relieved to find the waiting area empty, and we were escorted immediately into the ICU. We hesitantly approached his bed, and I looked down at the stranger, who was my dad. I had never seen him with gray in his, otherwise, jet-black hair. The lines on his face showed he had aged in the past eight years. He awoke, and it took him a moment to realize it was me, but when he did, he stretched his arms out toward me and called my name. We had a tearful embrace, and all was forgotten.

From there, we began a different relationship, one that would eventually center on Sean's football games. My dad would sit in the stands with Rich and I, Sean's dad, and other family or friends, enjoying the food I brought, and cheering as loud as anyone. My dad was at every one of Sean's football games, home and away, through junior high and high school. Until, one day, when he dropped out of our lives without a word.

****

Jamie was gifted. She was proficient at everything she tried. This girl was smart, funny, outgoing, artistic, and brave. She had a quick wit and was a natural leader. As Sean says, she lit up a room. I used to quip that she would be the first woman President.

Jamie was a natural athlete and played basketball and soccer, but her favorite sport was softball, which she started playing at the age of nine. The teams were full, and the season was about to begin. Luckily, there were a few new players, so a brand-new team was thrown together. We secretly referred to them as the Bad News Bears because, well - they were terrible. Most of the girls had never played past Tee Ball, and it pained me to watch the first few practices, resigning myself to the fact that this would be a very long season.

Jamie played first base, and her coaches soon began to refer to her as the vacuum, since she scooped up, or caught, nearly every ball that came her way. The girls came together and started to be pretty good.

By the end of the season, the Bad News Bears, formally known as The Rockies, were in the playoffs. It was indeed a long season after all. The team they were up against was full of experienced players (as experienced as you can be at nine or ten years old). Their pitcher's dad was a semi-pro player, who had his daughter throwing some ungodly number of pitches each day. Our pitcher was new to the game. Nonetheless, the Rockies won the championship.

Jamie went on to play select softball, and to play for her high school team. During her select softball days, we would spend entire weekends at the ball field for tournaments. It was a sacrifice for all of us (mostly Sean), but I loved almost every minute of those weekends.

****

Both Jamie and Sean played several sports and participated in many extracurricular activities. I was at sports practices, games, karate classes, volunteered on the playground and in the lunchroom during Sean's lunchtime. I volunteered at Jamie's middle school, to be the Choir Robe Mom. (I don't think that was the official title, but then, there probably wasn't one). It was a big commitment since there were a gazillion robes, and part of the job was to do some mending, and unlike my Nana, I can barely sew on a button.

My kids were used to a parent who made quick decisions. One Sunday, I was out, so Sean asked Rich if he could go to the movies on Friday, expecting an immediate answer. Rich told Sean he needed to think about it, so Sean checked in a couple of hours later, but Rich said he was still thinking about it. On Thursday, Sean was getting anxious and tried to get me to intervene, but they needed to figure out their roles in the new relationships, so I told him to be patient. When Friday morning rolled around, and Rich was still *thinking about it*, I told Rich he had tortured Sean long enough, but he made Sean wait until right before his friend's dad was leaving for the movies, to grant permission. From there on out, both kids avoided asking Rich for permission if they could ask me.

All torturing, and socks on the floor aside, we were working our way through the relationship challenges, without anybody losing a limb, or heading to divorce court.

****

Fear of public speaking ranks at the top of the list of fears in many surveys and articles. Really? More than death? Or spiders? Or birds?

The first time I did a formal presentation in front of a group of people was in a high school oral communications class, and I was scared half to death, even though I knew everyone in the room. It didn't help that I had chosen Spina Bifida as my topic. I was in a child psychology class at the time and was reading about children born with this condition, and it moved and interested me. Although I doubt the rest of the sophomore class shared my enthusiasm.

The first time I spoke in a business setting was at a meeting with around thirty people in attendance. I thought about my high school speech, and my nerves were on edge. But, then I remembered I had delivered Grandpa's eulogy, so I knew I could do this. Before speaking, I went around the room and introduced myself to every person I could, so when I stood in front of the room, I was looking out at somewhat familiar faces.

A year or so after that, I reluctantly agreed to co-emcee an event with several hundred attendees. The audience would include some very experienced and skilled speakers. I was scared, but I wanted to overcome another fear.

On the morning of the event, the other emcee came down with laryngitis. I was shaking when I took the stage, but I had planned to use humor (my go-to place) when asking the crowd to be mindful of cell phones, and some other event business. It was going great, and I felt pretty comfortable after about a minute or two on the tall stage when I heard someone down below whispering loudly,

"The National Anthem!"

"Oh no," I thought. The first thing this company always did was play The National Anthem, and I had gone right into my humor bit. Somehow, I had to eloquently get myself off the stage while the National Anthem played and then return as if nothing out of the ordinary happened.

We broke for lunch, and I wasn't feeling too bad about how I had managed so far when one of the seasoned speakers caught up with me and tapped me on the shoulder. He asked,

"How long have you been speaking?"

I looked at my watch.

"Since about nine o'clock," I answered.

He chuckled, then went on to tell me I was a natural and how impressed he was, especially considering it was my first stage appearance. Had I not stepped up and faced a fear, I would never have realized a gift that can be used to help so many others.

****

About the title of this section, "A Man Named Rich." I have a sarcastic sense of humor (I am part Scottish and Irish, so I can't help it), and one day I said to Rich,

"I prayed and prayed for a *rich* man, and God sent me a *man named Rich!*"

After he rolled his eyes, and said, sarcastically,

"Ha. Ha," I followed it up with,

"When you pray, you must be *very* specific!"

I couldn't help trying it out on family and friends, and it got some pretty good laughs, so it stuck. The poor guy has heard it now, about a hundred times. Recently, though, he brought it up to some new friends, so, after a couple of decades, I think my sense of humor is finally catching on.

My marriage was solid, and we were working to become a family, even with the bumps we had encountered. But, three short years after our wedding, Jamie would make decisions that would provide our little family with four free seats on the Roller Coaster From Hell.

All Hell Broke Loose

As a young girl, Jamie was concerned with doing the right thing and tried to stay on my good side. She was studious and did her chores without complaining. Sean didn't like doing his chores and liked it much less when he was in trouble.

Twice, Sean ran away from home; they were both very short trips. The first time he was four years old, and he made it less than a half of a block, before coming to his senses.

The second time, he was eight years old, and this time he was serious. He spent a great deal of time letting me know he was packing up, and that he was not coming back. He loaded up two department store shopping bags, with nothing but toys. I gave him a flashlight and told him he would need it because it would be dark soon. His eyes got big, but he snatched it from my hand and stuffed it into one of the overflowing bags. He asked if he could take some food with him, but I gently told him he couldn't because the food was for people who lived with me in the house.

Off he went, down the hill of our cul-de-sac, making it a total of about four houses, when one of his bags broke. Toys spilled out all over the sidewalk and onto the street. He was sitting on the sidewalk sobbing when I arrived to help him pack up his things and take him home, and to his surprise, back to being grounded.

Jamie knew where her bread was buttered and had no intention of running away; that was until she was fifteen. I grounded her for something, and in defiance, she took off without letting me know she was leaving. When I discovered she was gone, I was mad, but when it started to get dark, I was concerned. Jamie had recently switched schools, leaving behind all of her friends. So, she didn't have many new friends yet, and I was not sure where to start. As night turned into early morning, and Jamie had not returned, I started playing detective. Somehow, I made my way through a phone maze I couldn't have re-traced if I had to, and located a guy who said he knew where Jamie was, but he didn't want to rat out his younger brother. This guy was a grown man with children, so I spent a few hours playing junior psychologist, appealing to his role as a parent. Finally, he agreed to help, and we set up a sting operation. At eight a.m., Jamie's dad and I pulled into a fast-food parking lot to find a shocked Jamie, sitting in the back of the guy's car.

****

When Jamie was fourteen or fifteen, she went to bible camp and came back on fire for God. A week later, she was caught shoplifting with a friend. When I got the phone call from the mall, I was in shock and denial. Jamie wouldn't do such a thing. I raised her with integrity and honesty. She lived in a great home and didn't need anything. I thought it was the worst day of my life, which is almost comical, considering what we would endure in the coming years.

****

Rich and I reluctantly allowed Jamie to go with a church youth group to a shady area of Tacoma, which is south of Seattle, for a church outreach program. We lived on the eastside of Lake Washington from Seattle, and what seemed like a world away from Tacoma. The program took place in the late evening, and I was nervous, so I convinced Rich that we should take her to the location ourselves, and sit across the street in the car. We did the same thing a year or so prior, when she and her cousin, Shawnie, went to a Hanson concert in broad daylight.

Shortly after she started with the church outreach program, I found out Jamie had a boyfriend she met in outreach. I asked if he went to her youth group, or a different one, and was horrified to learn he wasn't in any youth group. He was one of the kids in attendance. The purpose of the outreach program was to reach at-risk youth in the inner city. We learned that many of the kids who attended were in gangs, but the leaders of the group assured us there was security, and that it was safe. As you can imagine, I didn't want my daughter anywhere near gang life, so we forbid her from continuing with the outreach program.

For unknown reasons, Jamie became fascinated with the people she was supposed to be reaching out to and wound up doing everything she could to enter a world she knew nothing about. During the time Jamie was in the outreach program, she attended a basketball game in Seattle, where she met and soon fell in love with a guy who was bad news. In the years that followed, I would spend a great deal of time in guilt over my decision to allow Jamie to participate in the youth group program.

We tried everything we could to get Jamie away from Terry, but she was determined. Before she had a driver's license, she and her friend, Megan, took one of our cars out on a dark winter night and headed the twenty miles from our home to the Central District of

Seattle, returning with Terry and his cousin in tow. I still cannot imagine what she was thinking, knowing we were only out to dinner, and would not be gone long enough for her to make the return trip before we got home.

We knew immediately she had taken the car as we followed the tire tracks in the snow dusting up our street, down the driveway and into the garage. I screamed so loud at Jamie that Megan ran out the door and all the way home.

Rich had to get up early for a business trip the next morning, so I told Jamie we were going to bed, and I would discuss this further with her the next day. Sean was at a friend's that night, so I set the alarm, and we went to bed. In the morning, I discovered I had unknowingly trapped Terry and his cousin in my house when I set the alarm.

I was furious, swearing at this tall teenage kid, and pointing my finger up in his face, warning him what I would do to him if he ever hurt my daughter.

By the time Jamie was a junior in high school, she had refused to go to school and quit the youth group and sports. I became certified as a homeschool teacher and set about handling my duties. The first order of business was to do some placement testing. Jamie tested at college level in every subject, except for math, and that score was high enough. She wasn't going to go for any more schooling with that report, and I was too weary to fight anymore, so I issued her a home school diploma, and that was the end of my illustrious career as a home school teacher.

It was time for Jamie to get a job and grow up since that is what she thought she already was. Jamie was into hair and makeup, so we paid for her to go to a high-end cosmetology school, but after a few weeks, she decided it was not for her. Out the door she went, leaving behind all of the expensive tools and supplies and the non-refundable schooling.

I was losing my daughter and had no idea how to get her back. If somebody had told me that their daughter was out of control by the age of fifteen, I would have thought they needed parenting classes. I wished there was a class to help me navigate the unchartered waters with Jamie. If only I could find that imaginary parenting manual.

****

For Jamie's eighth birthday, my mom and I took my kids to Disneyworld, and on a cruise to the Bahamas. I secretly packed suitcases for Jamie and Sean, and woke them up very early the next morning, telling them to hurry up and get ready, because we were going to Disneyworld.

The ship was docked, going through the preparations for setting sail, while a big party took place on the upper deck. The Disney characters were out, and Jamie and Sean held hands and danced in circles to the music. My heart was bursting, watching the pure joy on their little faces.

Suddenly, the music stopped, and the Captain announced over a loudspeaker that we needed to report to a specific place on the ship for a mandatory safety drill before the ship could depart. Based on what he said, we didn't have much time to get to our cabins, put on life-jackets, and report to the designated spot. We raced toward the elevators, but couldn't remember exactly how to get to our cabin. We had only been there once, and the ship was undergoing a renovation, with parts of it being blocked off. It took us some time to make it to our cabin, only to wonder, "where are the life-jackets?" I pulled open a closet, and about a dozen life jackets tumbled out onto my head. I started to laugh, and that made mom laugh, and before long, we were each lying on a bed, holding our stomachs. As we laid there laughing, six-year-old Sean joined in. Jamie, on the other hand, was hopping mad. She was yelling at us to stop laughing and put on our life jackets, and get to the safety meeting. Apparently, at eight years old, she was the only adult in the room. It wasn't entirely our fault, though. Aside from the ship undergoing construction, they had been foolish enough to serve the grownups *Bahama Mama* welcome drinks, right before asking us to do something that serious.

We were the last passengers to arrive, huffing and puffing, fumbling with our life jacket buckles, and trying not to laugh, while Jamie gave us disapproving looks. What happened to that little girl?

****

One day, we were arguing over her relationship with Terry when Jamie said,

"So, what you are saying is that I have to choose between Terry and my family."

I replied,

"I guess that's what I am saying."

I was terrified of what her answer would be. Her eyes were dark and cold, and I swore I could see little horns poking through her hair when she said,

"Then, I choose him."

****

Jamie was living with her dad by the age of seventeen and didn't want much to do with me unless she needed something, which was often. A part of me was relieved I didn't have to deal with her daily, but I was still worried sick about Jamie. My heart would jump into my throat whenever the phone rang, and it would sink when it did not ring.

I was working in my home office late one morning, when a strong feeling came over me – something was wrong with Jamie. There was nothing tangible, but I couldn't shake the feeling. I finally picked up the phone and called Jamie's dad, but he said she was at her nanny job, and everything was fine. I called Rich at his office, and he tried to assure me I was worrying about nothing.

I tried to ignore the feeling and get back to work, but I couldn't; I knew something was very wrong. So, I started making calls to strangers, as I had the day Jamie ran away. My detective skills panned out, and I wound up on the phone with a man, who was the father of a friend of Jamie's, whom I had never met. After I told him who I was, I said desperately,

"Jamie's in trouble, and I need your help."

His reply shocked me.

"Yes, she is, and I know what she's done."

I was too upset to yell, "I told you so," at Jamie's dad or Rich. Instead, I asked her dad to pick me up so I could be with him when he retrieved Jamie from her nanny job.

She walked toward the truck we were sitting in, and the moment she saw me, Jamie knew the jig was up. We drove straight to the Seattle police station. The goal was for Jamie to turn herself in for the check fraud scam I had learned about. We stood with her but made her go up to the counter and tell them what happened. The officer at the desk looked puzzled.

"Do you have a case number?"

I stepped in and explained that there was no case number, but we were trying to get in front of this. The confused look on the officer's face had me wondering if he was about to pull out his police manual from behind the counter and look this one up. He explained there was no way to take someone into jail without an arrest or a warrant. I was trying to keep my daughter out of prison, but I had no idea how these things worked.

Jamie was never arrested for her involvement in the check fraud scam, since they were far more interested in the adults who ran the show, than idiot seventeen-year-olds who were putting themselves in jeopardy by cashing fake payroll checks, using their personal identification.

Jamie didn't seem phased by her near-miss with serious jail time. Her life continued down the path of drama and chaos. Someone poured ketchup and mustard into the backseat of her car and scratched a not-so-nice word into the door. She went from job to job or no job at all. Jamie wore a police-monitoring ankle bracelet instead of going to jail. She appeared to have the *worst* luck, which was easier to believe than the fact that my daughter was on a freight train headed toward a brick wall. I will spare you all of the drama-filled details; you get the point. All hell had officially broken loose.

Who was this person who looked like my brilliant daughter, but acted nothing like her? She was supposed to be the first woman President.

****

Jamie went to stay with my parents in Palm Springs, California, the summer after she turned eighteen. They all came back to Seattle together at the end of August. Jamie was returning home for good, and my parents had come for a visit. The Saturday of my parents' stay, Rich, my siblings, their spouses, and I had thrown a surprise seventieth birthday party for Chips. Jamie was there, and she seemed much more like her old self. I was hopeful.

Three days later, we got a very different surprise. I was on my way home from a breakfast meeting and called Rich. I mentioned I had been unable to sleep the night before, and was super tired, but needed to stop at the grocery store for the ingredients for enchiladas and some party supplies.

Throughout Sean and Jamie's childhood, I had thrown "cousin parties," where some, or all, of their cousins, would come over and play, or have a sleepover. That night, the cousins were coming over to our house for a nostalgic cousin party, and my infamous enchiladas. Now teenagers, they still thought cousin parties were cool. It was my parents' last night in town, so it was going to be an awesome night all around.

Rich insisted that I should wait to get the groceries, and instead, go home and take a nap. I agreed, and we hung up.

A few minutes later, I pulled into the garage to see Rich's car in the stall next to mine. It flashed through my mind that when we spoke, he said I should *go* home, not *come* home. I had tried to convince him to take the day off and be there when the cousins arrived that afternoon, but he insisted he had to go to the office. When I saw his car, I thought he had decided to surprise me by staying home. "Pretty clever, Rich," I thought, "making me think you were at work when you were at home."

As I opened my car door, Rich came out of the house and into the garage. The moment I saw his face, I knew there was no happy surprise waiting for me. There would be no cousin party. No enchiladas.

He came toward me, shut my car door, and said,

"He shot her Val; he finally shot her."

I knew who Rich was referring to - it was Terry.

Rich steered me toward the passenger side of his car, saying,

"We need to get to the hospital."

"No! No! No!" I shouted, over and over again.

Rich attempted to usher me into his car, but I resisted.

"Is she alive?"

No matter how many times he assured me that Jamie was alive, I kept whimpering,

"Is she alive?"

Each time, he told me she was, but that I needed to get into the car so we could get to the hospital. I wanted to get to the hospital, too, but I was afraid to get into the car, for fear this was not just a bad dream. It couldn't possibly be my reality. The safe life I worked so hard to create for my kids was far from one where people shot each other.

Finally, I allowed Rich to pour me into the car, and we headed for the hospital in Seattle, about thirty minutes from our home. The drive felt like thirty hours. I needed to get to my baby, who had nearly bled to death, while I tossed and turned in my bed.

The surgery was hours before, but Jamie had not woken up yet. I sat in ICU, holding her hand and watching her chest rise and fall. There were tubes everywhere, including a breathing tube. Her face appeared swollen, but I couldn't recall the last time she looked so peaceful.

The surgeon explained she was hit by a single bullet that entered through her backside, barely missing her pelvis, and her tailbone. We would learn later on; it barely missed her iliac vein, which would have caused her to bleed out before she made it to the operating room. They never located the bullet during emergency surgery, which confused me, so I asked the surgeon why they didn't find the bullet.

He replied,

"We weren't trying to find the bullet; we were trying to save her life."

He went on to say,

"Abdominal gunshot wounds are fatal. We spent hours cauterizing vessels and veins. She's lucky to be alive."

The row of nearly fifty staples extended from her breastbone to her pelvis, taking a slight turn around her belly button. My daughter had been fileted open like a fish.

When Jamie woke up, her first words to me were,

"I'm sorry."

I told her I didn't care about anything right then, except for wanting her to get better. I told her we would get through this together.

Late that night, Jamie was finally breathing on her own and was taken to X-ray to locate the bullet. It was lodged in her abdominal wall, near her belly button.

In the ICU family room, where I stayed alone that night, I laid there trying to wrap my head around the situation, but I couldn't. I thought about the time I stood screaming and threatening Terry when I found him in our home. He was wearing saggy jeans, and a baggy coat, and was probably carrying a gun. That night I told him I would kill him if he ever hurt my daughter, and sitting in ICU, it's precisely what I wanted to do to him.

I couldn't understand why Jamie kept choosing to be a part of that world. Where had I gone wrong? Was it the one time I slapped her? Perhaps if Rich had moved instead of us, and she didn't have to switch schools, this would never have happened. If I wasn't a single mother all those years and worked so much, I could have prevented this. Maybe I should never have married Rich. The thoughts spinning around in my mind were the same ones that invaded my daily thoughts. I wondered how life could get any worse than it was at that moment.

I learned during those first days in the hospital that this was not the first time Terry had abused Jamie. I suspected this was the case, but to hear it from her friends and the victim's advocate assigned to Jamie, made me sick. My daughter was strong-willed, a leader. She had never witnessed domestic violence. I have even been known to tell a guy or two, tongue in cheek,

"If you ever hit me, you better make it a good one, because there won't be a second chance."

Jamie was more headstrong than I am. She was the least likely person to be in an abusive relationship, or at least, that's what I thought. Maybe I didn't know my daughter anymore.

My mom's purse was stolen from the ICU family room. It happened a couple of hours into our hospital ordeal, adding to the stress my poor mother was already going through. To make matters worse, she had a feeling it was a young teenager, who was the brother of one of Jamie's friends. I couldn't fathom this, so I was sure she was wrong. Who would come to visit someone who nearly died, and then steal their grandmother's purse? My mom insisted something was off about the kid and questioned why he was wearing an oversized winter coat in the middle of August.

I should have listened to the psychologist who once told me people are not as honest as I believed them to be. A few days later, camera footage at a convenience store showed the boy with the credit card, passing himself off as "Sandy."

That day, my faith in humanity took a severe blow. I wanted to go back to believing in Santa Claus, the Easter Bunny, and the Tooth Fairy. I wanted to turn into an ostrich and bury my head in the sand. But that wasn't an option. I needed to be strong for Sean, Rich, my mom, and Jamie. I had to fix this. So, I tightened up my Supermom Cape, shifted into high gear, and tried to figure out what to do.

Sean was just sixteen years old when his sister was shot. He took one look at Jamie lying in her hospital bed and turned toward the wall. Sean placed his massive arm against it, cradled his head in the crook of his arm, and sobbed. Then, he left and didn't return to the hospital. He stayed a few days with his cousins and tried to pretend it never happened.

Sean's high school football team was practicing for the upcoming season, and everyone at the school knew about the shooting. It was in the news, and word travels fast. Sean would tell me later that he was embarrassed his sister was a "gang-banger wannabe." He knew what his parents' friends must be thinking about Jamie, our family, and about Sean. Each time someone asked him if he was okay (which was a lot of times), Sean would say he was fine and change the subject. His way of dealing with the trauma was to stuff it down and allow the anger to build. One of my many regrets would be not getting some professional help for Sean.

When Jamie was out of the woods, they moved her to a room on the trauma recovery floor, registered under a fictitious name for security measures. For eight nights, Jamie laid in her hospital bed, and I in the recliner chair that served as mine. It was hard as a rock, and my body ached from trying to sleep on it, but there wasn't much sleep that long week anyway. The room was large, with enough room for both "beds," but she insisted mine be butted right up against hers.

Jamie had been distant for many months, and rude and demanding in the hospital. She refused to talk about the night she was shot, until one of those sleepless nights, as we laid staring at the ceiling when Jamie asked,

"Mommy, will you pray with me?"

Finally, the moment I had been waiting for – a sign that Jamie was coming back to me. We held hands in the dark, and I prayed my brains out. Afterward, Jamie told me what happened that night.

She was hiding on one side of a duplex after Terry had arrived uninvited and assaulted Jamie and her friend. He left and returned with his friend - and guns. They stood on the street firing round, after round, into the duplex. It would be described by the detective on the case, as "you wouldn't believe the number of bullet casings we found." Jamie was still alone on the one side of the duplex when the gunfire erupted. Not being accustomed to gunfire, she didn't immediately drop to the ground or run for cover. Jamie was the only one shot that night. One lone bullet in a spray of bullets, intended for anyone in their path, hit my daughter.

Once she realized she had been shot, Jamie dialed 9-1-1 from her cell phone, went to the front of the house to read off the house numbers, and then laid down on the carpet, to wait for help. It is still hard for me to speak or write about that moment without becoming emotional. I don't like the thought of Jamie lying there alone, in a pool of her own blood. It wouldn't be the last time.

As the EMT placed Jamie into the aid car, she asked him if she was going to die.

He replied,

"Not in my truck."

That's the last thing she remembered about that night.

While I would rather have been having about five thousand different conversations with my daughter, than this particular one, those few minutes were unexpected and treasured. They gave me hope that everything was going to be okay. Mommy was here, with her Supermom Cape, and she was going to get her daughter back. Nothing could have been further from the truth.

Jamie came to live with us after she was released from the hospital. For a month, I slept with her in her old room. She was afraid of the dark, so we slept with the lights on.

One morning, I awoke to hear Jamie in the bathroom, so I got up to see if she needed help. It was a painful recovery, having the muscles of her abdomen sliced open. Yet, I found her standing in the bathroom, dumping her pain pills into the toilet. I asked her why she would do that, and her reply was,

"I don't like the way they make me feel."

It would turn out to be ironic since it was opiates she was first addicted to, and it was that very prescription that started her addiction.

I would need to buckle my seatbelt and strap down the shoulder harness because my ride on the Roller Coaster From Hell was about to get a lot worse. Over the next decade, Jamie's life would spin further out of control, and mine would spiral into darkness. I would ride that roller coaster painfully up one hill and screaming down the next, caught in a cycle of hope and devastating disappointment.

****

The shooting ordeal was so surreal that it didn't occur to me until after she was released, that my dad never showed up at the hospital, or even sent flowers. That didn't upset me since it wasn't as if he had been there for me in years, but it did surprise me. The new relationship was mainly about football, but the season had started, and my dad had not even called. It turned out he couldn't – he was in jail, and to this day, I have not heard a word from him. Through my brothers, I learned my dad claimed he was innocent of the charge, one that I would rather not put into writing. He never allowed me to look him in the eye or to decide whether or not I believed him. Once again, I forgave him and let him go. Little did I know, this cycle of connection, forgiveness, and then letting go of my dad was training for using the "F" word in unimaginable ways in the years to come. (You will learn about the "F" word later, and why you need to use it as much as possible).

****

One evening, Jamie came upstairs, with her bags in hand, and announced she was going back to her dad's. I was upset and pleaded with her to stay. I told her she needed counseling and someone to help her get back on track, and, and, and. She said,

"I'm fine mom!"

I couldn't believe how nonchalant she was acting. She had been shot – with a gun! I told her how scared I was and reminded her,

"But, Jamie, you were shot!"

"I know, mom. I was the one who was shot, not you."

With that, the girl who was afraid of the dark told me she loved me and walked out the door.

I would learn later that she went immediately to the District Attorney's office and recanted the testimony she had given them while she was in the hospital.

I tried to get back to some semblance of "normal," but there was a pending attempted murder trial, and Jamie was right back on the same track she was before the shooting.

I attended Sean's football games and wanted to be excited, but my mind drifted to Jamie. I would try to focus on the football game, only to find myself watching the cheerleaders, especially those that had been Jamie's friends. Jamie should have been a cheerleader.

****

Rich was an executive and shareholder for a startup company that was struggling under the weight of a downturned economy. He and another executive were writing personal checks to keep the company going; to preserve stock value for the other shareholders. The tech bubble burst, leaving our stock portfolio (which was our retirement fund) depleted.

They finally sold off the company, with zero profits. Our house was now upside down, and we needed to *right the ship*, so Rich went to work for a consulting company, and was eventually invited to be part of a team on a long-term consulting engagement in Miami, so we sold our house and moved to Key Biscayne, Florida.

It was a fantastic experience living on a tropical island near Miami. I spent mornings walking the white sandy beach, looking at the turquoise water, and marveling at the never-ending sunny days. It was a far cry from the gloominess of the Seattle area, yet I longed for home.

Sean came to live with us shortly after we moved to Key Biscayne, which warmed my heart, but he was only with us for less than a year before he returned to Seattle. We brought Jamie to visit a few times while we lived there, but each time, I noticed how much she was changing.

Rich was busy consulting, and any friends we had, we met through his business. I was more than three thousand miles, and a day's travel, from Sean, whose anger was building, and Jamie, who was crashing.

I had forayed into the direct marketing business a few years prior and tried to keep that going in Florida. The fact was, I am not great at sales, and the leadership portion of the business was the only place I excelled. I wound up starting my own one-woman consulting company and went back to what I knew and was very good at – business operations and finance.

I tried hard to be happy and positive, and enjoy the experience in Florida, but I felt a bit lost the entire four years we lived there. The fact was, I was going to be lost wherever I was.

****

During our time in the Miami area, Rich had partnered with a couple of guys and worked with some banks to help them through the housing market fiasco, when those banks suddenly became property owners. Before long, the banks started to sell off their properties, so Rich's business was concluding, and it was time for us to leave Florida.

We landed in the Palm Springs area of Southern California, where my parents lived. Chips had undergone extensive open-heart surgery several months prior. The operation was successful, but mentally, he was declining. The dementia was likely caused by not wearing a helmet in his hockey years and accelerated by nearly seven hours on the heart-lung machine during surgery. It was heartbreaking to witness his decline and to be so helpless to stop it. We tried various things to help his brain, but nothing worked. My mom was exhausted and heartbroken while he slipped away, mentally, and physically. Rich and I helped out, but I would eventually add *not doing enough for Chips, or to help my mom,* to my ever-growing guilt list.

****

Meanwhile, I continued to spend money, I had no business spending and came to Jamie's rescue time and time again, much of it without Rich's agreement, or even his knowledge. I paid car payments, insurance, traffic tickets, rent, groceries, and more. I reasoned with myself that I was protecting Rich. It didn't seem as if he even liked Jamie, anyway. I tried to balance two separate lives, but during those years, I would have chosen Jamie and her chaos over Rich. My marriage was in big trouble. Sean wouldn't speak to his sister and was mad that I was trying to help her. My family was falling apart. Still, all I wanted to do was save Jamie, even though I failed miserably at every turn.

Jamie joined us shortly after we moved to Palm Springs. I thought spending time with us would make a difference. Plus, I told her I was not sending one more dollar to Seattle. Within twenty-four hours of arriving in the desert, she found *her people,* and the chaos accelerated.

Jamie was brilliant and likable, and could get a job, but couldn't seem to keep one. She was in and out of rehab, jail, took part in illegal activities, went missing for months on end, and lived in a world we could not and did not want to understand. We knew none of her friends, who seemed to change every few months. She was back and forth, living with us, her grandparents, and who knows who. As the years passed, I racked my brain, in an attempt to figure out how to fix her; how to make her leave the dangerous life she was living.

There were two occasions when she insisted I take her back to her drug-infested world, with nothing but the clothes on her back. I glanced at my daughter, who was going through withdrawals in the passenger seat of my car as I tried to convince her to go to a detox facility, but she only wanted one thing. Driving away, I had tears streaming down my face, and my heart physically ached as I watched my daughter disappear into the belly of her Beast.

If only she would stop, and there had to be something I could do to convince her. I cried, begged, screamed, threatened, guilt-tripped, bailed her out of trouble, bonded her out of jail, paid living expenses, advised, prayed, ignored, cyber-stalked, and reasoned with Jamie.

Nothing helped. There were periods when she was clean, and we had hope that life would somehow get back to normal. But, down deep, I knew life would never be *normal* again. Our lives were forever changed.

****

My thyroid issues caught up with me, and after living years in a constant state of stress and worry, on high alert, I was diagnosed with adrenal fatigue. What that means is my metabolism button has nearly shut off, and I fight constant weight gain, fatigue, and brain fog. Menopause joined the party, and I was wiped out.

My inability to save Jamie was excruciating. I was supposed to keep her from danger and ensure she would make good choices. Not in my wildest nightmares could I have imagined how far off track my life would stray from my dreams and goals. There seemed to be no way out. I was trapped living a life of hopelessness, lack of faith, fear, doubt, jealousy, depression, shame, and guilt. I had somehow been handed a life-sentence, and I was terrified. This couldn't possibly be my life; it was supposed to be amazing.

I was a complete failure as a mother, a daughter, and a wife; as a human being. I had a dark cloud over my heart that was there twenty-four hours of every single day, no matter what kind of an act I put on.

For my siblings and friends, life seemed to be marching on in the natural order of things. Sure, they all have had challenges, but none of the magnitude I was experiencing. They had kids graduating from high school and college. Their children were on to careers and serious relationships. I attended niece and nephew weddings and celebrated the birth of their children. Everywhere I turned, life was happening. I felt as if I were watching a movie. I was in a bubble and could see what was going on around me, but I wasn't a part of it. I no longer fit in. I was confused, and envious, and felt guilty for not being as happy for other people as I should have been. I tried to figure out how to be a better person, so the crap would stop hitting the fan, but nothing seemed to bring relief.

With each beautiful event in the lives of family and friends, I became more depressed. It felt as if life was marching on without me. I didn't want to be a victim and didn't like people feeling sorry for me, so I tried to hide how I was feeling from everyone, including Rich. I walked around, with a smile, going through the motions of life, but I was worried, confused, helpless, and depressed. I would hide in the walk-in-closet, with the door shut, and sob until I was too exhausted to shed another tear. I was a good actress in those days, hiding my pain from those closest to me, but it wasn't going to be long before I had a breakdown. This actress was about to have her last curtain call.

There had to be a way to stop feeling depressed and defeated, but I had no idea where to start, even if I could find the energy to take even one step forward.

By the grace of God, I hit an all-time low, which turned out to be one of the best things that could have happened. I was standing in my kitchen when I blurted out to Rich,

"I don't want to be here anymore; it's too hard."

Standing Up

Those words had been on my lips a hundred times, but I had never spoken them out loud, until that day. It was the lowest point in my life, but the silver lining was that it scared me enough to move me to action. Somehow, I had to find a way to stand up, if not for me, then for my son, Sean. He was losing his only sibling to addiction, and the self-destruction of his mother was in full swing. I didn't care much about myself at that point, but I was not going to allow Sean to lose his mom in this way.

I did a great deal of praying, and dug down deep for every bit of insight, knowledge, and wisdom I could recall from my five decades on planet earth, and put them to use. I decided to change my thinking and to step out of the powerless world of victimhood.

I was tired of riding the Roller Coaster From Hell, but I had been waiting for it to come to the next stop, or for God to pluck me from my seat. Finally, I took responsibility for my circumstances, pulled the emergency brake, and got off the ride.

I stood up on extremely wobbly legs and began to claw my way toward happiness. I wasn't sure if I would get there, or where it was I was going, but I needed to be happy – even for an hour at a time.

I battled my way through heartache, desperation, and depression. I stood up and was knocked back down.

I stared fear in the face, turned and ran, came back, and took it on, again, and again.

I fought my way out of shame, victimhood, and lack of faith. I declared war on my Beast, no longer willing to stay in agreement with the lies. I decided to walk the rest of the way with God.

I learned to forgive myself for the many things I have said or done that I am not proud of; that I would have done differently had I been the person I am now.

It has been an epic battle, but I vowed to do everything I could to be my best and to make the rest of my life matter; to never give up trying to do good. To make meaning from the madness that had become my world.

Slowly, I got a little bit better. Then, I got a little bit better than that. I kept getting stronger. I stumbled, dropped to my knees, and then stood back up. It was a long process, but eventually, I built enough courage to keep standing – most of the time.

I documented what I was doing to become courageous, wrote my first book, and began teaching others to stand, but the hits kept coming.

****

Chips died while Jamie was in rehab. Although she adored him, she didn't even shed a tear when I told her. A couple of days later, she was kicked out of rehab, disappeared, and missed her grandfather's memorial service. Jamie's self-destruction was in process.

We had two memorial services for Chips, and I was honored to deliver his eulogies, to honor the man who chose to be my dad.

Shiska, my sixteen-year-old cat who helped me through so much, died, and I was heartbroken. He had renal failure, so I knew the end was near, but I needed him. He helped me through some of the hardest years of my life, and I adored that cat, and he adored me. Jamie would tell people,

"You know those commercials where a man and a woman are running in slow motion through a field of flowers toward each other; that's mom and Shiska."

Just two months after Shiska died, we lost my mother-in-law, Emily. She was suffering from serious issues related to congestive heart failure, so we moved Emily from the San Francisco Bay area to where we live in the Palm Springs area. My brother Rod, his wife Lynn, and my mom joined in our excitement to add another place setting to our family dinners. My mom and my mother-in-law were making plans to be neighbors. During the first two weeks, Emily was here she was in the hospital twice, the second time for a week. On that last hospital stay, a doctor told us she had eighteen months to two years to live. She died two days later, leaving us shocked and heartbroken.

A few short months after that, a friend, whom we had done business with in Key Biscayne, and considered family, betrayed us by stealing a significant sum of money from us, never to be recovered. It set us back again, financially, and was another punch in the face emotionally.

I was fighting hard to keep standing, but life seemed to be coming at me from every angle. Since I was teaching other people to stand, I had to get back up, grab my **9 Actions** toolbox, and get back to work.

The Home Invasion

Two months after our friend betrayed us, I would get the news, no parent can ever adequately prepare for, no matter how strong they become.

On August 29, 2016, an officer from the coroner's office arrived to inform us that the night before, on August 28th, Jamie, who was barely over five feet tall, and unarmed, had been shot multiple times, and she did not survive. My daughter lived for 30 years, 7 months, and 4 days.

It was around ten o'clock in the morning, the day the pretty blonde officer arrived. Rich got to the door first, and stepped outside, shutting the door, as I heard Jamie's name. I looked out my office window to see a white SUV parked in front of the house, so my first thought was that she was a bill collector. Something kept me from joining Rich on the front porch, but after a minute or so, I got up and went to look through the window, next to the door. The young woman held a metal clipboard, the kind that opens up, with a place to store papers, the type a bill collector might use. Then I saw it! The badge on her hip.

I stepped onto the front porch, and asked, not needing an answer,

"Jamie's dead, isn't she?"

Not wanting to deliver the news to Jamie's mother on the front porch, she asked if we could go inside. That was enough of an answer for me. I insisted she tell me right there on the porch. When she did, my knees collapsed, and Rich grabbed me before I hit the ground.

Inside the house, she asked me to sit so she could talk to me, but I couldn't sit down. I wrung my hands, and paced the floor, echoing what I had said so many times the day in the garage, exactly twelve years and twelve days earlier,

"No! No! No!"

As if saying it over and over would somehow erase the reality. I finally sat down and took in the news. No matter where Jamie's life path had taken her, it was a shock to face the reality that she was never coming back.

Neither the pain I experienced over losing Jamie repeatedly to the addiction Beast nor the loss of other loved ones prepared me to deal with the flood of grief that enveloped me. In an instant, my hope of having my daughter back, clean and healthy, was gone. I would never be the mother of the bride or have mother-daughter talks. I would never be a grandmother to Jamie's children. We would never tell our story together, as we had talked about doing. A bunch of "nevers" came crashing in. I was devastated, and I was mad at God.

I am one of the hardest working people I know, and I was working twice as hard as I ever have, to keep standing, to make a difference. I was trying to have more faith and live in peace. I couldn't understand how God could allow this to happen.

I was doing a good job keeping my Beast at bay, and while he would knock on the door of my life, often, I would recognize him and slam the door in his face before he had a chance to get in. That day he didn't knock on my door; he crashed through without warning. It was a home invasion.

I was right back on the mat with my Beast on top of me, the guilt flooding in. I hadn't seen or spoken to Jamie in the eighteen months before her death. It wasn't that I was mad at her or had banned her from my life, but I had drawn a line in the sand for sanity's sake. I had to do it for my marriage and our safety. Still, I couldn't help but wonder if this was somehow my fault. For the second time, I imagined my daughter lying alone in a pool of her own blood and tried to push the vision out of my mind.

Jamie and I had an email exchange a few weeks before the murder. I told her we had a treatment plan that we would help her with when she was ready. Guilty thoughts invaded my mind:

"I should have been more insistent about the treatment plan."

"Maybe I could have reached out more to her."

"I should have tried harder to make her get clean."

"A better mom would have never allowed us to be separated that long, no matter what."

My heart ached, and my brain was filled with couldas, shouldas, and wouldas.

When my mom heard about Jamie's death, she fell apart. Just as my reaction was to say, "no" over and over, she kept saying, "I can't do this." I assured her that I would help her through it. No matter how devastated I was over the death of my daughter, I now had to be strong for my mom, and others.

A day or so after Jamie's murder, I was at another crossroads. Sean had his arms around me.

"How am I going to live without her?" I said, without really expecting a reply.

"Because you have another child, mom, that's how."

His tone was not defensive or self-serving but gentle and loving. He spoke with such conviction that I accepted it as truth. The dark road of ongoing grief was calling me, but Sean reminded me there was another road. I would call it "New Normal," and it would be bumpy, but I was not about to head back into the darkness.

****

Rich had a younger brother growing up, named Bradley (yes, we both have little brothers named Bradley), who died when he was only fourteen, and Rich was sixteen years old. One day, he collapsed at school, and never even made it to the hospital. Rich has a half-brother, Scott, from his dad's second marriage, who was much younger than Rich. They didn't see much of each other, so for Rich, when he lost Bradley, he felt like an only-child, overnight.

Sean became an only-child overnight when Jamie died. Over the years, Rich and Sean have bonded over many more things than the San

Francisco 49ers, but the one they now share, having lost a sibling, is a bond that has brought them closer than ever.

I spent years thinking Rich didn't like Jamie when, in reality, he just wanted the chaos to stop. Rich was devastated, too, when she died. He quietly framed a photo of Jamie and put it on his nightstand. He tends to Jamie's memorial palm tree and garden. When those moments of disbelief crash in, and I say,

"She's really dead; she's never coming back,"

Rich simply says,

"I know."

He doesn't try to fix anything or to tell me not to be sad. He hugs me or holds my hand.

There were times when I wished Rich would ride in on a white horse and save me, but God knew I would need to save myself. He sent Rich to stand *with* me. Together, we have spent more than two decades, falling and standing back up. God sent me a *rich* man, after all.

It's How You Finish

I wasn't born with a silver spoon in my mouth; it was more like plastic. My life may have started with fear, worry, and uncertainty, but

I have learned it's not how you start that is important; it's how you finish.

While I left out some of the scariest and most painful parts of my story, every detail is not necessary to illustrate the point that life is messy. While that is true, the invaluable lessons we learn are worth the mess. The strength and wisdom gained allows us to turn messes into messages.

Every person will encounter many challenges on their trip through life. You come up against mean people, unfair situations, heartbreak, unmet expectations, loss of relationships, divorce, job or career change, death of loved ones, addiction, betrayal, health problems, financial challenges, and more.

With a heart shattered into a million pieces, and a dark cloud hanging over my heart, I decided to stand up and fight. I decided to stop making excuses, waiting for someone else, or something else to change. I was done living in fear. It was time for me to gather up my tools and get to work on living a courageous life.

I have come to believe that courage is more important than anything else. Okay, maybe not more than God, or oxygen, but it's right up there with oxygen. Unforeseen circumstances will smack us over the head, but unless we dare to live courageously, we are left helpless, hopeless, and depressed or trapped as a victim. Courage changes everything.

It is incredible how our lowest points can also be some of the best places to land. The day I told Rich I didn't want to be here anymore was a pivotal moment for me. It is what propelled me into a courageous life when I thought all was lost.

If not for living **The 9 Actions** that had become a part of my everyday life, there is no doubt in my mind, that I would still be struggling to stand, or would have dropped right back to the mat, and stayed there. Instead, I stood up soon after Jamie's death, more determined than ever, to make a difference. Jamie's legacy would not end with a murder. Mine would not end with depression and fear.

Anything worth having, doing, or being, will take courage. It takes courage to be happy, hopeful, and to have faith. Courage is what we use to push ourselves to try something new, meet people, or to walk away from destructive people or circumstances. It is courage that stands up when we feel like staying down. Courage sheds shame and gives up guilt. It is what we use to let go of the uncontrollable, and to choose peace instead. Courage allows us to embrace the holes in our hearts, and to overcome the losses. Courage is what we use to say *yes* to our purpose; to make the world a better place.

Jamie's murderer was finally arrested, nearly three years after her death. Now, we wait patiently for the wheels of justice to turn at the very slow pace they move. As we face the probability of a murder trial, it's more important than ever for me to be courageous.

On my journey to courage, there were plenty of moments when I wanted to quit on my life. There were times I wondered if I could keep going, or if I even wanted to try, but I did keep going. I share my story, and **The 9 Actions**, in hopes that you will build a life of courage, and learn to stand through anything that comes your way. Courageous people are not quitters. We might alter our course, but we don't quit.

In a million years, I couldn't have imagined living through even one of the many serious challenges, life tossed my way, but I did, and I am still standing. Once you cross the courage line, there is no going back.

What It Means to Overcome

For you to get on board with the idea that you can overcome anything, you first need to understand what it means. Some definitions are *1) succeed in dealing with a difficulty, 2) gain control over, or 3) master or tame.*

The subtitle of this book is, "How I Overcame Guilt, Shame, Hopelessness, Devastating Loss & Paralyzing Fear." Each one of these was keeping me from living a life of courage. Together, they had me down on the mat.

Nothing was going to get better until I decided to change. When I got started using **The 9 Actions**, *overcoming* was not even on my radar. It didn't occur to me that I could stop feeling guilt or shame. I wasn't sure hopelessness would be something in my past. I didn't know how courageous I could become.

I will never get over the loss of my daughter, and frankly, I don't want to get over her. I will live the rest of my life with a massive hole in my heart, but I believe our hearts are big enough to contain holes, and still have plenty of room for love, joy, hope, and happiness. Overcoming means the things that once held us captive, no longer control us.

I don't know where you sit today, or what you want and need to overcome. Maybe that word is a bit difficult for you to grasp right now, but don't allow that to deter you. One decision at a time, and using **The 9 Actions,** you will start living with hope. You will build the courage to keep getting back up. Over time, an hour of happiness will turn into days and then weeks. Make a commitment to the actions, and before long, you will have dealt with, tamed, or mastered, what had you down. You will be an overcomer.

Action #1: Decide to Stand Up & Fight

About the Action

Nothing is going to change in your life until you decide and then act.

Do you want more faith? Decide it's time to figure out how to do just that.

Would you like to have a better attitude? Decide to change your thinking.

Is it time to improve your health? Decide today is the day to begin the change.

Do you want to live in peace? Decide to stop creating or allowing chaos and drama into your life.

Do you want to be happier? Decide you are going to start making choices to that end.

As small children, Jamie and Sean began learning about the impact of thoughts. When they said, "I can't," I would ask them, "What did Henry Ford say?" I can still picture them looking up at me, replying,

"Whether you think you can, or you think you can't, you're right."

It is the same for me, and you. If you think you can't be happy, then you won't be happy. If you think your best days are behind you, then they are. If you think you can't change your thinking, then you can't. If you think you can't become healthier, then you won't. If you think you can't do anything, then you are right.

If you think you CAN accomplish something, then you CAN. A positive mindset results in speaking positive words, which will lead to taking positive action. Believe you can, and you can.

The American philosopher and poet, Ralph Waldo Emerson, is attributed with saying, "What you do speaks so loudly that I cannot hear what you say." Your actions will always speak louder than your words, to the point where your words will have no meaning if not backed up by corresponding actions.

Making a significant life change will require a fight. Don't look at this as a negative; it's merely a reality. You will be up against people who want to purposely or subconsciously keep you down. The Beast will do his level best to keep you where you are, for fear you might become all you are meant to be. Someone will irritate you. You will get a cold. Distractions will be everywhere. Your thoughts will convince you that you don't have what it takes. Life will get in the way.

This is why your initial decision is critical, but the subsequent decisions along the way are just as important. Every time you are discouraged and feel like giving up, make another decision. Get up off the mat and keep fighting.

Life knocked me down repeatedly. My choices dropped me to my knees. No matter how I got there, though, I kept getting back up.

One of my favorite bible verses is:

"Have I not commanded you? Be strong and courageous. Do not be afraid; do not be discouraged, for the LORD your God will be with you wherever you go." ~ Joshua 1:9

Too often, we are waiting for someone to save us, a situation to somehow turn around, or for someone to change. There is only one person you can change, and that person is you. No matter what you have experienced, or what you are going through today, you always have the power of your thoughts, and the ability to make decisions.

Standing between you and what you want is the decision to live a courageous life.

****

Time Flies, Whether We're Having Fun or Not

Time. We spend it, pass it, or kill it. We endure it and waste it. Yet, it's the one thing we cannot get more of, no matter who we are, what we do, how much money we earn, or how good of a person we become. Each time the clock strikes midnight, it's another day you cannot recover. Time is marching on, no matter what we do with it.

Often, Rich and I will look at each other and say, "I can't believe I am ___ years old." I didn't leave a blank because I am concerned you know our ages, but because we have been saying it for years, and probably will for years to come.

In our younger years, it seemed we had nothing but time left. The older we get, time seems to move more quickly, but, of course, time keeps moving at the same speed it has always moved. Maybe time seems to pick up speed because each day we move closer to the inevitable, and we start to recognize the value and preciousness of time.

The saying goes: "time flies when you're having fun." That is only partially true. In reality, time flies, whether you're having fun or not.

The speed at which life is going by comes to mind nearly every night as I get ready for bed. I wash my face, brush my teeth, apply my lotions and potions, and the rest of the twenty-five steps that is my bedtime routine (seriously, I counted them), and think, wow, another day crossed off the calendar.

Lyrics from "Who Am I" by Casting Crowns is a further reminder (as if we needed more reminding) of just how fleeting life is:

> *I am a flower quickly fading;*
> *Here today and gone tomorrow;*
> *A wave tossed in the ocean;*
> *A vapor in the wind.*

Today is the only day you are guaranteed; make it count. Every day after today is a bonus. The value of our precious time cannot be emphasized enough.

This action is all about deciding to act now - not tomorrow, and certainly not *someday*. Time is flying by, and you cannot afford to spend, pass, kill, or waste any more of your precious time.

TIP: *Time is the one thing you cannot get more of, no matter who you are or what you do. Value your precious time, and start making the most of it.*

Stand Up

As a parent, the most nerve-wracking sport for me to watch was wrestling. Typically, wrestling matches are one at a time, with the lone wrestler, pitted against an opponent. Sean was in the heavyweight division, and it would be the last match of the day, and often, the deciding match for the team. Team sports are much less stressful.

Sean's high school team was at a big meet in a large college gym. In the preliminaries, there were several mats on a large gym floor, where multiple matches were taking place simultaneously. During these particular matches, we were able to stand on the floor, next to the mat.

Sean was down on the mat with his opponent working to flip him to his back, while Sean struggled to get loose. Eventually, he made it to his feet but was still bent over, while the wrestler who was older and more experienced, worked to get him back down on the mat.

While the two boys struggled, Sean's coach paced, yelling until he was red in the face,

"Stand up, Sean! Stand up!"

With my family history of bad backs, I had visions of Sean's going out as he labored to stand. I had to bite my tongue to keep from saying something to the coach.

The battle wore on, and the coach continued to shout,

"Stand up!"

Eventually, Sean stood up, got the upper hand, took his opponent to the mat, and won the match.

We don't like to struggle; it's uncomfortable, and we don't want to be uncomfortable. Seeing someone we love struggle, is even worse, so giving up can seem like a far less painful option. A part of me would just as soon Sean had stayed down on the mat or even given up, so he could have avoided pain. It's a good thing his mom stayed quiet, and he listened to his coach, who knew that if Sean didn't stand up soon, he was going to be pinned.

I continually remind myself that I need to keep standing. If I do fall, I know I must stand back up quickly. The longer we stay down on the mat, the harder it is to stand. If you are down on the mat and don't make the decision to stand up, you will be pinned.

Just as Sean's coach told him, I am telling you – Stand Up!

TIP: It may seem easier to stay down on the mat, but that is not where you belong. Stand up!

Standing Up to Fear

Fear is a complicated emotion. One that is detrimental yet necessary. Fear alerts us to danger and can keep us from repeating painful mistakes, but it is also a nasty little culprit that keeps us from realizing our dreams, making changes, trying something new, or stepping out in faith. Excess fear can be paralyzing.

Fear isn't always rational. Many people are terrified of air travel. Based on statistics, people should stop and kiss the ground when they arrive safely at the airport, since driving in a car is far more dangerous than air travel. However, people who have a fear of flying continue to hop in their car every day without giving it a thought and require a tranquilizer before boarding an airplane. My advice to anyone afraid to fly is this – fly more. You may never be jumping up and down as you board an aircraft, but the more you take off and land safely, the less fear you will feel each time you fly.

Shying away from fears only serves to increase them. Standing up to fear gives us power over them. We cannot completely eliminate fear, but we can overcome the hold fear has over our lives.

Small fears are equally as essential to deal with as the big ones. Facing fear consistently builds courage. Learning to face little fears prepares you to meet the big ones.

While vacationing in Mexico a couple of decades ago, I met some guests who were temporarily caring for an escaped pet parrot that made its way to the resort. I was fascinated by the talking bird, but I wasn't excited about getting too close to it.

When I was young, I watched Alfred Hitchcock's horror/thriller film, The Birds. In it, a small town was terrorized by sudden, violent bird attacks. If I got close enough to this parrot, I wondered if I would suffer the same fate.

One afternoon, I was sitting in my regular spot on the beach under a palapa, anticipating a rousing game of cribbage with my husband, and nothing else but perhaps a cold drink and a bowl of chips with guacamole, when the couple with the bird showed up. They were completely aware I had no desire to hold their adopted pet, and yet they asked me to watch it while they went to lunch. Before I could protest, the bird was in my arms, and down the beach, they went.

I sat, trying to look brave as people stopped to admire *my* bird. After a couple of hours, the bird sitters returned and relieved me of my duties. I was proud of myself for my bravery, and happy the bird didn't peck my eyes out.

There is a couple in our neighborhood who walk their dog and their bird, which is a large creamy white cockatoo, with an orange crest. There must be some cosmic reason I need to get over this bird fear thing, as I finally stopped to admire the beautiful creature. Suddenly, the bird lifted its incredibly large clawed foot off of its owner's arm and leaned in toward me. I backed up, thinking, "here we go again with the birds."

They explained the gesture meant that Mr. Cockatoo wanted to sit on my arm., so I reluctantly held it out, and I stood there, trying to act nonchalant with this magnificent bird on my arm. Then, he made a similar gesture, reaching for my shoulder. I am all for overcoming fears, but that was not happening. If I thought the parrot in Mexico might peck my eyes out, this huge cockatoo could have eaten my head. But, I lived to tell about both of my bird encounters. The score is Valerie – 2, Birds – 0.

I have faced many fears such as heights, single motherhood, betrayal, a job I was under-qualified for, public speaking, and birds. I was becoming more and more courageous, but whatever courage I built up, was all but lost after all hell broke loose. My courage muscles were pretty wimpy by the time I pulled the emergency brake and got off the Roller Coaster From Hell. The good news is that they can be built back up, with time and effort.

After nearly three years, it appeared my daughter's murder was headed to the cold case files. Then suddenly her accused murderer was arrested. The first court appearance this guy faced was his arraignment, just days after his arrest. Our Victim's Advocate recommended that we not attend hearings, but rather to allow her to keep us informed. I appreciate her effort to protect and support us through our long ordeal, but I told Sherri I wanted, no, I *needed* to face the guy who took my daughter's life.

Standing outside the closed courtroom doors, I told Sherri I was ready, although my hands had begun to tremble, and my heart was racing. Taking a big breath, I nodded, and she opened the door.

It was hard to miss him as I entered the small courtroom; he was the one in orange. I burst into tears when I locked eyes with my daughter's accused killer. I had not planned the sudden outburst that occurred as I walked toward him.

"How could you?" I said, rather loudly.

The judge looked up, and a bailiff immediately came over and informed me I was not to speak to the defendant. All eyes were upon me as I assured him I was prepared to sit quietly during the remainder of the short hearing. For the next few minutes, each time the defendant looked over at me, I looked right back. I faced a big fear that day; I stared down pure evil.

Fear is the path to the dark side. Fear leads to anger. Anger leads to hate. Hate leads to suffering. ~ Yoda

The ever-wise Yoda, of Star Wars fame, said, "fear is the path to the dark side," and the first step on that path, is anger. So many people tell me that anger is a big problem, and they wonder how to stop being so angry. First, we must realize that anger is typically a by-product of another emotion. Often, it is fear, and a defense mechanism we employ is anger. If we stay angry, we don't have to deal with the emotions, but if we stay angry long enough, hate creeps in. Once hatred is ingrained in us, we suffer.

Fear is the opposite of faith, and it's not from God; it's one of the battle tactics the Big Beast uses to separate us from God. The more we give in to fears, the more control the Beast has over us.

On the contrary, fear backs down when we face it. Our Beasts back down when we stand up to them. When we're wearing spiritual armor (the next action), our Beasts shudder.

Overcoming fear does not mean you never feel afraid, but it does mean you face those fears. There will be some rather large situations you will have to deal with on your trip through life, things that will slap you in the face and force courage out of you, but that is not the only way courage is developed. You can choose to face your fears head-on.

TIP: *You will never completely eliminate fear, but you can overcome it. Stand up to your fears, big and small, and you will overcome them.*

Why Me?

Humans need to know. There is satisfaction in finding answers to the millions of questions that begin with, "Why."

When Jamie's Beast grabbed hold of her and didn't let go for years, I began to ask, *why?* I couldn't understand why my brilliant daughter was on her destructive path. If I could only find the answer, we could all go back to living happy lives.

During my entire Roller Coaster From Hell ride, and beyond, I asked *why* incessantly. Many times, my question *why* was followed by *me*. Why me?

I couldn't understand why my life had fallen apart when I had tried so hard to keep it together. I wondered what I had done to make God so mad that he would punish me like this. Why? Why my child? Why is this or that not working out? Why me?

Many of our questions are pure curiosity or a need to understand. But, the questions we are most desperate to answer are those that will often elude us forever.

Two necessary actions were taken to help me stop asking *why* incessantly. First, I looked into the mirror (while I was running the *why me* question in my mind), and out loud, I asked the woman staring back at me,

"Why *not* you?"

I would rather have drawn a different card from the deck of life's problems, but there I was with *these* problems. So, why not be the one who stands up? Why not prove it is possible to be happy again? Why not be a role model? Why not prove my teachers right, and be a leader? Why not *me*?

The second significant action I took was to stop trying to figure out the answers for all of my *whys*. As part of Action #7, which is all about letting go of control, I started filing the questions I beat my head against the wall trying to answer into the "Some Things Don't Make Sense File."

TIP: If you are asking "why" with no answers, do one of two things (or both): 1) ask yourself why not you, or 2) start using the Some Things Don't Make Sense File (see Action #7).

No More Excuses

We come up with a multitude of "reasons" why we don't act to bring about positive change. Call them what you want, but the reality is, most of our reasons are simply excuses, and they are keeping us from moving forward.

One of the most common excuses I hear is,

"It's easier said than done."

Well, of course, it is! Everything is easier to say than to put some effort behind.

I am an action-oriented person and not big on excuses, but life's two-by-fours have a way of changing us, and often, not in the right way. As I was losing my confidence, I began to make excuses. I was waiting for Jamie to change. I was waiting for the economy to improve. I was waiting for Rich to do this or that. I was waiting. While I waited, I slid backward, and the more I backslid, the more excuses I made. I was in a vicious cycle of excuses, and one of them was, "it's easier said than done."

The vast majority of reasons we have for not doing something, or continuing a destructive, or unhealthy lifestyle, are nothing more than excuses, neatly packaged to look like reasons.

There may be some realities you are facing that are temporarily preventing you from doing certain things, but you are an intelligent and creative person and can find a way to overcome in spite of the realities. What excuses do you have for not making changes to get what it is you want? Are they indeed reasons, or are they excuses? It's time to be honest with yourself.

Making excuses is easy. We could make about a hundred of them right now. You could make an excuse for not finishing this book, but you didn't begin reading it for the easy way out. (I told you, if you are looking for a quick fix, I am not your girl.) You picked it up because you want to change something about your life. Change takes time and effort, and a fight against the opposition, including our patterns of thinking and behavior, and those pesky excuses. It is time to set aside all of your excuses, wrapped up as reasons. It's time to find reasons to stand.

TIP: Most reasons are nothing more than excuses. It's time to stop the excuses for not doing something and start finding reasons.

Finding a Reason to Stand

My first reason to stand was Sean. He was going through enough. He was losing his only sibling, his first friend, to the addiction Beast. His family was fractured, and he was hurting and struggling to find his way. The last thing he needed was his mom falling apart. No matter how much I pretended, I was okay; Sean knew I wasn't doing well. He could sense I was changing, and not in a good way. The more I changed, for the worse, the madder Sean was at his sister. My self-destruction was affecting Sean in ways I didn't see, for far too long.

While our own experiences teach us the most, we also learn from others. My life had a significant influence on Sean's, and it was my responsibility to teach him one of the most important lessons he could ever learn. This lesson was not one that could be explained with words. It had to be shown by example. Nobody was in a better position than me to prove to Sean that no matter how hard life gets, he could choose to stand. If I didn't step up and show him, who would?

If you don't feel you can stand for yourself right now, find a reason. Initially, my self-worth was so low that I didn't think I could stand for myself, so I stood for Sean. Whatever reason you can find, to stand, find it. Remember that time is precious, so make today the day you decide to stand up.

TIP: *Find your reason to stand. Eventually, you need to stand for yourself, but right now, find whatever reason it takes to get you up and standing.*

Fear of Making the Wrong Decisions

I have always made decisions quickly, but after all hell broke loose, I was having difficulty with even the smallest of decisions, much less the important ones that needed my attention.

To get back to being a decision-making machine, the first thing I did was to decide. As Nike says, I had to "just do it." That was the key to getting the decision-making engine revved up again. I had to go with what I knew at the time, decide, and live with the outcome.

I accept that I will make decisions I would not have made if I had a crystal ball, but I don't. You don't have one either, so go ahead and make the best decisions you can with the information you have today, and then try not to worry about it.

It is not as if we get an allotment of decisions. We are always in decision-making mode, and there is no limit to how many we can make, so stop worrying about one single decision.

TIP: *You will make the wrong decisions, make them anyway. Let go of the outcome, and remember, there is no limit to the number of decisions you have the ability to make.*

Sitting at a Crossroads

At many points in your life, you will be at a crossroads, with decisions before you. Certain paths might be easy to figure out, while others might cause you confusion, or fear.

The day I told Rich, "I don't want to be here anymore," and scared myself into action, I was sitting at a crossroads that would define the rest of my life, one way or another. I glanced at the two roads before me. The one I was currently traveling, was filled with pain, sadness, fear, self-doubt, shame, and chaos, but it was familiar. The second was unfamiliar and contained roadblocks, mountains, and monsters. They both had Beasts. It was scary, and I was apprehensive, but I was willing to head down a new path, just in case it was the road to freedom. With a tiny bit of hope and a shred of self-confidence, I chose the new route.

I wonder how many times my mom was sitting at a crossroads when life was difficult for her, barely getting by with four mouths to feed. I wouldn't blame her one bit if she felt like running down a different path. Thankfully, she chose the path of courage, setting an example for my own crossroads moments.

When you are sitting at a crossroads, not sure which path to take, be careful not to take the familiar road, simply because it's comfortable. A new way might be scary, but it could also be the road to freedom.

TIP: When you are tempted to stay on a particular path because it's comfortable, or the new way might be too scary, dig down and find some courage. Be willing to take an unfamiliar road that might lead to freedom.

Stay in the Ring Until the Final Round

It is easy to quit, and there could be valid reasons to do so. But, most of the time, we give up before we should. We stop because it is hard, or taking too long, or we are scared.

I am not a big football fan, knowing just enough about the game to not make a fool of myself watching with real fans. One thing I know for sure is that getting down the field and into the end zone is the ultimate goal during each possession.

We have all heard the football analogy of not quitting on the one-yard line. When you are that close to the end zone, i.e., your goal, don't stop. It is said that this is precisely where most people throw in the towel - right before they reach victory.

Recently, I watched not one, but two football games on the same day. During my football watching extravaganza, it occurred to me just how difficult it is for the offensive team to move the ball one single yard when they are at the goal line. They have already moved the ball as many as ninety-nine yards, yet one single yard appears harder than all of the ninety-nine yards before.

It seems the more we work toward something good, the more opposition we face. The closer we are to the *goal line*, the more our opponents try to block or tackle us.

When I feel the Beast fighting me, I picture myself in the boxing ring with him. He throws a few jabs at me, and I jab back. He lands a punch, and I land two. The Beast can throw as many punches as he wants my way, but I will keep hitting back, and I will keep standing. I have decided to stay in the ring until the final round.

What if you are on the one-yard line, ready to cross the goal line? Stay in the ring until the final round. It doesn't matter how many times you are knocked down, as long as you keep getting back up.

Fight as if your life depends on it because it does.

TIP: *It is easy to quit, but that's not why you are reading this book. You desire a life of courage, full of possibilities. No matter how many times you are knocked down, get back up. Stay in the ring until the final round.*

Action Reminder

Time is flying by. Each time the clock strikes midnight, it's another day you cannot recover. No matter what you do with your precious time, it marches on. Today is the only day you are guaranteed. Every day after today is a bonus. Use your time wisely.

Whatever the size of the challenge in front of you, it will be somewhat of a fight. Anything worth having, doing, or being, will take work. You will need to break habits, consider new perspectives, change your thinking, and take different actions. The Beast will get ahold of you, others may try to deter you, or you might knock yourself down. No matter how it happens, you will become discouraged, scared, or frustrated. Expecting the road to have roadblocks, will keep you from turning around and running, the first time you hit a small speed bump.

Face your fears, no matter the size. Don't allow fear to control you.

Stop asking *why me* and start saying, *why not me*. Stop making excuses, and start finding reasons to stand.

Decide that you will stay in the ring until the final round. Stand up every single time you are knocked down, discouraged, and tempted to give up or give in.

There is freedom on the other side of your decisions. Living a life of happiness, peace, courage, faith, and purpose will be a battle, but it is worth it. Fight as if your life depends on it because it does.

Action #2: Get On Your Spiritual Armor

About the Action

Make no mistake about this – whatever challenges you face, or Beast you are dealing with – this is a spiritual battle as much as anything else. The forces of darkness work overtime to keep you from living with courage, confidence, faith, and peace.

If there is a school of Beasts, Satan is surely the headmaster, and he teaches his students well. I don't like to give enough respect to Satan by using his name, so I call him The Big Beast.

I wasn't raised in a particularly spiritual home, although I am grateful my childhood did include a few church visits, a baptism at six years old, and some Sunday school. In my great-grandma Fannie May's bible, I found index cards, with the 23rd Psalm not-so-neatly printed by eight-year-old Valerie. I distinctly remember asking my mom to help me memorize that verse. It includes "walking through the valley of the shadow of death," so I am not sure why in the world I was so intent on getting that one down.

Your spiritual armor may look very different from mine or others. Since I can only present the spiritual side of my life from the perspective of my own beliefs, you will need to modify some of my terminology to fit yours. Don't allow our differences to trip you up or cause you to abandon this or any of **The 9 Actions**.

We are made of body, mind, and spirit, but too often, it is our spirit that takes a back seat. We obsess over our physical appearance. The brain gets plenty of stimulation, probably too much at times. Our souls, however, are often left twisting in the wind as we obsess over our bodies, and our minds navigate the never-ending thought process.

In the darkest days of my journey, I couldn't put two thoughts together, was on the verge of tears every moment, and I was physically exhausted. During those times, it was a tiny bit of faith that kept me going.

Spiritual armor helps us to find peace and patience, overcome fear, and live in gratitude. God is our not-so-secret weapon in a battle with a Beast and the daily struggles of life.

****

Wavering Faith

I am going to tell you I am a super-duper church girl; I am not. I won't pretend I have always had complete faith in God; I have not. I've always admired people with a great deal of faith, who seem to float through life, leaving matters in God's hands.

During my darkest days, I prayed hard. I got out my sword and battled The Big Beast. I sought after God, but life didn't become more comfortable. The heat was turned up. Most of the time, I couldn't hear anything from God. It seemed the more I tried to stay in faith, the harder life became. As a result, my faith waivered - big time.

I begged, pleaded, and made deals. I cried out, petitioned, and even yelled at God. I wondered where he was and why I couldn't seem to hear from him, at least not in the way I had expected or hoped. I tossed my spiritual armor against the wall many times, and then picked it back up. I didn't struggle with my belief in God, but I did struggle with faith.

It's difficult enough to have faith when bank accounts are bulging, kids are doing well, relationships are reliable, and health is excellent. When the rug is pulled out from under us, our faith is tested in ways we couldn't have imagined.

But I decided I would much rather walk with God, not knowing what is around the next corner, than without him, pretending to have it all under control. I started to believe that no matter what was in my future, with God beside me, I could stand through anything.

I will never completely understand God's ways, but I am willing to keep my spiritual armor on and ride this thing out until the very end. I am working hard to trust that he knows a bit more about my future than I do.

Whatever your spiritual armor looks like, get it on and keep it on. You are going to need it.

TIP: *Your faith has probably waivered, like mine. You might be confused about where God is, and what he is doing, but stay in faith. Get on your spiritual armor, and keep it on.*

The Big "No" From Heaven

When you pray hard for something, and it doesn't happen, or worse yet, the opposite happens, it can cause you to question your faith.

I prayed for years each morning, for Jamie to beat her addiction. It was a prayer for a miracle because I knew that's what it would take. When Jamie died, my prayer was answered in the worst way possible. It felt like a middle finger from heaven. I was mad at God and gave him a piece of my mind – out loud – just in case he could no longer read my mind. I accused him of getting this one wrong. It would have been nothing for him to jam the gun, or cause a flat tire – he's God! He should have granted me my miracle.

Had I not already committed to walking this out with God, I may have given up on my faith, when the big "No" came down from heaven. It is so critical to keep your spiritual armor on, even when you are confused about what God is doing, or not doing.

It wasn't until after Jamie died that I saw clearly how God strategically placed certain people in my life, well in advance of when I would need them, or just in time. I received signs when I needed to know Jamie was near, and messages of encouragement, when I felt like quitting.

While I would opt for Jamie being alive and clean, I have come to accept that her life on this earth is over, but mine is not. Until my time on earth is over, I can choose to bring as much good from this tragedy as possible. After plenty of heavenly "Nos," I still believe that God will always provide opportunities for us to find the good, even in the worst of situations. He will always present us with yeses for our nos.

I have come a long way from yelling at God over Jamie's death, to being convinced she was on a collision course with disaster and went to heaven at the exact right moment. She was supposed to live 30 years, 7 months, 4 days. We were spared far worse than we had already experienced.

Incredible things can come out of the most devastating of situations if you are willing to believe and stay in faith when you have no idea what God is doing, or even if you get the big "No," from heaven.

TIP: God will always provide opportunities for us to find the good, even in the worst of situations. He will always present us with yeses for our nos.

Patience

We all have our strengths. Unfortunately, we all have weaknesses; one of mine is patience. I must have fallen off the assembly line in heaven when patience was being sprinkled in.

Impatience creates frustration, intolerance, and a great deal of disappointment. I have always admired people who had an abundance of patience, so I decided to get me some of that.

I literally got down on my knees, and boldly asked God for patience, and then I got back up and waited. I hoped I would wake up the next day as a patient person. After all, before I put in my request, I admitted my weakness, apologized, and asked for forgiveness. Hadn't I checked all the boxes?

I no sooner asked for patience when the $#*! really hit the fan. God could have waved his mighty hand over me, but apparently, that's not how it works. It appears God prefers we develop patience through trials and tribulations, and continuously choosing our feelings and reactions.

I process information very quickly, so I would be very impatient with other people who did not. It wasn't that I thought I was smarter, or better; I was just impatient.

God has all the time in the world, and we are stuck here on earth with these annoying things called clocks and calendars. We start to realize the clock is ticking, and days are being checked off of the calendar, and we become impatient. My patience process wasn't a downhill ride, but rather an uphill battle. With little patience, to begin with, I was impatient with the process of becoming a patient person.

I was playing a children's board game with a cousin. She was having a hard time grasping the rules of the game (or I didn't give the poor girl a chance to figure it out), and I was overheard, saying,

"Tammy, why don't you understand? It's so easy."

How rude. I want to issue an official apology to my cousin, Tammy. We haven't seen each other in decades, but four-year-old Valerie owes four-year-old Tammy an apology.

That is what happens when we are too impatient. We can wind up being rude, even if we are nice people.

The person I was most impatient with was myself. The expectations I place on myself are always higher than on others.

Slowly, over time and with a great deal of effort, I have developed a much higher level of patience with myself and others. Now, don't get the wrong impression. I tend to move at warp speed, so I am not exactly at the Buddhist monk level, but I am far more patient than I had ever pictured myself being.

Be mindful of your patience level. Take a deep breath when you find yourself becoming impatient. Be more tolerant and understanding of others who would otherwise test your patience. By the way, patience has a great deal to do with peace, so, stay tuned to the next section.

TIP: *Be mindful of your patience level. Take a deep breath when you find yourself becoming impatient. Make a conscious effort to be more patient with yourself and others.*

The Quest for Peace

Life is full of things to worry about, but I knew God didn't want me to worry. Of course, it was easy for him to say; he's God. I was just little Valerie, floundering around, trying to make some sense of the storm my life had become.

I tried not to worry, but it was nearly impossible. I tried to resist the temptation to Google Jamie's name when she would go missing because all it did was add to my stress, no matter the search results.

We worry about our children, no matter their age. We worry about the economy and our finances. We worry about what other people are doing or saying. We worry about worrying too much. None of it gets us anywhere.

It felt wrong to live in peace when Jamie was living with drug users and dealers. I would be a terrible mother if I sought peace – *my* peace. Besides, I needed to stay on high alert.

Unfortunately, I have learned what high-alert accomplishes. I wound up with adrenal fatigue from living on high alert for so long, with my adrenals working overtime. I am suffering the consequences of my flawed thinking and the choice to stay on high alert.

For the longest time, I desired even a moment's peace, yet I was still living in the chaos. We can pray for peace all we want, but we have to meet God somewhere on the road to peace.

I stepped up and drew my line in the sand with Jamie. I told her I loved her as much as I did the day she was born. I painted a picture of what my life looked like, and assured her I wanted her in that life, but it did not include illegal drugs, dealers, lies, deceit, or people shooting people. It was honesty, integrity, family, hard work, peace, and purpose. I took a stand, for my sanity, and it was up to her to decide whether or not she saw herself in that picture.

I kept praying for peace and then making conscious choices to meet God on the road to peace. I weaned myself off of searching the Internet for Jamie's name or trying to locate her secret Facebook accounts. I started focusing on my journey and how I could make a difference. I never lost hope, but I stopped obsessing over Jamie's life.

Slowly, but surely, peace entered my life, but because I had lived with little peace most of my life, I expected it to vanish at the drop of a hat (or a Google search), but it stayed with me, even after Jamie's murder.

I had heard about that *peace that surpasses all understanding* and never imagined it would apply to me. I am not sure if that is what I have, but I can tell you without reservation that what I do have is peace that surpasses *my* understanding.

It is a lifelong process to remain peaceful, so I keep working at it, no matter what is going on around me.

Too often, the level of peace we experience is in direct proportion to how well things are going in our lives. Hardship, heartbreak, disappointment, and troubles will hit all people to varying degrees. They are unavoidable, a part of the deal that comes with living on planet earth. The key is to get to a place where you can find peace during times of trouble or devastating loss.

TIP: We were not created to worry, but to have faith, to live in peace. Pray for peace, and then do your part to meet God somewhere on the road to peace.

Blessing and Miracles

During my worst years, any time I heard somebody with their seemingly perfect life, say, "I'm so blessed," I cringed. I recall wondering why God would bless others and not me. It made no sense that I was seeking him daily and working hard to find my purpose, and yet others, who didn't even seem to know God at all, were blessed all over the place. It has taken me some time to realize that there is no scoring system in heaven.

I have no answer for how or why God dishes out, allows, removes, or holds back on blessings, but I do know when we spend time focused on the blessings of others, we can miss those staring us right in the face.

Miracles happen too, but unless they come with six-figures or a bolt of lightning, we often miss them.

The bullet that was lodged in Jamie's abdomen came out nine months after the initial shooting. She found it in the toilet and called to tell me. That didn't sound right, based on what I knew about where the bullet was located, so I called our family doctor, who had hospital records in hand. He told me there was no way that was the same bullet since there was no migration path between the abdominal wall and the colon. After an x-ray, nobody was more surprised than our doctor; the bullet was gone. He suggested we take the x-ray to the surgeon because it would undoubtedly be documented as a medical miracle.

There was that three-week window for me to meet Rich. Any number of things could have kept me from our meeting, and plenty of things stood in the way of us winding up together. I don't know if that would be considered a miracle, but it certainly was a blessing.

I still live with significant challenges, so it would be easy to fall right back into the trap of missing my blessings and miracles. We can find people everywhere that seem more blessed than we are, but it doesn't do any good to focus on that. I use Action #6 a great deal, to keep my focus where it needs to be.

Be open to and aware of your blessings and miracles. They happen, but it is up to you to recognize them.

Aside from learning to adjust your focus, learning to live in gratitude will make a huge difference in you not missing out on blessings and miracles.

TIP: Blessings are all around us, and miracles happen too, but we are often too fixated on other people, or what we don't have, that we miss them. Don't miss your blessings and miracles.

Gratitude

It is easy to be thankful when everything is going well. How grateful do you feel when things don't go your way, or when all hell breaks loose? That is when your faith is genuinely put to the test. It is when you begin to understand that not all blessings come in the form of big bank accounts, great jobs, big houses, or amazing children.

When I started to work on my attitude and focus, I was once again able to recognize blessings, and not all of them looked like one might imagine.

Some of the most valuable blessings come in the form of a roadblock, hurdle, or challenge. Or, even in the form of a heavenly "no." We have to look harder to find blessings when times are tough.

It is easy to get into a routine and forget about being grateful. One thing I do is thank God out loud for even the tiniest of things.

I have a gratitude box where I place little slips of paper that contain my gratitude and the date. Often, they are one word. On particularly hard days, I will often place several gratitude slips in the box. There are now hundreds of dated notes in my gratitude box, and sometimes, I take some out and read them. It is fun to recall something I had not thought about recently or to recognize the number of times I have been grateful for the same things, situations, or people.

I believe gratitude gets God's attention far quicker than grumbling and complaining, or continually reminding him what we need, or want.

Living gratitude-minded helped me to change my attitude and adjust my focus.

I highly recommend you grab a jar, basket, shoebox – anything – and start a gratitude container. Remember to speak your gratitude out loud. There is something powerful about the spoken word. Try to remember to drop at least one thing in the container daily. On particularly tough days, put in ten! It is a quick way to change your attitude and adjust your focus. Share with others, so that they can experience the power of living gratitude minded.

Be sure to acknowledge gratitude throughout the day. Speak it out loud. This one simple practice will shift your mindset quickly.

TIP: *On good days, write down at least one note of gratitude and on tough days, ten. Verbally acknowledge gratitude throughout the day.*

Action Reminders

Whatever you are dealing with may seem impossible. It might feel as if it is too big for you to handle, but the good news is that no matter what you face, it is never too big for God. Stay in faith when God doesn't answer your prayers the way you want, hope, or pray. You don't know what might be going on behind the scenes.

Put your spiritual armor back on after you have jumped up and down on it, or tossed it into the closet. Don't lose faith when God says, "Not yet, or even, "No."

Work on having more patience with others and with yourself.

Do as I did, and go on a Quest for Peace. When you do, make sure you are not only praying for peace but meeting God on the road to peace.

Start making choices that help to develop patience. Pray, but be willing to make choices in line with your requests.

Don't miss your blessings and miracles. They happen all the time, but we are often too focused on what is going wrong, to notice them.

Develop a gratitude mindset. Throughout the day, acknowledge what you are grateful for, out loud. Get yourself a container to use for daily gratitude and then use it. Living in appreciation changes your attitude, focus, and so much more.

Action #3: Put On Your Oxygen Mask

About the Action

The purpose of this action is to bring attention to self-care, and the oxygen mask is a great example. It may seem unnecessary in today's self-indulgent society to discuss self-care. However, there is a big difference between self-indulgence and self-care. Plus, no matter how self-centered a society becomes, there will always be those willing to sacrifice their well-being in an attempt to save another person or to be a people-pleaser.

If you have traveled by air, you're familiar with the safety demonstration the flight attendants go through before takeoff. One crucial part is regarding your oxygen mask. We are told in the case of a loss in cabin pressure; your mask will be released from the overhead compartment. Instructions are given as to how to properly place the oxygen mask on your face and exactly how it will react as you begin to breathe. You are further instructed to put the oxygen mask on your face before trying to assist others around you.

Taking care of number one (you) means you will have the energy and proper mindset to be available for service to others. To be in a position to help other people, you must keep your *well-being tank* full. It is a balance between self-care and being of service to others.

This action is not solely for those who are out of balance, caring for others. It is also about general self-care. It is why I have included getting outdoors, exercising, sleep, and laughter.

While self-care includes mental, emotional, physical, and spiritual well-being, we will not emphasize the spiritual side in this action, since we dedicated the previous action to that aspect of self-care.

Give yourself permission to matter. You have one shot at this journey called "life," so take care of the one and only, You.

****

It's *Your* Oxygen Mask

Some of us concern ourselves with the welfare of others at the expense of our well-being. This only results in mental fatigue, or physical and emotional exhaustion. Often, serious health issues surface. Some head into full-on self-destruction mode.

Others burn themselves out in an attempt to please everybody, which is impossible. The moment you please one person, you will displease the next. In all of the flurry to please everyone else, you will find yourself unfulfilled and wiped out.

The so-called oxygen masks of life are given to each of us for breathing our own oxygen.

Imagine for a moment, that situation no airline passenger wants to think about – a need for oxygen inflight. If it were to happen, your first instinct might be to help somebody else with their mask before even thinking about yours. But, we all know what would happen if you ran out of air, attempting to secure another person's mask.

For some people, especially women, and certainly moms, it is counter-intuitive to put ourselves anywhere near the top of the self-care list. Sometimes we are not even on the list. It is noble to care for others, but self-destructing because of them is not. We are responsible *to* people, but not *for* them. We are responsible for inspiring, motivating, empowering, loving, guiding, and encouraging other people. We are not responsible for their happiness or choices, and they are not responsible for ours.

If you care for children or an adult who is disabled, of course, you need to put their needs near the top of the list. But, you have to be on the list too, or at some point, you might find yourself unable to provide care for them, and then everybody loses.

I saw this with my mom as she attempted to care for Chips, whose dementia manifested into anger much of the time. An ordinarily kind and gentle man was frustrated and angry. She finally had to admit she needed help, or she might not be with us today.

My oxygen mask spent far too much time on Jamie's face, for it to be healthy for either of us. She needed to find her own oxygen mask, but why would she, when she was sucking up my oxygen?

You are not a super-hero, although some people might consider you just that. The fact is you are human, and you have an emotional and mental fuel tank, and only one body, just like everyone else. Placing your oxygen mask on somebody else's face for too long will result in you becoming wiped out mentally, emotionally, physically, and spiritually.

Your "mask" is for breathing *your* oxygen. To be there for someone else, you first have to be there for yourself.

TIP: *We are responsible to people, but not for them. It is critical, especially in times of high stress or crisis, that you practice self-care. Be mindful of your oxygen.*

The Healing Power of Nature

"Go outside and play" is what our parents told us when we were kids, and we did. My brothers and I would go on a "pack lunch" on Saturdays, or during school breaks. We packed a lunch and left for the day, not venturing too far from home, since we lived next to the woods, where we played all day, stopping only for our lunch.

Times have changed in favor of playdates or going outdoors mainly for organized sports. Many people do not go outside much more than to and from the car.

Nature is a fantastic setting to de-stress, think, or connect with God. There is nothing like the solitude of an early morning walk where the only sounds are birds chirping (I do like birds from a distance), or a breeze through the trees. Few things rival a mountain hike or a walk along a beach or a river. Nature is where I always feel closest to God.

In the Hoh Rain Forest in Washington many years ago, I was mesmerized by the giant trees that canopy the forest. My spirit was so happy that I hugged a gigantic, moss-covered tree. A few months later, I hugged a huge oak tree in Baton Rouge, Louisiana. Several of us held hands around its enormous trunk and gave it a group hug.

My favorite place to work out is anywhere outside. I live in the desert, where high temperatures are in the hundreds during summer months and the lows in the mid-eighties. During those months, it takes creativity to keep my outdoor workouts going, but it is important enough to me that I find ways.

One excuse many people use for not going outdoors is the weather. I saw an article about which states in the U.S. have populations that consider themselves as "outdoor recreationalists." The states with the highest self-proclaimed outdoor recreationalists were Alaska, Montana, Idaho, North Dakota, Wyoming, Utah, Vermont, and Washington. Not exactly the sunbelts of the country. We can dress for nearly any weather.

My journey to courage included finding as much time as I could to be outdoors. I exercise, write, read, or walk in the outdoors as much as possible. There is something special about communing with nature, breathing fresh air, and marveling at the miraculous signs of God.

Get outdoors as much as possible. Go hug a tree.

TIP: Go outside and play. If it is raining, put on your raingear, or grab an umbrella. Spend time at a river, a lake, or at the ocean. Take a walk in the forest or hike up a mountain trail. Take an early morning or evening walk around your neighborhood. Go hug a tree.

Exercise

My trips to the gym began in high school. It was how my friend Janet and I justified downing a plate of nachos afterward. In those days, I could have skipped the workout since my metabolism was in high gear, but it's a good thing I got into the habit early on because my metabolism button has all but turned off since.

Rich, on the other hand, rarely exercises, and barely has an ounce of fat on him. Still, even naturally thin people need exercise for the heart, to keep blood circulating, and for all of the other amazing benefits of moving our bodies.

We find many excuses not to get our bodies moving. If you are not able to go outdoors, or to a gym, you only have to be able to get online. There are YouTube videos, for free, for every fitness level, and any exercise you can imagine.

I typically exercise a minimum of five days a week, which might lead you to believe I love working out, and you, on the other hand, hate it. The truth is that I'm not as excited about working out as you might think, but I am motivated to keep working on my metabolism and to stay healthy as I age. Plus, I love how I feel afterward, so it's worth deciding to do it, even when I would rather have my gums scraped.

There is plenty of research and proof that exercise not only benefits us physically but has incredible psychological benefits as well. When you exercise, your body releases endorphins, and one of the benefits of endorphins is the trigger of positive feeling in the body. They act as analgesics, so they diminish the perception of pain. Endorphins have been proven to reduce stress, ward off anxiety and depression, boost self-esteem, and improve sleep. That list right there should be enough for you to lace up your sneakers or get out the yoga mat.

TIP: In today's Internet age, there is no good excuse for most people not to exercise. You don't even have to leave your house. There are countless videos for any fitness level, and for every type of workout you can imagine, and some you didn't know existed. If you don't have an exercise routine, it's time to get started now.

Sleep

Sleep is critical for healing and energizing the body, mind, and soul. Back when I could sleep through the night, and spring out of bed the moment the alarm went off, I didn't appreciate sleep as I do now. I thought of it more as a waste of time.

Mornings are still my favorite time of day, but I don't exactly spring out of bed since my thyroid / adrenal issues started to cause me tremendous fatigue, and difficulty sleeping. Now, I covet sleep.

There are numerous methods people use successfully to get a good night's sleep, and I have tried several in the past few years, even counting sheep. I gave that up after the time I counted five thousand of those little buggers jumping over a fence.

My sister told me to count backward, so I do that sometimes, but I have become adept at counting and thinking through my to-do list at the same time.

I rarely take naps since my brain has a hard time shutting down, but if I could master the fine art of napping, I would do it as much as possible.

The sleep method that has helped me the most is learning to live in peace. I still struggle with sleep, but I am working on it diligently.

Everyone is different, so there is no one-size-fits-all for finding a good night's sleep, but make it a priority. On the other hand, if you are sleeping too much, it is likely you are depressed, or not wanting to face something. In that case, it is time to do something about whatever it is that is keeping you in bed. Sleep is precious, but so is time.

TIP: *It is the inability to quiet our minds that causes us the most trouble in getting to sleep or staying asleep. While I think we should do what we can and need to do to get precious sleep, none of the methods I have tried have been nearly as effective as learning to live in a peaceful state of mind.*

Laughter is the Best Medicine

Studies suggest that laughter stimulates organs, reduces stress, improves the immune system, relieves pain, and improves mood. Laughter is the best medicine, and you don't need a prescription or an expensive health plan. I look for ways to laugh several times a day.

The sitcom, Seinfeld, was referred to as "a show about nothing," but in reality, it was a show about everything. Each episode dealt with a subject or several subjects that were relatable. It allowed us to laugh at the characters and ourselves. A co-worker once told me I was like a female Seinfeld because I found humor in everyday life. That is something that has served me well through all of my challenges.

A few years back, I was helping a friend of my friend, Pamela, at a charity event. Carolyn sells a line of high-end clothing at discount prices, so the women flock to the clothing racks, and it is a lot of work from start to finish.

The event was at a resort hotel in a huge ballroom, with vendors located outside the event space. Carolyn's clothing was stationed at one end of the long lobby, while the bathrooms were at the opposite end, around a corner.

After the event, I headed to the bathroom past all of the vendors. They barely noticed me since they were busy breaking down their spaces. On my return trip, everyone seemed to take notice of me. My feet were killing me, but it put a spring in my step, and I smiled, nodded, or said hello. I must have been rocking that awesome black skirt I was wearing.

Carolyn was perched on a barstool, going through her receipts, as I approached. Suddenly, she burst out laughing and pointed at me, causing anyone in earshot to look over.

"Your skirt!"

I looked down and saw that my skirt seemed to be intact, but something didn't feel right. I reached around the back and found the entire backside of my skirt was caught up in my undergarments!

In these moments, we have a couple of choices. We can run screaming from the room, dying of embarrassment, or we can laugh.

Once I pulled my skirt out and made sure everything was in order, I laughed as hard as Carolyn and Pamela.

Learn to laugh with yourself, and even at yourself. The value of the skirt story and the number of laughs it has provided over the years as it has been re-told is worth a few minutes of potential embarrassment.

Laughter comes easy for me, but you might not be the type of person who laughs a great deal. If you are not a particularly funny or humorous person, get around some witty people. Watch a comedy show or movie. Lighten up and laugh more. Find humor in everyday life.

TIP: Get around some humorous people. Watch a comedy show or movie. Lighten up and laugh more. Find humor in everyday life, and be willing to laugh with, and at yourself. Remember, laughter is the best medicine, and it is free.

Action Reminders

Even the best of intentions can result in the worst of circumstances. We confuse self-care with selfishness. Too often, we give until there is nothing left of us. We people-please constantly or lay down like a doormat. Nobody, not even you, can take that for an extended period without disastrous results.

You are not a super-hero, although some people might consider you just that. The fact is you are human, and you have an emotional and mental fuel tank, and only one body, just like everyone else. Placing your oxygen mask on somebody else's face for too long will result in you becoming wiped out mentally, emotionally, physically, and spiritually.

Using yourself up in the service of others is a very short-term vision. Over the long haul, you will need to put yourself first, or there won't be anything left of you to serve others.

Putting yourself at the top of the self-care list is not selfish, and one could even argue that it's selfish not to care for number one. Put on your oxygen mask, first. To be there for someone else, you first have to be there for yourself. Get outside. Exercise. Sleep. Laugh. You deserve it.

Action #4: Build Your Circle of Strength

About the Action

Some of the biggest blessings are the people we get to go through life with; they can also be the source of much frustration.

Disappointment is a part of life, and much of it comes from the expectations we place on ourselves and others. While we do need to manage the expectations we place on ourselves, most of our frustration comes from those we place on other people. I created the Circle of Strength as a tool to help you sift and sort through your relationships and ensure you are putting people in the right place, and therefore managing expectations of those people.

The Circle of Strength represents your people. This action is all about analyzing your relationships, gaining new perspectives on them, and developing proper expectations of them.

© The Still Standing Group   ValerieSilveira.com

You will be encouraged to stand with the right people, and learn to identify people to avoid, if at all possible. If you are unable to stay away from them, you will learn about the benefits of interacting with those people who are difficult.

The Inner Circle

© The Still Standing Group   ValerieSilveira.com

At the core of the Circle of Strength is the Inner Circle. This group of people includes your foxhole friends, trusted advisors and mentors, supportive family, and hopefully, your spouse or partner if you have one. Ideally, you should spend the most time with those people in your Inner Circle. However, circumstances may prevent you from doing so. Despite the amount of time you spend with the people in your Inner Circle, be sure you are the most <u>influenced</u> by them.

It would stand to reason your spouses or partner would automatically be part of your Inner Circle. However, based on what the Inner Circle represents, they may not fit. They may even be preventing you from standing up or moving forward.

It took me two tries to get it right, but I now have a husband who is in my Inner Circle. If your spouse or partner is not part of your Inner Circle, you need to determine why they are not. You deserve for that person to be in your Inner Circle.

These people might also hold us accountable or speak a truth we might not be ready to hear. People who are standing with us in our Inner Circle should not be bobblehead dolls, merely agreeing with us. They should challenge us to go higher. If we are looking for excuses to stay where we are, we don't need an Inner Circle person to help with that.

Foxhole Friends

A foxhole is a small pit used by soldiers in battle. Foxhole friends will be at your side during the battle, and in the foxholes of life with you. But more than that, they would be willing to go out onto the battlefield and drag you back into the foxhole.

We expect a great deal from a foxhole friend, so they will be few and far between, but worth their weight in gold. If you don't have at least one foxhole friend, the best way to gain one is to be one.

Trusted Advisors and Mentors

Your Inner Circle will be comprised mainly of your family and friends; people you know well, but some of the most valuable people in your Inner Circle, might be trusted advisors or mentors.

Often, we confide in spiritual leaders, counselors, life coaches, or mentors more than we do with others in our Inner Circle. You may feel more secure sharing your innermost feelings with one of these people. You might gain perspective from them that others closest to you are unable to provide.

Family Members Who Support You Unconditionally

Family members in your Inner Circle support you unconditionally. They are the same as foxhole friends. Hopefully, there will be members of your family who <u>are</u> a part of your Inner Circle, but it's not necessary to include someone simply because they are your family. I love every person in my family, but most of them do not reside in my Inner Circle.

TIP: *Choose very carefully who you allow into your Inner Circle. It is critical to have the right people standing with you.*

Ring of Courage

The first ring surrounding the Inner Circle is the Ring of Courage. It is comprised of good friends, positive family members, and people who are bonded to you by a similar experience. These are the people who should have the most influence over you, next to those in your Inner Circle.

© The Still Standing Group   ValerieSilveira.com

Good Friends

We have all heard the notion that we can count our real friends on one hand. Friends in this ring are good friends, but they are not quite at the foxhole friend level. You will likely have more of these types of friends than foxhole friends. Good friends might even be in the foxhole with you on occasion.

Positive Family

While a few of your family members may support you unconditionally, others will simply be a positive influence. They will express genuine concern, but they are not likely to jump into the foxhole without some pushing or pulling.

Too often, family members cause us the most stress, or we cause ourselves unnecessary anguish by trying to stuff them into the Inner Circle. If most of your family reside in the Ring of Courage, consider yourself fortunate.

Bonded By Experience

On occasion, you will meet people who understand your unique challenge. With some of these people, you will develop an instantaneous bond.

As close as you may be to some family and friends, most of them have not walked in your shoes. A unique bond exists among those who have shared similar challenges, heartbreak, or loss.

For most of my journey through my daughter's addiction, I didn't have any family members with the same experience. Thankfully, nobody in my family has lived through the death of a child. While it would be helpful if family and friends could truly understand your challenges, some you would not wish on them for any amount of understanding.

The bond of life experience can be powerful, so support groups might be where you find common ground with someone. A few people you bond with this way will end up here in the Ring of Courage, or elsewhere in the Circle of Strength. One word of caution, however. Many people have no real interest in improving their lives, and we know misery loves company. Make sure these people are also standing up and not merely trying to suck you into living their suffering.

TIP: *Most of the people you consider real friends and your close family members will likely reside in this ring. If you bond with someone due to collective experience, be sure they are working on standing, and not pulling you down.*

Ring of Influence

In the Ring of Influence are your friends and acquaintances, ambivalent or non-supportive family and people with whom you have momentary connections. This section of the Circle of Strength will include people that should influence you less than those in the Ring of Courage.

© The Still Standing Group   ValerieSilveira.com

Friends and Acquaintances

Most of the people we refer to as "friends" may actually be acquaintances. These types of friends are less vested in you or your life, but they can be a great source of new perspective or wisdom for a challenge you might be facing. They can also give you a much-needed break from the seriousness of life. We don't need to spend all of our time thinking deeply about everything, or only spending time with people who know about our problems.

Ambivalent or Non-Supportive Family

Some of your family members will be non-supportive. Don't get confused by this wording. It doesn't mean they are necessarily negative but more ambivalent.

Many family members will go through the motions of showing concern, but they are not really in your corner. It could be that you have always been strong, so they are not used to offering support, or perhaps they are unsure how to help or what to say. Remember, some family members are selfish or self-absorbed. Your family members are living with Beasts too.

Momentary Connections

One morning I was at the checkout counter at Trader Joe's. I noticed the checker was happy and positive as she took care of the customer in front of me.

When it was my turn, I commented on how cold it was in the store, nearly killing the positive vibe. Cara, the checker, told Valerie, the motivational speaker, she had not even noticed the cold. She went on to tell me she loved her job and stated that attitude was about the only thing she could control and that it is a choice. I wondered if she had a copy of one of my books under her counter. Or maybe I should read hers! The teacher became the student in those few precious moments.

She asked me about my work, so I gave her a brief rundown. Cara had a tear in her eye and came around the counter to hug me.

I said goodbye and was about to push my cart toward the door when the customer at the next checkout counter said,

"Don't I get a hug?"

We hugged and laughed. Another guy was in line behind him, and I had the impression they knew each other. If not, two complete strangers embraced.

I started toward the door, but before I got past the third counter, a woman stood looking at me with the "what about me" look on her face. We hugged, and more people took notice of the morning hug-fest.

I steered my cart out of the store, to what sounded like a party going on behind me. I smiled all the way to the car, wishing I had turned around and taken a quick video.

That was a momentary connection on steroids. Those few short minutes made a difference for me, no doubt Cara, and the others who participated or witnessed the interactions that morning.

Momentary connections are impactful in unexpected ways. Kindness from a stranger is a reminder that there is still good in the world. One brief nugget of wisdom can stay with us for the rest of our lives. Momentary Connections are in the less influential ring, simply because they are chance encounters, but don't discount the importance of these moments.

The next time you go shopping, out to dinner, or meet a stranger while on a walk, smile and say hello. Ask how the other person is doing. You never know when these transformative connection opportunities will present themselves.

TIP: *Momentary connections cannot be planned or forced, but they can be missed if you are not open to them. Be on the lookout for some of the most meaningful interactions you will have with strangers.*

Ring of Fire

I used to tell Jamie and Sean, "if you hang out with bank robbers eventually, you will become a bank robber." You are influenced by the people you spend time with, so take care not to be around people who drag you down. Some people need to be avoided as much as possible, and others should be loved from a distance.

Your Ring of Fire is where the problematic people reside. They might be family, an acquaintance, or coworker. Typically, the people in your Ring of Fire are those people you can't easily avoid. If you can avoid them, and are choosing not to, you may want to ask yourself why. When it comes to people that are negative or cynical or those who don't believe in you, consider respectfully removing them from the Circle, or spending as little time as possible with them.

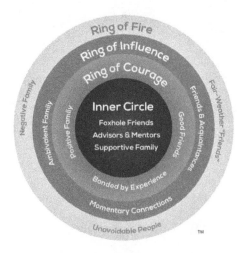

© The Still Standing Group   ValerieSilveira.com

If there are people you absolutely cannot avoid, then you will need to turn into Teflon, so you don't allow their words or behaviors to impact you. On the upside, you can choose to learn a great deal from the Ring of Fire.

Fair-Weather "Friends"

Fair-Weather Friends are those who are your friend only when it is convenient and easy, or when it benefits them. If a person is your friend when everything is going well but is conveniently absent when you're going through a rough patch, an argument could be made that they are not a *friend* at all, but rather, a fair-weather *acquaintance*.

Fair-weather people may be hard to remove from your life, or you may not choose to do so. If a fair-weather friend is in your life by choice, then don't be surprised by the inevitable disappointments.

Negative Family

Newsflash - not all family members will support you. It is said that "familiarity breeds contempt." The more acquainted one becomes with another person, the more that person's shortcomings are known, resulting in a sense of disrespect. Who knows us better than our family?

The bond family members have with one another can be some of the strongest imaginable, or the most challenging.

Since we all crave the approval of our families, it can be devastating when those you were sure would be the most supportive, end up letting you down. We need to have realistic expectations when it comes to family or anyone else.

There will invariably be people in your family that, given a choice, you would never have chosen. Typically, these people are negative, cynical, or miserable. Worse yet, they are probably looking for company.

Ring of Fire people are hard to deal with in general and can be more of a challenge when they are family. You may love these family members, but for your sake, limit the amount of time you spend with them.

Unavoidable People

Unavoidable people could be friends or family. Many are coworkers since most people spend more time with coworkers than nearly anyone else. Unavoidable people could be a customer or a member of a church or club. If these people rub you the wrong way, or worse yet, really get under your skin, you will need to dig down deep to not be negatively impacted by them.

Do whatever you can to stay away from the people in your Ring of Fire, or at the least, take them in small doses.

The Ring of Fire Silver Lining

After all of the warnings about the Ring of Fire, there is a silver lining. For much of the time, it may feel like more of a rust lining. Some good can come from the people you're "stuck with" in the Ring of Fire.

First, negative or cynical people can act as a mirror. If you don't like what you see when you look into the Ring of Fire, be careful, you don't see yourself in its reflection.

Another benefit of the Ring of Fire is that it allows (or forces) you to develop patience, empathy, and tolerance.

If you can't avoid certain people, why not take the opportunity to learn and grow from them? When you look back, you might attribute some of your most significant growth to the Ring of Fire.

TIP: *Do your best to avoid people in the Ring of Fire. If you cannot, then be careful, you are least influenced by them, and be willing to learn from them.*

Managing Expectations

The exercise of examining your relationships and placing people in the proper sections of the Circle of Strength is so you can manage the expectations you put on them.

We should have certain expectations in our relationships. I expect my husband will be faithful. He should treat me well and speak to me in ways that encourage me. When he talks about me to others, his words should be positive and respectful. He should expect the same from me. Friends should be truthful, caring, and speak highly of us. Our children should treat us with respect. These are all realistic expectations.

Sometimes, we have unrealistic expectations of people. I have been guilty of wishing, wanting, or even trying to make Rich more emotionally expressive. I want him to hand out more compliments or to be intuitive. He is not wired for those things, and I spent many years disappointed as I tried to make my husband fit into an idealistic mold

I had created. It caused me a great deal of frustration, put pressure on him, and left me less focused on all of his amazing qualities.

Think about your various relationships and the expectations you have of them. Don't make your expectations too low, or you might wind up with someone that you cannot count on at all. On the contrary, don't make your expectations too high, or you will be in a constant state of disappointment.

TIP: *Learning to manage expectations could be the most critical thing you do to improve your relationships and reduce frustration.*

Moving Around in the Circle

Even after you get the Circle of Strength figured out, it will change. A person who once resided in the Ring of Influence may wind up in the Ring of Courage, or even the Inner Circle.

Relationships change, and situations arise, so it could also be that someone who was once a Good Friend, or even a Foxhole Friend, moves into the Ring of Fire, or out of the Circle of Strength entirely.

The friend who betrayed us was once considered a Foxhole Friend. While we have forgiven him, he no longer resides anywhere in our Circle of Strength.

When you apply realistic expectations to each of the people you interact with, it will save you a ton of frustration, disappointment, and resentment.

I had a Foxhole friend for ten years, and due to something ridiculous, she bounced herself out of my Circle. Rather than being upset, I chose to treasure good memories. If we were to reconnect, she might wind up somewhere in my Circle again, but not likely in the Inner Circle.

You might meet someone you bond with due to common experience, and they turn into a good friend. Over time, they might even become a foxhole friend.

Nothing is permanent, so be open to changes in relationships. Some people are meant to be in our lives forever, others for ten years, ten months, or ten minutes.

TIP: *Remember that people and relationships change. Be open to changes in the Circle of Strength. Some people are meant to be in our lives forever, others for ten years, ten months, or ten minutes.*

People Who Don't Belong in the Circle

Relationships are challenging in the best of circumstances. Antagonistic, excessively critical, negative, or abusive people have no place in your Circle of Strength. While you can learn from those in the Ring of Fire, the types of people described in this section do not serve you in any way. Spend even a small amount of time with these people, and they will pull you down.

Maybe your Circle is small, and you are concerned that eliminating even the most negative of influences will leave you lonely. Possibly it will, for a time. But, it's not worth hanging around the wrong people to avoid being alone. Your purpose is too important to allow people to drag you down. There are several billion people on the planet, so you can find the right people to fill up your Circle.

TIP: *Removing people from your Circle of Strength might be necessary if you want to live in peace, build your confidence, or stay positive. We are far too impacted by the words and actions of others to take a chance on being around someone who will pull us down. Don't be afraid to let go of people who no longer belong anywhere in your Circle of Strength.*

Action Reminders

Take a look at the people you know and see where they currently reside in the Circle of Strength, think about where they actually belong, and then be willing to make some changes.

Develop and strengthen those relationships with people who will stand with you, encourage you, and even challenge you to go higher.

If a relationship is pulling you down, or creating chaos, consider walking away, even temporarily. We can love people from a distance. If the person needs to be removed entirely from your Circle, do it. It is *your* life, and you only get one time around.

Once you have people where they belong, place the proper expectations on them. Don't make your expectations too low, or you might wind up with someone that cannot be counted on at all. On the contrary, don't make your expectations too high, or you will be in a constant state of disappointment.

Allow for changes in the Circle. If a relationship ends, try to let go in love. If they are antagonistic or abusive, you might not feel like letting them go in love, but you can let them go with forgiveness.

Action #5: Change Your Attitude

About the Action

Right smack in the middle of **The 9 Actions**, is attitude; a perfect placement since attitude is so instrumental for the other eight actions to be effective.

You were cautioned in the last action to avoid negative people as much as possible. It will be even more challenging to avoid a negative person when that person is you.

Unless you change your thinking, you will never be able to change your circumstances. There is nothing you can do to change what has happened in the past. There will be situations that occur in the future, for which you have no control. There are very few things you have control over, but attitude is one thing you can control daily, in every situation, and each moment.

This action will provide perspective and tips to help you start kicking the negative attitude habit, move out of victimhood, and more. Harness the one thing you have complete control over – your attitude.

****

The Logic of a Negative Thinker

Disappointment is a part of life. If we live with hope, anticipation, or have dreams, we will be disappointed at times. My childhood was full of disappointment, which led me to a self-protective way of thinking, I refer to as, "the logic of a negative thinker."

My philosophy was that if I thought the worst, I would never be disappointed. If something good happened, I would consider it a bonus.

Not only did I begin to live by ridiculous thinking, but I am horrified to admit, I shared it with anyone who would listen.

Negative thinking may help to avoid disappointment, but it sure is a waste of a lot of time. If you have subscribed to this line of thinking, consider the number of hours, days, weeks, months, or even years in between disappointments that were filled with destructive, self-defeating thoughts, holding your breath, waiting for the worst to happen. Not to mention, we tend to attract what we put out, so it shouldn't come as a surprise when negative people flock to our negative mindset.

If you are living by the logic of a negative thinker, you need to shift your mindset ASAP. Some of the other sections in this action will help you do just that.

TIP: *Thinking the worst might seem logical, but it will also attract more negativity. Ditch the logic of a negative thinker mentality.*

My First Motivational Speaker

Somewhere amid my negative logic years, I encountered my first motivational speaker. He wasn't onstage in a big auditorium full of people, but rather in his kitchen, with only two people in attendance.

My friend Chris and I sat at the kitchen table, taking in her dad Ron's speech. The only part I remember was,

"When you have a bad attitude, you can't eat right. You can't sleep right. You can't poop right. You can't do anything right."

For two eleven-year-olds, that was hilarious, but Ron was right. It is hard to do anything right when you are living in negativity. With that type of mindset, we hold on to anger and unforgiveness. We are resentful and sometimes hateful. We don't eat right, or sleep right. And, we might not even be able to poop right.

Ron's message was impactful since I still tell that story decades later, but there is an even more critical point to the story. We all have the same opportunity Ron had that day in the kitchen. You don't have to be a motivational speaker, author, life-coach, or anything else, to spread messages that matter. You can impart wisdom to other people that will last a lifetime. Decades later, a word you spoke to a young girl, who rolled her eyes, and laughed, could be part of the message she uses to help change the world.

TIP: *Stay positive in every situation, then spread that positivity around, no matter if you are in front of a huge crowd, or around a kitchen table. Be like Ron.*

Find Your Positive Attitude Muscles

We develop habits over time and with experience. One of them is our attitude. It is necessary to build up your positive attitude muscles, but they may be hard to find at first, especially if they have not been used for some time.

I have had back problems since I was a teenager. At age twenty-six, I had two bulging discs in my lower back, causing tremendous pain and the inability to walk upright. For years after, I sought the help of physical therapists to heal and strengthen my back. One told me I had some atrophy in the muscles of my lower back, next to my spine. To get a muscle working again, she would have me in some contorted position, with her fingers on a spot, and then ask me to engage the muscle. "Engage it," I thought. "I can't even find it." Of all of the work I did to heal and strengthen my back, this was the most difficult. At first, I wondered if it were possible for me to engage muscles my brain seemed to have no connection to, but eventually, they came to life. Over time, and plenty of effort, my attitude muscles came back to life as well.

You came into this life with a great attitude. Kids are happy and hopeful, and you used to be one. Your positive attitude muscles might be atrophied due to lack of use and may be difficult to engage at first, but they are still there.

The key is to be aware of your words and thoughts. When you speak negative words, take them back and restate them differently. Do the same thing with your thinking. Sometimes they pop into your head without conscious thought, but you can consciously change them. It is a habit you can break. Find your positive attitude muscles, and put them to work.

TIP: Just as you developed a negative attitude habit, you can create a positive mindset. Each time you catch yourself in the negative zone, immediately change your thoughts and re-phrase what you said before, this time in a positive light. Do this repeatedly, and before long, your first thoughts will be positive, and you won't need to correct your words.

Resist the Mob Mentality

The people we spend time with can influence us, but so can strangers. The mob, herd, or pack mentality describes how people can be influenced by others to adopt certain behaviors, based on emotions, rather than on a rational basis. We have witnessed violence escalate when this mentality kicks in, but it can also happen in much more mundane settings.

I arrived at the post office one morning to find quite a few cars in the parking lot. I appreciate the postal service and find it remarkable the vast majority of letters and packages get where they need to be in a reasonable amount of time. Speed, however, is not a pre-requisite for employment at this particular post office. I pushed down my negative thoughts that were trying to surface, set my attitude right, and stood at the back of the long line.

Off to my left, a cheerful-looking postal worker and an angry customer stood on either side of Dutch door, with the top half open. The customer yelled at the postal worker about her package taking too long to arrive at its destination. The poor guy stood there trying to show compassion, but he probably wanted to slam the top part of the door in her face.

I could feel the people in the line ahead of me, which had yet to move an inch, starting to become agitated. I could see their body language and the looks of agreement on their faces toward the angry customer.

To diffuse the negativity, I stated just loud enough for those around me to hear,

"It's not *his* fault."

The woman in front of me turned around and began to voice agreement with the angry customer. She told me she mailed a package which had taken three whole days to arrive!

I was about to tell her at least she was not in a remote part of Africa walking for hours with water on her head, but instead, I told her a story.

I was in Calgary, Alberta, for a family reunion when I was a teenager. After jotting down a greeting to a friend back in Seattle, I dropped my postcard in the mailbox attached to the house, just outside the front door.

A few hours later, my great-aunt, Dorothy came into the house with the postcard in her hand, and asked in a sarcastic tone,

"Who's the idiot who put the postcard in the mailbox?"

"I did," I answered.

She went on to interrogate me further,

"What did you think the postman was going to do; take the postcard?"

"Uh, yeah, that's exactly what I thought. How else would I mail something?"

She looked at me like I had lost my mind.

"You go down the street and find a mailbox. Wait a minute. You are telling me that in the States, they pick up your mail from your house?"

I told her, "Yes, they do. If they are delivering anyway, doesn't it make sense they would pick up the mail at the same time?"

"Let me get this straight," she said, "they come to your house and deliver the mail, and pick it up, five days a week?"

I answered,

"No, they do it six days a week!"

My reply may have also been slightly sarcastic, but it was a long time ago, and Aunt Dorothy is gone now, so you have no proof.

We can decide to look at things in any way we choose. About the mail, for instance, we can focus on that one letter that was lost in the mail ten years ago or acknowledge the thousands that have made their way to their destination.

What happened in the post office line that day was a shift in thinking, and a choice to step up and step out against the growing tension of the crowd, and help to avoid a mob mentality of negative thinking.

Oddly enough, I read recently, where it took Canada Post forty-five years to deliver a letter from one Calgary woman to another. They lived just two-hundred-fifteen kilometers away (that's less than one-hundred-thirty-four miles for us Americans). In fairness to Canada Post, the address was incomplete, and it is pretty impressive the letter was not sent to the trash decades ago. I would love to have a forty-five-year-old letter delivered to me. It's all about choosing our thoughts, words, and attitude, and resisting the negative mob-mentality.

TIP: Be mindful you don't get caught up in the negative mob-mentality. Be willing to go against the crowd.

Be An Optimist

In my early thirties, I worked with some men who helped to shape my attitude. They introduced me to motivational speakers and authors. I read books and listened to tapes, working hard to change the negative mindset I had developed over the first part of my life.

I got pretty good at this positive thinking stuff, and then I met my Beast. Little by little, the habits I formed disintegrated, and I was right back to my negative thinking logic.

After many years of living in fear, doubt, and all of the other defeating emotions and thought patterns that invaded my heart and mind, I decided to start again. I reached back into my memory bank and recalled what it felt like to live as an optimist. It took time and conscious effort, but I am back. However, I am very aware of how easy it is to fall right back into a negative mindset. One phone call, knock on the door, or comment from someone, can catapult us right back into negativity and fear. I choose to live my life as an optimist and am willing to do the work to stay there.

Live your life as an optimist. Look for and expect the best, no matter what life looks like today. It might set you apart from most of the people you know, which is why you will have to use all of **The 9 Actions** to build up the courage to continue choosing optimism and to go against the crowd or find a new one.

Don't bury your head in the sand and ignore your issues, but dare to face your fears and obstacles, and choose to believe for the best outcome, no matter what anyone else thinks, or what you currently see.

Many people will disagree with your positive outlook, mainly because they haven't chosen to live with a positive mindset. I have been called *Pollyanna* on a few occasions, but I receive that as a compliment, no matter how it was pitched out. After all, *Pollyanna* is *an excessively cheerful or optimistic person.*

Negativity is the path of least resistance and believing the worst is easy. Have the courage to be optimistic when others wouldn't dare.

TIP: No matter what anyone else thinks or what you currently see, choose to believe for the best outcome. Be an optimist or even a Pollyanna.

Two Types of Victims

You might recall me mentioning that I don't care for victimhood. The Beast wants us living as victims, so we don't stand up and shine our light. Certain people would just as soon we jump into victimhood with them. There were many reasons for me to become a victim over my lifetime, but I refused. It wasn't me - until it was.

There are two types of victims, and you might recognize yourself in one of them.

Poor Me Victim

Poor Me Victims regularly solicit sympathy either directly or indirectly. Some Poor Me Victims will make it clear they want and expect your pity. Others take a more passive-aggressive approach stating they don't want sympathy but talk nonstop about their problems without working on solutions.

Initially, people will respond with sympathy, but eventually, they will grow weary, especially if the victim is not trying to change their circumstances or attitude. Over time, a Poor Me Victim will be left with either other Poor Me Victims, or with people who feel obligated to be in a relationship with them.

Victim in Disguise

Victims in Disguise are typically people others rely on for strength and support. Not wanting to be needy, the Victim in Disguise is skilled at hiding their victim status.

Unlike the Poor Me Victim, these people try to convince themselves they don't need or want support, then find it hurtful when nobody checks on them. To the outside world, these victims seem as if they are fine when, in reality, they are far from it. I was a Victim in Disguise.

Neither victim is a healthy way to live. Whether a Poor Me Victim or a Victim in Disguise, it is time to step out of victimhood.

My friend Jimi was the victim of childhood sexual abuse. In his young life, he didn't have an opportunity to get the type of support he needed to process and overcome what happened to him. He wound up, numbing his pain with alcohol, drugs, and dangerous choices.

By the time I met Jimi, he was long past the years of drug use and bad choices. He is one of the most positive and faith-filled people I know, so it came as quite a surprise when he told me about his past, which included a four-year stint in prison. Jimi was a victim in his childhood, but he chose to discontinue living as one. He took responsibility for his choices and completely turned his life around. He stepped out of victimhood.

A few years ago, Jimi's only child died of breast cancer after a long battle. He could have quickly headed to victimhood, but he chooses to honor the hole in his heart, but not fall into it. He spends his time encouraging others.

There is nothing wrong with acknowledging you have been victimized and permitting yourself some time to process the emotions that come along with being a victim. There may be medical, psychological, financial, and legal issues to wade through, but refuse to take on any permanent label that reinforces victimhood.

When my daughter was killed, she was labeled a *murder victim*. As her family, we are considered *victims* by the justice system. When our ex-friend betrayed us by stealing money, the justice system called us *victims*. While those labels are necessary for the justice process, we refuse the victim label.

It is vital to begin shedding shame and guilt (more to come on this topic), which is going to assist in moving you out of victimhood and get you standing <u>on</u> your story, not in it.

People become *victims* for many reasons, and not always connected to a legal case. Victimhood can even be self-imposed. Becoming a victim may not have been your fault, but remaining one is your choice.

Choose to look at what has happened as an opportunity. Use it to build courage in yourself, and to demonstrate to others, how to overcome a victim mentality.

TIP: Neither of the two types of victims is a healthy or productive way to live. Becoming a victim may not have been your fault, but remaining one is your choice. There is power in choosing to live as a victor instead of a victim.

Pity Party

It's easy to find a Pity Party; they are everywhere. If there were actual buildings, Pity Parties would have grand, well-lit entrances, and greeters at the doors. The minute you arrive at a Pity Party, you feel welcome. Strangers only moments before will become long lost friends. Pity Party attendees are not solution finders, but rather sit helplessly, re-living every offense, and running the movie of their unfair life, over and over. Pity Parties are full of self-proclaimed victims. I lived in a Pity Party for years. While I rarely hosted one, I did have plenty of parties for one. Feeling sorry for myself only caused more grief, sadness, and hopelessness.

If we allow our circumstances to dictate our level of happiness, we might be in big trouble. The road I have traveled is one thousand times harder than any I imagined, yet I am happy. I chose happiness, and then I fought for it, and continue to fight for the good things in life, no matter what life looks like at the moment.

Misery does love company, so finding an exit from a Pity Party will prove challenging. In contrast to the warm welcome, few people will help you locate the exit door. The closer you get to leaving, the more resistance you will have from the other attendees. If you do find an exit, it will be a small, unmarked door at the end of a maze. Once you locate the exit, run for the door and don't look back. Better yet, decline the invitation to attend in the first place.

TIP: *If you find yourself at a Pity Party, run for the door. Importantly, stop hosting them.*

Coulda, Shoulda, Woulda

Listening to a funny or inspiring story from the past can be captivating. Sharing an extraordinary experience is the next best thing to being there. Remembering a hardship can remind us to be thankful. Even recalling our mistakes can help us make better choices.

Short trips to the past are fine, but spending extended periods agonizing over what you could have, should have, or would have done is counter-productive to living courageously.

During my Roller Coaster From Hell ride, I visited Coulda, Woulda, and Shoulda so often, they became my imaginary friends. I called them Mea Coulda, Shirley Shoulda, and I. Woulda. They were more like imaginary enemies.

We understand 20/20 to mean perfect vision. You can actually have vision better than 20/20, but the term has stuck nonetheless, and "hindsight is 20/20" was born from that idea of "perfect" vision.

We don't have perfect vision, nor can we see the future, or anticipate every potential outcome, so we have to go with the best information we have at the time. Once all the facts are in, and we are looking back, it is far easier to see what we should have, could have, or would have done had we known what we know now.

I have kicked Coulda, Shoulda, and Woulda to the curb, so when I do take a trip into the pain of my past, I utilize it mainly to grab nuggets of wisdom. The past is a great teacher.

Go ahead and take a trip into the past to gain perspective, or learn from previous choices. Just be careful not to "Coulda," "Shoulda," and "Woulda" yourself to death. These three live in the past, and that is exactly where Coulda, Shoulda, and Woulda belong.

TIP: *Short trips to the past are fine, but spending extended periods of thinking endlessly about what we could have, should have, or would have done erodes your self-esteem. Stay away from Coulda, Shoulda, and Woulda.*

Ten Percent of My Life

I reconnected with some of my high school friends whom I hadn't seen in a couple of decades. Glancing across the large round table from Paula, I was struck by how beautiful she looked with her very short hair. She had always worn her thick, dark, wavy hair, in a long hairstyle.

"Paula, I've never seen you with short hair; you look great."

After that conversation ended, Laura, elbowed me and whispered that Paula had battled cancer - twice.

I said to Paula that I wished she told me about the cancer so I could have at least offered a word of encouragement. Her reply was life-changing. She said,

"I purposely didn't tell a lot of people about it, because I didn't want *this thing* to take up more than 10% of my life."

She only wanted cancer to take up 10% of her life!

My Nana was a 10% of My Life person. All the years she suffered from emphysema, she had a smile on her face. I would call her on the telephone and ask how she was doing, and she always replied,

"I'm fine, dear. How are you?"

Her body craved oxygen more and more, and her heart was getting larger, invading her tiny chest, but Nana didn't let emphysema take up more than 10% of her life.

If you want to change your attitude, get around some people like Paula, or my Nana - the 10% of My Life people. Better yet, become one.

TIP: Make a vow not to allow your troubles, challenges, hardships, heartbreaks, or Beasts to take up more than 10% of your life.

Self-Talk

There are times when we can use constructive criticism to realize a need for change. However, studies suggest we need as many as eight times more positive comments to every one negative.

Even if we get more positive than negative feedback from others, we tend to hang onto negative comments forever, yet dismiss positive ones quickly. This fact reinforces the need to receive far more positive feedback than negative.

Unfortunately, we are unlikely to receive what we need from others. Get around people who lift you, encourage you, and remind you of your value, but you cannot rely on even the most uplifting of people for your positive reinforcement.

Don't sit around wishing or hoping someone will praise you at least eight times more than the criticism or negative comments tossed your way. Step up and start talking to and about yourself more positively. Smile at yourself when looking into a mirror, and be generous with the compliments (out loud) for the beautiful soul looking back at you. It will seem silly at first, but this is powerful. It will help you to see yourself in a new light, and your brain will begin to identify those positive statements with the person your eyes are seeing.

I developed the habit when I dropped or broke something to exclaim,

"You dummy," or some other negative comment that shouldn't be in print. Now I try to catch myself and cancel the comment.

Many years ago, I worked with an older gentleman who had been a junior high school principal. Harry complimented me on how nice I looked, and immediately, I began to discount what he had said. He asked me,

"Why do you do that?"

"Do what?" I asked.

"Why do you not accept compliments?"

Harry went on to explain to me that it was rude to discount a compliment. It was like someone handing you a gift and you shoving it back at the person, saying,

"No, thanks. Keep your gift. I don't want it."

My friend Adrien is on the Autism Spectrum and is very matter-of-fact. Whenever I tell him he looks great, he responds with,

"I know."

Adopt Adrien's attitude. It is not arrogant but honest.

Throughout the day, acknowledge your gifts and talents, and don't be afraid to speak about them. If you are concerned with coming across as arrogant, stay tuned to the section on Humble Confidence in a future action. Accept compliments; after all, they are gifts.

TIP: Start seeing yourself as beautiful, talented, strong, capable, and courageous. Then, start speaking these things out loud. Your brain will begin to believe what it hears, especially from the sweet sound of your voice.

Banana In, Bad Mood Out

We have a German family, not by blood, but by blessing. Raphi was an exchange student and Sean's friend in high school. After living with us for only a short time, he was family.

Now, he has an incredible wife, Mona, and two kids, each of whom would take an entire book to describe. Emilia Val, who is six-years-old, is my Goddaughter and is impressive in every way. She was such a character, that when Mona was pregnant again, we secretly wondered how the second child would follow in Emilia's footsteps. Then Lennard arrived, and we knew he would create his own "footsteps." Not only is he adorable and smart like his sister, but his personality is off the charts.

Lenny is happy ninety-nine percent of the time, but he was upset one night around our dinner table. The foreign meal I made did not appeal to him, but his dad was attempting to convince him to eat it. Lenny was tired and began to cry and plead his case. I have no idea what he was saying since I don't speak a word of German, but whatever it was, he was emphatic. His mom left the table and returned with a banana. After one bite, a huge smile spread across his adorable little face, and he exclaimed (translated to English),

"Banana in; bad mood out!"

As adults, when we get ourselves into a bad mood, it can take an act of Congress to change it. Little kids can be sobbing one moment and laughing the next. We could learn a great deal from children if we would realize that while we are the teachers, we are also students.

Next time you are in a bad mood, remember, "Banana in; bad mood out."

TIP: When you get yourself into a bad mood, remember you can change it in an instant. It takes a split-second decision. Banana in, bad mood out.

Action Reminders

You can have a lasting impact on the people you come across on your trip through life if you harness this one incredible force – your attitude.

Kick the negative attitude habit by making a conscious effort to become an optimist.

Resist the negative mob mentality. Have the courage to step up and change a negative atmosphere.

You have a responsibility to the people in your life and those you interact with daily. Your attitude impacts people one way or another, so choose how it will affect them.

You never know when someone might tell a simple story about something you said, and how it impacted them decades later like I do with the Ron story.

It might take you some time to stop living with a victim mentality, but the first step is to recognize that you belong standing strong as a victor, not a victim. There is no power in being a victim, so stay away from Pity Parties, Coulda, Woulda, and Shoulda.

Try not to allow your troubles to take up more than 10% of your life.

Speak highly to and about others, and yourself. Accept compliments – they are gifts.

Remember – Banana in, bad mood out.

Action #6: Adjust Your Focus

About the Action

What you focus on becomes magnified. Stare at a minor issue long enough, and it becomes a major problem. The battle is for your mind, your thoughts. Since thoughts turn into words, and actions, or lack thereof, we must guard our thoughts and where we choose to place our focus.

When you suffer a loss, it is easy to become fixated on those who have what you have lost or never had.

In this action, you will gain some persepctive and find tips on re-focusing. Since focus is closely related to attitude, Action #5 will be especially helpful for this action.

An old Cherokee told his grandson,

"There is a battle between two wolves inside us all.

One is evil.

It is anger, envy, jealousy, sorrow, regret, greed, arrogance, self-pity, guilt,

resentment, inferiority, lies, false pride, superiority and ego.

The other is Good.

It is joy, peace, love, hope, serenity, humility, kindness, benevolence,

empathy, generosity, truth, compassion, and faith."

The grandson thought about it and asked his grandfather,

"Which wolf wins?"

The old Cherokee simply replied,

"The one you feed."

~ Unknown

Decide now which *wolf* will win in your life. Use the power of focus to harness your thoughts and your attitude.

****

Don't Believe Everything You See

The obsession with other people's lives is evident in the way television has drastically changed over the past couple of decades. Reality shows exist for anything you might imagine, and some you would rather not. Reality television should more appropriately be called *Scripted Reality Television*. I am not in the entertainment industry, but I'm certain producers don't set up cameras in hopes of catching some juicy footage. They are likely prompting and even scripting much of the interaction between the *actors*. Yet, people cannot seem to get enough of what they perceive to be reality.

You might be focusing on somebody else's life to avoid facing something in your own life. Or, when life takes a turn for the worse, you might find yourself comparing your life to others, to prove just how unfair your life is. When we spend a great deal of time comparing our lives, we most often conclude that *everyone else* has what we don't have, or what we lost.

The more loss I felt as Jamie moved deeper into her addiction, the more it appeared *every other mother* had a perfect daughter. It wasn't just the *perfect daughter* social media posts; it was everything. To my aching heart, it was as if half the world had the best husband, drank the finest wine, went on weekly dream vacations, swam with the dolphins, drove the coolest cars, had the best friends in the world, and bulging bank accounts. The postings were not the problem. I was out of focus.

While social media might not be as scripted as Reality Television, people are predominantly posting the highlight reels of their lives. Rarely do you see a photo of your friend looking like she just got out of bed. You will never see one of her cleaning toilets. Not many will brag about their time off work unless they are ziplining in Costa Rica. You don't see videos of arguments with spouses.

There is far too much negativity in the world and the media, so it is refreshing that people tend to post the best parts of their lives, but we need to be discerning. Otherwise, we come to the false conclusion about the lives of others, in comparison to ours. It's why I issue this warning:

Lives lived out on social media may appear better than
they really are.

If you keep focusing on sadness, you will be sadder. If you continue to focus on what you don't have, you might never get what you want. Choose to focus on everything wrong in your life, and you will miss what is right.

During tough times, you will need to re-focus constantly to gain and maintain perspective. Some people have what you don't, but it's futile to focus on other people's journeys. Most of them are not what they appear to be anyway. Keep other people's lives in perspective. Don't believe everything you see.

TIP: *Be careful not to get yourself into the trap of believing everything you see or hear. You are comparing your life to what you think someone's life is about, when in fact, you don't know the whole story.*

Everybody Has a Story

Everybody has challenges, hurdles, heartbreaks, disappointments, and unfair situations. Sure, we all know people whose lives are more comfortable than ours, but it's useless to spend valuable time attempting to figure out why.

When you are going through a tough period, it will seem as if everyone around you is doing well. While you are stuck dealing with your struggles, you begin to believe everybody else is on a beach sipping a Piña Colada. Life happens in cycles, and there will come a time when each person will have challenges. You could find yourself in a great place, while someone you thought had it all, goes through a tough season.

I know firsthand how difficult it is to keep from focusing on what other people have when it seems you keep losing what you love or need. I spent years doing just that. Life was unfair, and I was adding up the score, or at least what I assumed the score was, but I found that when we are peering through the window of somebody else's life, and it looks perfect, chances are they haven't cleaned their windows in a while. Nobody has an ideal life. Nobody has a perfect "anything."

The truth is not always what it appears to be, and the more time we spend focused on another person, longing for their life, the more convinced we become, that our lives are never going to change. The gap between the imaginary *perfect* life you assume others are enjoying, and yours will continue to widen. Before long, it will feel as if you are standing at the Grand Canyon. On one side, you sit with your troubles and disappointments, your Beasts. Eighteen miles across, stand the people with those imaginary perfect lives, who seem to have escaped life's misfortune. You look longingly across the vast expanse, straining to see the faces of those you believe are more fortunate. Sitting there feeling alone, turn around and look beside you and behind you. As far as your eye can see, will be those who have been where you are, or worse. The fact is – everybody has a story.

TIP: *No matter how much you think you know about another person's journey, everybody has a story. Nobody has a perfect life.*

Looking Forward

We have a lot of rabbits in our neighborhood. One sat in a yard, staring straight ahead as I approached from his left. As I moved past him, and out of the sightline of his left eye, he picked me up with his right eye, without moving a muscle. For a defenseless rabbit, eyes on either side of the head come in handy while trying to look like a garden statue.

Owls don't have eyes on either side of their heads, like rabbits, but even better, their necks can rotate two-hundred-seventy degrees, allowing them to see side to side, and even behind them, without turning their bodies. It is like having eyes on the back of their heads.

When they were very young, Jamie and Sean became convinced I had eyes in the back of my head. They would run into a room in our small house and ask me to guess where they were, then scream in delight when I guessed right. Of course, I didn't have eyes on the back

203

of my head, but it would come in handy, especially when my kids became teenagers.

While it would undoubtedly be useful to have rabbit eyes or an owl's neck, humans have limited peripheral vision, and no ability to see behind without turning our bodies. Perhaps God knew that if our vision capability were like that of a rabbit or an owl, we would spend too much time looking every direction, but forward.

I spent years looking back, wishing my life was different. I longed for the good ol' days. I looked around at other people's lives and wished I were them. I finally realized that *these are the good ol' days.* I stopped wasting my precious time looking around and looking back and started to look forward.

When you begin to look forward and to focus on your journey, it will change your perspective on the present. It will put you in a position to start improving your future.

TIP: *Be careful not to spend too much time looking side to side, fearful of danger. You don't have eyes on the back of your head, and the past is the past. Keep looking forward - to your future.*

Gaining Perspective

We barely notice, or even disregard other people's imperfections, but tend to zero in on our own. Who doesn't go straight to their image in a group photo? If it happens to be an excellent shot of us, we are satisfied, but anything short of remarkable, and we notice every flaw. Stare at that photo long enough, and we become hideous.

There are times when a friend will point out a blemish, gray hair, or some other flaw that I never even noticed until they brought it up. That is the way they are looking at us – they don't see us with the same critical eye as we see ourselves. We are our worst critics.

I am sliding down the backside of my fifties as I write this, just a couple of years from the big 6-0. Adrenal fatigue and missing thyroid glands have left me with metabolism and weight challenges. No longer am I able to indulge along with friends and family, as I am negatively impacted more than most by what I eat. It is frustrating to work out more than anyone in my social circles, and to struggle with the inability to lose fat, even when I try drastic diet measures. I don't want to live my life in deprivation, unable to enjoy my social life, so that means this blob that appeared on my abdomen might be here to stay.

Recently, I had a dream I was walking in a field toward a mountain, with another person. It was unspoken, but I knew I was walking toward the end of my life. I wasn't sad or worried; I was peaceful when suddenly, I remembered something and stated,

"Oh no! I didn't have a chance to get rid of my belly fat before I died!"

Immediately, I had another thought, and said casually,

"Oh well, I guess God didn't want me to lose it before I left this earth."

I was about to add this dream to the long list of bizarre Valerie dreams, but it had a positive impact on me. I highly doubt belly fat would be one of my death bed regrets. The other reason it won't make the bizarre, meaningless dream list, is that I wasn't walking toward a fiery pit, and I'm hoping that was a big thumbs up from heaven.

Many things used to bother me or upset me before Jamie died. Losses are opportunities to gain a great perspective. When you are tempted to get upset about something, especially something that is not life or death, find some perspective on the situation. You don't need to wait for a devastating loss to start doing just that. In all circumstances, consider whether it is something worth being upset over.

Whatever your life looks like, there is someone out there who would give anything to have your life, troubles and all. Keep things in perspective.

TIP: *Try to keep everyday situations in perspective. Decide whether it is worth being upset over.*

Choosing Your Focus

Recently, Rich was involved in a serious car accident, where three cars, including his, were totaled. Eleven people walked away from the crash, without one being taken by ambulance to the hospital. Too often, we come away from these types of situations feeling grateful, but when the adrenal rush is over, we quickly forget.

The photos of Rich's beautiful, pristine car, sitting on top of the tow trailer, are a reminder of how that day could have ended. Just the week before, his BMW received its first shiny new set of replacement tires. There wasn't a scratch on the car or as much as a leaf on the floorboard. Rich loved that car, so I would have anticipated his regret over the loss once the dust settled, but it never happened.

When you start living **The 9 Actions**, you will be able to have the proper focus right through the hassles of cleaning up after an accident or other serious situation, and you will gain perspective on daily life.

Strangely, I am grateful for the accident. While Rich and I already live gratitude-minded, the near-tragedy took it a new level.

There are probably times in which you would rather somebody else oversaw your life, but it's you who is in charge. You and you alone are responsible for your thoughts. If you can choose your thoughts, then you can choose your focus, and you can learn to do it instantly.

One exercise I have used over the years to train my brain for awareness and focus is to look for a specific color while out on a walk. I pick a color (usually not green since that might explode my head) such as blue or white, one that I am not likely to see everywhere. Then I purposely heighten my sense of awareness, searching as I walk for that color. You will be amazed at how many things you notice that you never did before. You can use the same discipline when your mind wanders to negative or unproductive thoughts.

When fear pops in, focus on hope. When you find yourself thinking the worst, switch your thoughts to the best possible outcome. If you start descending into the pit of grief, allow your heart a moment, then shift your focus to happy memories. Like negative thinking, your focus is a habit. It will take some time and consistent effort, but you absolutely can train your brain to focus in the right way. You don't need to wait for devastating loss, to start gaining perspective, and shifting your focus.

TIP: *When you are tempted to focus on other people's lives, or on your problems, stop and take stock of your thoughts. Remember, what you focus on becomes magnified.*

Action Reminders

What you focus on becomes magnified, so be mindful of your thoughts and where you choose to place your focus.

Don't believe everything you read or see, especially on social media. People are posting the best of their lives – the highlight reels while you are living your life of ups and downs. (By the way, so are they). Remember that "Lives lived out on social media, may appear better than they really are."

Everybody has a story.

Try to focus on the here and now and look to the future. Focus more forward and less, side to side, or backward.

Gain some perspective on what is important and focus less on what is not. In every situation, you can learn to re-focus in an instant. You are in control of your thoughts, and therefore your focus.

Action #7: Stop Being a Control Freak

About the Action

The title of this action might resonate with you in a big way, or you might be thinking, *heck no, not me! I am passive and quiet, not a control freak.*

I have a strong personality, so I am influential. However, I don't feel as if I try to control people. So, how in the world did I come up with this title? Well, because I realized I was a control freak!

This action is about understanding what we do and do not have control over. It is about learning to let go of what we cannot control and focusing on what we can.

211

This action might be the most challenging for you to use, or initially, to even want to attempt. It hits us in places we have not wanted to go, and in emotions, we don't want to face. It exposes stuff we have been holding onto for years, perhaps decades. While it might be the most difficult of the actions, the freedom you will experience will be worth what you might have to face.

****

The Illusion of Control

By attempting to control things, we have a sense that we can change, or steer an outcome. Unfortunately, though, there are many variables far beyond our control, leaving us with very little control over most situations. We don't directly control the economy or the government. Nobody can control the weather or the seasons. We have almost zero control over other people's actions unless they are under two years old. We have no control over what people think or say about us, no matter their age. We can influence people, but not control them. There is a big difference.

We are surrounded by people and circumstances we cannot control, big and small, every moment of every day. We interact with people daily who do not have our best interest at heart or don't even know we exist. There are people and situations right now that you are attempting to control, with little, if any, results. To a large extent, control is an illusion.

I spent years attempting to control the direction of Jamie's life. I did everything I could to push, prod, force, or make her change her ways; to control her addiction. After years of beating my head against the wall, and facing one disappointment and heartbreak after the next, I came to a painful truth:

If I had the ability to save Jamie from her addiction Beast, I would have done it long ago.

This reality did not unbreak my heart, but it allowed me to start letting go of the uncontrollable. It helped me to let go of unwarranted guilt.

No matter how many bridges Jamie burned, when she did get clean, I wanted everybody to welcome her with open arms. So, I tried to manage what people thought of her or even felt about her. I was attempting to control the thoughts and feelings of others, which is impossible – and wrong.

We would all like everyone to agree with us, to see things our way, and to have the same logic we do. Unfortunately, we don't often come across those people.

Rich and I agree on most things, but he has certain ways of thinking that make no sense to me. No doubt, he feels the same way about me. Ouch.

There is a good chance you are expending energy attempting to steer or control a myriad of things. Since you have so little control, you are left feeling frustrated, and surprisingly, out of control.

You do have control over one person, and that person is you. You can control your thoughts, words, feelings, and actions. Changing yourself is where you should focus your control. It is the only chance you have to see some results for your efforts. So, let go of your need to control others. There is power in letting go of what you cannot control.

TIP: Let go of those things you have a white-knuckle grip on, but little chance of controlling. When you do, it will free you up to manage your own life, resulting in increased confidence and peace. Give up the illusion of control.

Use The "F" Word

The most freeing thing I have ever done is to start using the "F" word. That other word might come to mind, considering what you are dealing with, but the "F" word I am referring to is forgiveness.

Forgiving people isn't natural. When somebody talks badly to or about you, it hurts your feelings. If a friend or family member lets you down, it leaves you disappointed. You may have been robbed of money, or your innocence; betrayal can be devastating. These offenses can leave you scarred, but what heals the scars is forgiveness.

What holds you back from doing so is feeling the offender doesn't deserve to be forgiven. If you forgive, you are justifying bad behavior. You believe a person should deserve it, for you to even consider doling out a portion of your precious "F" word, so you hang on to the offense for years, often for a lifetime. That's how I used to live. Stubborn and unwilling to forgive certain offenses.

For you to jump on board the "F" word train, you will have to come into agreement with the truth, or at least be willing to consider it might be true. That truth is this - forgiveness is not for the other person; it's for you.

The word "forgive" means to stop feeling angry or resentful. You get to decide whether you allow the anger or resentment to continue. When you refuse to forgive someone, you re-live the offense over and over and over.

The first time Jamie was shot (I know, it's weird to read that sentence because it's strange to write it), I was beyond mad. Terry needed to pay, and I couldn't wait for the day he would be sentenced to prison for nearly killing my daughter.

Nine months after the shooting, Terry received a ten-year sentence. I had come a long way from my revenge feelings in those nine months, to a place of forgiveness. When I got the news of his sentencing, I didn't dance in the street, or throw a party, as I had voiced. Instead, I bawled like a baby. Rather than feeling vindicated, I wept for the whole situation; and I forgave him.

Keep remembering forgiveness is a gift you give to yourself. It is, so YOU stop feeling angry or resentful. To be happy and free, use the "F" word on every person who has hurt you.

After you forgive someone, something might trigger an old feeling, and you will snatch the forgiveness back in a fraction of the time it took you to hand it out.

The beautiful thing is that God has given us a pretty good roadmap when it comes to the "F" word. He forgives us for everything. That's right – every single big, or little thing we do, say or think. I started to realize that if forgiveness is good enough for God, then it is good enough for me.

No doubt, one of the people you need to forgive the most is one that hurt you the most. It is also the one you might have no intention of forgiving.

On several occasions, I witnessed parents on television forgiving their child's killer and thought *no way*. I would *never* forgive them. They don't deserve forgiveness. I couldn't understand how a parent could forgive someone for killing their child. Yet, here I am, living that reality, and now I know. It is the only way to peace after such a horrific experience. I have already forgiven my daughter's killer, and justice has yet to be served. While I hope and pray the guy goes to prison, I will not allow what he did to take up any more space in my head. He already blew a hole in my heart, and I need the rest of it to keep loving and living.

There is a difference between forgiveness and justice. Allow God to deal with your offender. If your situation is a legal one, let the law handle the outcome. You are not in the justice business, but you should be in the forgiveness business.

Using the "F" word includes using it on yourself, which may prove to be more difficult than forgiving someone who truly hurt you. I beat myself up for years over Jamie's addiction; my mind was running through the list of my *offenses* continuously. I finally forgave Jamie for everything, and I stopped placing the burden of my happiness on her shoulders. But, I still had not forgiven myself for known or unknown offenses. I knew I was a good mom, but not a perfect one. God had forgiven me for my shortcomings in the parenting department. Jamie told me her addiction had nothing to do with me. So, I went ahead and forgave myself.

There is no expiration date on forgiveness, so keep at it. The important thing is to keep forgiving until you have nothing left to forgive.

TIP: Use the "F" word every chance you get, on every person who has wronged you, and importantly, on yourself.

Codependency

I didn't pay much attention to the word "codependency." Sure, I had heard it in passing, but it had nothing to do with me. Codependency is an excessive emotional or psychological reliance on someone. That wasn't me.

Finally, I took a look at my life and had to admit that codependency had been a part of my life forever. While I might not check many of the codependency boxes, I had begun adapting to it in my childhood. I carried it into my first marriage and then lived in full-on codependency in my relationship with Jamie.

I was now married to Rich and didn't have to do this alone, but they were *my* kids and *my* responsibility. Jamie made poor choices, and I rescued her, much of the time without Rich's knowledge. I reasoned that I was shielding him from the chaos. Plus, I had my trusty Supermom Cape, so I would find a way to make things right.

Jamie's situation got worse, and I continued to bail her out. She lied, and I chose to believe the lies. Her bad choices resulted in a series of significant problems, and I tried to solve them for her. I had to figure this out; she was my daughter, and it was my responsibility, no matter how old she was.

We needed each other. Jamie needed me to help her stay in her addiction, and I was addicted to saving her. It was an unhealthy, codependent relationship. It was a vicious circle, with nobody getting better or stronger.

When I decided to stand up and fight, it included retiring my Supermom Cape. The thing was ripped, torn, and faded, with holes everywhere. No matter, I had worn the cape during some of the most challenging years imaginable, so it felt like a part of my body, and it was painful to remove. But, I kept reminding myself that it had never worked anyway. Plus, it had practically strangled me.

If you are in a Codependent relationship of any kind, it's not helping anyone in the long run. It may well be time for you to take off your Super_____ Cape.

TIP: *Our need to save other people makes us sick. As much as another person depends on us to fill a need, we become addicted to keeping them in their situation. Around and around we go, and nobody is getting better, or stronger. If that is the case, it may be time to remove the cape.*

Never Say Never

We take a hard stance on things, and often, not important things. I used to say I didn't like broccoli or cauliflower (and the list goes on), but the truth is that I had never tried them. When I was twenty-one, on a flight to Fairbanks, Alaska, I was served a small meal consisting of a couple pieces of cheese, a chunk of salami, raw cauliflower and broccoli, and ranch dip. The flight was behind schedule, and it had been hours since I had eaten, so after I plowed through the good stuff, I decided to soak the vegetables in the small amount of ranch dip and take a chance. It turns out I do like broccoli and cauliflower.

A guy I dated asked if I liked sushi, and my instant reply was a resounding,

"No! I like my fish cooked."

I liked the guy, though, so off to sushi we went, along with a couple of his friends, I had never met. We no sooner sat down when the first dishes arrived. One of them was a bowl of what appeared to be guacamole. Now, if I had been thinking, guacamole in a Japanese restaurant would not have made sense, but I was so happy to see something familiar that I popped about a teaspoon or so of the *guacamole* into my mouth, and nearly came out of my chair. That was my first encounter with wasabi, a Japanese horseradish. I sat there with the *I meant to do that* look on my face. My mouth was on fire, and my sinuses were burning. After that incident, what did I have to lose? I tried some sushi, and it was tasty. After I got over my preconceived notion about what it might taste like, and the new textures, I became a regular Sushi eater, and now, Japanese is my favorite ethnic cuisine.

For most of my life, I stated I would *never* get a tattoo. I had no desire to *mar* my body with permanent ink. It's not that I have anything against tattoos on other people, but that they didn't appeal to me.

When Jamie came home with her first tattoo, I was furious. We had talked many times about it, and I forbid her to do it while she was under my roof. The reason was not as much that I didn't care for tattoos, but what a young teenager chose to be a permanent part of her body, would likely not be what she would want in her forties and beyond.

When Jamie was around sixteen, she started negotiating for one. Of course, I explained my logic, but it didn't take her long to come up with the perfect tattoo, one that would shatter my logic. She would get a symbol of a cross. Jamie is quick, but she had met her match. I told her that whatever *style* of cross she came up with at her young age would not be the same one she would choose later. Boom!

I assumed I won the tattoo chess match until she showed up with a tattoo, and it was not a cross. The words *Jamie Lynn,* in large script, were now written permanently across the inside of her forearm. At least it wasn't a tattoo of skull and crossbones, but still. After the initial shock and anger, I expressed how foolish I thought the choice was and sarcastically asked why in the world she would put Jamie Lynn on her arm; was it in case she ever forgot her own name? Considering where her life would head in the ensuing years, maybe the tattoo proved useful.

It is interesting how much we change over time. Between age and experience, our viewpoints can soften or change altogether. Two months after Jamie died, I was in a tattoo shop in Phoenix, with my sister-in-law, Suzanne, getting matching heart and wing tattoos above our ankles. So much for *never.* I smile at the thought of Jamie telling her angel friends how much I disliked her tattoos, and then pointing down to me laying in the chair wincing as the permanent ink settled onto my skin.

I was *never* going to get a tattoo or eat raw fish. We can close our minds to new things, and miss out on valuable life experiences, or even broccoli and cauliflower.

TIP: *There are things you can be pretty sure you would never do, but for the most part, we don't honestly know until we try, or at least consider the possibility. Never say never.*

Standing on the Soapbox

We are all guilty of playing judge and jury on occasion. Convinced we know how we would act or react under certain circumstances, we make judgments. We make them based on our experiences, values, opinions, and viewpoints, even if we have not been in that particular situation. In matters of integrity or principle, it might be fairly cut and dried. However, nobody can guess with certainty how they will feel or react in a situation they have not experienced.

Opinionated minds lead to closed minds. Like me, you probably consider yourself a person with an open heart, but when we have strong opinions on things, like tattoos, we are demonstrating a closed mindset, and closed minds lead to closed hearts.

My judgment of parents of addicts was very harsh. I stood on my soapbox, loudly, and vocally proclaiming that it was the parents' fault if kids went astray. If you raised them right, they would make good choices. When Jamie met her addiction Beast, I fell off of my soapbox and nearly broke my neck when I landed.

There are times when we do need to take a stand, and maybe even step up onto a soapbox but most of the things we find ourselves standing in judgment of, are not important enough, or understood well enough, to risk, taking the big fall.

It would serve us all to walk a mile in another person's shoes before judging or believing we understand. If not a mile, then at least a good walk around the block.

TIP: *Be careful when you get on your soapbox; it is painful when we fall. We should walk a mile in another person's shoes before we judge, or at least a good walk around the block.*

Overcoming Loss

Life is full of loss, and when we lose something or someone we value, we grieve. Grief is a part of life. We might mourn the loss of a relationship, a period of time, or even our youth.

Anything we obtain, we have a chance of losing. That includes the people we love. The only way to avoid loss is to try nothing, take no chances, own no possessions, or love nobody.

After years of beating my head against the wall and getting nothing but a headache, I began to adjust my focus. Instead of focusing on the heartbreak of my daughter's path, I started to focus on my purpose. Rather than spend countless hours each day wondering why all of this was happening to me, I decided to figure out how it could serve me or others.

Too often, when we think of overcoming something, it conjures up thoughts of getting over it. The loss of certain friendships, jobs, our youth, and money, we can get over. The loss of certain loved ones, we might never get over, but we can overcome loss and grief. We can *succeed in dealing with it*. We can *gain control over* the feelings that keep us depressed.

Some of the smaller losses we encounter, we blow up into huge losses. Remember, in the last action, what we focus on becomes magnified. Try to keep your losses in perspective.

I miss Chips, who had such a positive impact on me personally, and was a big part of why I have the extended family I cherish. Grandpa and Nana have been gone for decades now, but I still miss them at times. A smell might trigger a memory buried deep in my subconscious, and I feel a moment of profound sadness.

Waves of grief come over me, and I miss Jamie so much that my heart physically aches. I cry. Then I stand back up and keep going. The key is to embrace the hole in your heart without allowing it to swallow you up. The price we pay for loving someone is the risk of losing them. But, it's worth the risk.

While one half of Jamie's life was a $#*! show, now, I mainly talk about the best parts of life with Jamie. I recall her incredible qualities, and who she truly was under the weight of her addiction Beast. I choose to leave the sad memories behind because they don't serve me.

Losses are a part of life and something we have to learn to manage, or they can destroy us. You have suffered losses of all magnitudes, but learn to ride out the losses, without allowing them to spiral you down into the pit of depression. Be assured that your heart is big enough to contain breaks and holes, along with joy and happiness.

TIP: *Overcome your losses. Take control of them, so they don't control you. Honor the hole in your heart, but don't get swallowed up by it.*

"Some Things Don't Make Sense" File

No doubt, you have wondered why certain events have transpired in your life, and have been unable to make sense of the circumstances. You have so many questions and few answers. One of the most significant sources of frustration are the events we cannot seem to wrap our heads around; those that leave us perplexed. They keep us awake at night, sorting through the details, looking for answers.

You set goals, plan, strive, and push to make your life all that you imagined it could be, and suddenly, out of left field, everything changes. You find yourself living a life that is far different from what you planned, wished, hoped, dreamed, or expected.

We want answers; to make sense of things. So, we analyze, compare, and judge. We need to understand how and why; it's human nature. We agonize over tragedies or a sudden loss, finding it hard to reconcile what has happened, versus what we anticipated or expected. It goes back to asking the question that so often goes unanswered, "Why?"

We all start out with hopes and dreams, and then life happens. As John Lennon sang, *"Life is what happens to you while you're busy making other plans."*

If life has happened to you while you were busy making other plans, then you will need to make new plans and dream new dreams.

I know approximately one person whose life appears to be going exactly as planned. I hope she has flexibility built into her life plan, as not even she will escape life without hardship, trials, or heartbreak.

The *Some Things Don't Make Sense* file is where you should start to file the events in your life, for which you have no answers. It is a way for you to acknowledge reality, without allowing the unanswered questions to drag you down, or keep you in constant agony. It is where I have filed Jamie's addiction nightmare and her murder. It's where my biological father's desertion is filed. It contains our former friend's betrayal and much more. It is the place for you to file those "whys" that will likely never have an answer.

Doing this will allow you some peace and open your mind and heart to focusing on new and different things.

TIP: *The "Some Things Don't Make Sense" file is the best place to file those events and losses for which there are no answers. It is where many of your questions that begin with "why," belong.*

Action Reminders

Let go of the illusion of control. The fact is you have very little control over most situations, and all people (unless they are a small child). Start focusing on the one person you can control – you! That means *your* thoughts, *your* words, *your* feelings, and *your* decisions.

Use the "F" word every chance you get, and be sure you are using it on yourself. Forgiveness is freeing.

Speaking of freedom – free yourself from the self-destructive cycle of codependency. Untangle yourself from codependent relationships, which don't help anyone in the long run.

Never say never.

Don't stand on your soapbox, unless you are sure you won't fall and crack your head open.

Overcome your losses, but don't fixate on them. Focus on the good memories.

Stop asking *why me*, and consider – why *not* you? For the other *why* questions that have no answers, file those in the "Some Things Don't Make Sense" file.

The only thing we have control over is our thoughts, feelings, words, and actions. Let go of your false sense of control and allow yourself to focus on what you can control – you!

Action #8: Stand <u>On</u> Your Story

About the Action

It would be easy to focus on all of our failings, shortcomings, or our past. I could consider myself the poor little girl from the broken home, with a dad who abandoned her repeatedly. It could be my teenage party years that I blame for Jamie's addiction. I could be the victim of betrayal or the sad mom of an addict. It would be easy to live out my days with the "mother of a murder victim" label stuck to my forehead. Who would blame me?

I would blame me.

Instead, I choose to consider myself a warrior. The lessons I have learned on my life's twisty, messy path, I couldn't have paid any amount of money to learn. Yes, much of it came at a cost much higher than what I would like to have experienced, but most of it is invaluable.

You are different than you were before life clobbered you over the head. Experiences change us, but the good news is we get to decide what they will turn us into.

Standing up will change you as well, and in positive ways, that may be hard to see right now. I would be lying if I said I am happy with the way certain things transpired for me, whether by no choice of my own, or based on my own decisions. If it were possible, I would rewind the clock and change much of my story in a heartbeat. You probably wish you could turn back the hands of time, too.

Since there are no do-overs, we must own what has happened without shame, guilt, or regret. Climb up out of your story and stand on top of it. Certain events have occurred, and this is your reality. A heartbreak knocked the wind out of your sails. A betrayal or loss dropped you to your knees, or flat onto your back. You live with a hole in your heart. Fear has gripped you. You became complacent. But none of this needs to define you.

This action will help you to own your story and use it to become all you are meant to be on your way to making the world a better place. It will have you standing <u>on</u> your story, using every experience as a building block to climb higher.

****

Your Value & Self Worth

We place value on things, experiences, situations, and even people. In considering a purchase, you might compare similar products, or evaluate how much you want or need such an item. We put a price tag on relationships and people, based on love, need, or the connection we have to the person. We apply value to jobs, status, achievements, or past mistakes.

It has become commonplace, almost expected, in meeting someone for the first time, to ask,

"What do you do?"

It is a good conversation starter, but it also creates an instant judgment, based on the answer, as well as potential discomfort for the person in the spotlight.

If you met someone who worked as a rocket scientist, you would be immediately impressed and conclude this is a person you might like to know or at least tell others you met. I met a rocket scientist, and I guess I should have been more impressed, as I cannot even recall who it was.

On the contrary, if you met a middle-aged man who worked as a janitor, you might immediately think that he's not highly motivated.

The rocket scientist is likely to be very intelligent, but it is also possible she is arrogant and self-centered. The janitor might be the most kind, generous, and motivated person you will ever meet. You don't know her story.

Sean and I were talking about this point, and he suggested that it would be much better if we met someone and asked,

"Who *are* you?"

Can you imagine the strange looks you would get if you started doing this? Most people wouldn't even know how to answer that question.

We must take care not to place immediate value on another person based on their job, career, financial status, family, or the wealth of their parents. In the same way, we should not allow ourselves to be defined by one part of our lives.

Sean came home from elementary school one day and told me his friend was rich. After his initial comment, our conversation went something like this:

"Wow, that's amazing. What does he do?"

"Mom! He doesn't have a job; he's only ten!"

"But, you just told me he was rich. "

"He is. His dad is a brain surgeon."

"Oh, I see. So, he's not rich at all; his dad is rich."

"Mom! You know what I mean."

I knew what he meant, and he got my point.

A portion of your self-worth, or all of it, might be based upon your loved ones - *their* status, talents, abilities, success, or even looks. If your sense of self-worth is too tangled up in others, then it is a false sense of worth, and over time, it will diminish your value.

Shortly after we took that company public in the early nineties, we started to build the company by acquiring other companies, and I led the due diligence team that traveled the country and into Mexico, investigating and auditing the potential acquisitions. I was off on another self-taught adventure. All of my team members had degrees, as did the auditing firm staff. I was barely over thirty and had only taken two community college accounting classes.

At one of the first dinners, conversation turned to colleges and degrees. I squirmed a bit in my seat, reasonably sure they were not wondering which high school I attended, and probably wouldn't have been so impressed with the two community college classes. I was the only woman and the youngest person there.

The conversation went around the table, with each person talking about their alma mater and which letters followed their names. They had names that ended in a CPA or MBA.

When it was my turn, I said,

"I never went to college."

I braced myself as the table fell silent. It turned out that rather than looking down on me for my lack of a degree, the others were blown away by my accomplishments.

College is a worthy goal, and certain degrees can be incredibly useful, and the process of obtaining a degree teaches discipline. People are impressed with letters like "Dr." before a name, or those that follow a name, such as "Ph.D." I just had my name; that was it, but I didn't let it stop me from standing up and standing on the story I did have. The girl who used to put her hand over her heart when she passed the Big Red R on top of the brewery, was leading a team full of alphabet soup letters.

Esteem comes under attack from many directions. Kids can be hurtful to each other, with teasing, or worse. Often, teachers or coaches say something that stings and sticks. Parents can knowingly or unknowingly damage self-esteem. Bosses and coworkers can beat down your value.

Resist the temptation to wallow in self-pity, shame, guilt, or fear. Fight the urge to give up or to give in. Reject the notion that you have *become* your story. Refuse to stay down on the mat. Shake off the stigma that society has thrown at you. Dig down and find the courage to become the person you would not have become, had you not been a part of your life's story.

Don't be fooled into thinking that you are supposed to carry around shame and guilt, or wear your obstacles like a badge of honor. That is the Beast's attempt at keeping you down.

It is called "self" worth, and you should place a very high value on yourself. This action is all about learning to Stand <u>On</u> Your Story, whatever that story may be. Everything you have been through can serve to build your value if you will start using this action. Life gets better when we get better.

TIP: It is called "self" worth, and you have the power to lift yourself and to put a high value on you. From this day forward, you can choose your worth. Nobody on the planet has the same abilities, talents, lessons, and experiences that you have, and that makes you valuable beyond measure.

Humble Confidence

Kids are confident. They continuously make statements such as,

"Look at me!"

"Look what I can do."

"I can do it myself."

Somewhere along the way, we lose our confidence. The world beats us up. We become self-aware, and that leads to fear. We begin to say, or to think:

"Don't look at me."

"I can't do it."

"Someone needs to do it for me."

That is sad. We are all capable beyond our wildest dreams, but fear has us believing otherwise. We have become so fixated on what other people think, or the criticism we might receive, that, unlike children, who will try until they exhaust themselves, and then try again, we quit.

We stop having dreams of becoming Spiderman or Wonder Woman. We no longer think of ourselves as brave. Instead, we shrink into obscurity or fall in with the masses. We stop trying new things, and we stop believing in ourselves.

For years, I was confident; I believed in myself. Then, all hell broke loose, and life beat me up enough, that my confidence was hanging on by a thread.

So, what do we do to re-build our confidence?

You probably know what my first piece of advice is going to be by now. Here it is – you decide! It would be nice if you had a magic wand or a genie pot, but you don't. So, it will take some work, but nothing is going to happen until you decide that you want to build your confidence; it all starts with a decision.

Confidence has much to do with courage, and these actions are full of tips on building courage.

You might be able to gain some confidence by reading about it or hearing courageous stories, but the best way to build confidence is to stand up to fear. Start taking bold action. Speak about yourself confidently, and accept compliments.

Three-year-old Lennard, whom I told you about before, busted through the door after a walk, arms spread as wide as his smile, and announced in a perfect English accent,

"Hello! Hello!"

We should all walk into a room, believing we are a gift. For too long, we have thought that any amount of confidence or positive self-talk is stuck up or conceited.

You don't have to announce yourself when you enter a room the way Lenny does, but remember that you are valuable and that value starts with believing you are.

Our gifts come from God, as does the grace to make mistakes and still be loved, forgiven, and valued. That is what keeps us humble, but humility does not include playing small; that does not honor God, or serve other people. If we genuinely love and believe in ourselves the way God does, we should be strutting our stuff. Not in arrogance, but with humble confidence.

Forget the noise, what people have spoken over you, and the lies the Beast has fed you. Start believing you are loved, cherished, valued, and capable. Stand up and go out into the world with humble confidence.

TIP: We should walk into a room saying (or at least thinking), "Hello, hello!" Start believing you are valuable and carrying yourself with humble confidence.

The Thief of Joy

We compare things. It is one way we make sense of the world around us. Comparing gives us perspective and information with which to make decisions. There are many good uses for comparison, but comparing your life to your perception of somebody else's life is not one of them. When you are always comparing, you will miss out on the marvelous journey you are on, and the only one you get. Comparison is the thief of joy, and it will rob you of your happiness.

It's possible to compare yourself to someone else and feel better, but more often than not, we compare ourselves with people we think are better looking, more talented, have more money, or are more successful. In those instances, we always come up short and are left feeling lousy.

Growing up, I knew girls named Kathy, Julie, and Patty, not Valerie. I also had red hair. My friends were brunettes and blonds. I write with my left hand, and do a few other things left-handed, but mostly everything else right-handed. I was different: red-hair, freckly, sort of left-handed, Valerie. I didn't want to be different; I wanted to be like everyone else.

I tried endlessly to get a tan. It was before sunscreen, so all I did was burn. As a teenager, my friends laid out in the sun with baby oil slathered on their skin, and I sat in the shade with a t-shirt covering my swimsuit.

When I was old enough, I planned to dye my hair brown, find a miracle cure for my freckly white skin, and do something about that name. I didn't have the patience to deal with the left-handed, right-handed situation, so I would have to let that one go.

In high school, I worked and paid for most of my clothing, entertainment, and personal care. While I wasn't old enough to change my name, I could start working on the other stuff. I hit the tanning booth, but it proved fruitless for gaining that bronze skin I so desired. The red hair, I could do something about, but while I had waited for the day to arrive, my orange hair turned into a coppery red color, with natural highlights. It became one of my best features, attributing to the most compliments about my looks to date.

I read that blue-eyed redheads are the rarest combination on the planet, and only ten percent of the population is left-handed. Now, I like being rare and different. Once I realized how awesome it is to be unique, I started to love my name, too.

In trying to be like everybody else, we only serve to discount what makes us unique. There is only one you, and the more you attempt to change the real you, you lose what makes you unique. There will always be someone taller, skinnier, more prosperous, funnier, more athletic, better-looking, more successful, and, and, and…so what. You are the way you are for a reason, and you have something to offer the world that nobody else does. Do *you* to the best of your abilities.

We also compare our troubles, and our Beasts, which is equally as debilitating. If you read this book and your problems appear to be smaller than mine, you will discount yours. If you have gone through more, you will run the risk of heading straight to the Pity Party. Remember: comparison is the thief of joy.

TIP: Don't waste time comparing yourself with others. Embrace your differences. Comparison is the thief of joy, and it will rob you of your happiness.

Give Up the Guilt

A certain amount of guilt is okay as it can make us realize when we have done wrong and can help to avoid repeating the offense.

Whenever my brothers and I had a few cents, we would head to the Little Store and buy penny candy. I had collected a few coins, so off I headed to the Little Store, but it was not for penny candy. I bought myself a chocolate bar. On the way home, I tore open the candy, dropped the wrapper to the ground, and started to devour the chocolate. I didn't get two houses down when I felt too guilty to take another step. My five-year-old conscience knew I was not supposed to litter. I turned right around, went back, and scooped up the wrapper.

Some guilt is good, but it becomes a big problem when you live in a constant state of guilt. Giving up guilt is not to be flippant, or disregard past behaviors, but rather, to relieve yourself of your never-ending guilt.

Many people are carrying guilt for other people. I felt guilty being the mom of an addict, when, in reality, I had nothing to do with Jamie's decision to start and continue taking drugs, or put herself in dangerous situations. I made it about me when it wasn't.

Some of your guilt might belong to another person. Initially, you felt terrible for that person, but over time, you morphed their problems and choices into your guilt.

You are not doing anyone any favors by carrying the blame for them. Torturing yourself with guilt over your choices only serves to keep you in self-contempt, doubt, and shame. Stand up and claim your rightful place in this world, as a woman or man of courage, leaving the guilt behind.

TIP: Giving up guilt is not being flippant about, or disregarding your past behaviors, but instead, it is about forgiving yourself and letting go of the past. It is not serving you, or anyone else, so give it up.

Shed the Shame

"I'm ashamed of you."

"You should be ashamed of yourself."

We have heard those stinging words, and have probably said them. Parents often use these statements as a way to correct behavior in their children. When our parents told us, they were ashamed of us, we paid attention. Most times, we changed our behavior.

When I was eleven years old, my friend Karen (the one who taught me to smoke) stole a candy bar from the neighborhood grocery store. I didn't know she had done it, but when I saw the candy, I wanted one too, so back to the store we went, to get my candy bar. Obviously, I was not much of a criminal mastermind.

We walked around the side of the store happily eating the candy bars, and were nearly off the property, to freedom, when we heard shouting behind us. We turned to see the mean lady from the store, walking toward us. My heart was beating out of my chest as I started toward her, breaking up the candy bar behind me as I did. The mean lady was too focused on the evidence Karen held in her hands to notice the candy trail behind me.

My friend was in big trouble, but since I wasn't caught with anything, I was only sent home and asked not to return to the store. I could have kept my life of crime hidden from my mom, but I had a big problem. I shopped at that store weekly with her. It was a big store, but it wasn't as if they wouldn't notice me – I was the redhaired, freckle-faced girl.

My confession went as well as I had expected. I would have preferred my mom yelling at me, and then grounding me for the rest of my life as opposed to the looks of shame. She barely spoke to me for a whole two weeks, but it felt like an eternity. In that case, the shame worked. It was the end of my crime spree.

There is a different kind of a shame that sticks to us, and it is hard to wash off.

When I realized Jamie was addicted to drugs, I suddenly had this unwanted label of *mom of an addict*. I accepted the shame, knowing what other people were thinking of me since I had plenty to say about "those parents" before my daughter became addicted to drugs.

One of the Beast's favorite tactics is shame. If we remain covered with it, we are far less likely to stand up and use our story to make a difference. Shame keeps us isolated. Isolation keeps the shame intact. Around and around we go. Not being able to live in the truth of our story keeps us from being whole.

Once I came out of the cave of my self-imposed prison of depression and fear, I slowly shed my shame. Helen Keller said,

"Never bend your head. Always hold it high.
Look the world straight in the eye."

No matter what has transpired in your life, stand up tall and look the world straight in the eye.

If you think you have made too many mistakes or don't measure up to other people, it will serve you well to consider that every sinner has a future, and every saint has a past. Everybody has made mistakes and wrong choices, but not one person is beyond redemption.

TIP: No matter what has transpired in your life, stand up tall and look the world straight in the eye. The layers of shame will start to peel off of you when you stop slinking around in shame.

Your Piece of the World's Puzzle

When I was a teenager, I put together a puzzle with what seemed like a million pieces. It was a mostly white snow leopard, laying on – you guessed it - white snow. For weeks, I worked that puzzle, painstakingly, having mainly the shape of each piece to go on. As I neared completion, puzzle anxiety kicked in – I feared getting to the end of the puzzle only to find one piece was missing.

Thankfully, none of my puzzle pieces were missing but imagine for a moment working your way through a puzzle such as mine, only to realize three spaces remain, but you have only two pieces in front of you. Placing them where they belong, you stare at the hole in the puzzle where the last piece belongs.

You grab the puzzle box and shake it just in case you missed a piece, but hear nothing but silence. Perhaps the elusive piece is stuck to the top of the box, so you open it and search every corner to find the box is empty.

Down on the floor, you go, crawling around frantically searching for what has become the most valuable piece of the puzzle.

You recall using the vacuum cleaner a few days ago, so you run for the laundry room and dump out the contents, digging through dirt, food particles, and furballs, only to come up short.

Off to the closet you go in search of any item of clothing that you may have worn in the past few weeks.

Maybe the dog ate it - not going there.

All the work you put into the puzzle, weeks of eye-crossing focus, only to come up a piece short. You wanted to frame your masterpiece, but you are finding it difficult to get past the missing piece. One piece of thousands shouldn't matter, but it does.

I carefully chose matting and a frame for my puzzle masterpiece and hung it on the wall, where it was for years.

If even one piece of the puzzle were missing, though, I would never have framed it. Instead, I would have tossed every piece back into the box and headed straight for the trash. The picture would not have been complete without that one small valuable piece of the puzzle.

If you don't step up and become all you can be, then the world's puzzle won't be complete. Yes, the world will keep turning, whether or not you stand <u>on</u> your story and become the awesome person you were created to be, but it will not be the same. The world needs your piece of the puzzle. The world needs you!

TIP: The world will keep turning without your awesomeness, but it will still have that missing piece. The world needs your piece of the puzzle. The world needs you!

Fly Like an Eagle

Eagles are some of the most fascinating, majestic animals on the planet. They are a symbol of bravery, courage, honor, and determination. The Bald Eagle is the symbol of the United States of America.

Unlike other birds that hide from the storm, Eagles fly right into it and use the wind to soar higher and higher, without expending energy flapping their wings.

When our mighty winds blow, we either run for cover or flap our wings until we are exhausted. It takes tremendous energy to battle through our storms, but rather than fighting the winds; we should use them to lift us higher.

What I wouldn't give to have the expended energy back that I used fighting against the storms. What you wouldn't give to retrieve your wasted energy.

Sure, a part of me would like relief, but another part of me has begun to embrace challenges. It might sound crazy, but there are instances when I receive difficult news or am struggling with a situation, and suddenly – I get a happy feeling. I am tempted to think I might be headed around the bend, but I believe this is the personal growth that comes from using these actions.

The Beast whispered, "You can't stand through the storm."
The warrior shouted, "I am the storm."

Don't hate the storms; use them to lift you, rather than to defeat you. Every event that is allowed into your life is there to serve you in some way. You can withstand the storm. You are a warrior.

TIP: Embrace the storms and use them to lift you higher.

Action Reminders

Use your obstacles as stepping stones to stand up and stand <u>on</u> your story. Everybody has made mistakes. We all have a past. Don't allow your story to keep you from becoming all you can. Use your experiences to build more character.

Live with humble confidence – that you are enough. Stop slinking around in shame, playing small. Hold your head high and look the world straight in the eye.

You don't have to stand in the muck of your story, like a victim after a storm. Stand up tall, put your shoulders back, and declare that you are going to become a better person, not in spite of, but because of your story.

Don't compare yourself to others, or use other people to determine your value. You are one of a kind, and it is time to start acting like it.

Decide today that you are going to make the absolute best of the rest of your life. Use every situation and challenge as a learning tool to become more. Harness the power of experience to propel you to places you might never have gone, if not for those experiences. The world needs your piece of the puzzle. The world needs you!

Stand up and fly right into the storm. Spread your wings and allow the storm to lift you higher.

Action #9: Make Meaning From the Madness

About the Action

You might be tempted to blow through this action or skip it altogether. Making meaning might not be on your radar right now, because you are trying to figure out how to be happy yourself. You may be trying to survive; to get by. You might believe it is best for everyone if you wait until you have it all together before considering meaning or legacy. If you wait for that time to come, it will be – never, because you will always be a work in progress, just like everybody else.

While I did encourage you to take care of number one, in Action #3, it is also essential to be of service to others. Taking care of yourself is vital so that you can be healthy and whole for other people.

You don't have the luxury of waiting because somebody needs what you have to offer, and they need it now. People are waiting to be inspired by your courage and perseverance.

In every grade school report card, my teachers wrote, *"Valerie is a leader."* With leadership comes responsibility. We can use our influence to negatively impact others, as I did with my negative attitude, or we can accept the responsibility of helping others find their potential.

After standing up and giving my first formal speech in oral communications class, I vowed I would avoid public speaking. God had other plans, starting with delivering my Grandpa's eulogy. Imagine if I had allowed fear or shame to keep me from my mission. The world would be missing a valuable piece of its puzzle, and I would be missing out on the incredible opportunity to become more by serving others. When you take even a tiny step forward to reach out to someone else in need, you will get back far more than you give.

****

You Don't Have to Be Mother Teresa

Whatever you do to give back does not have to be a huge mission. It truly can be the simplest of gestures. Think of all you have been through and how much knowledge, wisdom, and perspective you have gained. Consider how much you have to offer. Don't wait until you come up with an earth-shattering venture to begin making meaning. Little things are *big* things.

Several years ago, I decided to make it my mission to get people to smile at me. I was at a store where the checker didn't even acknowledge me, let alone smile back. My first thought was, *how rude; I am the customer!* Hey, no judging; I was a different person back then. I was about to show her that I could be as rude as she was, but instead, I asked,

"Is everything okay?"

She stopped in mid scan, and tears welled up in her eyes. She went on to tell me her granddaughter was in the hospital, and it was a serious illness. This poor lady was at work when she wanted to be at the hospital with her granddaughter. She thanked me for caring enough to ask.

Recall the *Momentary Connections* from Action #4: Build Your Circle of Strength? These are meaningful minutes or even moments we have with strangers.

It was an opportunity for me to show a little kindness and compassion, and to learn a valuable lesson. People are in pain, and even the smallest of service can make a difference. Maybe that brief encounter was enough to help the grandmother make it through that day, or beyond.

Those connections can be difference makers to people whose lives you touch in those brief encounters, and to you. Don't take these moments lightly, or for granted. You don't have to be Mother Teresa to make a difference.

TIP: *Even the smallest of gestures can make a massive impact on another person who needs your kindness and caring at that moment. Little things are big things. You don't have to be Mother Teresa to make a difference.*

People Are Watching You

People are watching us, and they want and need to be inspired by us. Your resolve to stand is not just about winning the battle for yourself; it's also about the opportunity you have to inspire others. They can find hope by watching you stand.

Sean and Jamie had a strained relationship for years because Sean was angry. He was in pain, watching his sister self-destruct, so he masked his emotions behind anger. Sean built a wall to protect his heart and tried not to even think about her. He swore she had never been kind to him his whole life and had almost no good memories of her. For years, I tried to get Sean to recall the good times and to convince him to forgive Jamie. I would tell him that she never judged him or held anything against him. No matter, he hung onto his anger and unforgiveness, and then Jamie died.

Sean now had a flood of emotions he had stuffed away. One of them was guilt. He spent more than three years working through the process of opening his heart, letting go of anger, and forgiving – mostly himself.

There was one person he was not about to forgive – the guy who killed Jamie. Initially, Sean was so angry that he scared me with some of the comments he was making about what he wanted to do to the guy.

Over the past couple of years, I noticed a change in Sean, but the biggest came just weeks before I typed these words. Sean told me he had forgiven the guy awaiting trial for Jamie's murder. He is still sad and misses his sister every day, but he has let go of the anger. The most important gift I could receive was to know my son has unburdened himself. I told him he doesn't have to give me another gift as long as I live.

Sean told me,

"I talk about Jamie all the time, mom; but, I never talk about him."

He went on to tell me that he is in such a good place in his life, listed his blessings, and explained that this guy was no longer welcome in his thoughts.

When I told him how happy I was, he told me,

"It was all of the forgiveness B.S. you have been talking about for the past three years!"

We both chuckled, but this is the part I want you to hear. Sean was watching me. He said something to this effect,

"I got here because of you, mom, because of the work you are doing. If you weren't who you are, I would never have made it to this place. I would still be wanting to show up at the courthouse with a gun."

There could be one or many people watching you, searching for hope from your decision to stand. The world has never needed leaders more than it does today. Warriors willing to lead the way.

The people who truly inspire us most, those that captivate our hearts are the people who have been to hell and back. The world cheers for the heroes who have, against all the odds, risen off the mat. It is the person who has battled their Beast, and won, whom we admire most. People like you.

TIP: *People are watching you and needing to be inspired by you.*

Well Done

Some of us have taken the harder road through life. Mine has been a mixed bag of awesomeness, mediocrity, terror, success, failure, peaks, valleys, confusion, and hope. The ups and downs of life.

Hunter S. Thompson said,

> *Life should not be a journey to the grave with the intention of arriving safely in a pretty and well-preserved body, but rather to skid in broadside in a cloud of smoke, thoroughly used up, totally worn out, and loudly proclaiming "Wow! What a Ride!*

One day I will skid broadside in a cloud of smoke, totally worn out, and my ride will be over. Someday your ride will be over too. When mine is over, and I stand at the gates of heaven, first, I hope my name will be on the list. Assuming heaven's gate angel finds my name, I understand I will have to take a little trip down my life's memory lane with my maker.

I'm hoping I heard it wrong, and God and I don't have to watch the movie together; after all, we have both seen it. If we do, there will be scenes in my life story that will cause me to cover my eyes, and to plug my ears. I may have to watch much of it peeking through my fingers. As the scenes of my life unfold, God will smile, and a time or two, He will no doubt chuckle. Knowing my life, he may downright laugh out loud. During certain scenes, God might close his eyes or shake his head. While watching other memories, tears will stream down both of our cheeks. As the last scene flashes by and the credits roll, I will look sheepishly at God, holding my breath in anticipation of what he might say. He very well might say,

"Wow! What a ride!"

My hope and prayer is that with all things considered; the whole messy movie, that was my life, he will whisper,

"Well done."

Like mine, your life is far from perfect. The good news is that as long as we are breathing, we still have time to add more scenes to our life's movies; to make our lives more meaningful.

When the credits roll on your story, there is no doubt you will want to hear,

"Well Done."

There are many things for which you should hear, "well done." For starting to implement even one of **The 9 Actions** -well done. You have gone through hardship, heartbreak, and disappointment, but you have decided to stand – well done. No matter how you feel today, you have not given up – well done. You are near the end of the book – well done. You are going to go out and shine your light and make the world a better place - well done.

TIP: There are many things you have accomplished, for which you will, no doubt, hear "well done." Life is messy, but you still have time to make more meaning.

Legacy

Life is short, no matter how many years you live. We are here for a fleeting moment in comparison to eternity. Life is short in time. But life is also long. It is long in possibilities and hope. It is long in potential, and in the people, you have impacted during your lifetime. It is long because your legacy can live on in other people long after you're gone.

One of our greatest needs is the connection to something bigger than ourselves. You have an innate need to know you matter; that the world is a little bit better because you are in it.

Each person has a unique mission. Maybe you know what yours is, or perhaps, you have no idea. Your purpose could turn out to be far different from what you imagined, or maybe even wanted. Mine sure did.

When I was young, I loved red licorice so much that I told my friend I was going to make a million dollars and buy a licorice factory. Perhaps, I was already on my road to entrepreneurship, but at that age, it was more likely about the licorice.

Making a difference has always mattered to me. In my very early thirties, after we took the company public, I watched the stock soar upward and had dreams of cashing in and starting a non-profit to empower single parents and their children. Through a series of events, including a stock plummet, that particular mission was not carried out.

After all hell broke loose and there was no relief in sight, I began to believe I had missed the purpose boat; it sailed without me. How was I supposed to start leaving a legacy when I could barely stand for myself? The actions I have shared in this book are how I was able to go from depression, hopelessness, helplessness, confusion, self-doubt, and paralyzing fear, to living a legacy. And, I started right in the middle of a storm that kept gaining strength.

If you are in a similar situation and cannot imagine anything good coming out the other end of your current tunnel, hang on. It can, and it will, if you grab onto a tiny bit of hope, and start to use **The 9 Actions**.

Most people don't think much about their legacy. I posted something about legacy on social media recently, and somebody asked,

"What do you mean by legacy?"

It hadn't dawned on me that someone might not understand the meaning, but I have since realized many people don't consider they legacy they are leaving behind.

When we think of legacy, we think of leaving something for someone. We can leave a legacy *for* people, but it is even more important to leave a legacy *in* them. The imprint of *you* that lasts long after you have left this earth.

A couple of generations from now, we could be forgotten unless we have some type of public platform that outlasts us. But, a public platform is not required to leave a lasting legacy.

It's no secret that one half of Jamie's life was a mess, yet she still left an imprint on those around her. I have had many of Jamie's friends contact me, and each one describes her in the same way. She was a true friend. She would give you her last dollar. Even in the messiness of Jamie's life, she left a positive imprint.

Every person will live on in other people. In the wisdom we impart, the hope we offer, and the belief we have in others. You can leave invaluable pieces of *you* in people, who will, in turn, make their mark, and on and on it goes, leaving a little of *you* in the world forever.

The fact is, you are impacting people, even if you are not focused on leaving a legacy. Why not *choose* the legacy you leave behind?

If you are sowing seeds of fear, negativity, lack, hopelessness, helplessness, or anger, that is the legacy you are leaving.

When you sow seeds of courage, integrity, faith, positivity, hope, peace, and purpose, *that* will be your legacy. You may not get direct credit fifty years from now, for sowing those seeds, but do it anyway, with the knowledge that you are leaving a lasting legacy of courage and hope.

Whatever level of madness you have experienced, make meaning from it. The world is waiting for you!

TIP: *You can leave invaluable pieces of you in people, who will, in turn, make a mark on others, leaving a little of you in the world forever.*

Action Reminders

You can make meaning from the madness of life with even the smallest of gestures. You don't have to be Mother Teresa to make a difference.

People are watching you, and they are waiting to be inspired by you. It is your responsibility to lead the way for others. Show them it is possible to move out of the darkness or to get up off of the mat.

We all need to know we matter and that our legacy will outlast us. Time is going by quickly, and life is short, but it is also long in the fact that you can leave a piece of you in those you touch on your trip through this life. You are leaving a legacy right now, so make wise choices. Your imprint will be in the world forever, so don't place a period at the end of your troubles. Stand up, and go out in the world, and make meaning from the madness.

Keep Standing

I told you a great deal about my life, and how I used **The 9 Actions** throughout it, even before they had a name, and how I consciously applied them to some unbelievable situations, once they did. Now, it's time for you to use them to improve your life in any way you can imagine. Here are some things you can do to keep standing:

√ Continue using **The 9 Actions**.

√ Join Valerie's **Facebook Group (find it at her page: Valerie Silveira)**.

√ Get a companion **Still Standing Journal** (or two).

√ Attend an **event**.

√ Get on Valerie's **email list**.

√ Visit **ValerieSilveira.com** for resources, news, and links to social media.

All of the books are on Amazon. Find links to books and all of the Programs and Resources is **ValerieSilveira.com.**

Keep standing! I am standing with you.

Still Standing Journals

Still Standing Journals are the perfect companion to this book. Each Journal contains 30 of Valerie's most powerful quotes and nuggets of wisdom. There are short but powerful sections for your use each morning to get your day started in the right direction. Return to the Journal to reflect on your day and set your intention for the next.

Journal topics align with the principles of **The 9 Actions** and the message in **Still Standing: How I Overcame Guilt, Shame, Hopelessness, Devastating Loss & Paralyzing Fear.**

Find Links to the Still Standing Journals, and all of Valerie's books at **ValerieSilveira.com.**

About Valerie

Valerie Silveira is an award-winning author, courage coach, and motivational speaker. She is the creator of **The 9 Actions (a.k.a. The 9 Weapons of Hope**™.

Valerie has faced childhood trauma, abandonment, loss, divorce, health issues, and betrayal. She stood up during her darkest day, riding the Roller Coaster From Hell with her daughter, Jamie, and the addiction Beast she lived with for half of her life.

All of Valerie's challenges combined did not add up to the heartbreak and devastation she faced, losing her only daughter to addiction, and eventually, to a senseless murder.

At a very dark time in her life, Valerie found a shred of hope, and a tiny bit of courage, and made a decision that saved her life – she decided to Stand Up and Fight.

Valerie has had a diverse career in finance, business operations, consulting, training, and speaking.

She is passionate about helping others put the pieces of their lives back together. Valerie is on a mission to help others find their courage, no matter what they are facing.

Valerie has an incredibly relatable style, a great sense of humor, and her courage is contagious. **The 9 Actions**, her books, empowerment programs, are invaluable for anyone struggling to move through or past a difficult life situation.

We want to connect with you! Find Resources and Social Media links to Valerie at **ValerieSilviera.com.**

LEARN TO LEAP

Praise for Learn to Leap
How Leaders Turn Risk Into Opportunity

"I've known Kip for many years, as one of the stories in here attests, and I still don't know whether things happen to Kip Knight or Kip Knight happens to things. You'll get plenty of examples of both in this book. It's a story lover's delight by a storytelling master, but not just that: underneath are many memorable and transferrable lessons of leadership. This is a wild, wonderful, and very wise read."

> —**Stan Slap,** *New York Times* bestselling author of *Bury My Heart at Conference Room B* and *Under the Hood*

"This is a highly entertaining yet pragmatic book on what it takes to win friends and influence people in the 21st century. In a world where one is likely to face unexpected challenges and setbacks daily, *Learn to Leap* gives the reader just the right perspective and attitude adjustment to keep on going no matter what happens."

> —**Klon Kitchen,** Author of *The Kitchen Sync* and former National Security Advisor

"Kip shares some timeless principles of leadership through personal stories presented with cinematic quality and impact. There are parts of it I enjoyed immensely—his stories brought me smiles that went beyond smiling to outright laughter."

> —**John Pepper,** Former CEO of Procter & Gamble, former Chairman of the Walt Disney Company

"Kip Knight is a great storyteller, and *Learn to Leap* is abound with life and business lessons collected from a remarkable career. Well worth a read."

> —**Greg Macfarlane,** President and CEO, Jackson Hewitt

"Kip's book is like a Disney ride where you go inside many Fortune 100 companies and meet the CEOs and executives you have read about in one turn, then around the bend learning about leadership and emotional intelligence from his personal experiences and stories. The ride in *Learn to Leap* gives you practical skills embedded in Kip's stories of courage, creativity, perseverance, resilience, and gratitude that will inspire you to be your best."

> — **Relly Nadler, Psy.D.,** MCC Author of *Leading with Emotional Intelligence*

"*Learn to Leap* brings a wealth of Kip's wisdom to readers through the rich stories and life lessons Kip and his cast of supporting characters share about leadership, the importance of never losing one's love of creativity, the influence of creativity on risk-taking, and how to innovate with success and humanity."

> — **Sandy Climan,** Founder & CEO, Entertainment Media Ventures, Inc.

"From Louisiana to spots across the globe, Kip Knight and an amazing cast of characters show us what good leadersip—and a good life—is all about. Keep moving, act fearlessly, and take the leap!"

> — **Maynard Webb,** Founder of the Webb Investment Network, *New York Times* bestselling author

"This is a compelling collection of stories about people united with a common purpose. Kip and his team created widely applauded training programs for U.S. diplomats, training hundreds of U.S. diplomats to create effective global communication strategies. *Learn to Leap* will tell you how they did it as well as how you can apply this same 'can do' spirit in your own life."

> — **Michelle Giuda,** Former Assistant Secretary of State, U.S. State Department

LEARN TO LEAP

How Leaders Turn Risk into Opportunity

KIP KNIGHT

This book is dedicated to my wife Peggy
and my sons Tom and Chris
who were always there to hold the net.

LEARN TO LEAP
How Leaders Turn Risk into Opportunity

ISBN 978-1-7377964-0-4 (hardcover)
ISBN 978-1-7377964-1-1 (ebook)
Published by 1845 Publishing

Cover and interior design by
Monica Thomas for TLC Book Design
TLCBookDesign.com

Printed in Canada

TABLE OF CONTENTS

Prologue

*Bob Pearson, author and chair
of The Next Practices Group*

The experiences we encounter in our lives shape what we will do next, often without us being conscious of their impact.

Kip Knight, the author of *Learn to Leap*, has always had a keen sense of self-awareness. He possesses a unique ability to learn about a "moment," while it is happening, and reflect on what he should do to take the next "leap," both personally and professionally.

I have listened to Kip's stories over many dinners and have always found them to be interesting, often funny, and inspiring. They make me reflect on my own life and remember how I have learned to leap.

In my own career, I was once told that I would probably fail at my next job (gee thanks and I didn't), and I have been presented with awesome opportunities that were a bit scary at first. Both types of moments required me to think about what I can do and somehow summon up the courage and confidence to take the next step.

I still laugh at myself when I think of my first job. When I called Carl Byoir & Associates to inquire about an entry-level job, I was told they did not hire people out of college. In this case, I made the leap to not listen well, send them my writing samples, and keep calling, leading to a job as an assistant account executive. Years later, two long-time friends and colleagues, Bob Feldman and Bill Heyman, talked to me about joining Bob to create a new healthcare practice from scratch at GCI Group. Just me, a houseplant, a desk, and a plan. I am glad I took them up on their offer. In both cases, it required taking time to reflect on the situation, understand what I wanted to accomplish, and then doing my best to make it happen.

We can try to plan life, but it is rare that it works that way. How we embrace these moments defines our journey.

Of course, not every leap works perfectly. Nothing in life does. And that is ok. A great baseball hitter only gets a hit three out of every ten times. No one wins every time, yet we still learn from these moments as well.

What I have discovered over the years is that we learn the most when we listen carefully to the stories that have shaped others. They are remarkably similar and parallel to our own decisions. When a situation is new to us, it often requires the most reflection.

Entering stage left is our friend Kip, who reflects on stories from childhood to working at Procter & Gamble to teaching for the U.S. Government.

Kip's exceptional storytelling skills are captured in the style he has written in this book. When you start reading, imagine yourself sitting at the dinner table with Kip, thinking about how a scenario developed, what his reaction was to the situation, and how he learned to leap. If you are like me, you'll also laugh more than a few times.

As you read each chapter, just keep reminding yourself that taking a risk is easy. Anyone can do something silly. But taking educated risks requires thought. We need our friends to talk it out so we can think through what makes the most sense.

Of course, sometimes risks impose themselves in unwelcome ways, such as bullying, where it may be uncomfortable, yet a positive lesson can still be embedded that can carry on for many years.

Helen Keller once said, "Life is either a daring adventure or nothing at all." I have always interpreted this quote as a reminder that we make choices every day on how we interpret and handle a new opportunity or issue that has been presented to us.

Whether you are the one asking others to leap, or you are considering doing so yourself, the mindset presented by Kip inspires us to ask simple questions that can guide our decisions.

Should we trust a new process? Is this new job the right one for us? How do I go from "wanting to give back to society" to actually doing it? How do I give back to the next generation to share the wisdom we all have gathered? How do I protect those who might be bullied by society? Should I accept this new job? And much more. There is always a core question to consider.

Of course, questions are not enough. It is the start of a decision-making process to build the internal confidence to embrace life's risks and opportunities and make the leap that is right for you.

Learn to Leap, in my view, is about refining and rethinking how we prepare, how we become more self-aware, and how we give ourselves the confidence to take chances in life that are meaningful. It's all about learning how to assess and adapt to risky situations, so we make the most of every interaction along our personal journey.

Enjoy!

INTRODUCTION:
Change of Plans

"I advise you not to mess with me. I know karate, kung Fu, judo, Taekwondo, jujitsu, and 100 other dangerous words." —Skylar Blue

It had been a long flight from Los Angeles to Seoul, South Korea when I landed in mid-afternoon. I was ready to get off the plane after a 13-and-a-half-hour non-stop flight. I managed to get a bit of sleep but was looking forward to getting a full night's rest in a real bed. One rule of international travel I learned over the years was "sleep when the locals sleep," so I was going to have dinner with the Kentucky Fried Chicken (KFC) marketing team in Korea before getting some desperately needed shuteye.

Since taking the VP of International Marketing role several months earlier, this would be my first visit to their market. I was looking forward to learning about the great work they had been doing—the Korean team had a reputation of being one of our best in all of Asia. I was also excited to be in Korea for the first time, the "Land of the Morning Calm," an ancient country with a fascinating history.

At the time, KFC was owned by PepsiCo. We were part of a corporate division called PepsiCo Restaurants International, which included KFC, Pizza Hut, and Taco Bell. I'd been with PepsiCo for about five years. Even though international travel could be physically demanding, I never complained about their corporate travel policy. I was allowed to fly business class and stayed at incredible hotels. For this trip, I was booked at the Four Seasons in downtown Seoul. As standard practice, the hotel would be sending a limo driver to the airport to pick me up right outside the immigration area inside the airport.

Before leaving on this trip, an email explained that as I walked out of the immigration control area at the Seoul international airport into the main lobby, I should look for a tall "Four Seasons" sign with my name on it. Despite a huge crowd waiting in the airport lobby, I was pleased to see the tall Four Seasons sign with my name written in large letters. I approached a man in a suit holding the sign.

"Hi, I'm Kip Knight."

The man smiled and shook my hand. "I'm Mr. Park from the Four Seasons. Welcome to South Korea. I'm your driver. Do we need to go and get your luggage?"

I shook my head. "No, I always travel with just carry-on luggage. I'm ready to go."

We started walking down the hallway to the airport parking garage. One thing I couldn't help but notice is although Mr. Park was wearing a suit, it was of poor quality, especially for someone working at the Four Seasons. His gaudy polyester tie wasn't much better. Limo drivers are usually sharp dressers, but I tried not to be too judgmental. Maybe he was new to the role, or perhaps he didn't have enough money yet for a tailor-made suit.

As we walked to the airport garage, Mr. Park indicated a slight problem with the Four Seasons limousine. It had developed engine problems right before he left the hotel for the airport to pick me up. The only vehicle available to pick me up on such short notice was his van. He apologized as we approached his vehicle. I glanced inside—the interior of the van was a total mess. It looked more like something a painter would drive to a home remodeling site.

Mr. Park told me if I preferred, he would call for a limo to come to pick me up, but it would probably be about a one- or two-hour wait. I already knew it would be about an hour's drive to the Four Seasons hotel from the airport. All I wanted to do now was to get to the hotel, take a shower, and maybe sneak in a short nap before dinner with the Korean team. I told Mr. Park his van would be fine, and we hit the road.

As we left the airport, I started to notice the highway signs were in Korean as well as English. I always try to pay attention to how the roads are laid out any time I'm in a new city. We passed a directional sign indicating to turn off on an exit road that would take you to central Seoul, where I knew the Four Seasons was located. For some reason that wasn't clear to me, we kept going straight and went right past the exit. Oh well, I thought, Mr. Park must know a shortcut to avoid traffic.

We'd now been driving about ten minutes at a leisurely pace and drove past a second directional sign that indicated to exit here to go to central Seoul. I was starting to wonder what was going on.

"Excuse me, Mr. Park, I'm new to Seoul, but are you sure we are going in the right direction to go to the Four Seasons? All the highway signage says central Seoul is in the opposite direction we are heading."

Mr. Park kept driving and didn't say anything.

I thought perhaps he didn't hear me or didn't understand what I was saying. "Excuse me, Mr. Park, where are we going?".

Mr. Park glanced over his shoulder at me in the back seat of the van and stated, "There's been a change of plans. We're not going to the Four Seasons."

I'm a trusting individual—some would say too trusting—perhaps even bordering on naive. So, I started to panic for the first time since leaving the airport and wondered what was happening.

"What the hell are you talking about?" I exclaimed.

Mr. Park was very calm. He continued driving the van and glanced at me in the rearview mirror.

"I'm not the driver from the Four Seasons. I was in the airport lobby and saw the limo driver holding the sign with your name on it. When he went to the restroom, he left the sign outside the bathroom, and I grabbed it. Then you came out of Immigration."

My mind started racing. Who the hell was this guy? Where were we going? What did he want?

Mr. Park continued. "You're going to pay me $1,000 in US dollars or else."

At this point, as I sat in the crappy van, I quickly concluded several things:

- This guy was probably not a professional kidnapper since he was asking for a small amount of money, unless kidnappers in Korea haven't figured out yet they could get a lot more than $1,000 for an American business executive, which didn't seem very likely.

- Maybe he'd pulled this scam off at the airport before, but I doubted it. My guess was he saw an opportunity and decided to go for it without first considering the pros and cons.

- Mr. Park knew absolutely nothing about me or my background, which I knew I could use to my advantage. For all he knew, I could be someone he absolutely didn't want to mess with. I decided to test this theory out.

I started screaming from the back of the van, "Do you have any idea who I am?"

Mr. Park looked confused and kept driving.

"The American and Korean authorities are already looking for me right now. If you don't turn this van around immediately and return to the airport, you will wish you were never born!"

My heart was racing, and I was close to freaking out. I didn't have $1,000 with me, but I'm not sure that would have satisfied Mr. Park even if I did. I had no idea if he had a weapon or not. My gut reaction was I needed to scare the hell out of him while we were still in his van and convince him I wasn't worth the trouble.

Mr. Park turned around and yelled, "Give me my money NOW!"

I yelled back, "Turn this van around NOW and go back to the airport. This is your last chance! You can't even begin to imagine the trouble you are in!"

Mr. Park violently turned the steering wheel and did a U-turn in the middle of the busy expressway. He started cursing in Korean and kept looking at me in the rearview mirror. He was now driving like a madman. I was beginning to worry I was at more risk of being in a severe car accident than being kidnapped the way he was driving.

We made it back to the airport in a very short amount of time.

As we approached the terminal, my heart was racing. I kept yelling at Mr. Park to keep going if he wanted to save himself. We reached the first drop-off area. He slammed on the brakes and told me to get the hell out of his van.

He didn't need to ask twice. I opened the van's side door, grabbed my suitcase, and jumped out as he sped off. I didn't even think to look at the van's license plate since I was in a semi-state of shock.

I stood there on the sidewalk with my luggage and finally calmed down enough to start walking back to the international terminal. When I reached the airport lobby, I started looking for the Four Seasons sign with my name on it. I eventually spotted it. The driver from the hotel was visibly relieved to see me. When I told him what had just happened, he was very upset since he felt responsible for leaving his sign unattended.

I told him not to worry about it. We went over to fill out some paperwork with the airport police. After meeting with the airport police, who had a lot of questions about what had happened to me, we finally left for the hotel, this time in a real limo.

I was relieved to be safe back at the Four Seasons and shared the story of my airport arrival with my Korean team later that evening at dinner. The rest of that trip was a lot more relaxing and enjoyable thanks to the beauty of a low base.

"Leap and the Net Will Appear"

Twenty years later, I was sitting in a fancy restaurant in New Delhi with Mr. Wadhwa, a well-respected business leader in India. I was now in charge of the international business at H&R Block. We were looking to expand into India, a country of 1.3 billion, where the government was trying to encourage more of its citizens to file their tax returns. Nobody knew more about the Indian tax code than Mr. Wadhwa.

I was creating a Board of Advisors for H&R Block India and was grateful Mr. Wadhwa had agreed to join. It was just the two of us at dinner—I hoped to get to know him better and listen to his thoughts and advice on starting a new business in India.

Mr. Wadhwa was in his late eighties, about the same age as my parents. I started the conversation by complimenting him on his excellent health despite his age.

"Age is just a number," he replied. "You are as young or old as you decide you are. It's all about your attitude about age and life—it's just a mind game."

I had heard about the various successful companies Mr. Wadhwa and his family had created in India over the years. He had also served in the Indian government and established several professional accounting and financial organizations during his long and successful career.

This was not the first time I'd been in India or the first business I had tried to start here. I'd worked hard to get KFC India established in the late '90s. It was a real struggle, but they finally began to prosper after a decade. I'd also worked here with eBay India, which eventually merged with a local e-commerce company called FlipKart to become the leader in that category.

Having worked in over 60 countries at this point of my career, I knew from experience India was one of the most challenging countries in the world to start and grow a business. I was curious to learn if Mr. Wadhwa had some insights on what it took to launch a successful venture in India.

When I asked Mr. Wadhwa that question, he paused and looked away from our table for a moment. Then he looked me in the eye and said, "If I had to tell you the secret of doing anything well, I would simply say believe in yourself and do your best. Whenever I had to do something I had never done before, even when I had no idea what the various challenges would be, my attitude was always simply this: leap and the net will appear."

His "leap" philosophy on taking calculated risks made a lot of sense to me. Over the years, I'd been keeping a journal of some of the situations I'd been in and lessons learned along the way. I thought to myself that evening, "If I ever write a book about what I've learned in life and business and the importance of learning how to push yourself to take a chance on something, this 'leap' concept could be a powerful unifying theme for my stories."

The Journey is the Reward

This is a collection of stories that made a lasting impression on me at critical points in my life. They are not all as dramatic as the one about my first trip to South Korea or as insightful as my dinner with Mr. Wadhwa. The one thing they all have in common is they taught me valuable lessons that helped shape me into who I am today.

An ancient Tao expression is "the journey is the reward." What I've collected in this book are personal stories about leadership and life. I've organized these stories by various virtues for each chapter, such as courage, empathy, and honesty. At the beginning of each chapter, I've included a dictionary definition of the virtue the chapter is about, as well as a relevant quote.

This isn't a novel or an autobiography or a book necessarily intended to be read sequentially. I invite you to look over the list of chapters, find a virtue of interest, then read that chapter. Some of these stories include things that have likely happened to you at some point in your life, such as dealing with a bully, being fired, or helping others who are less fortunate than you. I've also included some stories that probably haven't happened to you, such as being in the financial district in New York City on 9-11, producing a musical for your company's 150th anniversary, meeting with the National Security Council in the White House, or walking over hot coals in your bare feet at a Tony Robbins seminar. Still, every story offers a practical takeaway.

To help you decide which chapter you might want to read next, I've included a "Sneak Peek at My Leap" at the beginning of each chapter, summarizing the stories and lessons learned in that upcoming portion of the book.

At the end of each chapter, I've included some "Reflective Questions" for your consideration that cover some of the issues in the chapter—or, even better, for you to share and discuss with others. I've also added a "Leap into Action" section, which includes potential ways for you to start to apply some of the lessons from these stories to your own life.

I conclude each chapter with "A Moment of Zen." To create this, I asked some of my close friends and colleagues to contribute their thoughts to one question: *What advice would you give your 25-year-old self?* I was blown away by the wisdom they shared and hope you find it as powerful as I did.

CHAPTER ICONS

SNEAK PEEK AT MY LEAP

REFLECTIVE QUESTIONS

LEAP INTO ACTION

A MOMENT OF ZEN

One other note about my stories: While I've tried to be as accurate as possible, there is one exception. A few of the names have been changed. I've been fortunate to have had some fantastic and supportive bosses. There have been a couple of bosses who, unfortunately, I would not include in that category. When they are in a story, I'll introduce them by simply stating, "Let's call him (or her)..." and use a made-up name for the thankfully few bosses I would prefer not ever to have to work for again.

It's never my intention to embarrass anyone deliberately, but the lessons I learned from my handful of weak bosses are worth sharing. Ironically, I learned an incredible amount from my weak bosses in terms of practical ways to motivate employees and lead a team. This has meant doing the exact opposite of what they did when I worked for them.

Push Yourself and Enjoy the Ride

Each person's life is a unique, separate, and remarkable journey. We all have opportunities and situations throughout our lives that vary dramatically in risk and nature. Some are easy decisions; others pose difficult choices. Some challenges you can plan for; others you will have to trust your gut at the moment of truth on the right thing to do—like when you are in the back of a van in Seoul with a crazy driver demanding money.

What I've learned from the stories I'm sharing is that when these opportunities inevitably come along, it is usually better to say "yes" than "no." I'm not advocating for taking foolish chances. After all, the expression "look before you leap" started way back in the 14th century in English literature. I've always tried to weigh the pros and cons of any big decision I had to make before acting. Yet the inevitable conclusion I've come to—along with folks much wiser than me—is that when your life is all said and done, you are more likely to regret the things you didn't do much more than the things you did.

Take a chance. Make a stand. Share a vision of a better future. Lead from the front and trust that others will follow. Or if you must, go it alone—at least for a while. This is best summarized from the Latin expression from over two millennia ago: You must be willing to take a "Saltus Fidei" (leap of faith).

In the future, when you look back at your life, it's those fleeting opportunities you will inevitably come across that can make your journey uniquely rewarding—perhaps not always financially, but absolutely from an experience point of view. It's your level of willingness to "give it a go" that can turn a risk into an opportunity that makes your own journey much more satisfying than if you never took a chance.

When Neil Armstrong landed his lunar module in 1969 and was the first person to walk on the moon, his immortal words were, "That's one small step for man, one giant leap for mankind." My goal with this book is to give you the confidence and courage to make your own giant leap to do whatever it is that you have always dreamed of doing with your life. Now is the time and place to take that first small step on your journey that can lead to giant leaps later.

With that as my starting point, here are the stories about some of the fantastic people I've been lucky enough to work with throughout my life and career. This is how they helped me learn to leap and turn risk into opportunity.

01

Courage—
I'm Still Standing

Courage: Standing up for what is right,
even in the face of overwhelming odds

> *"It is not the size of the dog in the fight.*
> *It's the size of the fight in the dog." —Mark Twain*

SNEAK PEEK AT MY LEAP
How I Found the Courage to Stand Up to Bullies
(Both Big and Small)

There's a lot of discussions these days about the problem of bullying in school. It's a conversation worth having, and we should do everything we can to stop it. Kids can be incredibly cruel, and parents need to make sure their kids are protected from bullies. If you've been a victim of bullying, it's something you never forget. But sometimes bullies can teach you valuable things about yourself and life.

When I moved from Bogalusa, Louisiana, a tiny paper mill town—to Baton Rouge, a much larger city, I didn't fit in with the other kids. If you'd like to know what I looked like, imagine Buddy Holly at age 12. Only skinnier—a lot skinnier. With braces. Big metal braces. And eyeglasses. Big plastic-rimmed eyeglasses. You get the idea.

My first day of junior high school was a shock to me: there was a whole ecosystem of kids I was never exposed to in my life when I was in a small-town elementary school. The jocks. The cool kids. The outcasts. And long-haired dudes you didn't mess with if you had any sense.

Every day I'd ride my bike to school, and without fail, the long-haired dudes would be there waiting for me—my very own welcoming party. They would call me names. Spit on me. Spit on my bike. Push me around. I tried to ignore them, but it was getting harder by the day to get away from them. They seemed to get pure joy out of making my life miserable.

One day a group of them announced they were going to beat me up. Right then and there. I figured the only chance of getting out of this would be to appeal to their sense of honor, assuming they had any.

Looking around at them—or rather, *up* at them, since they were each a good foot taller than me—I declared, "What's the fun in beating me up, guys? You outnumber me five to one. Where's the sport in that?"

The greasiest of the lot, Brian Landry, sneered at me. "Got a better idea, stupid?"

I responded, "Sure, how about a supervised boxing match tomorrow."

Skinniest Boxer in the World

A bit of background would be helpful here. I had heard from some of the gym coaches that if a kid disagreed with another kid, they could have a boxing match supervised by the coaches. While that might be hard to imagine today, keep in mind this was in the Deep South in the late 1960s.

Brian's gang thought this sounded like a grand idea and urged him to be the honored one to pound me to a pulp. "Okay, Knight, you'll fight me. And I'll beat the living hell out of you."

This news made me feel good and not so good at the same time. Good in the sense I had just avoided being beaten up by five guys way bigger than me. Not so good since I had no idea how to box. The time between today and tomorrow was probably not enough time to learn. As if having a more extended time would make much of a difference.

I went home that night and didn't say anything to my parents. What could I say? If I told them about the pending fight, they would no doubt have called the school and not allowed it to happen. Which meant I would have to face these badasses outside the ring without any adult supervision at some point shortly after that. I figured it was time to face the music and at least try to box this bully.

The next day I went to my gym coach and told him that I wanted to set up a boxing match for after school.

He replied, "Okay, with whom?"

I told him, and he winced. "Brian? He's sleazy as they come and a lot bigger than you. Are you sure you want to fight him?"

I told him yes. The coach agreed to tell Brian, and he instructed me that we should both show up after school later that day in the gym.

Three coaches were waiting for us at the boxing match after the last class was over—one coach for me, one for Brian, and one as a general referee.

My coach looked me over in the corner of the mat where I stood in the most pathetic pair of boxer shorts you have ever seen. "OK, Knight, how many times have you been in a boxing match?"

"Well, coach, counting today: one," I replied.

He had a pained look on his face. "That's what I was afraid of. Let me give you three quick pointers. First, keep your gloves up near your face to protect yourself, like this." He put his fists up near his face and looked at me.

I held up my gloves, mimicking him. "Like this?"

My coach responded, "That's the idea. Next, always keep moving around the mat. Don't stand still, or you're a sitting duck."

"Okay, keep moving. Got it. What else?" I inquired with a growing sense that maybe this might not be a total suicide mission after all.

The coach leaned in and looked me in the eye. "Remember, this guy is nothing but a punk and a bully. Bullies thrive on fear. He will know if you're scared. You need to act fearlessly."

While I thought this was an outstanding suggestion, there was the practical matter that I was about to fight a slimy guy a good 50 pounds heavier, and a 12-inch longer reach compared to me. At least I had some adult supervision in case it got out of hand.

"OK, coach, I'm ready. Let's get this over with," I said with a shaky voice.

Brian and I walked to the middle of the mat, and the coaches went over the ground rules. The coach had me put in a mouthguard and took off my glasses. Then they asked us to touch gloves and wish each other luck.

Brian leaned over and whispered in my ear, "I'm going to kick your ass, you skinny loser." Oh, well, Brian, so much for the "Sportsman of the Year" award going to you.

I held up my gloves and started moving around as fast as my skinny legs could move. Brian came after me with a look of pure hate in his eyes. I let my guard down and tried to take a swing at him. He ducked, and I missed.

Brian didn't let that opportunity pass him by. He clocked me with a right hook that had me flying backward and landing hard on my back toward the edge of the mat.

I had the breath knocked out of me as I laid there absolutely stunned. Man, that hurt like hell! As if it couldn't get any worse, then I felt something wet and dripping all over my face. I reached up with my gloves. There was blood. A lot of blood. Despite the mouth guard, my lip was split open and bleeding like a water faucet.

I can't explain what happened next since something snapped inside of me. At that point, I didn't care how much I was hurt. The only primal feeling I had was that this Brian dude was going to pay for picking on me for all these months and now busting open my lip. I don't know what a shot of adrenaline feels like, but if the coach had come over and stuck a giant syringe in me at that time, that would be close to how I felt at that moment. It was as if someone else took over my body.

Brian was standing over me, laughing and telling me what a wimp I was. I honestly don't think he expected me to get off the mat. I know he didn't expect to see a skinny and crazed 12-year-old gushing blood to crawl over and start pounding his legs. He was shocked when he fell, and I then got on top of him, continuing to pound away at his acne-scarred face. He had a look of shock and gratitude when the coaches finally pulled ME off HIM.

After the boxing match story started to spread around the school in the weeks that followed, Brian and the long-haired greasers left me alone for the rest of junior high school. I guess they figured that I was more trouble than I was worth and would have an easier time picking on someone else.

I've never put on a pair of boxing gloves since or gotten back in the ring to box with anyone, even for fun. It's something I never wanted to do in the first place, but I felt I had no choice.

But I have never forgotten what I learned in junior high school that day: if you let a bully pick on you, you're done. From that day forward, I vowed bullies were never going to have the pleasure of me being afraid of them or succumbing to their scare tactics.

Stepping into the ring with Brian gave me a sense of purpose I carried with me from then on. Though I didn't realize it then, a mental switch had been flipped. I now knew how to mentally stand my ground in the face of intimidation.

This sense of purpose served me exceptionally well decades later when working as a brand manager at Procter & Gamble.

"So, When Are You Leaving?"

I was managing the Ivory soap brand when I was assigned a new boss. While most folks at the company were easygoing and played nice with each other, no one would ever think that of (let's call him Reeve), who was an associate advertising manager.

Reeve was a former college football lineman with all the charm and wit of Darth Vader. It always seemed that this guy was angry about something and quite willing to shred you to pieces if he felt like it, which was most of the time.

Reeve was very negative in how he worked with and motivated you. I had two experiences early on I should have seen as serious "warning signals" he would be a real pain in the butt to work for.

The first was during our first copy meeting with the advertising agency.

Typically, the agency representatives would come in and share their latest ideas on the next advertising campaign. This primarily involved presenting "storyboards" laid out in visual and text form to show what the commercial would look like.

The tradition in the P&G marketing department was that the most junior person in the room, typically the brand assistant, would comment on the storyboards. You'd work your way up the management chain until the associate advertising manager would proclaim judgment on the work, and this is typically the primary person the agency would pay any attention to.

We had finished the advertising portion of the meeting. As we were wrapping up, the agency indicated they had one more idea they wanted to share.

The advertising executive at our agency reached under the meeting room table and pulled out a small box. He opened the box and passed it to me. Inside were two bars of Ivory that looked like earrings.

"We were thinking that instead of running another price off promotion, you should have some type of premium in which you could get these limited edition Ivory earrings."

I smiled, thinking this would be a terrific way to get some excitement in the boring soap category. "I love it!" I declared as I passed the box over to Reeve.

Reeve was not smiling. He was turning several shades of red. He glared at me and barked, "Out in the hallway, Knight!"

I couldn't imagine what had set Reeve off like that. We walked outside the conference room into the hall.

I thought Reeve was going to punch me physically. "What the HELL are you doing in there?" he yelled.

"What are you talking about? I was just giving my feedback on what I think is a clever idea. Young women are our key target. I think they'd like this idea."

Reeve got even more agitated and continued, "That was a sacrilege in there. I've got half a mind to go in there and fire all of them. They do not understand Ivory—we would never do anything like that to disparage the brand!"

I was genuinely confused at Reeve's reaction and responded, "Reeve, I disagree. Since neither one of us is a woman, why don't we at least expose this idea to some female consumers and see what they think?"

Although I didn't think Reeve could get any redder, he did.

"Wait here and do NOT move!" he screamed as he went down the hall to parts unknown.

He returned a few minutes later with Vandy, the advertising manager, who oversaw all the brands in our division. Reeve glared at me, "I've told Vandy what you've done, and you are to go back in the room immediately and tell the agency that's the stupidest idea you've ever heard of."

I looked at Vandy and could tell he didn't want to be a part of this conversation. I looked at Reeve and stated, "I'll tell them we're not interested in the idea, but I'm not going to comment on what I think of it since I like it."

"Then I'll tell them!" he spit out the words as he went back in the room to yell at the agency. Geez, I thought to myself, just who the hell was this guy? He had some serious anger management issues.

After that awkward meeting with the ad agency, things got worse between Reeve and me over the next four months. My second big run-in with Reeve started when the product development team told both Reeve and me about a secret project; they had been working on a synthetic version of Ivory that would solve many of the problems the product had in "hard water."

As the brand manager of Ivory soap, I had a significant problem with a synthetic soap product since I thought it would confuse consumers on what the brand stood for, such as "99 44/100% pure" and "so natural, it floats." But wouldn't you know it—Reeve loved it.

The approval process for testing a new product starts with the brand team writing a test market recommendation. When the product development team asked me to do this for the "new" Ivory, I declined the request. Reeve insisted I write it up, and when I refused, he wrote the recommendation himself and forwarded it to our management for approval.

The art of writing a persuasive memo was something every brand manager aspired to master. Usually, an associate advertising manager would write a cover note to a Brand Manager's recommendation, then send up the chain of command for approval or rejection. Still, it was even more challenging to write a powerful cover note since you typically had a lot fewer words to do it with.

A test market recommendation would be no more than three pages plus exhibits, a cover note from an associate that would be one page, and the remaining cover notes from the advertising manager, division manager, vice president, senior vice, and president. These would all be on smaller and smaller pieces of paper.

By the time it got to the CEO, the cover note was pretty much down to one sentence, such as "This is a solid plan—we should proceed." And almost every time, by the time it got to that level, it was approved when the CEO signed "I approve" and sent it back down the line.

So, in a most unusual move, I separately sent a cover note to go along with Reeve's recommendation. I declared we should not test the new synthetic Ivory product since it was out of line with what the brand stood for, which was all about natural ingredients and purity. Both our notes went up the chain of command and came back down. Remember, this was before the Internet or email existed.

Everyone was surprised when the CEO agreed with me—he wrote a note that said "this was a dumb idea" on Reeve's recommendation, and we would not be proceeding.

Not surprisingly, my relationship with Reeve after that went straight downhill fast. I knew I was in for a hard time with him but was surprised one day shortly after that when he came into my office, slammed my office door, and sat down across my desk.

"Well, hello there, Reeve," I offered.

Reeve was already red in the face as he sat in the chair across from my desk. I sat back in my chair and did not say anything. For a moment, my emotions took me back to junior high school and the boxing match. Only this time, we were in my office, not a school gym, and I got the strange sensation that there was a severe beating about to take place. I figured I'd let Reeve take the first swing.

He glared at me as he declared, "I've been thinking a lot about you lately and decided this company is just not big enough for you and me."

This was not a total shock given the state of our relationship, but it was still a bit of a surprise to me when he said it aloud. I was quiet for a moment as I looked him in the eye, then slowly leaned forward and stated, "Reeve, I'm sorry to hear that. When are you leaving?"

Reeve jumped out of his chair and screamed. "That's the kind of disrespectful attitude I'm talking about. I'm tired of it. I'm tired of you. I'm going to enjoy firing you."

It was my turn to respond.

"Listen up, Reeve, feel free to try to fire me. I think I'm doing a pretty good job as Ivory Brand Manager. If anyone ought to be fired, it's you. You are far and away the worst manager I've ever had. You're mean. You're spiteful. And the only thing I've learned from you so far is what I will NOT do in the future when I'm managing people. But know this: I'm not leaving here without a fight."

Reeve smiled as he got up to leave, "This is going to be fun. You're toast, Knight." And with that, he got up and left my office.

My heart was racing. What had I done? What should I do now? I decided to get Reeve's other three brand managers together for a quick huddle, so I called them each on the phone to come to my office right away.

After I'd explained to them what had just happened, I turned to each one of them and said, "I am going to be fired unless I can convince our management this guy is poisonous. The way I see this, we either band together and go after this guy, or you can watch me get fired. But based on what I've seen, he's going to fire all of us. One at a time."

There was silence in the room for about a minute. Finally, Fran, one of my fellow brand managers, looked at the other two brand managers and me and said, "You know, you're right. This guy is the worst boss I've ever had. I say we tell his supervisors just what a bully this guy is."

My pulse started to calm down a bit. Thank God the other brand managers agreed with Fran.

It's a tribute to P&G when lower-level managers can go to senior management and challenge a group supervisor, such as Reeve. It took about three months and many meetings, but Reeve eventually agreed to leave the company. I have no idea what happened to him after he left P&G—maybe he mellowed out, maybe not. Let's just say he's not on my Christmas card mailing list, and I'm not on his.

I paid a high personal price for all this. My "political capital" in my division was pretty much exhausted by the end of the process that led to Reeve's departure. I was told I would give up the Ivory brand and now work in the Food and Beverage Division. I would be the first marketer to work on a secret new product that was a zero-calorie fat replacement called Olestra. This would have never happened if I'd had a different boss.

It's funny how things turn out sometimes. Getting to work on a new brand like Olestra was excellent training for what I ended up doing later in my career, plus I learned several new valuable skills in the process of working on a new brand. I *will* credit Reeve for teaching me a lot about managing people—by learning to do the exact *opposite* of what he did.

Courage is one of those virtues I prefer to use only when necessary. If you are a policeman or fireman, you'll need plenty of it regularly. For the rest of us, when the occasion arises, my sincere wish is that we all have the strength of mind and spirit to face these future threats with unmoving resolve and confidence.

> **CHAPTER ONE**
> **Courage—I'm Still Standing**

REFLECTIVE QUESTIONS

- Have you ever been a victim of bullying? How did you handle it?
- What advice would you give to someone who's in a situation where they are being bullied?
- What should parents do when it comes to protecting their children from bullies?

- What steps should companies take to ensure their employees aren't subject to bullying bosses or colleagues?

- When was the last time you made a stand for a cause or an individual being bullied?

LEAP INTO ACTION

Remember, bullies thrive off perceived weakness. When confronted by a bully, you must calmly stand your ground. Explain what about his or her behavior is unacceptable, and start documenting your interactions. Often, pushing back will be enough to make the bully think twice. But if not, don't be afraid to take your documented case to a supervisor or human resources. And ultimately, don't be afraid to walk away from a situation where you're being tormented by a bully.

A MOMENT OF ZEN

Be fearless and leverage your "beginner's mindset" whenever you start something new.

While you don't have as much experience, you have a fresh perspective—and that's valuable. You are learning and growing—and always will be, by the way—thus embracing "mistakes" and stumbles is helpful. Your mistakes and stumbles will make you stronger—and others can learn from them too.

Leverage your lack of experience. It is a great time to be fearless, push the envelope in business and personal life. Learn and experience new things. Don't let anyone hold you back because "you are not experienced enough."

There is no single correct answer to whatever problem is in front of you. Release the need for perfection and certainty!

02

Gratitude—
Lucky Breaks

*Gratitude: A readiness to show appreciation
and exhibit kindness*

> *"When eating fruit, remember who planted the tree."*
> *—Vietnamese Proverb*

SNEAK PEEK AT MY LEAP
**How I learned about gratitude from a fantastic
teacher (and felt immense gratitude for
several narrow escapes).**

Looking back on some of my teachers who've had a major impact in my life's direction, several come to mind. My marketing professor, Dr. Alvin Burns, who got me excited about marketing and marketing research. My fourth grade teacher, Ms. Carroll, who started my lifelong interest in foreign cultures. And a Catholic priest, Brother Carl Bouchereas, who helped me on my first trip abroad.

My grandfather, who we affectionately called PaPaw, had no interest whatsoever in travel. He was perfectly content running his grocery store and butcher shop—so long as he could go fishing on the weekend. According to my father, my PaPaw only took his family on one vacation.

"That's a Big Hole—Now Let's Go Home."

My dad and his two brothers had read about and dreamed of visiting the Grand Canyon. Such a sight was hard to imagine if you'd spent your whole life in the pine forests and swamps of Louisiana. After years of much discussion at the family dinner table, they finally convinced PaPaw to shut down his store for the first time and take a well-deserved vacation to see the fabled geographic wonder.

Keep in mind this was long before the U.S. Interstate highway system was built. They would have to drive over 1,500 miles of pre-World War II highways from Bogalusa, Louisiana, to the Grand Canyon in Arizona. And that's what my PaPaw did.

He closed the store on a Thursday afternoon and proceeded to drive the family car with my grandmother and his three sons for the next 30 hours—switching off periodically with my grandmother so he could get a few hours of sleep.

As dawn broke over the Grand Canyon on a Saturday morning, PaPaw pulled his car up to the South Rim. My dad and his two brothers piled out of the car to see the breathtaking sight of the sun rising over the canyon rim. PaPaw walked up to where they all stood, looked over the edge, and declared, "Yep, it's a big hole. Now let's go home." He instructed everyone to get back in the car, and they arrived back at the store on Sunday evening so he could open up that Monday.

An Urge to See the World

Unlike my PaPaw, by the time I started my senior year in high school, the urge to travel internationally had grown to the point of wanting to do something about it. Our family had gone on several camping trips across the U.S.—the most memorable one being a three-week adventure where we traveled from Louisiana to California and back.

My dream was to go to Europe because, as a lover of history, this would be a perfect way to see a lot of what I'd only read about in novels and non-fiction books. My cousin recommended a Catholic-sponsored tour of Europe that happened every summer. I wrote them for more information and was introduced to a fantastic individual leading the tour, Brother Carl Bouchereas, a teacher at Brother Martin High School in New Orleans.

The tour would be 26 days and was quite ambitious in scope. We would spend six days in Paris, four in Salzburg, three in Venice, five in Rome, and an ocean cruise to Athens, where we would spend four days. Best of all, we would get to spend four days in England with a final stop in London. I instinctively knew England would be my favorite country because my ancestors had left there in the late 1600s to settle in Jamestown, Virginia. I felt a solid connection to all things British. The timing seemed perfect—I would turn 18 while I was on this tour, and we could celebrate this auspicious occasion while we were in London.

The only catch for me was be how to pay for this. The cost was $1,290, equivalent to about $7,175 today. And I had all of $500 in savings when I learned about this whirlwind trip.

I asked my mom and dad if I could go, and they were in full support. Paying for it would be a challenge, however. We didn't have a lot of spare cash at the time, so if I wanted to go, it would be totally up to me to raise the remaining amount of around $800. Fortunately, I had started a lawn mowing business the previous year when I was a high school junior, which seemed to be the best way to earn the money I needed to finance the trip.

I charged $10 to mow a lawn and another $5 to do the edging. At $15 per customer, I would need to mow 53 lawns over the next five months to reach my goal, or about three yards per week. It's amazing what you can do if you are properly motivated. I raised the money along with some extra to cover any additional expenses. Fortunately, lawns needed to be mowed in Louisiana all year, so Mother Nature was on my side in this endeavor.

When it was time to leave for Europe, I was ready. I'd read as much as I could on all the places we would visit to appreciate the importance of what I would experience once I got there.

Paris was a fantastic place to start our tour of Europe. Brother Carl knew all the best places to go since he'd done this tour many times before. He took us to world-class museums such as the Louvre, the Rodin Museum—home of *The Thinker* statue—and Musee d'Orsay.

As you'd expect, all our meals were spectacular, especially those in the local, non-tourist restaurants, which reminded me of some of the French meals I'd enjoyed in New Orleans in the French Quarter.

After four days taking in the sights of Paris, we were off by train to Austria. The most impressive aspect of Salzburg was the mountains. Having grown up in a place where everything was at the same elevation, the soaring peaks of the Alps were gorgeous. And we especially appreciated the cool mountain air, a big contrast to the muggy heat we endured at home every summer.

Given our tight budget, the tour organizers arranged to stay primarily in inexpensive accommodations, such as with local families and in college dormitories. This turned out to be a much better way to get to know the local culture than staying in an expensive hotel. Keep in mind this was half a century before Airbnb came along.

We leveraged the fact we were traveling under the auspices of the Archdiocese of New Orleans, and our tour leaders were Catholic priests, including Brother Carl. For example, in Italy, we spent several days at a monastery. It was an excellent opportunity to stay where most tourists would never have been permitted.

In Austria, they broke us into small groups to spend the night with local families. As I got ready to go to bed on my first night, I looked upon my bedroom wall to study their family portrait. The whole family was decked out in traditional Austrian attire, except for the father. He was a military officer in WWII since he was wearing a Nazi uniform and an impressive array of medals. I thought it best not to ask too many questions about my host family during my stay, who were quite gracious and friendly.

I'd never been on an ocean cruise before, so I thoroughly enjoyed our trip from southern Italy to Athens. We didn't make it to the island of Delos, the setting for several stories in Greek mythology and the source of my first name which is—believe it or not—Delos Lavern Knight, III. I managed to glimpse the island on the horizon as we made our way through the Myrtoan Sea from Italy to Greece. Perhaps I'll be able to return there one day for a future birthday celebration.

Athens was as unique as I'd dreamed it would be, especially since I love ancient history and have read several books based on the Stoics' philosophy of stoicism. I could have easily spent several months in Greece soaking in all the culture, food, and history, but we only had four days. As sad as I was to leave, I looked forward to the tour's highlight when we visited London, England.

Welcome to England

The center of everything in the U.K. is London, and I expected it to live up to its reputation. As Samuel Johnson once said, "When one is tired of London, one is tired of life."

We flew out of Athens and landed at Heathrow Airport, where we would be returning in just four days to return to the U.S. We spent our first night in England, staying in Oxford at the campus where we stayed in the dorms. We walked around where students and teachers had been attending lectures since 1096, making this institution the oldest English-speaking university in the world. We were going to be visiting London for the final part of our tour since we were flying out of Heathrow airport in greater London.

As we were wrapping up our European tour on 7/17/1974, Brother Carl planned a special day for us. We would start by leaving Oxford early in the morning to visit Hampton Court, then contine on a bus tour of Central London, starting with a visit to the Tower of London. He wanted us to enjoy a British favorite for a late lunch—fish and chips, naturally. That evening, we were all going to go to a medieval-style restaurant to celebrate my birthday, which had officially occurred several days before. This celebration would include mead, an alcoholic beverage developed during the Middle Ages since I was now legally allowed to drink.

I'd done my homework on the Tower of London before leaving the U.S. The Tower was built originally as a palace and fortress on the banks of the Thames River in the 11th Century. It has been the setting for several key events in English history. First as the sovereign's residence, and then as a prison for the targets of the king's—or in some cases queen's—wrath.

In the present day, the Tower of London, a collection of 11 separate towers, is a major tourist attraction that features the Crown Jewels. It has a fantastic collection of armor, canons, swords, and other battle weapons. For all I know, some of my ancestors might have worn the suits of armor and swords on display to guard the palace.

Our first stop after leaving Oxford was Hampton Court. Hampton Court Palace was originally the home of Cardinal Wolsey in the early 16th century. But back then, having a fabulous house was a significant risk because the king, who was also head of the Anglican Church, could take it over along with any church property he wanted. That's what King Henry VIII did, bringing along all six of his wives over the years. For many of these wives, it would be their final resting place. The palace is surrounded by incredible gardens, including the Maze and the Great Vine. Queen Victoria opened the palace and grounds to the public in 1838, and it's been a favorite of visitors from the U.K. and abroad ever since.

Although it's only a 20-mile bus ride between Hampton Court and the Tower of London, in heavy London traffic, it's anybody's guess how long it will take you to get there. We wanted to make sure we had plenty of time for the short trip, so we had a snack at Hampton Court at noon. We got on our bus at 12:30 p.m., and our tour was scheduled for 2:15 p.m. This gave us over 90 minutes to get there in time for our tour. After the Tower of London, we looked forward to a traditional British lunch of fish and chips wrapped in newspaper and drenched in vinegar.

London traffic that day was terrible, and at 2:15 p.m., we were still stuck in traffic about a mile from our destination. Brother Carl was agitated as we rode on the bus because he knew we would probably miss our chance to visit the Tower that day since you had to show up at your appointed group tour time to be admitted.

At 2:30 p.m., we finally pulled up to the bus parking area, which was about a two-minute walk from the Tower of London. At the same time we arrived, a massive bomb in the Mortar Room of the White Tower exploded. The building structure wasn't significantly damaged, but given the room's layout—30 feet wide and 70 feet long—flying debris went everywhere. Cannons and mortars, cannonballs, spears, and armor instantly became lethal weapons.

The explosion in the crowded space hurled an ancient cannon five feet in the air and drove debris and a rack full of spears through the packed chamber. About 50 people, mostly Germans, and Scandinavians, were in the armory room when the bomb went off. Two of the victims suffered severed legs, and rescuers found a child's foot beneath the displaced cannon. One of the victims died later that night in a local hospital.

The IRA had been placing similar bombs in London since March of 1973, the year before. But in these instances, warnings had been given—in the Tower of London bombing, there was no warning at all. If there had been, Brother Carl would have canceled that part of our tour.

This had been the first bombing at the Tower of London since 1881 when Irish Nationals exploded a bomb there, but there were no injuries or damage. Some of the Tower buildings had been damaged in air raids during World War II, but that day's bombing was the bloodiest at the Tower of London in over 300 years.

We got the news that all this was happening over the British Broadcasting Corporation (BBC) news announcements as we sat in our bus at the Tower of London parking lot. Everyone on the bus was severely shaken since we had been scheduled to be on the tour about the same time as the explosion. This is one instance in which I was happy to have been stuck in traffic.

Brother Carl decided the best thing to do would be to head over to the restaurant immediately. There were 37 of us, including students and tour guides, led by Brother Carl. We were seated at long tables inside a vast hall. Having never eaten British fish and chips before, I became an instant fan. I devoured all my fish and chips and some of Brother Carl's since he didn't want to eat all his portion.

We were going to be staying in our only hotel for the tour that evening in Central London. Brother Carl called the hotel to see if we could check in early since some of our group indicated they weren't feeling very well after lunch. By the time we got to the hotel, most of our tour group were in serious gastronomical trouble, including Brother Carl.

While we will never know for sure, Brother Carl suspected our group got food poisoning due to the fish and chips we had at lunch. We were supposed to have about 20 of us go "out on the town" to celebrate my birthday that evening, but only three of the women from our tour and I felt well enough to venture out. The four of us agreed to meet in the hotel lobby at 7:00 p.m., catch a London cab, and head out to the medieval restaurant for what I hoped would be a (k)night to remember.

A Memorable Birthday Celebration

As we all stepped out of the hotel lobby onto the busy London sidewalk that summer evening, there wasn't anyone from the hotel to hail us a cab, since we were staying at a modest hotel that didn't have a doorman. Since I didn't want us to be late, I decided to take it upon myself to get us a cab. I looked to my left to check for oncoming traffic and, seeing none, stepped out onto the street to get one of those famous London cabs to stop and pick us up.

The one key factor I had neglected to keep in mind as I was doing this was Brits drive on the opposite side of the road compared to Americans. I had just stepped into heavy traffic, which would be coming *from my right.*

If it had been a double-decker bus, I wouldn't be writing this story today. Nearly one in three traffic deaths in Britain involves a pedestrian being run over by a car or bus—a disproportionate number of them tourists. For comparison, the number is about one out of seven in the U.S.

Another lucky break (no pun intended) was I didn't see the Rolls Royce that hit me. I've been told if I would have seen the oncoming car, I would have tensed up, and that's when you can break a lot of bones. I don't remember being hit, but according to my three tour companions, the car first knocked me onto the hood, rolled me over the roof where I landed on the trunk, then fell off the car trunk into the middle of the busy pre-evening London traffic. All this took about five seconds. It was still light outside at this time of the summer, so at least the other cars could see my body lying in the street.

This happened so fast all I remember is laying on the road with a crowd quickly gathering around me. I heard some yelling, *"Hey, I think that Yank is dead!"* I slowly started to get up when a well-dressed woman quickly emerged from the back of the Rolls Royce and ran up to me.

"Good lord, son, are you alright!" she exclaimed.

I was still trying to figure out exactly what had happened. "Yes, I think so," I muttered.

"My chauffeur tried to stop, but you stepped right in front of our car. Are you sure you aren't hurt?"

I slowly got up off the ground and stood up. Everything seemed to be in working order.

"Yes, ma'am, I think I'm fine."

She reached into her purse and gave me a card with her name and number on it. She asked me where I was staying, and I told her. She wrote it down and told me she wanted to have her doctor look me over. I promised I would let her know if I had any problems and walked back over to where my friends were looking at me in shock.

"Well, what are you guys waiting for? Let's get to that restaurant!" I declared.

We got back later that evening to the hotel, and by this point, I must admit I was starting to ache a bit. Looking back on this incident years later, I was foolish not to immediately go to the nearest hospital and make sure I didn't have a concussion.

But to my amazement, the woman who gave me her card sent her personal physician over to my hotel later that evening after I had returned to go to sleep. He gave me a thorough exam to ensure I was alright and ended his inspection by declaring I was lucky not to be permanently injured.

Gratitude for Amazing Teachers

My high school trip to Europe made me appreciate all of the hard work educators such as Brother Carl put into planning and guiding tours, such as the one we went on. I've still got the numerous handwritten letters he sent me while getting ready to leave on this trip. He was everything you'd ever want in a tour guide—well informed, locally savvy, and kept a cool head even when disaster struck. He would be a role model for me in my future international travels.

Teachers such as Brother Carl deserve a lot more gratitude from all of us. By telling his story, I hope you can think about a teacher in your own life and let them know how much you appreciate how they help make this world a better place for all of us.

This trip also taught me to be grateful for having a lucky break—in this case, two lucky breaks in one day. If our bus had been on time at the Tower of London, we might have been the ones in the armory cellar in the White Tower when the bomb went off. And if a larger vehicle such as a bus had been whizzing by our hotel when I was trying to hail a cab, I shudder to think about what might have happened to me.

I don't want to assume I'll always be lucky when I need to be, but I'm very grateful that on 7/17/1974, luck was on my side twice in one day.

CHAPTER TWO
Gratitude—Lucky Breaks

REFLECTIVE QUESTIONS

- If you could live anywhere in the world, where would that be and why?

- What's your favorite place you've ever been on vacation? Why is it your favorite?

- What's the most bizarre thing you've ever eaten?

- How comfortable are you going to different countries? Eating different foods?

- Are you open to experiences outside your comfort zone? Why or why not?

- Who have been some of the most influential teachers in your life? What were the most important things you remember about them? Did you, or can you, take the time to tell them what their help meant to you?

LEAP INTO ACTION

Too many folks wait until they are retired before going out to see the world. When you are young, take advantage of getting out into cultures and places that are a radical change compared to what you are used to experiencing.

Suppose you don't have the time or money to travel far. In that case, you can often get a lot of the same experience if you go to different parts of a large metro area where various groups of folks from other parts of the world have brought their culture and traditions to your backyard. You'll come away from these local adventures with a sense of gratitude that comes from expanding your worldview and appreciating the incredible diversity we all live in.

A MOMENT OF ZEN

Appreciate the need for giving back to people who help you along the way (as well as those who need your help).

I wish I knew then how special it was to support all those people who helped me over the years. Not all of them believed that what we were doing was wise or even right, but they believed in me. What I missed doing or knowing how to do was thanking them at the time and showing my appreciation for their confidence and support.

Leadership is in service of getting the best out of others, not always taking the hill from the front. Understand the energy and serenity that comes with giving back. I now spend most of my time involved with efforts that help others achieve their destiny. I've learned that it's not just the right thing to do, but that it brings me more satisfaction and joy than I could have imagined. I wish I started giving back to the world sooner.

03

Assertiveness— Boldly Going for It

Assertiveness: Achieving results by setting ambitious goals, asking for help when needed, and being confident and positive about your capabilities

> *"If you don't have a seat at the table, you're probably on the menu."* —Elizabeth Warren

---

SNEAK PEEK AT MY LEAP
How I rebounded from a disastrous start in college and discovered my professional career path.

Sometimes things don't go exactly as planned. It's what you decide to do after that which matters. Sometimes it takes a "door closing" to open up the next opportunity that can often make up for any short-term pain you went through.

My lineage at Louisiana State University (LSU) in Baton Rouge runs deep. My father and his two brothers all went there—so, it was assumed, I would, too.

The Naked Truth

In my senior year of high school, I got my first glimpse of life at LSU, and let me tell you, it was an eyeful. It was spring of 1974, and streaking—or running around naked—was a national fad reaching its peak. Rumor had it all the LSU fraternities and sororities would have the world's largest "streak parade" on campus. That sounded to me like something not to be missed.

At the dinner table the night of the rumored event, I asked my dad if I could borrow the car to see "history in the making." He told me it was okay with him and my mom under one condition: I could *not* be a part of making this history.

I've been to a lot of parades in my life, but that night is sure to be the cheekiest (pun intended) spectacle I've ever witnessed. Just as dusk rolled in, hundreds upon hundreds of students lined up. Think Macy's Thanksgiving Day Parade formation, with marching bands and all. But not one stitch of clothing.

The wildest Brazilian Carnival celebrations would have paled in comparison to what I witnessed that night. The most amazing part to me is that this happened in a very conservative town during a very traditional time.

The streaking craze crumbled about a week later, and suddenly, what was "cool" became grounds for arrest for indecent exposure. I left that parade thinking if just watching fraternity life from the sidelines was that much fun, I should join in. So, I decided to pledge to a fraternity at the start of my freshman year at LSU.

Blackballed for Life

For those who don't know, pledging usually consists of freshmen visiting all the fraternity houses. It's time for the fraternities to size up the incoming freshman class. It's a test to see who is cool enough to be a fellow fraternity brother.

Sadly, I was woefully unaware this would be a popularity contest. I showed up, ready to tour all the fraternity houses, with a clipboard in hand. Along the way, I took detailed notes on my clipboard. Unknown to me at the time, this was not cool.

Now I know what you must be picturing right now: Buddy Holly going around like he's doing a Consumer Reports cover story on *"Fraternities: Which One Is Best for You?—We've Got the Facts!"* Well, you would not be far off.

As I arrived at the last fraternity house, I was incredibly excited. This was the Sigma Chi house. My uncle Richard had been president of this fraternity. I was sure this would give me a golden ticket.

What's more, my uncle Richard was a prominent lawyer in Louisiana. I had entered LSU with dreams of my law career. And joining the fraternity that my uncle Richard once led was going to be the first step to my brilliant legal career path, which I hoped might eventually lead to me joining his law firm.

I stood in the Sigma Chi house, scribbling away happily on my clipboard. Suddenly, someone grabbed my arm and drug me to another room. My friend from high school, Jay, a few years older, was now part of the Sigma Chi fraternity and later was elected lieutenant governor of Louisiana.

"What do you think you are doing?!" Jay exclaimed.

"What do you mean?" I asked, genuinely confused by his question.

"What are you doing with that damn clipboard? Are you out of your mind? You're the laughingstock of the whole fraternity!" Jay stammered.

I was shocked. I had no idea my future brothers could be so opposed in principle to ensuring I made the best choice in my selection of fraternities.

I mumbled something about not knowing clipboards were forbidden.

He looked me in the eye with a mixture of pity and apprehension. "Look, I know you were hoping to join Sigma Chi, but I'm not sure this situation can be salvaged. I'll do my best, but I'm not very optimistic about you becoming a brother."

The news hit me like a ton of bricks. I walked back to my dorm room in the dark, crushed, still holding my clipboard.

Sigma Chi rejected me. And Sigma Nu. And Acacia. I didn't even cut with the infamous Delts, the fraternity that was the inspiration for the movie *Animal House* several years later. To my knowledge, I was the only LSU freshman who did not get a single offer to join a fraternity that year. Most got several and could take their pick.

I was devastated. It seemed my college life was over before it had even begun. The brilliant legal career I'd imagined with my uncle had also taken a major, perhaps fatal, hit.

A Second Chance: LSU Student Union

Trying to salvage my freshman year, I went over to the LSU Student Union to see if there might be anything for me to do there. I discovered they had student committees for activities such as concerts, fine arts, cinema, etc. That included a committee that oversaw lining up guest speakers. Surprisingly to me, no one wanted to be the chair. I volunteered and got to work.

For the next several months, I worked with a small group of students along with my student advisor, Shirley, to bring some interesting and contemporary speakers to campus. We had Alvin Toffler, author of *Future Shock*, tell us that over the next 30 years there were going to be unbelievable changes. He only scratched the surface in retrospect, as the Internet didn't even exist as an idea at the time.

Lawrence Peter, the author of *The Peter Principle*, came to tell us we were all going to rise to our level of incompetence. Time has proven how true this is, though some got there faster than others. For Halloween, I even managed to bring in an expert on vampires to tell us the real scoop on wooden stakes and garlic.

My favorite speaker by far was Margaret Mead, the world-famous anthropologist. I got to spend the better part of the day showing her around town and helping her before and after her speech. At the time, she was the most famous person I'd ever spent any time with, and it was a fantastic experience.

We got decent crowds, with usually at least a couple of hundred showing up. Toffler managed to attract almost 1,000 to come out and hear his predictions. Margaret Mead set a record of 1,300 in attendance (the maximum seating in the LSU Union Theatre). We got a bit of local TV and newspaper coverage for each event, but nothing we did made a big splash.

One afternoon, I came into the room where the Speaker's Committee met every two weeks. Instead of the typical group of 3 to 4 students, the place was packed with more than 20 students.

"Wow," I commented to the group. "What makes us the most popular committee at the Student Union all of a sudden?"

One of the students said they had heard we had a budget to bring speakers to campus. I told him that was true—we had a total of $35,000 for the year and had about $10,000 left for the balance of the year.

"We have all joined this committee to bring Gene Roddenberry to LSU," he declared.

"Who the heck is Gene Roddenberry?" I asked, thinking I'd heard the name before but couldn't quite remember who he was.

There was a gasp from the new members of the committee. "Why, he's the creator and producer of the greatest science fiction series of all time, *Star Trek!*"

Keep in mind this was late 1974. *Star Trek* had gone off the air five years before in 1969. While I had occasionally watched it in syndication, I had no idea why anyone would care about what Gene Roddenberry had to say in a speech. But maybe they knew something I didn't.

I looked around the room. "Well, let's assume we brought him here. How many people do you think would show up to hear him speak?"

There were smiles all around. One of the new members clued me in, "It would be a record crowd. We can't have him speak in the LSU Union Theatre—that only seats 1,300. We will have to have this in Pete's Palace." The arena was nicknamed for the greatest LSU basketball player of all time, "Pistol Pete" Maravich.

I was incredulous. "Are you kidding? It seats over 14,000 people. The biggest crowd we have ever had for a speech is 1,300. How many do you think we could get to come?"

The newly assembled team wasn't sure of the exact number, but there was one thing they were willing to bet on: it would be a lot more than the Union Theatre could possibly hold and would set a record in terms of attendance for a speaker event.

I can't remember how long we were in that room debating this idea, but it was a long time. I can't remember all the reasons they gave me that bringing Gene Rodenberry to LSU was a big idea. All I can say is by the time I left that room, I had become a "Trekkie." They were convinced this would be the biggest event in the history of the LSU Union Speaker's Committee. Now all I had to do was convince the rest of the world.

Looking back, I can see now this sparked something in me. Pulling this off would be a long shot. Heck, it would be a moonshot. But I was ready to give it my best shot.

Maybe it was because I needed a win after my rejection from the fraternities. Maybe it was because I knew my new team was counting on me to make this happen. Maybe it was a combination of these things. But for whatever reason, I'm certain this was the first time in my life I decided to be truly audacious. I was going to boldly go for something that was unlikely, even preposterous. I knew I was way over my head—but something in me was not willing to throw in the towel. I knew I could fail. But I also knew I might not. So that was good enough for me.

Over the next week, I watched *Star Trek* reruns on the local station in my dorm room to brush up on my *Star Trek* knowledge. Then I made an appointment to see Shirley, my program director, to tell her about what we wanted to do. I sat down in Shirley's office. "Have you ever heard of *Star Trek*?" I began.

Shirley thought for a moment and replied, "Perhaps. Why do you ask?"

I told her about my plans to bring Gene Roddenberry to campus in March. I told her about the enthusiasm of the Speaker's Committee for doing this—at least among all our newly acquired Trekkie members.

Shirley shrugged and said that, within reason, we could pick whoever we thought would be a good choice as a speaker. Then I dropped the bombshell, "And we'd like to have it in Pete's Palace."

She was shocked. "Are you crazy? Do you know how much that would cost? And why would you need a venue that big?"

My committee members had given me the confidence to be assertive. "This will work. We'll have the biggest crowd to ever attend a speaking event at LSU." I couldn't believe I'd just said that.

"And how are you going to get that kind of crowd out for this event?" Shirley asked as she looked me straight in the eye and suddenly got very serious.

I hadn't put a lot of thought into that question until she had asked it. "I will get the local TV station to sponsor the event!" I blurted out, not having any idea if that was even a remote possibility.

"Well, Kip, I'll give you credit for being assertive. Go ahead with your plans. You can spend the rest of your budget on this event. But if you don't have at least 2,000 people show up, that will be the end of your time as speaker's chair as well as with the Student Union. You're taking a huge risk. I personally would not do it, but you make the call," Shirley warned.

At this point in the conversation, I figured there was no turning back. "This will be an amazing event. You'll see," I replied.

I left her office with my head spinning. I had enjoyed being the head of the Speaker's Committee. Was I going to risk it all on a guy who produced some TV show about space travel that was canceled five years ago?

I now felt entirely outside of my comfort zone. I didn't know it then, but this is what the Hindus in India mean when they say, "Leap, and the net will appear." It was time for me to take a massive leap into the unknown.

The following day after my classes were done, I called the local TV station and made an appointment to see them in the late afternoon. As I walked into the TV station lobby later that day, I introduced myself to Mr. Smith, the station manager.

I figured I better make this sound like an incredible opportunity for this station. "Hi, I'm Kip Knight, chairman of the LSU Student Union Speaker's Committee. I'm here today to offer you the exclusive rights to be the sponsor of the upcoming Gene Roddenberry speech."

"Yeah, so what do you want from me?" he asked.

I knew this was "do or die" time. I continued, "It's very simple. All you have to do is create a commercial promoting the speech, run it on your station every day during the *Star Trek* reruns, plus create and distribute posters all over town promoting the event."

"What's your budget?" Mr. Smith wanted to know.

This was the question I was dreading the most. I was going to have to use the rest of my budget for the year to pay for Gene's speaking fee and renting Pete's Palace. I had nothing left for a marketing budget. And without heavily publicizing the event, there was no way I was going to have a successful event and keep my position as speaker's chair.

"Uh, well, frankly nothing. But this is going to increase your TV ratings so that it will pay for itself!" I responded enthusiastically. I had no idea if this was accurate, but I thought it *might* help his ratings, and frankly, it was all I had in terms of what was in it for him.

Mr. Smith stared at the ceiling for a moment. "Well, we don't get much for the ads on that show anyway. Oh, what the hell, sure. We'll do it," he volunteered.

My heart started beating again. One problem solved. Now I needed to figure out how to make this a newsworthy event that was going to get the attention of the local news media.

My first idea was to publicize that we would be beaming Gene Roddenberry on the stage. I had it all figured out in my head: smoke, flashing lights, the appropriate sound effects—and we could have him appear on a lift from underneath the stage. To this day, I still think it would have worked, but Gene's agent axed the idea.

As an alternative, his agent told me Gene was going to make a major announcement during his speech, plus he was bringing along a "blooper" film to show the crowd. So that's what we emphasized in the local publicity. The local newspapers ate it up and ran several stories about Gene, *Star Trek*, and the upcoming event at Pete's Palace.

The biggest unknown I was facing was that it was practically impossible to know how many people would show up for this event. Students were assessed an activity fee each semester, which was the basis for our funding. Tickets were free to students since they had already paid a student activity fee as part of their tuition and were given out on a first-come, first-served basis.

For certain events, such as this one, we would also sell the tickets at the door to the public for a nominal amount of $10 a ticket. But most of the attendees would be students, and we wouldn't know how many would be there until the day of the event.

My assistant committee chair and I drove to the airport in silence to pick up Gene. The Baton Rouge airport was still very basic at the time with passengers getting off the plane on steps that were wheeled up to the airplane's door.

Gene got off first, and then I was surprised to see a woman I recognized as Nurse Chapel on the TV series who was also married to Gene. We all went to dinner, but I had a hard time enjoying the moment since I kept wondering if anyone would show up for Gene's speech. Despite my stress over wondering how many people would show up to hear him, Gene Roddenberry was one of the nicest people I had ever met, and his wife was equally charming.

As we drove up to the gate of the university, Gene looked at me. "Well, Kip, how many folks are coming tonight?"

We were rapidly approaching the university's gates, and the truth was I still had no idea how many, if any, would show up. If I had gone to this much effort and the event was a bust, my LSU Union career would be ending later that evening.

Before I could answer Gene's question, we turned the corner and entered the campus. I looked out the car and saw the longest line of people I've ever seen in my life lining up to get into Pistol Pete's Palace. I looked at Gene with a huge sense of relief that this whole crazy scheme just might work. "We're going to have a terrific crowd tonight," I said with a confident smile.

We went inside and it *was* a great turnout—over 6,000 people (which to this day is the biggest turnout for a speaker event at LSU). Gene gave an incredible speech that night. At the end of it, true to his word, he announced Paramount Studios had just agreed to film the first *Star Trek* movie. We got national press coverage the next morning. Although various delays would mean the movie would not actually make it to the movie theatres until four years later, the world heard about it for the first time that night.

As I stood there at the end of the evening and the crowd was starting to leave, I made two important decisions about what I wanted to do next. First, I was going to work hard to become the president of the LSU Student Union and have a fun time doing it. Secondly, I was going to pursue a career in marketing instead of becoming a lawyer. Any career that allowed you to do what we had just done was a lot more exciting than any career I could imagine having in law. Lawyers were all about creating and enforcing the rules; my natural strength was in continually challenging the status quo and changing the rules.

That's what I proceeded to do over the balance of my time with the LSU Union. The following year, based on my success with the Speaker's Committee, I was appointed to head up all the academic programs on campus. For my junior year, I was appointed Vice President of Finance, which was invaluable training for the many budgets I was going to create and manage in the future.

Time to Change the Laws

During my senior year, I became the president of the LSU Student Union. I wanted to challenge several restrictions I had encountered during my time moving up the organization. The Union was prohibited from advertising in the local papers due to laws passed during the Great Depression. We were banned from serving wine in our restaurants due to laws dating back to Prohibition. And college students couldn't access cash on campus because of local banking restrictions.

With every one of these restrictions, I kept asking why and was told time and time again, "well, that's the law, and we have to follow it." When I finally got into a position where I could challenge the status quo, I declared to our LSU Governing Board it was time for us to make some changes to these laws for the university's good. When I was asked how I planned to do that, I told them we'd figure it out, but we were going to push to make these changes while I was still in this role.

I had one advantage when I started this effort. During the summers while I was in college, I'd worked in the Louisiana Legislature, first as a proofreader of Senate bills, then as a Senator's Aide. I knew enough about how state laws were created and passed to get us started.

We approached several legislators who were LSU graduates and explained what the situation was and what we wanted to change. It took me my entire term as president to get this work done, but by the time I left, we were able to advertise in the local paper, serve wine in our restaurants, and installed some of the first ATMs in the country on a college campus. Some of the folks I worked with initially didn't think we had a chance to make any of these changes, but by the end of our time together, they were all believers in the power of pushing hard to make smart changes to the status quo.

Being assertive has taught me that when you take risks, you learn something, regardless of if you succeed or fail. I also learned assertiveness is all about being *ready* to take risks with the right mindset—along with being fully *prepared* to act. If you have the time to "get your ducks in a row" like I did when I was president of the LSU Union, that's ideal, but there are also going to be unexpected situations like the one I had with Gene Roddenberry where you must trust your gut and make it up as you go along. If it isn't unethical or illegal, do whatever you have to so your efforts have a shot at success.

My advice is whether you've had years to prepare for something or just five minutes, don't hold back. When you feel like you're ready to take that moonshot, go for it, and do it with your whole heart. As the Romans said, "Fortune favors the bold." What I learned about being assertive during my time in college prepared me for the roller-coaster career that lay ahead of me.

CHAPTER THREE
Assertiveness—Boldly Going for It

REFLECTIVE QUESTIONS

- What's the most assertive thing you've ever done? What was the outcome? What did you learn from this experience? Would you do it again?

- Who are some of the most assertive people you know? Are they people you tend to admire or try to avoid? Why?

- How comfortable are you in taking a risk in your career, investments, etc.? What are some of the factors you consider?

- What's the biggest thing you have regretted not doing so far in your life? Why?

- What percentage of information on an important decision do you need before acting? Do you wish you would be more willing to move ahead with less information? Why or why not?

LEAP INTO ACTION

Accept that failure is part of life. Taking a chance of doing something you've never done before will embolden you to take more risks, even if you initially fail. Remember that every risk, no matter how it ends, is an opportunity to learn. If you have the desire, skills, and drive to truly give it your best, you'll gain something from taking that risk. If you need to work up the courage, start with smaller risks. Getting a few wins under your belt will help you build that confidence to lean into bolder risks.

A MOMENT OF ZEN

Let go of "should" and replace it with more love and less fear.

Eliminate "should." This one simple word can cause so many problems. Any time it's used, it almost always leads to disappointment where pain and heartache follow. "Should" limits your thinking. It keeps you trapped in a smaller world, stuck in old habits and patterns that may not be serving you well. Discover what's real for you. Feel it. Live in it. Own it. Draw power from it.

Whom you choose to love and to love you back is the most important decision you make. You don't have to get it right, but if you do, life and your career will be much easier. We are "trained up" to focus on success itself, but love is the catalyst we don't focus on enough. More love. Less fear.

04

Integrity— 99 44/100% Pure

Integrity: Acting in a way that inspires
confidence and trust in others

> "Waste no time arguing about what a good man
> should be. Be one." —Marcus Aurelius

SNEAK PEEK AT MY LEAP
How I got the most significant break in my career to
work at Procter and Gamble in brand management
(and learned a valuable lesson from my first boss).

One guarantee in business is you are going to have to deal with
unexpected setbacks. You also are going to likely have some
great bosses and others that are a challenge to endure. When
you have a setback and/or a weak boss, try to turn it into a
unique learning opportunity for you to chart a new path for
your life and career. But admittedly, sometimes it helps to be
lucky as well.

I was looking forward to getting a full-time job once I finished my MBA at the University of Cincinnati. I had been very fortunate to work full time in a fellowship program at Burke, a marketing research company, and get a full-paid scholarship to the University of Cincinnati's Graduate School of Business—paid for by my employer. I was seriously considering going into marketing research as a professional once I graduated.

As my graduate program fellowship with Burke was coming to an end, I went to (let's call her Louanne), an account executive and my boss at the time, for some much-needed career guidance. Up to this point, Louanne was a bit of an enigma as my manager, and I didn't have anyone to compare her to since she was my first boss. We didn't spend much quality time together since most of my work was done on my own. She seemed to spend most of her time meeting with her clients—lots of lunches and dinners and off-site meetings.

I was happy doing marketing research and assumed I was doing good work. I say "assume" since there was no process in place for any kind of feedback on how you were performing—we never had any one-on-one meetings, never discussed my career development plans, and never had an annual review.

It seemed to me that Louanne was an excellent role model on how to be a great people manager—just do exactly the opposite of what she did.

I finally ran out of patience and decided to ask her for some feedback with about two weeks left before I was due to graduate—and more importantly, when my fellowship and paycheck at Burke was going to end.

"Have You Ever Considered a Career in the Federal Government?"

I sat in her office. "Louanne, as you undoubtedly know, I'm finishing up my MBA later this month. My fellowship time is almost over. I was wondering if you could tell me what career opportunities I might look forward to here at Burke?"

Louanne looked uncomfortable and squirmed in her chair. After a couple of false starts trying to address my question, she finally blurted out, "Have you ever considered a career with the federal government?"

I certainly didn't see that coming. After mumbling several incoherent sentences, I got up and left her office in a state of shock.

Dave, my cubemate, was seated at his desk. He looked up and declared, "Holy cow, Knight, you look like a car hit you."

"No, Dave, I've been hit by a car before when I was in London. This feels worse."

He was equally surprised to hear the news about my job prospects but didn't have much to offer in terms of what to do next. I needed a "Career Plan B," and fast.

As my roommate and fellow Burke employee Kevin Martin and I drove home from work that night, I mentally kicked myself for making a fatal assumption I was going to stay at Burke following my graduation. How could I have been so stupid? Why didn't I have a career conversation with Louanne or someone at Burke a year ago when I would've had time to do something about it? I was in a world of hurt and wondering what I should do next.

We stopped at a stoplight in downtown Cincinnati at the intersection of Sycamore and Broadway.

The Procter & Gamble (P&G) headquarters building was to our immediate right. After listening to my tale of woe for the last five minutes, Kevin looked over at me and nodded toward the large P&G building. "Why don't you apply at P&G and work there? After all, they invented brand management. If you're going to be in marketing, I hear there's no better place in the whole world."

I snapped at Kevin. "And just how exactly am I supposed to do that? First, I already checked, and they don't recruit at the University of Cincinnati. P&G typically only interviews at a select number of schools, and most are in the Ivy League. Second, in case you forgot, I'm graduating in just two weeks. I am totally screwed."

I felt totally defeated. What a lousy way to start out my professional career!

"Hey, it's just a thought. That's what I'd do if I were you," Kevin replied.

The next day, I sat glumly at my desk and wondered what I should do next. My cubemate Dave mentioned that the Cincinnati chapter of the American Marketing Association (AMA) had their monthly luncheon meeting later that day. It just so happened it was held a couple of blocks from Burke's office building, so I could walk over during my lunch hour if I decided to go.

Luckiest Lunch of My Life

I figured now would be a mighty good time to do some "power networking." I went to the copier to make copies of my resume. Since I wore a suit and tie to work anyway, I figured I'd take a chance and see if I could meet someone, anyone, who might know someone at P&G who could give me a shot at interviewing for a brand management position.

I arrived at the AMA meeting just as over 200 folks were in the process of finding a table in the large hotel ballroom to sit. I found an empty chair and asked if I could be seated between two young women. They welcomed me to their table. I introduced myself and was shocked to discover on my left was Gloria, an assistant P&G brand manager for Cheer, and Mary, an assistant P&G brand manager for Tide.

When I learned who they were and, more importantly, where they worked, I immediately told them I'd like to apply at P&G for a position in brand management.

To my relief, after some initial questions and hearing my story about how much I loved marketing, they agreed to be my P&G coaches and see if they could help me get an interview, even though they both thought it would be a long shot. I got copies of my resume from my suit pocket. We proceeded to ignore the AMA speaker and rip my resume apart and put it back together.

As we were leaving the luncheon, I told Gloria and Mary just how grateful I was to have them helping me out. Gloria smiled. She said, "Don't thank us just yet. First, you must pass an intelligence test. It's hard and they only give you one hour to complete it—you probably won't be able to finish it. And unless you get a passing score, you won't be able to get any interviews."

My heart sank.

Standardized testing was not one of my strong suits. I could blame this in part on where I went to school—education was never a high priority in the small town in Louisiana where I grew up. But it didn't change my current reality. All I could do was give it my best shot and be focused on the upcoming task at hand. This was my best chance at changing my career trajectory, and I wanted to win.

I went back to my office and retyped my resume based on their suggestions. Then I walked over a few blocks to leave a copy for Gloria at the front desk at the P&G offices, where she would give it to a friend in the group that interviewed brand management candidates.

The person staffing the desk told me to come back at 11:00 am the next day to take the intelligence test.

I tried to get a good night's sleep that evening, knowing a lot was riding on how I did on the test. I checked in at the P&G front desk the following day and was told to go up the elevator to the floor where the human resources department resided. As I walked down the hall, a woman was typing and stopped to look up. She looked at me. "Wow, I could feel your energy as you walked down the hall."

I smiled weakly and told her I was here to take the brand management test. She had me go to a small, windowless room and wait. A few minutes later, a young guy walked in. He looked at me with a mixture of amusement and pity as he introduced himself.

"I'm Fred. Gloria is a good friend of mine. She asked me if I'd let you take the test as a favor to her, and I agreed. Here you go. Remember you've got one hour. Good luck."

With that, Fred left the room. I immediately got to work. He came back exactly one hour later.

"Well, how'd you do?" he asked with a smile.

"I finished it," I replied.

He looked surprised. "Congrats. Most people don't."

I looked at Fred and smiled. "I noticed there is a typo on question 154."

He laughed. "I don't think so. P&G has been giving this test for 20 years. I certainly think we would have found a typo by now."

So, I took the test and pointed out the typo. Now finding typos is not something I was born with a natural ability to do. I got good at doing this three years earlier when I was a rising senior at LSU and got a job in the Louisiana Senate proofing legislation.

This was not a job I had sought out, but I needed a job and did it for three long months. The prime directive in this office you were reminded of daily was that *any* typo could have substantial legal consequences.

I became good at spotting typos by working with someone who would read the proposed legislative language, including pronouncing all punctuation, to ensure everything was perfect. After doing this level of precise clerical work for an entire summer, I was surprised to discover I could pick up a typo now by glancing at a page. They seemed to jump out at me now.

To this day, I have no idea how I did on that test, but I'm convinced it helped me get an interview at P&G because I spotted that typo. As I was to learn later, at P&G, attention to detail in developing persuasive recommendations has semi-religious importance. So don't look down your nose at certain kinds of work you might have to learn along the way—you never know when it might come back and give you a natural competitive edge.

Fred called me later that day to tell me they wanted me to come in the following week for a series of interviews. This was a lot of fun compared to taking the test, and I enjoyed talking with everyone who interviewed me. Some of the interview panelists would become lifelong friends. At the end of a very long day of interviews, I got a job offer to start as a brand assistant, triple my salary at Burke.

I would have to rank that day as one of the four happiest events of my life, only surpassed by the day I got married to my wife, Peggy, and the birth of our two boys, Tom and Chris. For someone who wanted a career in marketing, it simply didn't get any better than this.

The associate advertising manager who made me the offer —Bob Morrison, who later went on to be the president and CEO of Kraft and Quaker Oats—asked me if I wanted to think about the job offer overnight. I replied I wanted to start as soon as possible. He smiled and suggested it would be a good idea to at least take a week off before starting my new job. I asked him if there was anything I could do in the interim.

"Yes, there is something you should do. Every time you watch a commercial on TV, I want you to analyze it. And the next time I see you, I want you to be able to articulate why you think it was either an effective or ineffective ad," Bob stated. I have followed Bob's advice and have been doing this ever since. If you love marketing, practice makes perfect.

I'm the only person I'm aware of who's ever walked "off the street" and landed a position as a P&G brand assistant, the entry-level job in brand management. If I hadn't met Gloria and Mary at that AMA luncheon, and if they hadn't taken me under their wing, getting my foot in the front door at P&G would've been a lost cause. Gloria and Mary later told me this was the first and only AMA meeting they ever attended. Sometimes it's better to be lucky than good—the marketing gods were smiling on me that fateful day.

But before I could start at P&G, I had one last thing I needed to do at Burke: quit. It was time to deliver the news to Louanne. I wanted to tell her in person since that seemed like the proper way to wrap up my fellowship that was coming to an end.

Timing Is Everything

I went to Burke early the day after getting my P&G offer to pack up a few items without being noticed. I left them in a box next to my desk. I then walked over to Louanne's office, but she was nowhere to be found. I surmised she must have been recovering from some late-night entertaining of whichever client happened to be in town.

I left her a note on her desk and went back to my cubicle to wait for her eventual return.

Jack, the president of Burke, who rarely frequented the hallways in my part of the building, came over to my desk. He asked if I could come to his office. I said sure but wondered what in the world this could be about this early in the morning. I followed Jack down the hallway.

When we got to his office, Jack walked over to his desk and picked up a yellow legal pad with many names on it. He then sat on the couch in his office and invited me to sit down next to him.

"Kip, I'm going to tell you something very confidential."

I was mystified as to what in the world he could be talking about. I looked at Jack and replied, "Okay, sure, I'll be sure to keep it quiet."

He showed me his yellow pad. It had a long list of handwritten names on it, including mine. All the names were crossed out except mine. "As of this week, we have finalized the purchase of a major acquisition. We will announce it next week. They specialize in doing eye-tracking research for TV and print ads—all very high tech."

While I thought this sounded somewhat interesting, I still couldn't figure out why he told me all of this and why my name was on a list.

Jack continued, "The founder of the company will stay on as the president, but we need to have a strong number-two person who can help him manage the business. We considered everyone here at Burke for this important role. I'm delighted to tell you: You're our guy!"

The first person I thought of when he told me this was Louanne. This whole situation was surreal but made me smile.

He smiled back.

"Jack, did you happen to talk to Louanne as you were working on this acquisition and your list of names?"

Jack shook his head. "Oh no, this acquisition has been top secret, as well as who's going to run it. She has no idea what we're doing. Why do you ask?"

I then told Jack of the epic career chat I recently had with Louanne two weeks earlier. I informed Jack that because of her counsel to seek employment with the U.S. government, I began a crash course to find another job, which recently came to a successful conclusion.

Jack, who was red-haired, started to get red in the face. He looked confused. "What are you talking about?"

"What I'm saying, Jack, is I'm going to work in brand management at P&G. Today is my last day here at Burke. I'd like to thank you for the opportunity to work here. Frankly, if you had asked me to take this job a couple of weeks ago, I would have been thrilled and accepted on the spot. But I've already accepted the position at P&G. I start next week."

I thought Jack was going to have a heart attack sitting there on his couch. His face was beet red—even redder than his hair. I figured this was as good of a time as any to exit. I wished him good luck as I left his office and closed the door behind me.

Louanne's office was in the building between my cubicle and Jack's office. I noticed she was back at her desk, checking her makeup in a pocket mirror. I walked into her office. "Excuse me, Louanne."

She looked up at me, rather irritated. "Yes, Kip, I saw your note. What do you want?"

I smiled at her. "I was just in Jack's office, and we were just talking about you. I think he'd like to see you now."

Her look of irritation suddenly turned into a worried look.

"And just what does he want with me?"

I smiled again and uttered my last words to her. "All I know is that it's very hush-hush—extremely confidential. You should see him as soon as possible."

She quickly got up out of her chair and pushed past me as she hurried down the hall to Jack's office. I went back to my cubicle and picked up my box of personal items. I left the building, put the box in my car trunk, and drove away for the last time.

Hollywood endings don't get better than that. I don't know who or what in the universe was looking out for me at that time. I did know I was given a once-in-a-lifetime chance to work for P&G and was determined to make the most of it. I appreciated my time at Burke—and that they paid for my MBA—but my gut told me I would be much happier as a client of Burke's rather than a vendor.

The Greatest Consumer Package Company in the World

A bit of background on Procter and Gamble might be helpful. P&G was started in 1837 by William Procter, a candlemaker, and James Gamble, a soap maker. The men were married to a pair of sisters, making them brothers-in-law. They set up shop in Cincinnati on a suggestion from their shared father-in-law. The new company treated employees progressively well over the years.

For example, in 1885, William Procter's grandson decided workers would be happier if they got Saturday afternoons off with pay, a revolutionary thought at the time. In 1887, P&G started the first profit-sharing program in the country, which continues to this day. In 1915, they made sure all employees had a sickness, disability, and life insurance plan. By 1923, the company promised all employees 48 weeks of employment annually.

I joined P&G 143 years after it was formed as part of the brand manager class of 1980 in the Bar Soap and Household Cleaning Products Division. There were 13 of us—one for each of the brands in the division—where we would learn how to be marketers in a series of classes, courses, and assignments over the next several years before we were eventually, we hoped, promoted to assistant brand managers.

P&G is the closest thing this country has to a post-graduate school in marketing. They have a systematic way of approaching business and marketing in practically everything they do. There was a standard way of setting up a test market and analyzing results. They used marketing research tools to evaluate new products and new advertising campaigns. There were rules of thumb and benchmarks on assessing the health of a brand developed over many decades.

More than any other activity, memo writing was an art form at P&G. This was based on the premise that clear writing was a sign of clear thinking. A memo could be no longer than three pages, not including exhibits. The memo had to go through every management level for review—called "niggling"—before going forward for the next level of approval.

There was a memo-writing course, which lasted a week. As a brand assistant, it would not be unusual for your first memo to go through as many as twenty rewrites before it finally made it to the ultimate decision-maker. Memo writing was a critical skill you were expected to be really good at.

As an incentive, one of the brand managers put up a "Wall of Shame" outside his office where he posted memos he didn't think were worthy. Talk about public humiliation if you were the author of one of those memos! But by placing such a high premium on this skill, you become pretty darn good at writing concise, persuasive memos.

One of my favorite executives at P&G was Tom Laco, who had the ability to point out fundamental principles I still remember four decades later. One of these principles was you are probably only going to do one or two things of significance in any given year, so it's worth putting a lot of thought into what you want that goal to be and focus on making it happen.

Tom was a big fan of keeping it simple when writing a P&G memo. As he observed, "Abraham Lincoln's Gettysburg address was 275 words long. Two hundred of those words were one syllable. I want to declare Abraham Lincoln English the official language of P&G and want to encourage that kind of simplicity. I think maybe 80% of the memos we write can be done on one page and maybe one exhibit." That became the norm of what was expected.

Making a Required Fashion Statement at Work

P&G was also a stickler for what you wore to work. Wearing a suit and tie was a given. The color and type of your shirt were also limited: white or blue; buttoned down or not buttoned down. I saw more than one of my fellow brand assistants sent home when they didn't wear the appropriate attire to work. None of these rules were written down—it was all part of the oral tradition that guided young brand management recruits on what was and was not acceptable at a conservative Midwestern company.

The rules about what to wear turned into a sporting event at our annual year-end meetings. There would be a betting pool. It worked like this. We would gather in a giant assembly room in the building. A huge stage was assembled that would hold all the company's senior management—senior vice presidents, CFO, CEO, etc.

Not surprisingly, at the time, they were all older white guys—a total of 25 of them, quite a change compared to P&G's management team today. And every one of them would have to be wearing a suit and tie. But there *was* something you could bet on: the number of white vs. blue shirts and buttoned-down or non-buttoned collars. So that's what all the brand managers and their teams did at every year-end meeting: put a lot of money on the line to bet on what senior management would be wearing that day on stage.

The shirt color was easy to confirm, but the buttoned vs. non-buttoned-down collars was tricky. There were official "spotters" in the audience with binoculars. They would verify the blue/white/button/no-button shirt of each person on the stage, then enter it into the official tally.

I don't know the total size of the betting pool, but I guess it was large enough to get your attention if you won. I placed my $5 bet before the meeting as "17 white, 8 blue, 21 button-down, 4 non-buttoned." I don't know the mathematical possibilities for this, but I'm sure some math geeks in the room did. Still, it made it a lot more exciting to go to what was generally considered a tedious affair.

P&G CEOs aren't known for their sense of humor. But as Ed Harness, CEO at the time, got up to begin his "State of the Business" remarks, he looked out over the crowd as everyone waited for him to get the meeting underway. "Before I begin, ladies and gentlemen, I did want to make one observation. (Long pause.) You can mark me down as a blue shirt, button-down."

Stunned silence. Then the crowd went wild with hooting and clapping. Maybe these guys weren't as stiff and serious as I'd been led to believe.

A Song about Memo Writing

Unfortunately, Ed's opening comment was the high point of the meeting. The presentations seemed to go on and on and on. I frankly lost interest by the time we got to the fifth division president droning on about his business.

I reached over to my notepad and thought it might be fun to poke a bit of fun at the whole P&G memo-writing process. Since "Carol of the Bells" was one of my favorite Christmas songs, I thought that would do nicely for the melody. Here are the lyrics I came up with:

"The P&G Memo Song"

Here's what I want

ASAP

A memo now

From you to me

Please hurry up

Don't dare be late

Associates

Don't like to wait

When you get through

Here's what I'll do

You'll learn to rue

How I love to

Niggle, niggle, niggle memos

Niggle, niggle, niggle memos

Words that you use

Take it from me

Are not in the

Dictionary

Words such as "net"

Are favorite

Open your eyes

And "prioritize"

When you get through

You'll want to sue

How I love to

Do this to you

Niggle, niggle, niggle memos

Niggle, niggle, niggle memos

When we came back over the holidays, I made some copies of the lyrics and shared it with my P&G friends. They then shared it with their friends. And remember. this is before the Internet. I was pleasantly surprised by how much everyone liked it.

This song ended up being such a hit, it was eventually included in the official memo-writing course taught to new brand assistants. And though I did not know it then, this would be the start of my quasi-musical career at P&G that was in my future.

While it was fun to satirize the whole memo-writing process, it was one of P&G's greatest strengths. No matter how complex, getting a business idea down to one to three pages required incredible discipline and focus. It made the writer eliminate anything that wasn't essential to getting their ideas across.

While niggling memos would sometimes become frustrating to a young brand assistant, it reinforced the importance of brevity and logically written persuasion to get the approval to launch a new product improvement or spend millions of dollars on a promotion idea.

The Price of Working Too Many Hours

At P&G, I also learned about setting personal limits. After being there for about six months, I was working late when Margo, my brand manager, came by and said, "Kip, I want to talk with you about your work hours."

I thought she was about to compliment me on how hard I had been working. "Sure, let's talk," I replied.

"I noticed you are working long hours." I agreed I had. What she said next surprised me.

"That's not good. I know you're doing good work, but it's going to make others wonder if you have to work longer hours because you can't keep up with the others."

I started to panic. Even though I didn't know the concept of "imposter syndrome" at the time, that was what I was dealing with. I was continually wondering if I was good enough to work at P&G and was trying to make up for that doubt by putting in longer hours than any of the other brand assistants.

She nodded. "I know you can do this. But you've got to start to set some limits on your work life and learn how to relax. Just something to think about." Then she said good night and left.

It was great advice from a boss who really cared about me. While my family would be the first to tell you today that I'm not the poster child for striking the perfect work/life balance, Margo's coaching was timely and wise. All those long hours and stress were starting to take a toll on my health—I'd recently broken out with a bad case of shingles, which was concerning.

After my chat with Margo, I did some soul searching and decided that I would make a change. I started leaving the office at the end of the workday with everyone else. I tried to get some exercise in as well, my favorite being swimming and bike riding. After a few months, my shingles had cleared up, and I started feeling a lot more confident leaving work at the end of the day. A great people manager such as Margo gave me the gift of candid feedback that made a big difference in how I managed myself after that one conversation.

The Importance of Training and Role Models

While I didn't fully appreciate it at the time, the time and resources dedicated to our training were terrific. There were customized seminars on all types of topics: effective trade promotions, how to work effectively with agencies, how to evaluate television advertising, etc. Later in my career, I would develop similar training courses for marketers—the inspiration for doing this was based on the value of the courses I had at P&G.

The senior management at P&G were role models for brand assistants. Most of the senior management of the company had started in the same position we started. And since P&G only promoted from within, P&G management was extraordinarily interested in ensuring there were training opportunities for all of us, including one-on-one meetings.

There was a heavy emphasis on improving the skills of its current employees rather than bringing in new ones from the outside. While it's not a perfect system, the business results P&G has achieved over the years offer a compelling case that this system has a lot going for it.

My role model for an executive at P&G was John Pepper, president of P&G when I worked there. He later went on to become the CEO. John started at the company just like I had in brand management after serving in the U.S. Navy for 3 years. And after 23 years had risen from the bottom of the organizational structure to the top. The amazing thing about John was his ability to focus and listen. I was invited to present to him several times when I worked on various brands and was always impressed that you had his complete and undivided attention when you were talking with him.

When John was promoted to CEO, he sent out a vision of the organization, which I've kept over the years. It isn't very long, but it's compelling. Here are the three key points he made:

1. All our operations are very close to consumers—we are all about meeting consumers' needs better than the competition with a constant focus on providing superior quality and value.

2. We are accountable for results, and our people love their jobs— they respect and trust and care for one another.

3. Our entire organization is highly flexible, highly entrepreneurial, and constantly learning.

How many companies in the world deliver on these three core principles? Once you find them, they are the firms to bet on for the long run.

"Walking the Talk" on Corporate Principles

The company lived by these principles that we based on integrity. Once three P&G employees stupidly decided they would spy on one of our key competitors, Unilever, to find information on the hair care category. These employees hired operatives to go through trash bins at Unilever headquarters and misrepresented themselves as market analysts to gain confidential information.

When John found out about what had happened, he immediately fired the three employees, quarantined the information they had gathered, and personally called Unilever to tell them what had happened. It was highly unusual to have a P&G employee sink to corporate spying. Still, when it was discovered, John took instant action since it violated the company's integrity principles. It showed me, and every other P&G employee, that integrity was not just words on paper. It was the core value everything was built upon.

At one point during my time at P&G, I was the brand manager for Ivory Soap, whose slogan is "99 44/100% Pure," which could also be a reminder of the importance the company placed on doing the right thing. It's worth pointing out that no company is perfect and gets it right all the time, but one valuable lesson I learned while working there is the importance of being very clear on what your core principles are and "walking the talk" daily.

In addition to honoring integrity, at P&G, I also learned about the importance of being a great people manager. My definition of a great manager is someone who believes in someone they are working with even when that person temporarily doesn't believe in themselves. Managing people is hard and time-consuming, and frankly, too many managers don't give this responsibility the time and effort it needs and deserves.

But when you do invest the time and effort to really care about your team and let them know it in your words and actions, it's amazing to see what they can do. During my career, I've been in some tough spots, and it's gratifying when you have your team rise to the occasion and overcome the odds you collectively are facing.

"Leave Us All Our People"

I've worked for many bosses during my career and can divide them into two basic types: those who rule by fear and those who lead by positive energy. By positive energy, I mean leaders who care deeply about their people and are willing to put the energy into helping develop each team member to their full potential. Teams with an "energy-based" leader will be rewarded with an incredible discretionary effort from their team when it comes to making things happen. Team members with a "fear-based" leader are primarily concerned about just keeping their job—and hoping their boss would move on, quit, or be fired.

This power of a strong leader with a united team is best expressed by Richard Deupree, the first president (1930–1948) and chairman of the board (1948–59) at P&G, who was not a Procter or Gamble family member. Here's what he said about the importance of the people on your team, "If you leave our money, our buildings and our brands, but take away our people, the company will fail. If you take away our money, our buildings, and our brands, but leave us all our people, we can rebuild the whole thing in a decade."

Rather than make running a business seem complicated, at P&G, they would tell you it was simple: it was all about people and business results. The tricky part was getting the balance right. If your people adored you, but you didn't deliver, you were doomed. And if you crushed your business results but destroyed your people in the process, you were going to fail in the long run. The truly great business leaders were the ones who could grow their people and business at the same time.

Do both things well with integrity, and there's no telling how far you can go in your career and business.

CHAPTER FOUR
Integrity—99 44/100% Pure

REFLECTIVE QUESTIONS

- Who are the best and worst bosses you have had? What made them great or horrible?

- What's your definition of integrity? What are some situations you encountered in which you had to make a tough call to protect your integrity?

- What are some ways we can teach children about integrity?

- Have you ever been in a situation where you had to make a tough call deciding the right thing to do? What did you learn about yourself?

- Do you think companies are getting better or worse about making sure their employees act with integrity? Why or why not?

LEAP INTO ACTION

One expression I can't stand is when someone says, "Can I be honest with you?" before telling me something. Does that mean they've been lying to me the rest of the time? We all need to be sensitive to how someone is going to receive whatever information we'd like to share, but let's all agree our conversations should be based on a fundamental level of integrity and honesty that is consistent no matter what the issue is.

A MOMENT OF ZEN

Be thoughtful in how and when you communicate.

There is value in being calm, especially under duress or stress. Amping up the concern, rounding down, getting mad never helps. Good leaders exhibit and stress composure in themselves and their people. Learn the mechanism to stay composed when triggered by stress or pressure.

I remember hearing something I disliked while still relatively new in my position as CMO of a major hotel chain. I immediately sent a memo to my boss, the company president. My memo was laced with more emotion and conviction than fact. I cringed when I reread it the next day.

My boss called me into his office the next day. He sat me down and had me read my memo out loud. I was horrified and thought my tenure as CMO was over. Instead, he calmly explained the damage resulting from acting out of emotion and used this as a learning experience.

He told me the next time it would cost me, which is why I never take any action while I'm dealing with an emotionally charged issue. I now always let a night pass before responding.

Never write what you can say. Never say what you can wink. Never wink when you can nod. Put simply: be careful with your words and never expose yourself more than is necessary.

05

Creativity –
From Sycamore
to Broadway

*Creativity: The ability to see the world in new
and different ways and act on it*

"Creativity is intelligence having fun." —Albert Einstein

SNEAK PEEK AT MY LEAP
**How I got to be creative at one of the most
conservative companies in the world
(and grew professionally from the experience).**

When you think of all the places you can be creative, the first
place you probably think of is in an artist or recording studio.
Or if you are in marketing, at an advertising agency. The last
place you would expect to leverage your creativity would be
at a conservative company such as Procter & Gamble (P&G) in
Cincinnati, Ohio. But that's where I got to experience some of
the most creative endeavors in my career.

My experience with creativity has taught me it's not about a place but rather your attitude or state of mind. I never looked or depended upon a physical location to be "creative"—it always started inside my head with the question "what if," and it would go from there.

Sometimes a spark or idea from someone or something would spur a new idea. Sometimes it would just pop into my head and form over time. Where a concept starts and where it eventually goes is all part of that creative process. And for me, at least, it would have been impossible to predict what specific creative path an initial idea would take. Going through the unexpected creative journey was a big part of the thrill and reward of doing it. And sometimes, the genesis for these ideas would come from the most unexpected of places.

Let's Make a Music Video!

For example, in August of 1981, Music Television (MTV) took the country by storm. The first MTV video aired was "Video Killed the Radio Star" by the Buggles. That first video had limited success in terms of viewers and was nothing compared to the premiere of Michael Jackson's first MTV video in February 1983, which featured "Beat It" from his Thriller album. This was the first music video by an African American artist to be played on MTV, and it was a huge global hit for both the artist and the network.

I've always enjoyed writing lyrics to popular songs, going all the way back to my high school years. The "P&G Memo" song I had written when I first joined P&G was subsequently shared broadly in the company and was even included in the official memo writing course taught to new brand assistants—see Chapter Four for the story about that.

When I saw Michael Jackson dancing in his "Beat It" video on MTV, I just knew I would need to create a version of it for work. Weird Al had a similar urge when he wrote "Eat It," a hilarious parody of the original "Beat It" video.

The first thing I had to do was think of a "hook" on what the song would be about. Since there was continual pressure at work for all of us to meet our sales targets for our brands, the title was easy to come up with: *Meet It*.

A little context here: As a brand manager at P&G, you were expected to deliver a certain amount of business every fiscal year, which was measured by "cases of product shipped." That number needed to be larger than the previous year—otherwise, why did they need you?

Your finance and manufacturing teams would work closely with you during the year to come up with a volume forecast, which, at a minimum, needed to meet—and ideally, beat—your official financial forecast. P&G's fiscal year ended on June 30, which could mess up your summer vacation plans if your shipments were lagging your agreed-upon targets. And God help you if you didn't meet your volume forecast—you ran the risk of being labeled "a problem brand," which would get you more attention from senior management than you ever wanted.

The lyrics didn't take very long to write since this was a topic I knew all my fellow P&G brand managers could instantly relate to:

"Meet It"
They told the Brand don't ever come around here
If your volume's shaky, better disappear
A firm forecast is set, and your volume base is clear
Just meet it, just meet it
You better try, you better do what you can
Don't want to see no drop, don't be a problem brand
Don't say it's been rough, better do what you can
And meet it, just meet it or the boss will be mad!
CHORUS
Meet it, meet it
Make your volume base or beat it

Show em you're smarter, show em you're right
Better not come in a little bit light
Just meet it, meet it, just meet it
Category up, but your brand share is bad
Your non-food shipments are looking sad
You have to ask yourself—is my brand just a fad?
Am I defeated? Defeated?
You have to prove it's not as bad as they feared
When third-quarter shipments are looking weird
You better say your prayers when the end of June is near
Just meet it, just meet it or get the hell out of here!
CHORUS (twice) and fade out

In my mind's eye, this was going to be a fantastic music video with high-quality production values, professional dancers, and professional editing. My only problem was Michael Jackson spent $150,000 to produce his video, and I had the grand sum of precisely zero. I had no idea if anyone would be interested in creating this version of his song, or what we could possibly use it for, but after mulling it over a few days, I came up with a crazy idea on how we could produce it.

I knew P&G had an in-house photography department with outstanding professional photographers, videographers, and editors. I had worked with them before, and they did excellent work. If you had a project with them, your brand budget was cross-charged for the work, and that could be very expensive. But I was always pleased with what they produced. Since music videos were the latest rage, I wondered if they might be interested in turning my lyrics into a music video to show off what they could do—and pick up the tab for doing this.

I called up (let's call him Sam), the head of the P&G Photographics Department, and invited him to lunch. I brought a copy of my lyrics along and told him what I was envisioning—his department could be part of P&G history and make the company's very first music video!

Sam looked at me, confused. "What on earth would you use a music video for here?" he asked.

I was prepared for that question. "Oh, it will be perfect for our year-end meetings. They could use something like this to liven things up a bit." I was imagining the video being shown to the entire company as I made my pitch.

Sam leaned back in his chair, thinking it over. He looked back at me. "And you have the funds to pay for this out of your brand budget?" he queried.

I shook my head. "Sam, you know I couldn't justify doing this for just my brand. It only works if it's a company video..."

Sam cut me off. "You are out of your freakin' mind. There is no way I'm doing this. Nobody has ever done anything like this here, and it would cost at least $50,000. I don't want to waste my team's time or energy on something this stupid. Forget it."

With that declaration, our lunch was over, and we went back to our respective offices. I was bummed out. This would have been a chance for P&G to do something a bit "cutting edge" and make those drab, long year-end meetings a bit more energetic and entertaining. But without a way to pay for this, I was stumped on what to do next.

About a month later, fate intervened. There was a major scandal in the Photographics Department. It seems Sam had been submitting fake invoices to benefit himself and got caught. He was led on a perp walk out of the building in the middle of the day to face formal felony charges.

This was a scandal of significant proportion at a company such as P&G, which had a stringent policy on what you could and could not do. For example, if you met with a vendor, they could not buy you lunch since that might influence you to favor them in the future. I knew what happened with the head of the Photographics Department would significantly negatively impact their reputation.

I waited a week and called Eric, the new acting head of the Photographics Department. I knew Eric from when he and I worked on several brand projects.

"How's it going, Eric?" I asked.

"Horrible. It's like we all contracted leprosy over here. Nobody wants to have anything to do with us." Eric was despondent over the sudden drop in work for his team.

"Eric, I have an idea that might help your Photographics team out. Are you available for lunch tomorrow?" Eric agreed to get together and said he was interested in anything that could revive his team's workload.

We met for lunch the next day and had the same conversation Sam and I had the previous month. But this time, the outcome was different. Since Eric had to employ his team whether they were busy or not, suddenly, the Photographics team had plenty of free time available. He liked the lyrics and thought this could be a fun project to work on.

Success! Well, at least it was a start. The next thing I had to figure out was who to put in the video.

I didn't want to hire professional dancers—that would cost money I didn't have. Besides, I thought it would be a lot more entertaining to a P&G audience if actual brand managers were doing the dancing and singing.

My strategy was to include as many P&G people in the video as possible. I knew higher participation would make it more likely to catch on and become popular within the company.

But my top priority was to find someone who could dance like Michael Jackson, who also worked at P&G. What were the odds I could find that person?

After asking around, I was pleasantly surprised to learn that Pete Carter, a brand manager in the Beauty Care Division, had been a featured dancer at Busch Gardens in Florida during his college years. While he worked there, he was "Mr. Bud" and danced along with the Busch Garden Dancers. Rumor had it that he could bust a move like no one else in the company.

I went to meet with Pete and explained what I had in mind. At first, he was skeptical but gradually became enthusiastic. Both of us were somewhat concerned about what this might do to our professional reputation as marketers but figured it was worth the risk. It helped reassure Pete we were all in this together when I offered to be one of the video dancers, even though this would be a first for me—and I instinctively knew dancing was not one of my God-given talents.

Surprisingly, it wasn't tough to recruit the rest of the cast for our production, including about 50 people in all. Most P&G folks were on camera for just a few seconds of lip-synching and dancing in a wide variety of settings, including the company boardroom, hallways, bathroom stalls, and in front of the newly completed company headquarters.

We thought it would be fun to come up with a name for anyone involved in our video production. *Saturday Night Live* had been around on the NBC television network for almost a decade and called their performers the "Not-Ready-For-Prime-Time Players."

Since no one in our video would be promoted to senior management anytime soon—nor get an office on the hallowed 11th floor of the headquarters building where all the bigwigs congregated—we decided an appropriate name for our troupe would be the "Not-Ready-For-The-11th-Floor Players." The name was an instant hit and made it that much easier to recruit who we needed.

The rumors about Pete's dancing ability were no exaggeration. He was terrific and had dance moves even Michael Jackson would have admired. In the video, Pete transforms from a brand manager in a suit and tie to a badass dancer in a red leather outfit; he was a real pro.

I kept my promise and was part of the line dancers but made sure the other dancers—who were my fellow brand managers—were prominently featured in the final edit. My appearance in the video was a bit like an Alfred Hitchcock appearance in his films—you can spot him if you look closely, but you must know where to look. I've never wanted to be in front of the camera—I am a lot happier creating an idea and letting others bring it to life.

When the filming and editing were done, we premiered the video at the next P&G year-end meeting. It was a monster hit. No one had ever seen anything like this before at a P&G meeting. Pete became the talk of the town among his fellow brand managers and other company employees.

P&G TV: All Commercials, All the Time

Once the video bug bit me, I was hooked. Over the next several years, I came up with several new ideas for the Not-Ready-For-The-11th-Floor Players. We created a spoof of current television commercials for the following year-end meeting, which we put together on a reel called "P&G TV." The network slogan: *"All commercials, all the time."*

We thought it would be fun to get some of our senior management in one of our videos. The head of the advertising for the entire company was Bob Goldstein, who oversaw one of the most significant advertising budgets in the world. Unlike many other senior executives, he insisted on being called "Bob" rather than "Mr. Goldstein." If you tried to call him Mr. Goldstein, he corrected you and told you that was his father's name.

Bob was delighted to volunteer to be one of the "stars" in our video. He would be featured in a spoof commercial based on a TV campaign American Express (Amex) was running called *"Don't Leave Your Home Without It,"* which featured various celebrities.

Since you had to carry your P&G ID card everywhere you went while you were at work, it was natural for us to create a commercial that looked very similar to the Amex ad that featured the P&G ID card with the slogan, *"Don't Leave Your Workspace Without It."* The star of the commercial would, of course, be our beloved head of advertising, Bob Goldstein. Even though he had an office there already, we made Bob an honorary member of the Not-Ready-For-The-11th-Floor Players, which he proudly accepted.

When P&G TV aired at the following year-end meeting, I looked at Bob when his commercial aired. He burst out in a big smile as the crowd went crazy—seeing a senior company leader show a sense of humor at such a serious meeting was refreshing, and everybody loved it.

Cincy's Nice

After we'd finished "P&G TV," I thought my video production days were done. I figured it would be best to focus on my job as a brand manager. However, a new NBC TV series launched nationally called *Miami Vice*, which featured two detectives in stylish clothing fighting bad guys and drug dealers every Friday night. I found the urge to do something with this new trending TV show was just too much for me to resist.

I called Sheila, the head of recruiting for brand management at P&G. I started the conversation by asking what it was like trying to recruit candidates on the East Coast and West Coast to come and work at P&G in Cincinnati.

As expected, Sheila told me it was one of the most challenging parts of trying to attract the best candidates. The Midwest had a reputation of being boring and not a great place for a young, ambitious marketing person to move to.

"What if the Not-Ready-For-The-11th-Floor Players could produce a video that could start to change that image?" I asked.

Sheila said she'd love to hear how we could do that. I shared the idea I had that would play off the hit *Miami Vice* TV series. We would call it "Cincy's Nice," and we would have our version of the two stylish detectives just like the TV show.

But instead of solving a murder mystery or drug bust, the video would be focused on showing two new job candidates all the fun aspects of Cincinnati—including being driven around the town in a Ferrari F355 Spider Convertible, which we could borrow for an afternoon from a friend of a friend.

Sheila was enthusiastic about the idea and agreed to fund the production cost. Just like the "Meet It" and "P&G TV" videos, "Cincy's Nice" was a lot of fun to make and got a great reception from everyone who saw it, including college students across the country, especially since it was a direct contradiction to what they were expecting when the P&G recruiters showed up on their campus.

But after I finished "Cincy's Nice," I absolutely thought this would be the end of my video production adventures. We had Thomas, our firstborn one-year-old, at home, and the workload from being a brand manager for a new test product was growing by the week.

Let's Put on a Show!

Later that same year, I got a message to meet with John Pepper, president of P&G, who had an impressive corner office on the 11th floor. I had no idea what he wanted to talk about. I didn't have any recommendations awaiting senior management approval, so I went to his office with a mixture of curiosity and dread as to what he wanted to discuss.

John welcomed me to his office and asked me to sit down.

"Kip, we've enjoyed the videos you and the Not-Ready-For-The-11th-Floor Players have made over the past several years. They've all been terrific."

I breathed an internal sigh of relief and smiled.

"Thank you very much. It was a lot of fun making them," I said, wondering where this conversation was going to go next.

John continued, "As you know, every September we have our annual Dividend Day, where all of our families come out to Kings

Island *(note to readers: this was a local theme park)* to celebrate. But what you probably didn't know is that Dividend Day featured a talent show put on by employees for many years. We haven't done that in a very long time, but since next year is our 150th anniversary, we thought it's time to bring back that tradition."

Several thoughts were racing through my mind at that moment. If John wanted me to do an employee talent show, what idea could I possibly come up with that could work? And how would I find the time or resources to pull this off since it was less than a year away?

Sure enough, John wanted me to develop a creative proposal to bring back some type of employee-based entertainment for our upcoming 150th anniversary. He wanted it to be a live production and be very memorable since this would be a special occasion for the entire company. And to make sure everyone around the world could see it, he wanted us to produce a video of it as well, which we could share with P&Gers worldwide.

I asked if this would be my new full-time job.

John laughed. "No, you need to keep doing your regular brand management job. But we will make sure you get the budget to be able to do this right. Think about it and let me know if you'd like to be the producer of an employee-based show for our 150th anniversary."

I left his office excited and a bit frightened. I had never done a live theatrical production of anything before. My high school didn't even put on a school play. Although I loved the theatre—especially musicals—I instinctively knew a world of difference between being a member of the audience versus creating and producing a live musical.

The additional workload this would create for me was also a significant concern. If I didn't continue to deliver as a brand manager, this new creative endeavor would harm my career. I couldn't use producing a company musical as an excuse for poor business performance.

On the other hand, how often does the CEO of a Fortune 500 company ask you to do something this audacious? And after all, I'd tried crazy ideas before, and they somehow worked out. And this time, we would have money to work with to create this production—woohoo!

What finally convinced me to say "yes" to John was I knew if the Not-Ready-For-The-11th-Floor-Players could pull this off, it would mean a lot to thousands of P&G employees worldwide and be a significant career highlight for anyone involved in the production.

After talking it over with my wife who was pregnant with our second child, I decided to sign up for what promised to be my most creative adventure ever. My total lack of experience in doing anything like this would not get in my way—I knew we could figure it out as we progressed.

An All-Volunteer Army of Singers and Dancers

The first thing we had to do is to take a ballpark guess as to how much money this would cost. Our budget would only be as good as the assumptions we made. We knew a significant expense would be getting the music rights for the songs we would want to use. There would also be the cost of creating multiple scene changes. A budget for recording original music. The expense of designing costumes for the all-employee cast—how many, we could only guess. The cost of filming and video production. And many other items we knew we would find out only after we'd agreed on a budget.

One area we knew we would not have to spend any money on was talent. This would be an "all-volunteer" army. The question was how many people would we need and how many of those would have the skill required to put on a great show?

After considering and debating many different assumptions and calculations, we told John we would need $200,000 to do the show. He said to us that it would not be a problem. That was a relief. This was the first P&G production in which we had an approved budget before starting any actual work.

Once we had agreed on a budget, at the year-end company meeting, Tom Laco, vice chairman of P&G, announced to everyone the Not-Ready-For-The-11th-Floor Players would be performing their first "live" show at the next Dividend Day, nine months away. He promised this would not just be an employee talent show but an incredibly fast-paced, near Broadway-quality extravaganza.

Game on, I thought. At this stage, there could be no turning back. It was going to be showtime of the highest order for all the Players and me.

The next big issue we needed to tackle was what the show would be about since that would determine everything else, including songs, cast, sets, and so on. I got together with Pete Carter, of "Meet It" fame, and Shawn Coyne to develop ideas on what you could do in a 30-minute live show.

We knew there were a couple of things we had to keep in mind when writing this musical. We agreed it needed to:

- Involve different functions of the company, not just the advertising department.
- Feature music the audience would readily recognize and like.
- Have a big emotional finish since the whole point of the musical was to celebrate 150 years of creating and selling branded products to consumers around the world.

A Musical Journey

Peter, Shawn, and I knew nothing about writing or producing musicals, but having watched many of them in college and New York, the one thing I knew was all musicals were about a journey of some sort. After kicking around several ideas, we eventually decided to make the musical a story about three brothers who had read in the newspaper that P&G would be celebrating its 150th birthday. The three brothers would travel to Cincinnati and visit various company departments to figure out where they could be a part of its upcoming sesquicentennial celebration.

Since P&G company headquarters was located at the intersection of Sycamore and Broadway, we thought it would be fun to call the musical, "From Sycamore to Broadway: A Musical Celebration of Procter & Gamble People and Products." Since we now had the basis and premise for the musical, we needed to figure out what songs to feature and what the musical plot would entail.

We decided to break the show into six separate parts, requiring a different stage set, costumes, crew, and music. This would allow us to have six songs lasting between three to five minutes each. Set changes would have to be done in less than 30 seconds between each scene, as the brothers continued their journey to find out where the celebration was being held.

The three brothers start the show by arriving at P&G headquarters. The traveling brothers in our story were a spoof of a popular CBS series, *Newhart*, in which only one of the brothers, Larry, could talk. He was constantly introducing his two hapless siblings as, "This is my brother Darryl, and my other brother Darryl." That line was guaranteed to get a good laugh from the first scene and get the audience into the story.

That first scene would be set in front of the company building with many folks on stage singing new lyrics from the song "Comedy Tonight" featured in the movie *A Funny Thing Happened On The Way To The Forum*. The revised lyrics to this song would be called "Party Tonight" and establish an upbeat mood for the rest of the show.

The second scene would pay homage to everyone who worked in product development. Quick trivia point: At this time, P&G had more PhDs on their payroll than any other company in the world. Whitney Houston was at the peak of her popularity, so we picked "How Will I Know If He Loves Me?" as the song, and I wrote new lyrics to a song we called "How Will I Know If They Love My New Brand?". The setting was in a colorful laboratory. Everyone would have lab coats with bubbling smoke from test tubes all over the stage.

The third scene was the most ambitious one in terms of choreography and logistics. The setting was a major P&G manufacturing and distribution center. It featured sixteen skaters moving products around while they were skating around the stage singing "Get It There" to the tune of the WWI song "Over There." At least we would save some money on music royalties for this number.

The fourth scene was all about how great our sales teams were. It would be set in a grocery store and feature Pete Carter, doing his best Tom Cruise imitation. Just like in the movie *Risky Business*, Pete would come sliding across the stage in his shirt and boxer shorts, singing new lyrics to the tune of Bob Seger's "Old Time Rock and Roll." To give you a flavor for this song, here's a sample of the lyrics:

Now don't tell me that the shelf is full
Cause this new brand's got lots of pull
Latest advertising and a grand deal
Yeah, I'm the P&G Salesman!

The fifth scene would spotlight just how vital advertising was to the company and included a character dressed up as our very own Bob Goldstein. The stage set for this number was going to be wildly ambitious—it would consist of an enormous boardroom table in which "Bob" would dance up and down the table singing about the merits of world-class copy to ensure the success of a new brand launch—sung to the tune "Tell Her About It" with apologies to Billy Joel.

The finale of the show was going to feature the only original song of the show. We had planned on using the song "We Built This City" by Jefferson Starship, which I wanted to turn into "We Built This Company (on Soap and Suds)." But the music house that owned the rights to this song wanted an outrageous amount of money, which we didn't have in our budget. So, we contracted to have an original song written for the last number.

That turned out to be a smart decision. The original song we created was very emotional and hit just the right notes with our target audience. The song's title summed it all perfectly: "We Are a Part of It All." It was the best song you could have wished for to end our musical.

Now that we had a musical written and music rights secured, it was time to put out the call for talent auditions. We figured we would need a huge cast—about 150 in total, including the backstage crew—but we had no idea how many employees would be interested in trying out. Or more importantly, how many would have the right talent we needed?

An Abundance of Talent

We placed an article in the monthly company magazine, appropriately entitled "Moonbeams" since its original company logo was the Man in the Moon, announcing tryouts would be held the last weekend of that month at company headquarters. We were going to schedule tryouts over a Saturday and Sunday if we needed the extra time, since we had no idea how many people would sign up for an audition.

We needed the extra time. Over 300 people came to try out from every Cincinnati P&G plant and office location—eight areas of the city in total—and some even mailed in applications from different parts of the country. We were blown away by the level of talent. There were incredible singers and dancers, as well as folks who wanted to help build the sets that all happened to work at P&G.

The most challenging part about all of this was deciding who to cut. After talking it over with our musical director and fellow P&G employee Eric Light, we decided anyone who had the guts to try out for this show would be in it.

To do this, we decided we would put on a total of 24 live shows for 30 minutes each. That would maximize the number of P&G

employees who could see our live production at the theatre in Kings Island, which could accommodate 500 people for each performance.

We decided we would create two entirely staffed casts of 100 singers and dancers each. We would also have a core team of 100 who would oversee building all the sets and changing them between numbers. This core team would also create props, costumes, lighting, sound, make-up, and costumes. We were now fully staffed at 300 employees and ready to get underway.

There was fantastic camaraderie in pulling all this together, which quickly consumed many weekends and late nights for the next eight months. We even had John Pepper come out one Saturday afternoon as we were building and painting some stage sets.

Given the amount of musical talent we wanted to be a part of this show, we also decided to create a band to entertain the audience before entering the theatre. In a tribute to the man who made it all possible, we decided to call the group *Mr. Pepper's Lonely Hearts Club Band.*

Tragic Turn of Events

As we got closer to show time that September, my brand manager workload got even heavier. Since my brand was still in the test market, I didn't have the luxury of running an established business, which would have been a bit more predictable. My test market results were not where they needed to be, which meant even more late-night meetings to figure out what we could do to turn it around. With one month to go before Dividend Day weekend, I was beginning to wonder if I had signed up for too much this time.

I was driving into work on a Monday in early August, listening to the local news. The announcer said over the weekend, there had been a rafting accident in British Columbia, Canada, in which five American executives had died. One of them was P&G's own Bob Goldstein, who was only 50 years old.

This was devastating news to me and the entire company. Bob was universally liked and admired by everyone, especially anyone associated with the advertising department. Bob had been on this boating trip with several other friends, including some advertising agency executives he worked with, when 11 of the 12 people in the boat were thrown into the rapids. Six managed to make it to shore, but five of them, including Bob, didn't survive.

At our next rehearsal, we decided to dedicate the show to Bob and kept the song that featured him as one of the main characters. Our collective judgment was that Bob would have wanted the show to go on. Bob told me several times during the year he was honored to be featured in our musical. As we entered the final weeks before we went live, we re-doubled our efforts to make this show something he would have loved.

Showtime!

After nine months of planning, tryouts, and rehearsals, the big weekend (9/25–26/1987) finally arrived. Our first son Tom had just turned two years old, and his brother Chris was just three months old. Peggy and the boys came to several of the live shows and loved it. While that was gratifying, I was looking forward to spending some quality time with them again when this was all over.

The whole Dividend Day weekend was a blur. Twenty-four live performances over two days have got to be a world record for an amateur theatrical endeavor, but we wanted as many employees and their families as possible to see the show in person.

We had standing ovations for each performance. Thank God we had two casts—I don't think it would have been humanly possible for one cast to do that many performances in that short amount of time.

After the 24th show was finished late Sunday night, the entire crew and cast gathered backstage to celebrate. The mood was euphoric. Everyone was pumped up about how well everything had gone. There was a growing feeling among many of the cast that we needed to do something like this again.

Leave Them Clapping

That's when I made the firm and definitive decision that this would be the end of my video and musical productions at P&G. If I had wanted a career on Broadway, I would have headed to New York City after that and given it a shot, an admittedly very long shot. But I enjoyed working in brand management, and even though this had been a lot of fun, there is a lot of merit to the concept of "leave them clapping" and stop when you are at the top of your game.

According to the archivist at P&G, who I recently talked with (yes, they have someone who does that), this was the last time P&G employees have put on a show anything like what we did that year. They are happy they have the video footage available for future generations to watch, and I am delighted the video starts with a dedication to Bob Goldstein.

What did I learn from these creative adventures at P&G, which started with writing some lyrics to a Christmas song at a year-end company meeting and ended up with a 300-person live musical production? I have several key takeaways from this unexpected journey:

- **Don't Be Discouraged by Initial Rejection**—If you're excited about a new creative idea and think it has merit, keep at it. You might have to wait for a while or take a different approach, but if your gut reaction is that your idea deserves to move ahead, your persistence will be the crucial reason it gets to the next development stage. Ignore the skeptics—keep going!

- **Be Open-Minded as to What Your Creative Options Are**— Coming up with new ideas is a lot more productive and fun if you do it as a team. Be open to taking your original idea in new and different directions. For the P&G musical, we played with several wild and crazy ideas before settling on what we ultimately produced. The outcome was a musical that was a lot better because we were willing to give and take on what we thought would work—"we" is always better than "me" in creating something new and original.

- **Know What to Leverage and When to Wrap It Up**—Leverage what you are good at and enjoy doing while also acknowledging what you aren't good at. For example, I know I'll never be able to dance like Peter Carter—I'm OK with that! Knowing when to move on to another idea or phase of your life is also critical. If you are doing something because you are still learning and having fun, keep at it. Otherwise, savor what you've accomplished, then move on to your next creative opportunity.

Having had the incredible opportunity to produce some music videos as well as a live musical production, I'm in awe of the people who do this for a living. Most of the audience watching a live theatrical or musical event will not know how much work goes into their creation. I can understand why a scathing review can hurt so much to the folks who take the chance and try to make something original happen.

So, here's to all the creative people out there who make all our lives a bit more entertaining and enjoyable—well done! And for the rest of us, keep your minds and hearts open to leveraging all the creative talents all of us are born with. It's amazing what you can do with your creativity if you just let it flow.

CHAPTER FIVE
Creativity—From Sycamore to Broadway

REFLECTIVE QUESTIONS

- Do you consider yourself creative? Why or why not?
- What's the most creative thing you've ever done in your life? What did you learn about yourself? How did it make you feel?
- How important is creativity in your life? Is it essential or not a big deal? Discuss.
- Do you wish you were more creative? Is there anything you are considering doing to enhance your creative side?

LEAP INTO ACTION

Children are naturally creative. In our attempt to educate them, we take away a lot of that natural curiosity and creativity. The two most powerful words at the beginning of a potentially life-changing sentence are "what if ...?" Be willing to fill in the rest of that sentence with the same level of imagination and wonder you had while you were growing up.

A MOMENT OF ZEN

Recognize the importance of play and curiosity in everything you do.

When I was 25, I was almost all work and no play. Relationships were mostly transitory as my career involved major geographical relocations. Potentially essential focus areas, like personal growth, continued learning, and spirituality, received zero attention. Back then, my definition of success was extremely narrow. I had my "success formula," and it did not include these areas. These areas would have been seen as success distractions and inhibitors.

Play harder and play longer. I was in such a rush to get everything done that I forgot to recognize that youth also wouldn't last forever, and I should make the most of each moment. I wish I spent more time outside chasing balls and having fun.

06

Perseverance – It Ain't Over till It's Over

*Perseverance: Taking the necessary steps to
reach your desired objective despite significant
challenges and difficulties*

> "Nothing in this world can take the place of persistence.
> Talent will not: nothing is more common than unsuccess-
> ful men with talent. Genius will not; unrewarded genius
> is almost a proverb. Education will not: the world is full
> of educated derelicts. Persistence and determination
> alone are omnipotent." —Calvin Coolidge

SNEAK PEEK AT MY LEAP
**How I outlasted a tough boss, reaffirmed the
value of hard work, and learned a powerful lesson
about thinking "outside the box."**

Sales training at Procter & Gamble (P&G) was a time-honored tradition. The four-month, off-site training assignment marked your
official passage from a lowly brand assistant to an up-and-coming
assistant brand manager. When it was time for me to go, I ended
up learning a lot more than just how to sell soap.

It was typical for the incoming class of brand assistants to obsess over how quickly someone could finish being a brand assistant and get promoted to go on to sales training. Taking 18 months before being promoted was considered excellent, while 24 months was a bad omen. The company record was 12 months and was the first sign of an imminent CEOship—more Fortune 500 CEOs have started at P&G than any other company in the world.

Where you were sent for sales training was also of high importance to all brand assistants. According to brand assistant lore, the genuinely great and fortunate brand assistants got to pick from fantastic sales territories—places such as Beverly Hills, San Francisco, New York City, and Miami Beach.

From what I'd heard, these sales training assignments were better than paid vacations. You'd get up late, call on a couple of stores, have a long lunch, check a couple of store displays in the afternoon, and knock off early—especially on Fridays since it was considered bad form to call on the trade during the start of a busy weekend.

A Waiting Game

When the big day finally came for me, I was nervous. My brand manager, Rob Malcolm, called me into his office.

"Congratulations, Kip, you're going to sales training," he said.

I could barely contain my excitement. "That's fantastic!" I practically shouted. I was waiting for him to say, "Envelope, please," but decided to go ahead and asked directly, "Where am I going?"

"Dayton, Ohio," he replied.

Of all the places I could have worked, Dayton, Ohio, would have come in dead last. But at that point, I was just happy to get my sales training completed so I could continue my career track to brand manager.

Sales training, which lasted four months, was designed to transform you from thinking just as a marketer and start thinking more like a salesperson. The "final exam" of sales training included a field visit by the sales district manager.

In a typical sales training situation, this field visit would not have been a huge deal, consisting of a few polite visits to some grocery store offices, a few superficial trips to some supermarkets to admire your hard-earned end aisle displays, and a rousing lunch to celebrate what a wonderful experience those past four months had been. Your district manager would then send in a glowing report on how well you'd done. This was all that was needed to complete your promotion to assistant brand manager.

That is unless you were assigned to Dayton. I was assigned to work with Mr. (let's call him Barker), sales district manager with over 30 years of experience. I never found out the reason why, but it seemed to me Mr. Barker had taken a sacred oath many years ago to destroy all advertising folks assigned to him for sales training.

I knew I was in big trouble when my fellow brand assistants and other marketers didn't come over and offer their congratulations about me going on sales training in Dayton. Instead, they offered their sincere condolences about working for Mr. Barker.

"You are so dead," one veteran brand manager offered. "When Mr. Barker comes to visit you in the field, you'll wish you'd never been born."

"Why is that?" I asked.

"Because this guy eats brand assistants for lunch," he said. "He's been beating the crap out of people like you for the past 20 years and loving every minute of it."

"Any suggestions?" I asked, hoping to receive some last-minute enlightenment that would make the next four months survivable.

"Yeah, you might want to start thinking about getting another job. This guy has caused more than one brand assistant to quit. You'll never get a favorable review at the end of your sales training."

I was determined to make the most of this lousy assignment and focus on being a great salesman. I soon found out exactly what that would require. I'd never worked so hard in my life. I worked six days a week from 6:00 a.m. to midnight. I was responsible for more than 200 grocery stores and made it a point to visit every one of them at least once every month.

The one advantage Dayton had was that there were no distractions. None. Zero. Zilch. So, I could focus totally on the job.

I went out of my way to form alliances with my key accounts in the grocery trade, knowing the dreaded day would come when Mr. Barker would come out and pay them a visit. Most store managers wouldn't give you the time of day if you were from P&G sales. They would see you coming and literally head in the other direction. But I was able to establish some close relations with a few of them and hoped I could count on them as my best shot at impressing Mr. Barker when the inevitable day came for the field visit.

See You at Dew Drop Inn at 6:00 a.m.!

After four incredibly long, insufferable months in sales training, I got a message. Mr. Barker wanted me to call his office. Immediately.

I nervously dialed his office, and his secretary put me through to his line. "Knight!" I heard Mr. Barker yell over the phone.

I gulped and replied, "Yes, sir!"

"It's time for my visit to your territory. Meet me for breakfast at the Dew Drop Inn at 6:00 a.m. tomorrow," he said.

My first thought was there really couldn't be a restaurant with a name that corny.

"Tomorrow!" I blurted out. "Could we make it a little later in the week so I could be better prepared?"

"You mean you're not prepared!" he roared back over the telephone.

"Of course, I'm prepared," I replied. "I just wanted to make sure we had everything perfect."

"See you at 6:00 a.m. Don't be late. And it better be perfect," he shouted. Then the phone line went dead.

This was bad. After working my ass off for four months, it was all going to be for naught in less than 24 hours. If I didn't get a decent review from this guy, my P&G career was officially over.

I made a few last-minute phone calls to try to set up some appointments. After a restless night of tossing and turning, I got up at 4:30 a.m. and arrived at the Dew Drop Inn at 5:30 a.m. to make sure I beat Mr. Barker to the restaurant.

It was too late: He was already there drinking his coffee and talking with a cute waitress.

"Well, Knight, I hope you're ready for a full day."

"Yes, sir, it's going to be a great day!" I lied.

"Grab a cup of coffee to go. We're outta here," he declared as he rose from his chair and headed for the door.

We left his car behind and headed out in my beat-up excuse of a car for our first sales call of the day.

My strategy to get through the day was simple: I'd start with a couple of my best accounts and show Mr. Barker that I was not the total waste of skin he thought all brand assistants were. We'd finish off the day with a rousing tour of another dozen or so stores. With any luck, I'd wear Mr. Barker out and be outta Dayton within the week with at least a passing field review.

Our first stop was my very best store out of the two hundred I called on. The store manager's name was Mr. Phillips. The store was independently owned in a small town north of Dayton called St. Mary's.

I don't know why Mr. Phillips was so helpful to me. He would go get me a cup of coffee when he'd see me approaching and was always agreeable to putting up end aisle displays and running ads in the local flyer for my products. It didn't get any better than that.

As luck would have it, Mr. Barker and I entered the store and saw six end aisle displays of my latest promotions. My shelf space in the bar soap section was overly generous compared to the competition, and shelf space is something salespeople live and die for. I even had several featured ads in that week's advertising circular.

After saying goodbye to Mr. Phillips, we went back out to my car. Mr. Barker offered his assessment.

"Knight, that was the sorriest excuse for selling our products I've ever seen," Mr. Barker said.

Wow. If he wasn't impressed by this store, there was no hope the rest of my stores we visited would pass muster.

"What are you talking about?" I sputtered. "I had six end aisle displays, three ads in the circular, and great shelf space."

"A real salesperson would have had at least eight end aisles, a front-page in the ad circular, and double the shelving," he said. "Besides that, his pricing was way out of line. Too high."

"I didn't think we were supposed to set retail prices," I countered.

"You can't," he said, "but you sure as hell can influence them. And I can see by his prices you've got no influence with Mr. Phillips."

This was going to be the longest day of my life.

Agony and Ecstasy...in One Meeting

My next shot at redemption was our next call. Mr. King was the buyer for Stumps Market, a small regional grocery store chain. The promotion I was pitching was for the Publisher's Clearing House mailing. Each year for the past five years, P&G contributed up to one million dollars to Special Olympics based on the total number of coupons redeemed, with a contribution of a nickel for every redeemed coupon.

Mr. Barker and I entered Mr. King's office. I pulled out the Special Olympics and Publisher's Clearing House sales material and started my pitch.

"Now, Mr. King, as you know, each year Procter & Gamble does a tie-in with Publisher's Clearing House and Special Olympics. P&G contributes a nickel to the young athletes of Special Olympics for every coupon redeemed. Last year, P&G contributed over one million dollars..."

Mr. King held up his hand and stopped me in mid-sentence. He leaned over and looked me right in the eye as he said, "Just a minute. You know, it makes me sick how you people at Procter & Gamble use innocent people with learning difficulties to sell more of your products."

If Mr. King had punched me in the stomach at that very moment, I don't think he could have taken more air out of my lungs. I never expected this kind of reaction from any of my accounts, especially with my boss seated next to me.

"But it's a worthwhile cause!" I argued.

"That's the sickening part, how you take this charity and make it look like you care, but all you want to do is sell more soap," he replied.

So, this is what the bottom of your career felt like. This was about as bad of a day as I could have imagined. But it was just about to get worse. I could tell by looking at him that Mr. Barker was about to save the day, at least for himself.

"Mr. King," Mr. Barker began, "I'd like to apologize for Mr. Knight."

"How's that?" Mr. King replied. Funny, I was thinking the exact same question.

"Well, it's like this. I haven't been totally honest with you. Knight is not really part of the P&G sales organization. He's in advertising and has been in sales training the past four months in this territory. But he's finished with this job and probably this company. First thing Monday morning, we're going to get a real salesperson in here and straighten this whole mess out."

Mr. Barker glared at me in total disgust.

If I had some cyanide tablets and a glass of water at that moment, I would gladly have exited this planet for that happy brand management cubicle in the sky.

But just when I thought my career at P&G was over, something was about to happen that would reaffirm my faith in hard work and teach me the value of not totally panicking in the middle of what seemed to be a pending disaster.

"Oh, is that a fact, Mr. Barker?" Mr. King inquired.

"Yes, sir, that is a fact. I'm sorry we didn't tell you Knight was on sales training. That was my fault, and I take full responsibility for it. It won't happen again," Mr. Barker said with a solemn look on his face.

"Well, Mr. Barker, let me tell you a few things," he said. "First, Knight is one of the finest salespeople I've ever had the pleasure of working with from your company. He's hard-working, delivers on what he says he will do, and goes above and beyond what I expect. That's a lot more than what I can say about some of the other salespeople you've sent here before."

At this point, it would be hard to say who was more shell-shocked: Mr. Barker or me.

Mr. King continued, "Furthermore, don't even think about taking this out on Knight. My concern is over this promotion, not his ability to be a great salesperson, which he is. You can send whoever the hell you please. I want nothing to do with you or them. Good day and get out of my office now," Mr. King ordered.

And with that, Mr. King escorted us to the door. Mr. Barker was speechless. We walked out to my car and sat down.

"That was a total disaster," Mr. Barker said.

I was feeling extremely bold at this point. "No, it wasn't. If the purpose of sales training is to teach me how to be good at selling, you've just heard from one of my biggest accounts how well I've done."

Mr. Barker shot back, "But you didn't make the sale."

"I will. Mr. King might have some personal objections to this promotion, but I checked, and he's tied into it for the past five years. I'm sure he'll do it again when I call him back," I insisted.

At that point, I could tell Mr. Barker didn't have the energy to beat me up anymore. The tone of his voice was one of total dejection since he knew that whatever else happened that day, he couldn't make me feel like the worthless excuse all brand assistants were supposed to be in his eyes.

"Take me back to my car, Knight. We're done here." And we drove back in silence so he could pick up his car at the Dew Drop Inn. It was only 9:00 a.m.

The following week, I got back in touch with Mr. King, and, as predicted, he bought into the promotion and bought a record amount of product behind it.

With that out of the way, I finished my sales training, got a "passing grade" from Mr. Barker, and headed back to Cincinnati to continue my quest to become a brand manager.

I lost touch with Mr. Barker after my sales training was over—well, truth be told, I doubt either one of us wanted to stay in touch. I would love to know how his next meeting with Mr. King went, but that's just one of those mysteries I'll never know the answer to.

My only hope is if any future brand assistants had to put up with Mr. Barker's version of Sales Training Hell after my time with him, they were blessed with a sense of humor and the wisdom of knowing "this too shall pass."

While my sales training was rough, it did galvanize my belief that hard work pays off. From my first day in Dayton, I could feel the weight of work before me. I chose to laser focus on the prize. I doubled down, put in the long hours, and when push came to shove, the strong relationships I had built with the grocery store managers saved me.

That was an important lesson I would take with me as I began my next chapter at P&G as a newly minted brand manager.

"You Have 24 Hours to Come Up with a New Idea."

One of the benefits of being in brand management at P&G is you are given an incredible amount of responsibility at a very young age. The part they don't tell you in the job description is you don't have much authority. That's because you were the brand manager of one of many brands in a division. For example, there were 13 brands in the Bar Soap and Household Cleaning Products (BS&HCP) Division when I was a brand manager.

As one of 13 brands—and one of about 80 brands in the company at the time—you were in constant competition for resources. Support from sales, artwork, media buying, marketing research, advertising strategy counsel, etc. were all "shared resources." This means if you were a small brand, you had your work cut out for you.

That's because if you were lucky enough to oversee one of the "mega-brands" such as Tide or Pampers, you could pretty much get anything you needed—you were too important to ignore. But if you oversaw one of the smaller brands—such as the ones I had, Spic and Span and Ivory—you could not assume anyone was going to go out of their way to help your brand. What you lacked in budget or sales, you had to make up for in creativity, charm, and focused determination.

A great example of this principle in action was when I was the brand manager of Spic and Span, and we were working on our marketing plans. Given the long lead times to get a promotion manufactured at the plant and sold in by the trade, you had to have everything agreed to well in advance. Sometimes this was as much as a year ahead of when the product was going to be "on the shelf" and available for purchase by consumers.

So, you can imagine my chagrin when my boss's boss at the time—Ross Love, the advertising manager of my division—called me into his office.

"Kip, I've been thinking about your next sales promotion for Spic and Span in February," he said, frowning—which was unusual for this normally upbeat guy.

"Sure, we're almost done with everything that's needed. It's 40 cents off a 64-ounce price pack promotion," I responded.

Ross looked at me. "That's just so boring," he declared.

"Well, I'll admit it's not the sexiest promotion we've ever run in the business, but we've done it plenty of times before, and it's worked," I countered.

Ross leaned across his desk and asked, "How much is it going to cost you to run that promotion?"

I opened my trusty Brand Fact Book, which I always brought to management meetings, and quickly found the answer: "If you include the value of the price pack and the television advertising, it comes to about half a million dollars."

Ross leaned back in his chair and stared at the ceiling: "I want you to imagine half a million dollars sitting in the corner of this office. And I want you to imagine lighting a match and watching it all burn. Because I think you're going to waste that much on a very tired price-off promotion. As I said, it's so *boring!*"

At this point I tried to appeal to his logic, explaining it was too late in the production process to make any major changes.

Ross cut me off and said, "Be quiet. Listen carefully to me. I've heard folks tell me you're a creative guy. I'm going to give you a chance to prove it. You have 24 hours to come up with a new idea. And it better be a lot more exciting than a boring 40 cents off price pack."

I didn't know what to say. And then Ross added, "Or I'm canceling your event."

I told him I'd be back in 24 hours and walked back down the hall in a state of shock. If I didn't pull this off somehow, I knew there was no chance of meeting the annual sales forecast. Canceling one of our key promotions would surely spell trouble for my brand as well as my career. Still, I was determined to try something—anything—to avoid that fate.

I instinctually knew I needed to tap my assistant marketing manager for Spic and Span, Doug Hall, who I had helped recruit to P&G several years before. Doug was one of the most creative folks I'd ever worked with, and I was counting on him to save the day for our brand.

I gave Doug the gloomy download from my meeting with Ross. He calmly replied, "Let me think about this tonight and let's talk in the morning. This could be fun."

I admired his positive attitude but was still nervous when we met for coffee the next morning.

Grinning, Doug asked me, "Have you ever heard of cubic zirconia?"

"No, I have not, and what does that have to do with Spic and Span?"

He explained he remembered Spic and Span had its 60th anniversary this year, which traditionally is the "diamond anniversary." His brilliant idea was to celebrate our brand anniversary by sprinkling "fake" diamonds (cubic zirconia) in the powder and liquid versions of the product. He'd already made some calls and calculated we could get these mock diamonds for about 10 cents each.

I was starting to get excited. "But we'd need thousands of them. Can we get enough?"

Doug smiled. "We'd have to pretty much buy up the entire world's supply of cubic zirconia but it's possible if we move quickly."

I continued to think about how we could pull this off. "What about getting the cubic zirconia in the product?"

Doug got up to write on my whiteboard. "I thought about that as well. You haven't heard the best part yet. We're going to mix real diamonds in with the fake ones. Diamonds have a huge markup—if we buy them wholesale, I figure we can buy 1,000 real ones and mix them with 50,000 fake ones. And we'd still be within our current budget!"

I was confused again. "But how would you be able to tell a real one from a fake?" I asked.

Doug continued, "I wondered that myself. So, I called a jeweler friend of mine and learned there's a machine in every jeweler's office where you can tell a real diamond from a fake. We could do a tie-in with the jewelers and drive traffic to their stores."

I was now starting to get very excited. "Doug, do you really think we can pull this off?"

"Well, given the choice of trying to do this or getting our promotion canceled, we don't have much of a choice here, do we?" Then he broke out into a huge grin.

I had to agree with that. Then another idea occurred to me.

"Wait a minute. Since this is a February event, let's tie it into Valentine's Day. I can see it now: Give your sweetie a box of chocolates, a dozen roses, and a package of Spic and Span for her big day!"

Doug loved the public relations tie-in to Valentine's Day. We ran down the hall to tell Ross. He agreed it was a big idea and to go for it. We had our work cut out for us, but I had to agree with Ross—this *was* a lot more fun than creating another boring price-off pack.

Over the next three months, what happened was a true testimony to the determination of my team to make this work, especially Doug. As you can imagine, the manufacturing team thought we had lost our minds. We ended up having to have security guards on the manufacturing line as the diamonds, both real and fake, were inserted into the product.

Our campaign—the "Spic and Span Diamond Jubilee"—proved to be a rousing success. *Consumer Reports* in later years claimed it was one of the "most audacious consumer promotions of all time," which I'll take as a compliment. We earned record levels—I'm talking hours—of TV coverage during Valentine's Day and hit an all-time sales record as well.

This reaffirmed in me the value of perseverance. I will always be grateful to Ross for challenging me and my team to think outside the box.

Sadly, Ross passed away years later at the young age of 55. I will always remember and admire him as someone willing to challenge the status quo. In hindsight, I see how he made waves in the name of helping us become better marketers. As the saying goes: "A smooth sea never makes a skilled sailor."

CHAPTER SIX
Perseverance—It Ain't Over till It's Over

REFLECTIVE QUESTIONS

- What's the toughest situation you've ever been in at school or work? What did you learn about yourself and the value of perseverance?

- What advice would you give about perseverance for someone facing a big challenge at work or school?

- When does it make sense to give up? When should you stick with something and push ahead?

- As you get older, do you find yourself being more determined or more flexible about getting the original outcome you desired?

- Complete this sentence: Every day I will become more _____. Discuss.

LEAP INTO ACTION

Everybody loves a comeback story—it's the most common plotline for Hollywood movies. When you are having a tough time dealing with whatever life is throwing at you, keep that "comeback" image alive in your mind in which the hero of the story—which is you—overcomes whatever it is that is out there trying to defeat you. Make your mental attitude of perseverance the award-winning soundtrack of your own life's movie.

A MOMENT OF ZEN

Be patient and play the long game.

Don't be in such a rush. Your career is a marathon, not a sprint. Take your time, learn as much as you can, and don't feel you have to race to get to the next level. Building a solid base of skills will more than pay off in the long term.

Be patient. Keep setting big goals and keep in mind that six months or a year doesn't matter in the long run. Always remember HOW you do things matters at least as much as WHAT you do. The people you touch, the relationships you build, are everything. They are the ones that will both hurt you (a couple of times) and help you repeatedly.

Don't waste time trying to find the wisest path for your professional life. Your instincts about what you really want to do with your life are better than you assume; abandon the voices of supposed wisdom telling you to ignore those instincts and warning you to not be foolish. Try to muster the courage to walk away rather than take the path that's more lucrative but wrong for you. Try to pursue what and whom you love, not what will best pay off.

Play the long game. There is no keeping score. Only a joint feeling of satisfaction and happiness from being of service.

07

Tolerance – When in Rome, Do as the Romans Do

*Tolerance: Allowing people to have their own opinions
and accepting ideas different from your own
without compromising your values*

> "The openness of our hearts and minds can be
> measured by how wide we draw the circle of what
> we call family." —Mother Teresa

SNEAK PEEK AT MY LEAP
**How I came to appreciate the value of different
cultures and people (and what happens when you don't).**

Despite advances in technology and travel, tolerance for people
different from our "tribe" unfortunately seems to be on the
decline. That's a real shame—there is so much we can come
to appreciate about ourselves when we try to learn about and
understand different cultures. Especially when there's such a
lot of world to see.

Growing up in Louisiana, I was exposed to French-Cajun culture at a very young age. I grew up with a real sense of pride in how Louisiana is different from the other 49 states. For starters, Cajun food is like nothing else in the U.S. It features a unique blend of spices from all over the world, mixed with seafood, poultry, blood sausage, and some fantastic ways of serving it all up—such as using a colossal paddle to stir the giant pot of jambalaya over an open flame.

Louisiana also bases its legal system on the Napoleonic Code, while all the other states were based on the British legal system. Even local governments are organized as parishes rather than counties.

I took French in junior high school rather than Spanish, which I would regret because knowing even basic Spanish would have been convenient later in my career. But I still love how the French language sounds.

In college, I earned money one summer going door-to-door doing survey work for the State of Louisiana. It was not unusual in Cajun country for someone to answer the door with "bonjour" rather than "hello."

A New Culture Awaits

While my upbringing made me very comfortable with French culture, I wasn't at all familiar with the Latino culture. But I didn't let that hold me back from an opportunity to become the general manager of Kentucky Fried Chicken (KFC) International for Northern Latin America. I assumed I could figure out Latino culture "on the fly," despite my total lack of Spanish language skills or familiarity with its culture or different geographic regions.

My territory was huge. It started in Bermuda, extended through the entire Caribbean, and included countries in Central and South America, including Costa Rica, Honduras, Nicaragua, Venezuela, Guyana, and Colombia. I would also be responsible for the company market of Trinidad. One of my primary goals was to establish the KFC brand in new markets in Central and South America, given the right opportunity and business partners.

Oh, and I should mention this was in the early 1990s when the illegal drug business was booming in South Florida. Colombia was one of the most dangerous countries in the world with ongoing "cocaine wars." I didn't fully appreciate any of this until I'd moved my family to Coral Springs, Florida. But at that stage, our moving boxes were unpacked, and it was time for me to get to work.

My weekly routine would be to head out either Sunday night or Monday morning to one or more of the countries I was responsible for overseeing. I would hopefully make it back to Miami International Airport (MIA), which I hoped wouldn't mean "missing in action" for me, by the end of the week.

This role was the most demanding job I'd ever had up to that point in my career. It was tough being on the road so much since both our sons were under the age of five. I was doing "on-the-job" self-training on how to deal with different people, languages, cultures, and issues along with the responsibility of managing my core team based in Fort Lauderdale, which included marketing, operations, finance, and so on.

The Most Intense Boss on the Planet

To top it all off, I was working for (let's call him Ben) one of the most demanding bosses I've ever had. To say Ben was intense would be an understatement. Everything he did, he did with total focus, including physical fitness. He took great pride in his physique and healthy eating habits, constantly reminding us he never consumed caffeine, even though he now sold fried chicken for a living.

One Monday at the office, he complained at our staff meeting that he had worn out his exercise bike over the weekend—one of my earliest recollections of a "humblebrag." He wrote to the manufacturer to complain. They wrote him back with a lot of skepticism that this could have happened. Ben then shipped them his exercise bike as proof, and they sent him a new exercise bike, declaring that no one in the history of their company had ever worn out a piece of their equipment. That was an excellent metaphor for what it was like working for Ben.

When you would go out on a trip with Ben to visit KFC franchisees, our day would start at 6:00 a.m., after Ben finished his five-mile morning run. You would not only see all the KFC restaurants in that city or locale—you would visit *every single fast-food restaurant*. It was exhausting.

Franchisees hated these visits since nothing was ever good enough for Ben. He was constantly criticizing them. You would be so wiped out after being on the road with him for a week you had to tag-team with someone else on the regional staff since two weeks straight with Ben would have been unbearable.

Ben's aggressiveness sometimes got us into scary, dangerous situations. For example, Ben and I were invited to come to Honduras to meet with some prospective franchisees. Pizza Hut had already opened restaurants there, so we figured it could be a potential market for KFC.

When Ben and I arrived in San Pedro Sula, Honduras, for our first visit, I was surprised to see Pizza Huts with security guards holding machine guns standing outside the front door—not exactly inviting for an outing with your family on a Saturday night. San Pedro Sula was, and unfortunately still is, considered one of the most dangerous cities in the world, with one of the highest murder rates anywhere and an ongoing plague of kidnappings, extortion, and corruption. And my dinner companion was going to be my boss, famous for his short temper and aggressiveness toward current and prospective franchisees.

Ben and I were scheduled to meet our franchisee prospects at a nice restaurant on the evening of our arrival. After landing at the airport, we had our driver take us around the town a bit before dinner. The tremendous poverty and lack of decent roads were shocking. The threat of crime was real. I was ready to get this dinner meeting over with and get the hell out of there.

Ben and I waited in front of the restaurant, and a huge Mercedes Benz pulled up. The chauffeur got out and opened the door for our host. As he got out, the driver went around to the Mercedes' other side to open the other rear door. So, I decided to close the car door for the driver. When I tried to close the car door, I was surprised at how heavy it was.

Then it dawned on me: This was a bulletproof car! What kind of franchisee needs a chauffeur and bulletproof car?

After some small talk at the table, Ben started laying out all the requirements to become a franchisee. While everything Ben was describing was accurate, it was the aggressive way he said it that concerned me. As the dinner progressed, I could tell our franchisee prospects were getting the same vibe.

Soon there was finger-pointing by Ben at our hosts and raised voices. When the conversation switched over to rapid-fire Spanish— which Ben was fluent in and I was not—I knew it was time for us to get out of there.

When I suggested we wrap it up since we had an early morning flight, our franchisee prospects insisted we drink a traditional local espresso before leaving. While I make it a strict rule not to drink any coffee other than in the morning, I was more than happy to drink anything short of arsenic to be able to leave for our hotel. I looked at Ben and could tell he was conflicted since he was always bragging about how he had never consumed anything with caffeine in it.

Thankfully, Ben didn't raise any objections, which would have significantly offended our hosts. We drained our shot glasses of a very dark beverage. It was the equivalent of drinking pure liquid caffeine and tasted horrible. I didn't care. All I could think of was how soon I could get back to the hotel and out of this scary city.

I was so exhausted from being with Ben all week, especially after a nerve-wracking dinner, I immediately fell asleep when we returned to the hotel. When I went to the lobby at 6:00 a.m for our regular departure time, there was no Ben in sight. I called his room—no answer. I turned around and saw him walking quickly down the hall. He looked like someone recovering from a major shock to the system—in this case, caffeine. He had not slept at all that night.

I almost felt sorry for Ben as we headed to the airport. Still, I was keenly aware of how easy it was to offend potential business partners from that point on. I vowed to try to be as open as possible to create a common ground to work together. Especially in places where upsetting the wrong person could have severe personal consequences. This was the start of my learning how to become more tolerant and adapting quickly to new business environments and situations.

An Incredible Place to Work

Since almost all my revenue came out of the existing markets in the Caribbean, that's where I initially focused my time and effort. Anyone reading this could be thinking, "This has got to be one of the greatest gigs in the world. You're getting paid to go to places that others pay big bucks to go on vacation!"

It's partly true. The Caribbean is a unique, beautiful part of the world. Every time your plane touches down, you are in a different country with a foreign language, culture, history, and heritage—every language from Spanish to Creole to French to Dutch to English. I had KFC franchisees in 16 countries in the Caribbean and visited all of them several times.

Most of my franchisees were an absolute pleasure to work with and get to know. I had never worked with so many millionaires in my life. You see, on many of the islands, KFC was the only fast-food restaurant available, and sometimes even one restaurant could generate millions in annual sales.

On paper, the airlines flew to all my markets. Some of the airlines were, shall we say, less than reliable. There were two airlines I tried to avoid if possible: BWIA or British West Indies Airways, nicknamed

"Been Waiting in Airport," which went out of business in 2006; and LIAT or Leeway Island Air Transport, nicknamed "Leaving Island Any Time."

Whenever I was traveling to the Caribbean, I would tell my wife Peggy every Monday, "I'll see you on Friday, I hope." That's because I knew I would be on "island time," which was not just a cute expression. It recognized that while travel schedules are an excellent idea in theory, sometimes they just don't happen the way they are supposed to. Navigating your way through the Caribbean or Latin America can be a weekly test of your personal tolerance for delays and unexpected problems that come up on a regular basis while traveling.

"You Have to Leave NOW!"

Let me give you an example. One Friday morning, I wrapped up a very productive week of island hopping, which concluded with my Martinique visit. I was sitting in a quaint cafe enjoying croissants with the franchisee in Fort-de-France, the country's capital. My plane was leaving later that morning, but it was just a short ride to the airport. So, I was relishing a rare moment of relaxation before hitting the road again for the flight home. The restaurant looked like something out of a travel commercial: sunlight streaming through the window of an old French cafe with delicious food and coffee. Perfect!

The peaceful quiet of the morning was shattered when the franchise operations manager came bursting into the cafe and ran up to our table, drenched in sweat, yelling, "MONSIEUR, YOU HAVE TO LEAVE NOW!!!"

I was baffled. It was several hours before my flight was due to leave. The airport was a short 10-minute drive from where we were seated, enjoying breakfast. I asked, "Why the rush?"

He looked increasingly frantic as he leaned closer to my face and exclaimed, "ZE TAXIES! ZEY ARE ALL ON STRIKE. YOU MUST LEAVE **NOW**, MONSIEUR!"

This request didn't make any sense to me at all. I could not for the life of me understand why he seemed so concerned. I took a sip of my delicious French coffee, still not registering why he was so frantic. I calmly asked him who would be willing to drive me to the airport if the taxis were not an option.

I thought the operations manager was going to have a heart attack as his face flushed red. He started waving his arms all over the place. "YOU DO NOT UNDERSTAND, MONSIEUR! ZE TAXI DRIVERS, THEY HAVE BLOCKED ZE ROADS!"

Now it was my turn to panic. I instantly recalled seeing news footage of infamous cab strikes in Paris. The taxicab union there had perfected the art of bringing traffic to a complete standstill. And by the sound of it, they had been sharing some best practices among their fellow French cab drivers here in Fort-de-France.

I instantly grabbed my luggage and headed for the door. "What are my options?" I yelled as we ran to the street. The franchisee and ops manager were running alongside me. "Your only hope is to go to the local bus station and see if you can get on a bus that goes near the airport. Sometimes the taxi drivers will give the bus drivers a break."

I was hoping my junior high school French class might prove to be of some use as I ran toward the bus station just down the street. After some awkward conversations in French with several folks waiting for a bus, I managed to get on one, supposedly heading in the general direction of the airport.

We didn't get very far. At the end of the Fort-de-France business district, the roads were already blocked. Not with cabs as I expected, but with big rigs that were much more effective at blocking both lanes of traffic as well as the shoulders. Oh no, these guys *were* professionals.

None of this deterred our bus driver. He turned the bus around and headed east in the opposite direction. We encountered the same scene on the opposite side of the business district with a fast-growing traffic mess. We headed north only to find the roads there blocked as well.

Same situation when we tried to get out of town on the south roads. These taxi drivers were downright brilliant in how they executed their roadblocks. No car or bus was going to get in or out of Fort-de-France during this taxi strike.

In the meantime, my comfortable margin of time was quickly slipping away. We had spent over an hour driving to the various roadblocks. I had a little over one hour left to figure out how to get to the airport for the one daily flight back to Miami.

The bus passengers were getting more and more agitated and urged the bus driver to keep trying. After initially declaring he had tried all the roads, someone suddenly yelled out something in French. At first, the bus driver looked back at the crowd with a look of surprise and hesitation but then shrugged his shoulders and turned the bus down a small alleyway toward the end of town. I wondered where we were going now.

Here's a fun geographic fact about Fort-de-France in Martinique, which is a French department or territory: the city is surrounded by an ancient chain of five volcanoes called Pitons du Carbet. They rise to a height of almost 4,000 feet. There were a few mountain passes leading out of town on ancient, narrow dirt roads, but they were more suited for a small car or motorcycle, and certainly not a bus.

The taxi drivers had systematically blocked all the main roads that allow traffic to go over these inactive volcanoes. The one road left was made of dirt many years ago that hardly anyone used anymore due to safety concerns. No one would be crazy enough to drive on that eroded road through the rainforest mountains, with the one exception being our bus driver.

I could not believe this guy would try to get on that dirt road with this overloaded bus. If our bus fell over the edge, the authorities would not even know it for a week, given the rainforest's thick undergrowth. But he was going to give it a try. So up and up we went. I decided it would be best for me not to look out the bus window over the road's edge, which dropped straight down into who knows what.

The ride up and over the volcano ridge took 45 minutes but felt like a lifetime to me. When we finally got on the other side of the mountains onto a flat paved road, a cheer from the bus passengers was offered to the driver. Five minutes later, I could see a sign indicating the Martinique airport and runway were very close. This was in the early 1990s, and the airport was the size of a Greyhound bus station in a small town in Iowa.

In very broken French, I asked the driver to please stop the bus. I sprinted the last 200 yards across the field to try to make it to the plane in time.

I burst through the doors of the small airport building and ran straight up to the counter. This was before travelers went through any kind of security in the Caribbean before getting on a plane. The attendant behind the counter smiled at me and asked how she could be of assistance.

Out of breath, I handed her my U.S. passport and ticket and told her I needed to get on the flight to Miami. She smiled and told me, "*Monsieur, une minute,*" as she disappeared inside another room behind the counter. I looked at my watch. It was just 10 minutes before takeoff. It was going to be close, but I just might make it.

The attendant was not gone for an *une* minute. It was more like *dix* minutes. I was getting frantic since my flight would be taking off any time now.

I practically yelled at her when she returned to the counter. "Where have you been? My flight is just about to take off!".

A look of surprise crossed her face. "Oh, monsieur, pardon. You want to go *TODAY?*" I could hear the engines starting up on the plane I was supposed to be on. I ran to a window to watch in frustration as it headed down the runway.

Just like the bus driver, I was not going to go down without a fight. I went back to the counter and asked the ticket agent if any other flights were leaving that day heading northwest toward Miami. There was a LIAT flight heading to Antigua, going in a couple of hours. We quickly looked in the printed flight schedule to find any connections from Antigua to Miami. There was just one late in the day, but I would still get back to Miami later that same day. Success!

When I landed in Antigua mid-afternoon, I was surprised that this "airport" was even smaller than the one I left in Martinique. Not even a regular size building—more like a shed next to a runway with one security guard watching over everything in a fenced airfield. I asked the guard to confirm when the flight to Miami left. Just like the schedule called for, it would be taking off in 4 1/2 hours. I thanked the airport guard, and he phoned for a cab to take me into St. John's, the main town of Antigua.

The KFC franchisee in Antigua could not have been more gracious. He was delighted to see me and was justifiably proud of his restaurant, which did over $1M in sales every year. His operations looked great, and his KFC team was excited to see me since they didn't get visitors from HQ very often. I decided to play it safe and get back to the airfield a full 90 minutes before my flight was scheduled to take off for Miami.

As I got out of the taxi at the airfield, the same security guard approached me and started laughing. I could see a twin-engine propeller plane heading down the runway in the fading light of day and heard the engine rev up.

I looked at the security guard, perplexed. "What is going on? Is that the flight I'm supposed to be on? That LIAT flight is not supposed to leave for at least another hour!"

The guard looked at me and smiled. "Hey man, the pilot, he's got a hot date in Miami tonight, so he left early." When folks had told me LIAT meant "leaving island any time," I had assumed it meant they were always late. I hadn't considered it could also mean leaving early for pilots looking forward to a hot date in another city. I thought to myself: *I had just been LIATed.*

I finally got back to my family in Florida the next day. Rather than get angry, I gradually learned this was just part of the job, and it didn't do any good to get upset. If you were delayed, just accept it and do the best you can. If you got home when you originally planned, that was a big bonus for the week.

Adventures in Latin America

As challenging as my Caribbean markets were, they were easy compared to what I had to deal with in South America. While the Caribbean franchisees and my company market in Trinidad provided a solid base of revenue for my region, the only way I could grow the total revenue was by opening at least one new market, such as Costa Rica, Venezuela or Colombia.

Given my lack of understanding of the Latino markets, I thought it would be helpful to spend some time in our Puerto Rico company market with Eddie, my general manager in Trinidad. We arrived at the office on a Monday afternoon, and I went looking for Angel, the Puerto Rico business head.

"Buen dia, Angel!" I declared in my best attempt to sound like I was at least trying to pick up some Spanish as we walked past all the others already in the office. I immediately headed to the main conference room and sat down. "Eddie and I are ready to learn!"

Angel was not happy. He asked me if I realized what I had just done. I told him we'd come to the office, and we were ready to get to work.

Angel looked at Eddie and me and explained, "You need to understand something about this culture. People will not want to work with you unless they trust you. And they will not trust you until they get to know you. And they will not know you unless you take the time to get to know them."

So, we went back to the open office area. We went to each desk and spent about five to ten minutes getting introduced to each team member. We learned about their families. How long they had been with KFC and what Angel thought was unique about that person.

This took us over an hour. When we finally made it back to the conference room, Angel sat down, smiled, and said, "Now we are ready to begin." This was the start of a close friendship with Angel, which I still enjoy to this day.

Learning How to Open a New Market

Once I had spent enough time in Mexico and Puerto Rico learning their best practices, I decided it was time to expand KFC into some new markets. Costa Rica seemed like an ideal choice, since it had a stable government, a booming economy, and a friendly business environment. The biggest challenge we faced was that it had been years since anyone had opened a new market for KFC International. In addition to opening this new market, we would have to create the process needed to do this successfully, since there was no existing documentation on how to plan market expansions.

One of the most talented operators I've ever had the pleasure to work with was Richard Eisenberg, and I was fortunate to have him join my team when he did. Richard was still in his 20s but already had some extensive experience in running KFCs in Florida. When he joined my team as head of operations, he was terrific at figuring out everything needed to open a new market.

We determined there were over 150 separate workflows that all needed to be coordinated. We documented everything from site selection to vendor qualifications to government permits to equipment procurement to crew training. Richard pulled all this together in a comprehensive document, which was the basis for our successful launch in Costa Rica and many markets that followed.

I was delighted when Richard bought out the Costa Rica franchise later in his career and started one of the most successful QSR (Quick

Service Restaurant) businesses in Central America, which included KFC and several other leading brands.

We decided we would tackle Colombia next. This was a market we had never tried before, and I thought it looked promising despite many problems with the overall country, which included crime, corruption, and lack of regulations. I was contacted by a chicken grower, Carlos, in Bogota and I decided to fly down to meet with him. Since kidnapping was a growing problem at the time, I went out of my way not to call attention to myself. I dressed like a college student, and Carlos picked me up at the airport in a rundown vehicle.

As we drove to my hotel, we passed by the local fried chicken competition. It was the weirdest-looking restaurant I'd ever seen. It had no windows and was built like a fortress. When I asked Carlos why they would make a restaurant like that, he indicated it was actually a massive money-laundering operation, and the chicken business was only an excuse for moving cash through the books. "OK," I thought, "So much for visiting competitor restaurants on this visit."

Carlos turned out to be a fantastic franchisee who created a profitable business through the vertical integration of his chicken farms and KFC restaurants. There are over 20 KFCs in Columbia today in a number of other cities around the country. I haven't been back to Bogota in more than twenty years, but I understand the tourist business is booming, and kidnapping is no longer a significant risk. Bogota was a beautiful city when I visited—at least from what I saw while driving around with Carlos, since I didn't dare do any sightseeing while I was there like I did in other markets. I'm happy the country is doing better now.

My favorite story about working in Latin America didn't even involve a Spanish-speaking market. It happened in Guyana, the only South American nation where English is the official language. Just like Carlos had done, a chicken farmer by the name of Paul called my office in Fort Lauderdale and asked for me to get in contact with him.

After several long phone calls, I decided there was enough potential there that it merited a visit.

I went to my boss Ben and told him about my plans. He turned his office chair around and picked up his copy of the *Economist World in Figures*. He turned the pages until he found what he was looking for.

Reading from the *Economist*, he stated, "Guyana is the poorest country in the Western Hemisphere." He closed the book and looked at me. "A trip down there would just be a waste of time and money."

I pointed out to Ben that many times those types of official reports didn't capture the real cash or underground economy, so I didn't think that information by itself was enough of a reason not to go. Ben looked at me and said, "It's your call, but you are wasting your time. Any restaurant in that market is doomed to fail." I figured one advantage would be Ben didn't want to go with me to visit the prospect, so that was a big plus in trying to make this work.

I set up a visit for my finance manager, Bob, and me to fly to Georgetown in Guyana. The only thing I knew about Guyana was the site of the infamous Jonestown massacre in November 1978. Jim Jones had created a religious cult in the jungle, which he called "Jonestown," that attracted many American citizens who followed him there. When Congressman Leo Ryan of California went there to investigate reports of abuse, he and his party were ambushed by Jim Jones's henchmen.

The congressman was killed along with a cult defector and three reporters who were with the group. Jim Jones then ordered everyone in the cult to kill themselves by drinking laced punch—hence the phrase "drink the Kool-Aid" even though Kool-Aid wasn't the actual beverage consumed. More than 900 people died in Jonestown, one of the worst mass killings of Americans in U.S. history.

As we flew into the Georgetown airport, I kept looking for the airfield in the jungle below. When I finally spotted the runway, I was shocked. It was a small strip of clearing in the middle of the Amazon. After we pulled up to the saddest looking "airport terminal" I'd ever seen—and I've seen some bad ones—Bob looked at me as we landed and declared, "Well, now when I die, I don't think I'll have to worry about going to hell. We just landed there."

Our prospective franchisee Paul was eagerly waiting for us inside the terminal. As we drove back to Georgetown in his Jeep, I noticed a knock-off "Kentucky Fried Chicken" in the downtown area. I asked Paul what that was all about.

"Oh, they have been here for years. We'll challenge them in court and win."

"Great," I thought, "not only does my boss think this is a bad idea, now we've got to fight just to get our trademark back."

The inside of Paul's office looked like something out of a Charles Dickens' novel. It was as if we had taken a time machine back to the late 1880s. Everything was old and dusty and looked worn out. But outside, there was a real bustle to the town. Many folks were buying and selling in the local marketplace, and no one had the look of abject poverty. Based on the number of food vendors who had set up shop, I could see how a KFC could be very successful.

We sat down in Paul's office. He was excited that we were there to see him. Paul looked at us and asked, "OK, how do we get started? What can I do to help?"

The fake KFC we had passed coming into town was bugging me, so I thought that would be an excellent issue to get out of the way. "Paul, it's going to be a real problem if we can't get that restaurant to change the name of its business." Paul asked what I recommended.

"Well, have you talked to anyone at the U.S. Embassy? Perhaps they could give us some advice on who to talk to about trademark enforcement."

Paul's face lit up. "Not a problem! Let's go see the U.S. Ambassador right now! I know him!"

This was not the response I was expecting. I'd never been to a U.S. Embassy before nor met an ambassador, and here was a chicken farmer in Guyana telling me we would visit one that morning.

Paul picked up his office phone and dialed a number. After a couple of minutes of discussion, he hung up and declared, "The ambassador will be waiting for us at the embassy."

As we drove to the grounds of the embassy, I was amazed at how big it was. I later learned in the mid-1980s, the president of Guyana started to strengthen relations with the Soviet Union and looked to form a political alliance with the local Communist Party. The Reagan Administration spared no expense in turning the U.S. Embassy in Guyana into quite the showplace when that happened.

We went through security and were ushered into the ambassador's office. We waited a few minutes in his office, then he came bursting through the door.

"I hear you are going to be bringing the Colonel and Original Recipe to Guyana! That's exciting news!" he declared.

Since I'm sure that the last time "The Colonel" was mentioned in this room it probably referred to a South American dictator, I could understand the launch of KFC here might have been a welcome addition to bringing America to this part of the world.

The ambassador and his team at the embassy were extremely helpful in getting KFC up and running. We were able to get our trademark back, and the local government was very supportive in helping clear the various permits needed to open the restaurant. It opened a year later, and I was pleasantly surprised when it set a world record in first-year sales for a single KFC restaurant in the Western Hemisphere—over $3 million in sales. It was satisfying to prove *The Economist* is not the best reference source when selecting where to open a new fast-food restaurant in a developing country. Sometimes you must trust your gut and just go for it.

The Personal Price of Ignoring Culture

Shortly after my trip to Guyana, my boss Ben was demoted to general manager of KFC Mexico. He had burned too many political bridges with his management back in Louisville. Even though he was originally from Canada, since he was fluent in Spanish, I figured he'd do just fine there and maybe even make a career comeback. But this was not to be the case.

Shortly upon arriving at the KFC headquarters in Mexico City, Ben issued three official announcements to the entire Mexican team:

- Everyone would now be coming to work in a branded polo shirt to show solidarity with the restaurant teams.
- Lunch would be no more than 30 minutes.
- Company holidays would be reduced from 21 to 12.

Given Ben's financial background, I'm sure he thought these were needed changes to the business. But the reaction from his Mexican team was predictable. Within a short amount of time, they rebelled. They had worked hard to get into a professional role and took pride in wearing a suit and tie to the office. They used long lunches to get to know their colleagues and discuss various business issues. The family was core to their lives, and not spending holidays with family members was deeply insulting.

Ben was fired six months after he took the new role, and the Mexican office went back to the way it had been run before. There's a lot of merit in the expression, "When in Rome, do as the Romans do." When it comes to being tolerant, I learned through Ben there are some things, such as local culture, that must be understood and respected if you are going to be successful in working with a team.

REFLECTIVE QUESTIONS

- How open and tolerant are you to new cultures and traditions? Are you curious to learn more about them or prefer to stick with what you are already comfortable and familiar with?

- How tolerant are you of people with different values and beliefs? Do you wish you were more tolerant, or are you happy with how you currently feel?

- What's the best thing about the country you live in? What's the worst aspect? Think of three other countries and ask/answer the same questions.

- Other than the country you are currently living in, which three countries do you admire the most? Why?

LEAP INTO ACTION

There are a number of key factors in your life totally out of your control—where and when you were born, who your parents were, what country you were born in, etc. Once you appreciate the randomness of how you started out in this world, you can more fully understand the importance of tolerance when trying to "walk a mile" in another person's shoes. Whenever you find yourself becoming a bit judgmental, just ask yourself, "What if they're right?"

A MOMENT OF ZEN

Beware of trying to get "wisdom" too quickly.

It is dangerous to talk about wisdom. Knowledge has to do with facts. Wisdom has to do with judgment. It is nuanced. For me, wisdom needs to be fluid and can often feel like mercury moving and reshaping every time it is touched. Knowledge is tangible, while wisdom is an art form.

Mistakes are how you learn and are the basis for what you become later in life. The value is in the journey itself.

08

Greatness – Stay Calm and Carry On

Greatness: Pursuing big dreams no matter how difficult the journey; a willingness to step out of comfort zones and doing what will benefit ourselves and others the most

> *"Life is not always a matter of holding good cards, but sometimes playing a good hand well." —Jack London*

SNEAK PEEK AT MY LEAP
How I learned about the power of being on a talented team with a visionary leader (and why you should always praise in public and coach in private).

Humans have a natural desire to be a part of something bigger than themselves and do something that will be here after their time on this planet is up. Other than children, one way to do this is to help launch a new business or help turn a failing business around. If you are lucky enough to be a part of a team that does this, it doesn't get any better in the business world.

I first visited the U.K. during the summer of my senior year in high school. I had always fantasized about going back to work there. In 1994, I got my wish.

As part of its overall business strategy, PepsiCo wanted to diversify beyond soft drinks and salted snacks, so it created one of the world's largest restaurant businesses. In 1977, PepsiCo's acquisition of Pizza Hut for $320 million, expanded to include Taco Bell in 1978 for $125 million, and finished with Kentucky Fried Chicken's purchase in 1986 for $850 million. Not only would these restaurant brands be a steady generator of cash; they would also be an ideal way to ensure the public was able to sample and purchase their carbonated beverage brands —just like Coke depends on McDonald's and other quick service restaurants, called QSRs, to achieve the same business objective.

I'd been working solely on the KFC international business since I joined PepsiCo in 1990, and it was relatively weak outside the U.S. The U.K. was KFC's first international market, which started in 1965 and was currently managed very poorly via a joint venture with a U.K. hotel management company. Some KFC restaurants were beginning to open in continental Europe, such as Paris, and there were plans to expand in Eastern Europe after the Iron Curtain's fall in 1989. But overall, the revenue in Europe was relatively small except for the U.K. business.

KFC also had a presence in South Africa, with the first unit opening in 1971. But the company had to sell its 60 restaurants to a local S.A. company, DevCo, in 1987 when the U.S. Congress voted to stop apartheid by passing a law outlawing American companies from owning any South African assets. By late 1993, there was every indication apartheid was coming to an end, and PepsiCo could plan to repurchase their restaurants.

Moving to London

The senior management of PepsiCo wanted to grow its global restaurant business significantly. PepsiCo Restaurants International's management decided to put together a team to relocate to London, set up shop, and manage all KFC businesses in Europe and South Africa. They asked me if I'd consider going over as the director of marketing. Even though I knew this would be a big challenge, I didn't hesitate to move to London. I flew over the first week in January 1994 to meet with my new boss, Peter Hearl—an Aussie—and the rest of the newly assembled management team.

Peter would turn out to be one of the best bosses I've ever had. But neither one of us fully realized how thoroughly messed up the KFC business was when we accepted our new assignments. As someone asked Peter shortly after he arrived, "Did you take this job because you couldn't get a real job in Australia?"

I initially visited with many of the teams involved in running the business, including franchisees who ran 220 of the 300 restaurants in the U.K. I was surprised to learn how bad it was. Most restaurants were located next to pubs, and the overwhelming number of KFC customers were young drunk males. KFC's popular nickname was "Kentucky Fried Rat" and was the constant butt of comedian jokes on local TV programs. Rumor had it the KFC bucket was a convenient package to throw up in after you stumbled out of the pub to get something to eat before boarding the train home.

After a couple of weeks of getting as much data as possible, I concluded the KFC U.K. business was in big trouble. Even though the brand had started in 1965, an entire decade before McDonald's or Burger King, the KFC business had fallen way behind in terms of outlets, revenue, and customer base. The facilities were run down and used "the hairy arm" to get the food from the kitchen in the back to the counter person in the front. That is to say, the kitchen was behind a wall, and when the food was ready, a hairy arm would hold the food for the counter person, who then gave it to the customer. There were no drive-thrus at all in the U.K., which was vital since drive-thrus typically generate half of a typical fast-food restaurant's volume.

The former managing director in charge of the KFC U.K. business was from the joint venture partner, Forte, and only had previous business experience running hotels. I count my blessings I never had to work for him. He was a hot mess in terms of leadership and management skills.

His workday started late in the afternoon and went until late into the night. His marketing plan was totally ineffective, and the previous year's marketing budget had been significantly overspent.

The U.K. economy was struggling with a recession with over 10% unemployment. Our franchisees were unhappy and not optimistic that this new team from outside the U.K. could figure out how to turn this business around.

What Do We Do Now?

With my mind reeling from all this bad news, Peter invited me to meet him in central London a month after arriving. I was a bit surprised when he told me to meet him at the McDonald's located at Marble Arch next to Buckingham Palace.

Peter and I ordered some food at McDonald's and sat down. Peter smiled and asked how I was doing. I decided to be blunt.

"Peter, this KFC business is a total disaster. We've got declining sales, unhappy franchisees, a lousy economy, and tough competition. Did you have any idea what you signed up for when you took this assignment?" I asked.

Peter continued to smile. He said he had something to show me. He pulled out a color sketch of Colonel Sanders, the KFC founder, standing on a podium. The Colonel was bending over to receive a gold medal. Standing next to him on a lower podium was Ronald McDonald, the mascot for McDonald's. Ronald did not look at all happy.

Peter gestured dramatically around the McDonald's dining area. "It's great to have a worthy competitor. These guys are good, but they are not unbeatable. We've got better food and a great story to tell. We've just got to get everyone on our team to believe we can win."

I thought it was crazy to think we could beat McDonald's in the U.K. but admired Peter for at least wanting to give it a try. I told him neither of us had a choice at this point—we were already here, and our families were on their way to join us—so we might as well give it everything we had and see what we could do.

Peter's optimism was contagious. I left the McDonald's restaurant feeling energized and started thinking about how we could begin to turn this business around.

Having worked on the KFC business in numerous Latin American markets, I knew there was a trio of fundamentals we could leverage in creating a solid business strategy to compete effectively against McDonald's:

- **Family Focus**—Colonel Sanders started his business by offering meals to folks passing by his gas station in Kentucky. He'd invite them to stay awhile and join his family for dinner. His Original Recipe chicken and sides were perfect for time-starved parents to feed their family.

- **Real Food**—One of KFC's biggest strengths was the quality of the product, including the delicious sides we offered. McDonald's was a desirable choice for lunch, but we could be the dinner choice among future customers, especially busy parents. We could highlight that all our products were made in-store from fresh ingredients, and our chicken had the Colonel's secret recipe of eleven herbs and spices. Beat that, Micky D!

- **Value**—Given the severe current economic conditions in the U.K., we would need to create a compelling, ongoing value offering if we were going to attract new customers to start getting their meals from KFC. Having great food would not be enough to be competitive—we needed to deliver it at a great value as well.

Robust business strategies should be simple enough to write on the back of a business card. This one certainly qualified: *Family Focus*, *Real Food*, and *Value*. Those three pillars could be the start of a comeback for KFC in the U.K. and could also be the foundation of expanding the brand in Europe.

The following week, I sat down with my marketing team and new advertising agency, and we started to work on what our marketing strategy would be in terms of a plan and execution. Since we didn't have many families currently using our brand, we decided we would need to shift our marketing efforts to attract them to come to KFC.

We came up with a simple idea: create a fantastic meal for a family of four at an unbelievable price. We would offer eight chicken pieces, two large sides, and a 1.5 liter of Pepsi for the incredible price of £9.99, equivalent to around $15. We would brand it as the "Family Feast." The aggressive price point was vital, since it would be easy to remember and screamed "What A Deal!"

I checked with the lawyers and was relieved we could get the trademark for "Family Feast." I made sure we secured the trademark before our first ad would air, since I knew our competition would mimic it immediately if it worked.

While the profit margin percentage would be lower than other promotional offers, the absolute profit per transaction would be higher. As I reminded our finance team and my franchisees when they balked at the proposed price, I reminded them you take money to the bank, not percentages.

An Important Lesson in How to Build Consensus

Before we could launch the Family Feast, I knew we would need our franchisees's support because they ran 220 of our 300 U.K. restaurants. Keith, the former head of operations for the company, was now a successful franchisee with a dozen restaurants in Norfolk, an area north of London. He was also head of the U.K. KFC Franchise Council, a group that could either give us the support needed to kick off our new marketing program off successfully or bring it to a screeching halt.

I asked Keith if I could come to the Franchise Council's next meeting and share our proposed marketing plans. He told me I was welcome to drive to Norfolk and pitch my plans at a local hotel where they would be meeting. My team put a lot of effort into my presentation and included all the compelling reasons this was worthy of franchisee support.

I made the drive to Norfolk, knowing what was at stake. After I finished my presentation to the Franchise Council, Keith told me to step outside and wait in the hallway for their decision.

I waited for what seemed like an eternity. When Keith finally came out to see me, he had a serious look on his face.

"OK, Kip, here's the good news. We like you, and we're willing to support your new marketing plan," he stated.

I felt like a huge weight had just been lifted off my shoulders. But then Keith frowned and continued, "But if you ever come in here again and disrespect us, we will never support you in the future."

I was baffled. I did not recall saying anything I would consider disrespectful during my presentation.

Keith explained that while I didn't say anything directly negative about them when I was summarizing the business's current state, it seemed like I was delivering an implied condemnation on all the hard work they had done in the past 30 years in building their business.

Keith continued, "Keep in mind the only reason any of us are here tonight is due to all the work we've done to create this business in the first place. It might not be perfect, but it's profitable and has plenty of customers."

Keith's counsel was some of the best feedback and business advice I've ever received in my life. What I learned from that encounter is that if you are trying to partner with someone working on a business that's in trouble, it's critical to acknowledge what IS working first.

The first step for a business turnaround is to authentically recognize the folks who came before you to create the business in the first place. In many instances, the answer to turning a failing company around is to go back and appreciate what led to its initial success. Only after you've noted what got the business this far can you then plot out where the opportunities might be for future growth. If you skip the appreciation part, you can forget about creating any kind of viable business partnership.

The Start of a Turnaround

Once the franchisees were on board with our new marketing strategy, we launched our first Family Feast promotion backed with a new TV campaign. One significant aspect of the QSR business is you don't have to wait long to determine if a new idea is working or not. You'll typically know in a matter of days. A new campaign can launch on a Friday night, and by Monday morning, you can be sharing the good or bad news with your management team.

We were all thrilled when the launch of the U.K. Family Feast was a hit! It quickly became 30% of the revenue mix, and half of that was incremental—in other words, we went from declining sales to double-digit growth in a short amount of time. We put our QSR competition in a tough spot, since there wasn't a comparable offer they could make for a family meal since they were in the sandwich business. This initial marketing win was critical to establishing credibility with our franchisees and the rest of the company. Everyone loves to be on a winning team, and this was strong evidence we could compete against McDonald's and the rest of the fast-food competitors in the U.K.

Once the U.K. business started to turn around, we turned our attention to the rest of our region. Peter oversaw all of Europe and South Africa, not just the U.K., so he knew he needed a management team that was collaborative, innovative, and had a shared sense of purpose. Since we were a multi-national team that had never worked together before, he wanted to have an offsite that would enable us to become a high-performance team in a short amount of time. He'd heard a local British company, Raeburn Keslake, was just the company to host such an event and begin this transformation.

Management Offsite in Hell

The overall philosophy of Raeburn Keslake was that to create a strong team, you must destroy the current one. They believed in tough-minded team development. As one of their facilitators later explained to me when I asked why they did what they did, he explained they did their best work when an organization needed to generate a new range of behaviors to meet future challenges.

In other words, imagine a vendor that creates a management offsite that is a combination of Outward Bound, Navy SEALs Hell Week, and *The Hunger Games*. We had no idea what we were signing up for but were about to find out.

Our offsite trip (i.e. a business team meeting held outside the office) was going to be held over three days in the West Country, a beautiful part of England located about five hours by car west of greater London. We would arrive by lunch on Wednesday and would leave by lunch on Friday. That is all we were told in terms of the schedule. The only other message we got was, "Get ready for an experience you'll remember for the rest of your life."

As I drove out to the hotel with our development director, we speculated on what we would be doing. He had been with the U.K. KFC company for a decade and was excited to join this new expanded European team.

We got to the hotel and were given our schedule. After lunch, the first item was a session entitled "Hope and Fears," where team members were to outline their expectations and anxieties for this offsite. I'd been to many management offsites before, but it seemed unusual to me that we would be talking about what we were worried about to kick off this offsite. Especially since the discussion wasn't about what you were concerned about regarding the business—it was about what you were personally worried about. What were we about to get into? A group therapy session?

After about thirty minutes of sharing our thoughts about our worries, we were told to go to the next room to change into the outfits we would need for the next part of the program called "Canary." Our clothing consisted of heavy overalls, gloves, boots, helmets with headlights, and a 20-foot length of rope. We were told to quickly change and get on a bus that was waiting outside.

After riding on the bus for about 20 minutes, we all got out at the mouth of a large cave. We were told to turn on our headlamps. We followed the guide into the cave, and it quickly got smaller. We had to get down on our hands and knees to start crawling into a series of smaller tunnels.

At this point, the guide from Raeburn Keslake told us to turn off our headlamps. We all did as he asked, and suddenly, you could not see your hand in front of your face. It dawned on me at this point that the agenda item called "Canary" must be code for "coal mine," which, for all I knew, we were now collectively laying in.

The Raeburn Keslake guide turned his headlight back on and crawled back past our team, eleven of us in all. He then yelled we had to find our way back to the surface, and we would not be allowed to use our headlights. If any of us turned on our headlamp, we would all automatically fail the team exercise. We had thirty minutes to get out, starting now. And with that, he continued to crawl out of the tunnel, and his light soon disappeared into the total darkness.

I was grateful I was not claustrophobic; otherwise, I would have freaked out. Everyone started talking at once, and finally, I heard Peter yell out for everyone to shut up. He asked who had the rope, and someone yelled out they had it. Peter instructed all of us to turn around—not an easy thing to do in such a tight space—and start passing the rope up the line. We were to collectively crawl out of the tunnel holding the rope so we would not get separated.

Once we all had turned around, we started crawling back to where we had started. The trickiest part of all of this was several points in the tunnel where it split up, and we had to debate among ourselves in the dark if we needed to go left or right. It didn't help that we had not paid much attention to whether we had gone left or right when we entered the tunnel.

Every time we would get to a split in the tunnel, we'd have a shouting match to go left or right and let Peter make the final decision. Peter had a fluorescent watch so he could at least keep track of the time. In the dark, you quickly lose all track of time, especially when you are on the verge of a panic attack. At the 25-minute mark, we realized we could stand up, and with about two minutes to go, we could see daylight coming in at the tunnel's mouth.

We raced out with about a minute to spare. We all felt relieved to be out of that cave and proud since we did it under the deadline. Looking back on it now, this was an early version of an underground "Escape Room," which is very popular for team building today.

However, if anyone in our group had been claustrophobic, this team exercise would have been a disaster, as well as humiliating for that person. Unlike an Escape Room, we were deep underground with no way of making allowances for personal phobias. And if this was Day One of our offsite, what kind of fresh hell was being planned for Day Two?

We got back on the bus and arrived back at the hotel in time for a late dinner at 8:00 p.m., followed by a late-night discussion on what we wanted our team to be. When I got back to my room, I was a bit concerned about what I saw featured on the agenda for Day Two: *Cliff Rescue* and *Abseiling*. I finally got to sleep around midnight.

We started Day Two with an early breakfast and an overview of what we needed to know about mountain rescue skills. We would be heading over by bus to a place called Dewerstone after breakfast for the day's activities.

I had never heard of this place called Dewerstone. I hurried through breakfast and snuck over to the hotel lobby area to see if they had any information that might be helpful. I found a mountain climbing brochure that claimed Dewerstone was based on the ancient Celtic word "Dewer," which in English means "devil."

It stated Dewerstone was a famous cliff over 200 meters high, about 660 feet. Legend had it that each night Dewer, otherwise known as the Devil, would gallop across the local moor and lead a phantom pack of hounds to chase weary or foolish humans over the edge to their death. I was starting to wish we would go back to the Canary exercise.

I heard a call to get on the bus. As I boarded, I thought to myself that I had overcome any fear of the dark or tight spaces so far. Today, it looked like I was going to find out if I had a fear of heights.

We arrived at Dewerstone after a 30-minute bus ride. We had arrived at the top of the cliff. It was cold and misty. We carefully ventured out to look over the edge. It was a straight drop down. A crew from Raeburn Keslake had already been there earlier in the day, setting up ropes, pulleys, and carabiners. A metal stretcher was placed at the top of the cliff.

The plan was for Peter to be the "victim" who needed to be rescued. He would be strapped to the stretcher, and four of us—two on either side of the stretcher—would rappel down the cliff while holding the stretcher. The rest of us would have the ropes that would lower the stretcher down the cliff along with the attendees.

Peter wanted the most athletic team to be with him on his trip down the mountain, including Michael Roberts, our head of operation and former member of the British Army. I was relieved to be assigned to help lower the ropes and stay on the cliff's top. I was not offended I would not be with Peter on his trip down the mountain and was thrilled to help on the top, holding a rope on level ground.

After thoroughly going over what everyone needed to do, the Raeburn Keslake leader told everyone to go to their assigned places to get ready. Michael Roberts walked over to me and asked if we could have a quiet word. I told him sure.

We walked away from the group, and he told me he had a serious fear of heights. He didn't think he could do this. He wanted to know if there would be any way I'd be willing to take his place. From the look in his eyes, I could tell he was serious. I hesitated a bit but then told him I'd be willing to do it. I don't think I've ever seen anyone as relieved as when I told Michael I would take his place. I instantly regretted my decision when I looked over the edge of the cliff into the mist. Damn, that was one long drop!

I walked over to tell Peter what the plan was. I assured him my only goal was to get us both off the cliff as safely and as quickly as possible. Peter looked at me and said, "Don't screw this up—if I fall, I won't even have the pleasure of holding my hands in front of my face since I'm strapped to this stretcher." I told him no worries; we'd probably both die of a heart attack before hitting the ground below.

To put this cliff's height in perspective, one story of a building is on average about 15 feet tall. So, we were about to rappel down 300 feet or the equivalent of a 20-story building in the wind and misty fog. And my previous experience in doing this was, well, *nada.*

We double-checked Peter's straps and made sure the ropes were all secure and attached to the stretcher. If you think rappelling is a scary thought, imagine you are Peter facing the sky strapped to a stretcher and then placed in a vertical position as you are being lowered down the face of a cliff. Peter said, "Let's get this over with!" and we all leaned back on our ropes to begin our descent.

The freakiest part of rappelling is in the very beginning, in which you are placing your feet against the cliff and leaning backward. That is the exact opposite of what you feel like doing since it seems like you are deliberately trying to fall off the cliff. Your mind is thinking, "WHAT ARE YOU DOING, YOU FOOL!" The next part is even scarier—you pump your legs up and down and then push off the cliff while dropping down a few feet as you plant your feet against the cliff again. And you need to do this in unison with the other three rappelers who are shouting instructions to the team above you who are holding the ropes.

I focused on looking at Peter and not at the bottom of the cliff. After the initial heart-stopping beginning, I started to calm down. We could hear everyone at the top of the cliff coordinating with the person looking over the edge to make sure they would let out a bit more rope every time we rappelled. It didn't help that I was suffering from a head cold before leaving for this offsite. The weather conditions and the altitude made my head feel like it was going to explode.

After about 45 minutes, which seemed a LOT longer, we finally made it to the bottom. Peter was cracking jokes the whole time we were going down the cliff, which helped us keep our cool as we rappelled down the cliff. Once we unstrapped him from the stretcher, he gave us all a big hug and a heartfelt thank you for not letting him crash to the bottom face first.

That afternoon we did a series of other outdoor activities, including abseiling, which in essence is descending a rock face or other near-vertical surface using a doubled rope coiled around your body fixed at a higher point. I was doing the same thing with Peter that morning, except I was now by myself.

The scariest part of abseiling is ensuring your gear is working correctly. I later learned this is a dangerous and sometimes deadly sport. The British Mountaineering Council did a study years later, regarding equipment failure. It concluded there are plenty of ways to kill yourself while abseiling, including your rope breaking or being cut, anchors becoming loose, and as quoted in their report, carabiners "mysteriously not controlling the rate of descent."

We headed back to the hotel in the late afternoon for dinner, followed by a team debrief. By this stage, my stuffed head was aching, and I headed to bed early. I woke up around 3:00 a.m. and could not figure out why my pillow was wet. I turned on my bedroom light to discover to my horror that my pillow was soaked in blood. My right eardrum had burst in the middle of the night, and there was now a persistent ringing in my ears.

When I went to tell the hotel staff, they told me there was nothing that could be done at that hour of the night and to try to get back to sleep. They gave me a new pillow in exchange for my blood-soaked one.

By the time I got up a few hours later, the bleeding had stopped, and my ears stopped ringing. I told Peter what happened, and we agreed I could go to a doctor once I got back to London, since you can't do anything for a burst eardrum other than letting it heal over time.

The final team offsite exercise was to take place at the hotel that morning. One of the Raeburn Keslake staff was a psychologist who interviewed everyone on the KFC management team the previous week to learn about each team member's strengths and weaknesses.

He gathered everyone outside a large room at the hotel, where the doors were all closed. He explained that eleven easels and chairs had been set up in the room, one for each team member. Our assignment was to go inside the room and figure out which easel was the one that had our strengths and weaknesses. He then went over to open the doors and let us in the room.

As we entered the room, I glanced around and noticed that ten of the eleven easels had an equal number of strengths and weaknesses listed. Except for one easel, which had twenty flaws listed. In fact, there were so many weaknesses that an additional piece of paper had been taped to the bottom of the first. It only listed three strengths.

We all quickly figured out which one of the eleven was our easel and sat down in the chair next to it except for our new business development director. He just stared at the remaining easel with its long list of weaknesses. This was the most humiliating thing I have ever seen done to an executive in my life. We were all very uncomfortable. Finally, he went over to sit down next to the last remaining easel.

The rest of that morning and our team leaving the hotel is a blur to me. The only thing I remember is the long drive home to London, since I had driven over with the new business director in my car. The entire way back to London, he kept repeating over and over how humiliating that team session had been, and he didn't understand why everyone hated him.

I told him that was not the case—I was shocked at what had happened and didn't understand why, at a minimum, the psychologist would have made sure everyone had an equal number of strengths and weaknesses listed.

Not surprisingly, our business development director left the company less than a month later. In talking to Peter later, he agreed with my assessment that while a portion of the offsite had been engaging, overall, it had been a disaster. Our business development director was a casualty of the ill will of a small number on the management team and a psychologist who didn't appreciate how much such an exercise could do to someone's self-perception and confidence. The Brits have an expression—"praise in public, coach in private"—and I saw firsthand at that offsite the importance of such a principle.

Mission Accomplished: Back to the U.S.

Despite this disappointing offsite, our management team eventually came together and delivered some amazing results over the next two years. Given the U.K. and other markets' success, I was going to be promoted to vice president of marketing for KFC International based in Dallas, Texas. While our family was going to miss all the friends we'd made during our time in England—and the boys would especially miss their friends from the British school they attended, Hall Grove—we were looking forward to being closer to our own extended family back in the U.S.

I learned a lot during my time in London and working in the various European and South African markets. I learned about the importance of partnering with franchisees to make sure they felt like a true business partner who was valued. I saw once again how important it is to understand your customer and try to deliver what they want and need from your brand. And I came to appreciate the power of testing something in one market and successfully expanding it to other markets.

The most valuable lesson I learned about greatness was the power of an optimistic vision of the future that a strong leader can provide. Peter never wavered from his original idea of transforming the KFC brand to becoming a legitimate competitor against McDonald's and other QSRs. His combination of listening, humor, and bias for action empowered his team to take chances and make great things happen. To be a part of a team like that is something I wish everyone in business could experience as part of their career path.

CHAPTER EIGHT
Greatness—Stay Calm and Carry On

 ## REFLECTIVE QUESTIONS

- What's your definition of greatness? How has it changed over time?

- When was there a time in which you were able to stay optimistic in trying to achieve something great despite the odds being against you? What did you learn about yourself in this situation?

- How can you as a leader create more optimism for your team in pursuing something great for the organization? What are some things to watch out for?

- What great things have you done in your life that you are proud of?

- What great things are you working on in your life right now?
- What are some great things you would like to work on in the future?

LEAP INTO ACTION

Two consistent characteristics of a great leader are persistence and an optimistic vision of the future, "a better place." If you are a leader—and that can apply to any group, including a business, community, organization, nonprofit, family, etc.—you need to take them to that better place. After all, who wants to follow a pessimist who isn't excited about the future? If you aren't in a leadership position professionally, look for opportunities in your personal life, such as your church, clubs, etc.

A MOMENT OF ZEN

Be thoughtful about who's on your team.

In my 20s, it was all about me. I wanted to be relevant; I wanted to be a shining star. I preferred working on my own—it was so much easier and faster when I could do it all myself. But I missed out on a lot. Collaboration makes everyone and everything better.

Play on winning teams—if your team is not winning, find one that is winning—do not waste time because you settle for a job versus a winning team, where you learn more, become available to other opportunities, and have more fun. Choose YOUR teams wisely, whether you are a team member or its leader. Only work with people you both LIKE and RESPECT. Emotional intelligence and self awareness are just as crucial as raw intellect. Have a "NO BOZOS" policy when choosing YOUR teams!

09

Respect – Seek First to Understand

Respect: Recognizing the worth and dignity of every single person, so we can live in harmony with others

> *"Seek first to understand, then to be understood."*
> —Stephen Covey

SNEAK PEEK AT MY LEAP
How I learned about the importance of understanding different points of view and working together to develop winning global best practices and strategies.

In the early 1990s, a new marketing team was formed to support all three PepsiCo International Restaurant brands: Kentucky Fried Chicken (KFC), Pizza Hut, and Taco Bell. There were over 10,000 restaurants outside the U.S. at the time in 83 countries. I was part of a group that was supposed to go and figure out how to get everyone to work together to build these global businesses.

Half of the restaurants in this new international network were KFCs, a brand I had plenty of recent experience marketing. I wasn't at all sure we would have enough best practices or wisdom to offer to get them to support us. Given some of the KFC markets would be responsible for had been in business for decades without any outside help, I knew this would be a significant challenge since most folks prefer the status quo. They would need to be convinced that working with our new group based in Dallas, Texas, would be to their advantage.

Dwight Riskey was going to be my new boss, and I instantly liked him. He had a background in marketing research. He had a Ph.D. in something called psychophysics, which is not a typical marketing background. Before becoming a research scientist with General Foods, he taught at several universities and then went on to have a long career with PepsiCo, and he knew the chairman, Roger Enrico.

A Global Listening Tour

During my initial meetings with Dwight, while we were excited about the opportunity to create a new team to help lead the marketing for three global brands, we also knew we had a lot of work ahead of us. Dwight wisely suggested before we created anything new, it might be a good idea for me to "hit the road" and go on a listening tour to some of our major KFC international markets. When I got back, we could start to figure out what our key priorities should be and what programs we might want to develop.

Having lived in the U.K. for the previous three years, I was already familiar with the European markets. Since KFC had a powerful presence in the Middle East—with over 400 restaurants—Dwight and I decided this part of the world would be one of the first markets I should spend some time getting to know. My first stop on my "around the world" listening tour would begin in Riyadh, Saudi Arabia.

The first thing I noticed when I landed in the Riyadh terminal in Saudi Arabia was there were three airport terminals: domestic, international, and royal. By royal, I don't mean some type of frequent flyer membership. You've got to be a member of the royal family to use the royal terminal. Since there are over 10,000 members of the royal family in Saudi Arabia, there were plenty of customers to keep that terminal busy.

I arrived late at the international terminal and joined my franchisees for a late dinner. As they dropped me off at my hotel, they said they had a present waiting for me in my room.

"What is it?" I inquired.

"Oh, just a little something as a remembrance of your trip."

When I got to the room, there was a wrapped gift lying on my bed. I was curious and tore into the box.

It was a traditional Arabian outfit, complete with a full headdress. I quickly put it on and looked in the mirror. Lawrence of Arabia would've been proud. I thought I might even be able to pass for a local. But as tempting as it was, the following day, I came down to breakfast in my KFC polo shirt and khakis rather than my new clothing.

"How did you like your present?" they asked.

"It's great. I like it a lot. Thank you for giving me such a thoughtful welcome gift. I thought about wearing it today but thought that might be a bit presumptuous."

"Thank you for not wearing it."

"Why?"

They told me this had been a bit of a test to see if I was sensitive to the local culture. They then told me what had happened to their last American visitor from PepsiCo.

"We gave him the same outfit you got. It was his first trip here to the Middle East, and he was very excited about wearing it. When we came down to the hotel lobby for breakfast, he insisted on wearing it on our store visits."

My host told him this was a terrible idea, and he really should go to his room and change immediately. But he was insistent and refused to change.

The franchisee grimaced a bit and continued his story. "When we walked out of the hotel, it was the time for the second call to prayer. The mutawa approached him and asked why he wasn't at the mosque to pray. He told them he wasn't really a Muslim and just enjoyed wearing the outfit so he could fit in better with the locals."

The mutawa wasn't amused at all. The PepsiCo employee didn't realize the mutawa—also known as the "morality police" or "fashion police"—are given the task of arresting women, and men as well, who they deem are improperly dressed according to the dress code.

The franchisee shook his head. "There was nothing we could do to help him. He was taken to the local mutawa station and questioned for five hours. When we finally got him out, he had to leave the country immediately and has never been back. He's lucky he was allowed to leave the country."

At this point, I realized it would be very easy to get thrown out of this country—or worse, into jail. So, I needed to be careful about what I said or did during this visit. This was going to be a listening tour as my first and primary priority.

Our first stop on our store visits was at a KFC restaurant connected to a convenience store owned and run by the same franchise organization. When I finished visiting with the KFC restaurant crew, I wandered over to talk with the convenience store manager on duty. Being a global marketing guy, I thought it would be interesting to find out what the best-selling brands were in this part of the world.

"What's your best-selling brand here?" I asked the convenience store manager.

"Oh, we sell a lot of Pepsi," the store manager replied.

I wasn't surprised. Saudi Arabia is one of the few international markets where Pepsi had a commanding lead over Coke.

"And what's your second best-selling brand?" I asked.

"Man-O-War Perfume," he replied.

This wasn't at all what I expected to hear. Why would perfume be a big seller?

I walked over to the counter to look at the perfume displays and was shocked by the perfume packages. They were all plastic and the size of a quart of motor oil! And with brand names, I never heard of: "Man-O-War," "Smell-So-Fine," and "Arabian Nights."

This made absolutely no sense to me.

I asked why the perfume containers were so huge.

"To mix with Pepsi," the store manager said with a slight smile.

Why would anyone mix Pepsi and perfume? Then it hit me: for the alcohol. Alcoholic beverages were forbidden for sale in Saudi Arabia. The only way you could get a "mixed drink" would be to get the alcohol wherever you could; in this case, from Man-O-War perfume. At this point in the conversation, I thought it would probably not be wise to offer any color commentary on this interesting local custom, so I thanked him and quickly returned to the franchisee's car.

In Saudi Arabia, there were no public cinemas, discos, nightclubs, symphony halls, or theaters at the time I was there. Women were not allowed to drive or vote—or go out in public with other women or be alone.

In the KFC restaurants, there were two separate dining areas. The first is for men only; no women could order from the counter or drive thru. The second area is the family dining area. It consisted of several tables wholly covered with curtains. Once the male head of the family gave the order, the food was delivered outside the curtain by a male waiter and was passed through to the other side of the curtain. The women were covered entirely in elegant wraps from head to foot.

Even though some of what I saw in Saudi Arabia was quite different from what I was used to, everyone went out of their way to help me. From a KFC business perspective, the restaurants were some of the best operations I'd ever seen—much better than many of the ones I'd been to in the U.S.

And as far as their social customs, as I reflected on what I'd seen, I realized the U.S. had gone through several significant social changes over the years involving what was acceptable and unacceptable at the time. Looking back on the history of the U.S., what seems outrageous to us in the present day at one time in our past was seen as perfectly normal. I tried not to be too judgmental about what I saw on this trip, since every country has the right to enforce its own values and norms. After all, countries often evolve to be more progressive over time.

As Stephen Covey says in his *Seven Habits* book, "Seek first to understand, then be understood." I try to keep an open mind on the different cultures and countries I visit, since it's easy to become an "ugly American" unless you actively work at not letting that happen to the way you react to places you've never been.

The next stop of my listening tour was Egypt. I had always dreamed of visiting Cairo. On my first day in town, I met with the Cairo KFC franchisee. Since this was my first visit to Egypt, he wanted to get things off to an exciting start. He offered to drive me out to the Great Pyramids, where he had a thriving KFC restaurant.

Based on all the famous photos, you probably think the Great Pyramids are in the middle of some vast sand-swept desert. You would be wrong to assume this. The pyramids are located at the edge of a giant expanse of housing in the outskirts of Cairo. It's quite a shock to be driving through a residential neighborhood, and then suddenly you see ancient pyramids nearby like they just landed from outer space.

We visited the KFC restaurant directly across the street from the Sphinx and the pyramids. The franchisee told me you could even sit on the roof of the restaurant at night and watch the laser light show. I didn't know what to think of this restaurant location. While it's great to take advantage of tourist traffic, it just seemed wrong for a modern restaurant to be so close to one of the ancient wonders of the world. But I kept these thoughts to myself since I didn't want to offend my host.

After we finished our restaurant visit, the franchisee asked if I would like to go for a horseback ride among the pyramids.

"Boy, would I!" I exclaimed. I thought to myself that all I needed to do now was pull my Lawrence of Arabia outfit out of my luggage, and I would be ready for my grand entrance.

The franchisee asked for several horses to be brought to the restaurant's front and told me to wait for our guide. A few minutes later, I saw the most magnificent Arabian stallion I'd ever witnessed. The rider on the white stallion looked down at me, smiled, and asked in a loud voice, "How the f*** are you doing?"

This was not the greeting I was expecting.

"Um, I'm well, thank you," I replied.

The rider smiled. "I'm doing f****** great today! Are you ready to go for a ride?"

"Sure. By the way, your English is excellent," I lied. "Where did you learn it?"

"Why, thank you. F****** American sailors taught me excellent English. I like to practice it every f******* chance I get."

As I got on my horse, I hoped his riding skills were better than his English.

"Okay, let's ride!" I shouted in my best John Wayne voice.

We started at a trot toward the Great Pyramids. I couldn't believe my good fortune. Here I was riding on a fine Arabian stallion along with my friendly franchisee host and our trustworthy, albeit foul-mouthed, guide.

After about ten minutes, the guide smiled at me and suggested we go at a slightly faster pace than our host. I reluctantly agreed. Once we put about a hundred yards between the franchisee and us, he turned to me again and asked if I liked to ride fast.

"Oh, no thanks. A fast trot is good enough for me," I shouted over the sound of the galloping horses.

"F∗∗∗ that! Ride 'em, American cowboy!" And with that, he produced a horsewhip, which I hadn't noticed before, and gave my horse a serious whack on the butt.

Up until this point in my life, I've never been frightened riding on a horse. But if there's an equivalent measure on a horse of going from zero to sixty in a car, that's what it felt like to me.

I hung on to my horse for dear life. We headed straight up a steep hill.

I pulled back on the reins with everything I had. The horse made excellent time, galloping up the steep hill. If this weren't exciting enough, I contemplated the fact I had no earthly idea what was on the other side. It might be a gently sloping area, or it could be a cliff where I would plummet to my death.

As I reached the top, I was immensely relieved to see it wasn't the sheer drop-off I feared. I turned to my side and was surprised to see the guide sitting on his horse right next to me.

"You want to go faster?"

Now it was my turn to practice some American sailor English. "Are you f∗∗∗∗∗∗ crazy? You could have gotten me killed. No, I do not want to go f∗∗∗∗∗∗ fast!"

The guide seemed pleased with my response. "Okay, okay, no problem. Oh, by the way, you know it would be very nice if I could get a generous tip for being your guide today."

This seemed a bit forward, especially since we hadn't returned from the ride yet, but I reached for my wallet and pulled out a U.S. $5 bill, equivalent to Egypt's average daily wage.

"Sure, here you go." I handed over the money.

The guide's expression was one of shock and disbelief. "You call this a tip?" At the same time, he raised the whip directly above my horse's tender butt.

I decided that I wasn't in much of a position to negotiate with the guide. "Here's the rest of it," I exclaimed as I emptied out my wallet. "You're a great guide and deserve a big tip!"

The guide looked relieved and a bit pensive. "You know, this will be our little secret. I wouldn't want the franchisee to feel insulted to learn he didn't pay me enough for this trip."

Perhaps the guide was telling me the truth, and he had been short changed for setting up the trip. I decided it wasn't worth figuring out who was telling the truth and who was taking advantage of naive visitors. I wasn't going to let it get in the way of learning as much as possible while I was with them.

I continued my trip to South Asia and Australia to get feedback from our other markets on what we should be focused on globally. When I finally got back to Dallas to meet with Dwight, my head was spinning.

"Buildus Globus Brandus"

The good news was we had a network of over 5,000 KFC restaurants in over 80 countries worldwide. Our company and franchise networks were expanding to new markets every year and growing restaurants in established markets. One competitive advantage of selling chicken products is that there are no major religions that forbid eating chicken, unlike beef among Hindus or pork among Muslims. There weren't any significant barriers for us to eventually get to every country on the planet—all 195 of them.

Now the bad news, or at least, the most significant challenges we would face as a new international marketing team. First, since there had not been any strong leadership for the KFC brand over the years, the global markets had done what they thought was best for their markets. The one item that was consistent in all markets was the Colonel's signature product: Original Recipe. Other than that, the menu was all over the place.

We didn't have any global marketing strategies for anything —for advertising, for promotions, for a kid's program—so we would be starting from scratch. Our biggest international competitor, McDonald's, was the role model for consistency. They were rigorous in what McDonald's stood for in everything they did and executed it brilliantly in all their markets worldwide.

And if a McDonald's franchisee got out of line, the remedy was simple: since McDonald's owned the land upon which the restaurant was built, they could take over quickly. Ownership of the building and land the restaurant is located on is so important that many financial analysts have commented McDonald's is actually a real estate company that just happens to sell hamburgers.

Perhaps the biggest challenge I was concerned about was change management. I knew from my experience in the U.K. that trying to go into an established business and make significant changes is extremely tough. I used to remind my team in Dallas that all the international markets had two huge advantages in resisting any changes we wanted: time and distance. If they didn't want to deal with you, it was incredibly easy to ignore what our Dallas team wanted.

When I laid out all my concerns to Dwight, he listened intently. When I got to the part of our discussion where I laid out all my worries about managing change, Dwight just smiled. He seemed relaxed and not very concerned.

I finally had to ask, "Dwight, you and I both agree it is going to be hard to get all of these different markets to follow us. We don't have any real way of mandating any of this. If they don't like what we are proposing, they can just keep doing what they've always been doing. What do you think we need to do?"

Dwight broke out into a big grin. "I can answer that in one word: education."

I was confused about what education had to do with any of what we needed to do. While I could appreciate that Dwight used to be a college professor, I didn't see how that had anything to do with running a global marketing team.

Dwight went on to explain his thinking. He agreed we could not force any of our recommendations to the international markets. Facts, force, and fear do not work when you are trying to create positive change. What we needed to do instead was create plenty of empathy and connection with the general managers and marketing leaders of each country. You could not do that with a mandate or a memo. You had to do it with education.

What Dwight had in mind was to create something he called "PepsiCo International Restaurants Marketing University." It would be a one-week immersive event in which we would invite our country's marketers to do a deep dive into each of our brands: KFC, Pizza Hut, Taco Bell. It was a bit pretentious to call it a university, but we thought it needed to seem more significant than a regular marketing seminar or meeting. Dwight even came up with a Latin motto for us: ***"Buildus Globus Brandus!"***

We would make sure all the marketing leaders would understand the history of each brand, what made our brands unique and special, what our global challenges were, and how we would like to work with them to help them be more successful in each of their markets. We wanted to make sure everyone on the marketing teams was familiar with research processes and tools for better understanding our customers. We also wanted to share core principles and best practices in making great advertising.

More than anything else, we wanted to begin to create a network of marketing professionals from around the world who could leverage our collective experience and talent. We knew this was not going to be easy or happen overnight. There were over 300 marketers from over 100 countries worldwide. Some countries only had Pizza Hut, others only had KFC, many had both, and a handful had Taco Bell restaurants. So even if we held a Marketing University every other month, it would take us about two years to get everyone to Dallas through this training.

Dwight instinctively knew we needed to keep each group relatively small—no more than 30 in a class—and we needed to get a representative group together each time so that no one region could dominate the group's thinking. The core belief in creating Marketing University was that if we could get a critical mass of international marketers to believe in and support global initiatives, we would be successful. It would take time and patience, but we were confident this would work by making it a big deal to attend Marketing University so that we created a positive distinction for students.

Launch of the First "Marketing University"

We created and launched our first Marketing University. We first reached out to all the regional and country managers to get their support, since they would be the ones footing the bill for the travel of their marketing teams—plus taking them out of their field role while they were with us. Given Dwight's reputation as a strong marketer and executive, selling this idea to the country managers went smoothly.

Since we were a part of PepsiCo, Dwight's critical insight was we needed to leverage all the intelligent marketing processes used by our sister divisions—Frito Lay and Pepsi Beverages—to grow our brands. The fundamental premise of how they managed their businesses was a strong belief the best way to predict the future was to understand the past. When I was at Procter & Gamble (P&G), they had a similar philosophy.

What does that mean in practice? It meant you needed to approach marketing from both a macro and individual consumer perspective. The macro analysis would start with understanding the category size and brand share mix over time along with historical growth rates. You need to understand what triggered historic growth, so you could figure out what to do to get that kind of growth in other markets. You also needed to understand what impact geographic and demographic differences had on your business.

The same type of analysis could be applied to TV advertising, which is the most challenging type of marketing spend to analyze. Just like at P&G, if you were disciplined, you could set up test markets where you could measure the impact of running advertising—for example, different copy and different media weights. Those would be the "inputs" to this type of testing—the "output" would be the changes in revenue, product mix, customer frequency, and amount per purchase.

As we were pulling all this together with the initial content for our first Marketing University, we already knew we had some valuable insights and marketing principles that would have practical value to the field. For example, we knew "product news" almost always worked in driving customers to restaurants. For media plans, we knew you needed to "front load" your advertising to get off to a strong start because the impact of advertising would continue even after the ads stopped.

This type of marketing discipline of applying guiding principles such as these could make a meaningful difference in markets around the world—and could give us a fighting chance against McDonald's, the dominant player in most of the countries where we competed.

As part of Marketing University, we needed a common culture in how we wanted to work together. Inspired by Roger Enrico, who was PepsiCo's CEO and probably one of the best marketers of the 20th century, we agreed to focus on three core principles:

- **Think Different**—Roger talked a lot about the "tyranny of incrementalism." He encouraged anyone in marketing to develop an idea, take it on the road, and turn it into a business idea. You needed to focus on "big change to big things," since these were the only ideas worth fighting for. Here's why:

  • Small changes to small things were a waste of time and talent

- Small changes to big things were dangerous, since they could mess up what's currently working

- Big changes to small things just gave you the illusion of progress

- So, the only things worth focusing on were big changes to big things—these were the kind of ideas that build the business over time and gave you a sustainable advantage over the competition

■ **Think Data**—We wanted everyone on our extended marketing team to get their hands "data dirty" and take a deep dive into it to see what new insights they could come up with. Look at the world through the consumer's eyes and look for new ways to connect and help them out. Seek the truth, not pre-arranged answers. And once you've done all this, have the courage to share your conclusions and answer the "What? So what? Now what?" that any valuable consumer research should trigger.

Developing and advocating a data-based point of view was not considered "nice to have"—it was considered essential. Too many marketers and executives make the mistake of thinking they *are* the consumer—this is seldom the case. It takes a lot of discipline to stay data-focused in understanding your target audience and developing a research-based perspective. It was definitely worth the effort—as Roger liked to say, "A point of view is worth 50 IQ points."

■ **Think Big**—Once you identified significant changes to big things and did your consumer homework, it was time to act. We wanted to encourage marketers to come up with consumer propositions and test them. Since we had an international network, we wanted to set up a system in which various brands in different markets could test other ideas, including new products, promotions, and pricing. We would take the results and share what worked. And, just as important, what did not work.

Doing this well is one of the most significant advantages global brands have over smaller regional or national brands—and we wanted to make sure we were leveraging this competitive edge to the max.

Once we got underway with our first Marketing University, we constantly asked for evaluations and feedback to enhance what was working and refine or eliminate what was not. We didn't see much of an impact during the first year of holding Marketing University, in part because we deliberately kept the size of each class small to make it easier for folks to network with each other during the week. But by the second year, we started to see a significant impact. Instead of feeling like we were "pushing" ideas from Dallas, we began to see a lot more "pull" from various international marketing teams who now understood the "why" behind our global strategies.

The Importance of Mutual Respect

One aspect of all of this I came to appreciate was the critical importance of showing mutual respect to all our teams worldwide. While I'm proud to be an American, it drives me nuts when I hear my fellow citizens talk about how we're the "greatest country on the planet."

Given that half of U.S. citizens have never traveled outside the country, they might want to consider those other countries also have a lot to be proud of—and in many areas are probably better than our track record to date—such as health care, paid parental leave, infant mortality, etc.

It all comes down to how much you are willing to respect another person or country. If someone walked into a crowded room and started yelling how great they were, how many in the room would want to have anything to do with that person? A little more humility and willingness to listen to what others have to say goes a long way in creating a better outcome, whether you're talking about personal relationships or international relations.

When I traveled to different markets, I emphasized the U.S. team did not have a monopoly on new or good ideas. We went out of our way to encourage ALL markets—no matter how big or small—to test new ideas and share their results with the rest of the world. We were at a severe disadvantage at doing this, since we didn't directly serve any consumers.

We also encouraged markets to help each other out. One aspect of working with international teams is that while they enjoyed competing against each other in terms of sales growth and customer satisfaction, they also got a lot of satisfaction in helping others out. To make sure they were recognized for these efforts, my wife, Peggy, created a giant stuffed hand made from cloth that I showed off at one of our quarterly international meetings. I announced we would be having a competition called the "Helping Hand Award." It would be given to the country's marketing team who had gone out of their way to help another market in the previous quarter.

When we kicked this competition off, I had no idea if it would work and was pleasantly surprised by how well it did. Almost immediately, we had several countries offering to help other markets—usually newer ones with small teams—on a wide variety of issues such as advertising, working with agencies, promotional ideas, etc. The announcement of the quarterly winner of the "Helping Hand Award" quickly became one of the highlights of our international meetings. The respect and appreciation of folks you work with are some of the most powerful incentives in the business world. It's too bad more companies don't recognize and leverage this insight—it costs nothing financially but is one of the most valuable things a company can offer their employees.

One other critical insight we realized was the importance of showing respect to international markets by delineating what was required and what was optional. Think about it: if somebody from the head office comes to a global market and presents a long list of demands, what do you think the likely reaction is going to be? Nobody likes ultimatums. If this is your approach, the two critical questions they will likely ask you are when your flight leaves and if you need a ride to the airport.

The approach we took on establishing global standards was "less is better." We came up with what we called marketing "negotiables" and "non-negotiables." We tried to keep the non-negotiable list as short as possible. Trademarks were non-negotiable, since a global trademark is worthless if you don't implement it consistently in all markets. Key advertising language—such as "finger licking good" and "secret blend of 11 herbs and spices"—were required as well as the image of KFC's founder, Colonel Sanders. Certain products such as Original Recipe were required.

But a long list of decisions was left to the discretion of the local markets—for example, other menu items. In Japan, they developed a deep-fried corn soup, which Americans can appreciate if you like country fair food where *everything* is fried. Given there are many veg-etarians in India, they sold Vegetable Strips instead of chicken strips and a Potato Krisper, a potato patty in a bun with a tangy sauce. Spicy porridge and egg tarts were sold for breakfast in China, Singapore, and Malaysia. By giving markets the freedom to market what their local markets wanted, total sales and customer counts grew. This was much better than insisting everyone had the same menu around the world as we had in the U.S.

A Winning Global Strategy Delivers Powerful Results

Dwight was a visionary leader for our international marketing team who taught me the wisdom of Stephen Covey's principle of "seek to understand, then to be understood." You must have that kind of mindset in everything you do in marketing, and frankly in life. Start with really trying to understand your customer based on data, not assumptions or preconceived ideas. Work with international markets to appreciate their culture and preferences, not insisting that you already know what they should do.

For all those skeptics who aren't sure marketing adds much to the bottom line, it's worth noting we enabled our three international brands, KFC, Pizza Hut, and Taco Bell, which were making $50 million in profits when we formed our group, to generating over $400 million in just four years—an eight-fold increase. This was a global team effort, involving all parts of the organization, but I'd argue marketing helped lead to this phenomenal growth in business success and profitability.

We invested considerable time and effort to work with all the markets as equal thought partners to demonstrate what Aretha Franklin used to sing about: R-E-S-P-E-C-T. The success we enjoyed in our international marketing efforts was primarily due to the mutual respect we had for each other. Imagine how much better the world would be if we all tried to do this in our daily lives.

CHAPTER NINE
Respect—Seek First to Understand

 ## REFLECTIVE QUESTIONS

- How do you define respect? Has this definition changed over time?
- What are some ways in which you try to create a feeling of respect for someone?
- Think of a time in which you felt you were not respected. How did you react? Would you have responded differently today? Why or why not?

- Who are some people in your life who deserve more respect? What are some ways in which you could demonstrate this feeling to them?
- Who are some historical figures you respect? Why?
- What are some ways you can deal with someone who's not showing respect for you or someone you care about?
- How open or accepting are you of people or cultures different from you? Are there new ways in which you could be more accepting of them?

LEAP INTO ACTION

Listening is the foundation to creating mutual respect in any relationship. When you're having a conversation, rather than focusing on what you're going to say next, take the time to really listen and understand where the other person is coming from. As Epictetus, the former slave who became one the most famous of the Roman philosophers, once observed, "We have two ears and one mouth so we can listen twice as much as we speak."

A MOMENT OF ZEN

It's all about relationships.

Success is all about relationships. It is who you know. More importantly, it is who knows you. Most importantly, it is what the most influential people say about you as you've earned their trust.

Keep your circle tight and do the work to nurture your relationships. Being the best friend, brother, or son requires effort. Be the one that reaches out to check in and listen empathetically. Be authentic and vulnerable with your circle as they will appreciate your trust, and those meaningful relationships will deepen.

Too often, people approach networking as though they're simply collecting a stable of contacts who might one day be beneficial to them. It reduces people to things, and I hate that. Instead, always ask yourself, "How can I help this person? Is there anyone I know that could be helpful to them?" Even if you're not sold on the human side of this advice, in a practical sense, you'll find people are a lot more likely to help you if you've already helped them a few times.

Remember, family is always number one, and don't lose sight of that in all the excitement and pressure of your professional career roles. I would also tell myself not to feel guilty for not having every-thing figured out about relationships when I am just 25 years old.

10

Resilience – When the Going Gets Tough

Resilience: The ability to recover quickly from adversity, stress, and threats

> *"Fall down seven times, get up eight."*
> *—Japanese proverb*

SNEAK PEEK AT MY LEAP
How I learned to grow professionally despite losing the role I had worked for my whole career.

If you work in a large business and you are very ambitious, you dream about becoming a senior executive. In finance, you want to be the CFO (Chief Finance Officer); in HR, you want to be the CPO (Chief People Officer); in marketing, you want to be the CMO (Chief Marketing Officer)—that was my long-term career goal.

The CMO role has a lot going for it: it pays well, you get to work with talented folks—both inside your company and at your agencies—and it allows you to have a significant role in the direction your company is heading. If you've been working your way up the corporate ladder in marketing, becoming a CMO is confirmation that all that hard work has been worthwhile.

My career goal was simple: Become a CMO and do whatever it took to earn this promotion.

Going for the Top Marketing Spot

In the late 1990s, I was glad I was able to relocate my family to Dallas, where I oversaw international marketing for KFC. Then my boss, Bill Cobb, told me in the spring of 1999 I would be promoted to CMO of Taco Bell, which was based in Southern California. It was a career dream come true. Taco Bell was one of the U.S.'s iconic brands and one of the top 50 in overall marketing spending—over $200 million a year at the time. It was a favorite of QSR fans, especially among young males. And it had a quirky, edgy vibe that helped it stand out from the competition, such as McDonald's and Burger King.

And best of all, Taco Bell was headquartered in Southern California. I'd always dreamed of living on the West Coast. It seemed everything new and innovative started in California. It would be an exciting place to be with my family, especially since my sons would be just starting high school.

My wife was not nearly as bullish on the idea of taking the CMO job and moving to California. She was concerned the role would be risky, since if the business didn't perform, it was way too easy to have the CMO take the blame and get fired. We had a comfortable lifestyle in Dallas. California would be an expensive place to live—housing prices were easily double what we were paying in Texas. Not to mention taxes, since California has the highest personal income taxes in the country, while Texas has none. So, there would be considerable financial risk in taking this role.

Her concerns were not enough to dampen my enthusiasm for the CMO job at Taco Bell. I'd had a very successful nine-year track record with PepsiCo Restaurants, which was now called Yum! Brands after we'd been spun off several years earlier. I'd done well in every role I was given and had been recognized by senior management at Yum! Brands for various accomplishments. I already knew and liked who my new boss would be, Peter Waller, the previous CMO of Taco Bell. Besides, if worse came to worst, I figured I could always find another excellent marketing role in SoCal.

Heading Out West (Where Things Quickly Go South)

We made a move to Orange County, California, and I started in my new role. Initially, it was a real thrill. I had a team of over 70 talented marketers, and we worked with a fabulous advertising agency, Chiat\Day, and the famous Lee Clow, who created the "1984" Macintosh television commercial. Taco Bell headquarters was a big step up from the offices in Dallas. It had a fully functional test kitchen, where you could sample the new creations the R&D team was continually inventing.

There were some fun aspects of the job that were special. Since each year Taco Bell did several major promotions with various movie studios, we were invited to attend movie premieres in downtown LA, including the party after the movie. I had always wondered what it would be like to attend the Oscars, and we managed to get some tickets to that as well—but truth be told, after the initial excitement of seeing all the movie stars in the lobby, once the program started, it was dull. Unless you were a nominee, I now know why no actor would want to go to any of these award events.

But as they say in the Spiderman movies, "With great power comes great responsibility." I soon started dealing with what seemed like a growing cascade of crises and unexpected problems.

My first crisis at Taco Bell seemed to come out of nowhere. I was driving to a meeting with my head of advertising to do my first monthly budget review. On the way there, I was flipping through an enormous document with pages upon pages of numbers.

I've learned over the years that when it comes to financial statements, the most revealing information is often found in the footnotes. When I came across an asterisk on one of the balance sheet items, I looked at the bottom of the page, where it said in fine print, "excludes the value of excess merchandising materials."

I asked her what that meant. She quickly dismissed my question and said it didn't matter. I refused to let it go and asked her again.

She looked nervous and finally told me that there had been a practice of printing up extra merchandising materials for every promotion over the years. Hence, they never had to worry about running out and upsetting our franchisees. That would have been fine if whatever merchandising materials were not used at the end of that promotion—or at least at the end of the fiscal year—were recognized and written off. Unfortunately, that's not what had been happening. Instead, all these materials were piling up in a warehouse for a decade and had not been accounted for on the P&L statement. When you added up the cost of all that worthless material, it amounted to over $1 million.

I usually don't lose my temper, but in this instance, I went ballistic since I knew what the financial fallout from this would be. This lack of following a standard accounting practice was a self-inflicted wound that should never have happened. Our budget meeting turned into a shouting match. What made it worse was that I knew our CFO was closing the books for the quarter the following week, and I was legally obligated to let him know about what I had discovered—otherwise, I'd be guilty of covering it up. After our meeting, I drove back to the Taco Bell offices and told the CFO about the bad news in person. I'll never forget the look on his face, since this would be an unexpected hit to our upcoming quarterly earnings.

I subsequently had to fire the head of advertising, since she knew about it and should have told me about this problem rather than have me discover it independently. It was a significant embarrassment to the marketing team but, unfortunately, was just the start of a series of setbacks to the business—and to me personally.

The next crisis was just as unexpected. E-coli is a real risk to anyone in the food business. That fall, about 20 children in several western states got sick from e-coli that was detected at several Taco Bell restaurants due to a supplier that wasn't following food safety protocols. Fortunately, all the children eventually recovered, but the resulting negative publicity hurt our sales across the country for several months.

We also had to deal with another crisis when one of our significant suppliers had to recall their corn-based products because there was a concern a GMO version of corn nearby had blown over into the area where our non-GMO corn was grown. When I asked Mary Wagner, our head of R&D, how many of our products were corn-based and might need to be recalled, she told me a better question to ask would be how many were *not* corn-based, since almost everything we sold included corn as an ingredient.

Next, our major food supplier, AmeriServe, went bankrupt. While the impact was mixed on our restaurants, it was an unexpected distraction and created angst among our franchisees, who were a significant part of our overall network.

Despite all these challenges, we were making progress on several fronts. We got approval to install a new grilling platform in the restaurants, giving us a range of new products. We had several products either in the test market or planned for a national rollout, including chalupas and a pizza-like product called Crunchiza. We were getting great publicity from our "Chihuahua" campaign from Chiat\Day. After the fiasco with merchandising, we created a new system significantly lower in cost and higher quality.

But our business results didn't reflect any of this progress. We were missing our monthly sales targets. Despite its cultural popularity, our television advertising wasn't increasing sales. It seemed viewers were more excited about our dog spokesperson than buying our food. Our bi-monthly meetings with our franchisees were getting more and more contentious.

The first victim of these setbacks and business results was my boss. Despite an impressive track record for over a decade at PepsiCo and Yum! Brands, my boss Peter was officially out. I was in shock and frankly felt some guilt, since the marketing results were not what we wanted them to be. Peter was a role model for me, including how he left the organization. I was always impressed by his optimism and "can do" attitude, which he continues to exhibit to this day. The senior team had a farewell event for Peter, which was bittersweet. Following his departure, I started to get concerned about what my future at Taco Bell would be.

Our CEO David Novak instructed me to fire our ad agency, since he didn't think the current advertising was doing anything for the business. He wanted us to hire FCB as our new agency, which had handled Taco Bell's advertising before with their "Run for the Border" campaign. The meeting I had with the head of the Chiat\Day advertising agency, Tom Carroll, was especially painful to me, since I liked Tom a lot and knew how hard they worked on our account. The Taco Bell account's loss would be a blow to their reputation as a leading ad agency.

My new boss was Emil Brolick from Wendy's. Emil had a no-nonsense personality and was very analytically driven. Given my background in marketing research, at first, I thought I'd be able to demonstrate my ability to figure out what needed to be done and be part of the turnaround team, like what I'd done with KFC in the U.K. But this time, there was one big difference: I had worked on the U.K. business *after* the previous management team had been dismissed. It was becoming increasingly clear to me you can't be on a former management team and the new management team as well if the business is in trouble.

"Dead Man Walking!"

Rumors started to spread that I was on the way out. One day, one of my marketing directors saw me walking down the hallway and yelled out, "Dead man walking!" While she was just trying to lighten the mood, I knew she was probably right.

A couple of months later, I got a phone call when I was in my office from a close friend who heard from a reliable source about me being fired. I didn't want to believe it. I called the head of HR, who told me it was not true. Five minutes later, he called me back and admitted the rumor was correct. I was more upset about finding this news out via the grapevine rather than in person. I went to meet with Emil, my boss, and started to discuss my exit plans.

My biggest concern was what I would tell my wife, since she'd had concerns about accepting this job and moving in the first place. I went home that night and didn't have the courage yet to tell her what had happened. I figured I could wait until I had more details on what my exit package would be.

I couldn't go to sleep at all that night. Around 3:00 a.m., she finally asked me what the matter was, and I told her I had been fired. She took the news surprisingly well, which was a significant relief to me, then she told me I'd figure out what to do and please try to get some sleep.

I had never had to negotiate a severance package before, so I was about to get some "on-the-job" training. Having gone through this experience, I'd offer the following observations and tips if you ever find yourself in a similar situation:

- **Leverage**—Keep in mind that unless you have a signed employment contract, which is rare unless you're the CEO, the company doesn't have to give you anything other than what is required by law, such as COBRA. So, you have minimal leverage in one of the most challenging negotiations you are ever going to have to undertake in your career.

- **Trade-Offs**—Ideally, you will get a severance agreement you think is reasonable, and the company believes to be fair to you as well. But it's doubtful you are going to get to this happy place without some back and forth. You shouldn't hesitate to counter whatever is initially offered but recognize it's their call on what—if any—concessions or compromises they want to make compared to their initial offer. And typically, you get to make one counteroffer before they tell you, in essence, "take it or leave it."

- **Legal**—I'd strongly recommend you have a labor attorney review your final document and let your company know you are doing this—ideally with them paying for this review. Your attorney can give you an objective opinion on how "fair" the offer is, since they've seen many similar documents and can advise you whether it's worth taking the deal or continuing to negotiate. Just recognize that once you've made a counteroffer and the company responds to it, that's probably as far as you are going to be able to push them.

In the end, after going back and forth for about a month, I ended up with what I thought, and my attorney felt, was a reasonable severance offer—other than having to give up a significant number of stock options that would have vested within the next 12 months.

My marketing team wanted to have a going-away party for me, which I welcomed since it would give me a chance to thank everyone who had worked closely with me during my time as CMO. We held the party near the beach, and at the end of it, someone had the idea that it would be fun for all of us to head out to the dock and jump in the water, which we all proceeded to do. The water temperature was in the high 50-degree range—talk about a shock to your system! But symbolically, it was an appropriate way to mark the start of my exit from Taco Bell, since my journey for the next 18 months, in some ways, was going to feel like jumping into that same cold water daily.

The first week after leaving Taco Bell was surreal for me. I didn't have any meetings to attend. No overnight numbers to review. No agency engagements. Nada. I got in my car and drove to the local Starbucks to have breakfast and clear my head. I brought along a copy of *The Wall Street Journal*, which included several stories about the growing likelihood of a recession and challenging job market. That didn't improve my outlook or attitude.

Part of my severance agreement included an outplacement service. Looking back on this now, I feel bad for Paul, who was my outplacement contact, since I shared many of my negative thoughts about my situation with him as we started working together. Paul told me we were expected to come into their offices, where we were instructed to go to a small cubicle and start dialing various organizations to find out if they were hiring.

I went for two days and found the entire experience so humiliating I told him that I wasn't coming back. I could do the calling from the house without all the negative energy from other demoralized executives.

If you are offered an outplacement service as part of a severance agreement in the future, you might want to see if the company would be willing to give you the cash they'd spend on that service, since I don't see much value in what they do if you have your personal network to work with.

I didn't know it at the time when I left Taco Bell, but I was about to start an 18-month journey to find my next job. That's a long time to be unemployed both from a financial and psychological point of view. You will quickly discover it doesn't take much time to go from "hero to zero" in the marketing world. In my previous role as CMO, I always got my phone calls and emails returned quickly, and everyone was eager to please. People laughed at my jokes and complimented me on my marketing insights.

Rough Transition

When you're a former CMO, not so much; it was disappointing some folks I assumed were on my side didn't seem to share the same belief once I was fired. I'm not the first person to go through this realization—it pretty much happens to anyone who's suddenly out of work. A lasting lesson from this experience is it creates a powerful empathy for you in the future to want to help any of your friends who are unemployed.

Never underestimate the impact you can have in reaching out to someone out of work and going through a tough time—that email or phone call you make to them just might be the best thing that happens to them all week.

As the economy worsened, I was starting to wonder how I would get back into any kind of senior marketing role. I was in the race for a CMO role in over a dozen different companies, only to come in second place, or at least that's what the recruiters told me.

Contrary to my going-in assumption when we moved to SoCal, there were *not* many senior marketing leadership positions in Orange County. Since my new job might be anywhere in the U.S., my family would have to move again, or I would have to start commuting. Given our sons were just starting high school, moving was not a very attractive option. I would probably need to begin long-distance commuting, and just how far remained to be seen.

My former boss in Dallas, Bill Cobb, had left Yum! Brands shortly after I'd gone to join Taco Bell to work for a start-up in Texas. But soon after joining, he got the opportunity to work at eBay as their CMO. To note, on Labor Day weekend in 1995, eBay was started by Pierre

Omidyar, and it had quickly become an e-commerce favorite under Meg Whitman, the CEO.

I stayed in touch with Bill during my time at Taco Bell, especially since he had recommended me for the CMO role. Even more important, Bill was one of the most networked people I knew and had always been a strong promoter of me. Soon after I left Taco Bell, I asked him about the opportunity to work at eBay, and he told me he'd get back to me. He called back later that same week to say that although there were no current openings available, we should keep in touch, and we did on a regular basis.

After 18 months of searching for a new marketing role across the country, I started to have real concerns. My severance package was almost exhausted. Our boys were both in an expensive private school, and there was a sizable mortgage for our house. The national economy was suffering, and if anything, companies were shedding executives, not hiring them.

My marketing job prospects were looking slim. There was a head of marketing for a regional chicken chain and a CMO role at a company specializing in salads and soups. These positions were very different from heading up marketing for a multi-billion-dollar business, but it was getting to the point where I needed to figure out how we would pay the bills.

Meg and eBay

My wife Peggy suggested I check in with Bill one more time, since it had been several months since he and I had talked about eBay. I gave him a call, and Bill indicated there might be an opening we could explore. He invited me to come to San Jose to meet with him and Meg Whitman, the CEO.

When I arrived at eBay, I sat down with Meg, whom I'd read about in the business press but had never met. We shared one thing in common—we had both worked at P&G—and she had been CEO at eBay for the past four years. When Meg joined eBay in 1998, it had 30 employees and $4 million in revenue. Within the same year she joined, they had an IPO, and the stock exploded, going from a listing of $18 per share to $53 on the first day of trading. Since then, it had become the "darling of e-commerce" of Wall Street and added millions of fans to the rapidly growing e-commerce category.

I'd signed up as a member of the eBay community the same year Meg joined as CEO. I remember my first reaction when I heard how eBay worked was disbelief. You were supposed to send money to someone you had never met, and they were going to send you something that they had listed on the site? While I was initially skeptical, I tried it a few times and was impressed. The online auction format was fun, and I started to try my luck at selling a few items at a time.

At our meeting in San Jose, Meg told me she wanted me to complete an assignment before she would consider hiring me. The goal would be to field research to better understand what was working and not working in the sellers' and buyers' eBay communities. The whole concept of eBay was built on the premise that the founder of eBay, Pierre Omidyar, had that "people were basically good."

Meg wanted to ensure we had enough insights into what the eBay community appreciated and what they still wanted and needed. Otherwise, she was concerned company management might start taking their success for granted, which could ultimately lead to a decline in the business.

I was thrilled to tackle this assignment and grateful I had a background in marketing research. I started by interviewing Pierre Omidyar and Jeff Skoll, eBay's co-founders, on what they thought about eBay's growing community's history and current state. I then fielded surveys among buyers and sellers, which included rating and open-ended questions.

The most surprising aspect of this research was the response rate. Usually, you hope for a 10% survey response rate—in other words,

10 out of 100 would fill out and return the survey. I had never seen response rates like the ones I was getting at over 50%! And the enthusiasm for eBay expressed in the open-ended questions was off the charts from both buyers and sellers.

It took me about a month to field the eBay research and report back to Meg. At the end of my presentation, she smiled and said they would like to create a role for me at eBay. I was delighted to work with Bill again, and we agreed I would soon be joining his marketing team in San Jose.

What To Do If You Are Out of Work (Especially for a Long Time)

It had been a long 18-month journey between leaving Taco Bell and starting at eBay. Since these are not the kind of lessons you typically are taught in school, I wanted to share some of the insights I gained during this journey:

- **Attitude Is Everything**—Being out of work for an extended period will wear on you mentally and physically. If you're used to being in a position of power, it will get lonely in a hurry.

  You will start to doubt your abilities and run the risk of this lack of confidence hurting you when it's time to interview. Do whatever you have to not fall into that trap: read inspirational stories, listen to positive podcasts, and regularly talk to friends and family. Visualize what it's like when you get back in a new role, which you will appreciate more than ever before based on your recent experience.

- *Dig Your Well Before You're Thirsty*—This is the title of a book by Harvey Mackay, which focuses on networking's critical importance. Although his book was written several decades ago, its key points are still valid today. Talent and experience aren't enough to get you ahead on your career path—it also depends heavily on your network. Developing one today is easier than ever with platforms such as LinkedIn, but it's still time-consuming and requires attention and effort. Like the title of Mackay's book suggests, the time to create your network is long before you need it. No one can succeed entirely on his or her own. Your network will be one of the critical factors in how well you ultimately do in the business world in good times and bad.

- **It's Not Personal, It's Business** — One of my favorite books is *The Four Agreements* by Don Miguel Ruiz. The second agreement he talks about in his book is "don't take anything personally." This principle is essential to keep in mind when you're still employed but looking for your next role. While it's important to be loyal to a company, it's much more important to be faithful to yourself.

  There are going to be times in which, due to circumstances beyond your control—such as the economy, a company reorg, a shift in corporate politics—you are going to be shown the door. I've learned it's a lot more productive to focus on what comes next and not waste a lot of energy playing the "blame game" on why it happened. When it's time to move, make sure you act professionally and exit in a manner that is a role model for others to follow.

- **Plan Ahead (and Pay It Forward)**—In today's competitive environment, the odds you will be unemployed—either via layoff or being fired—at some point in your career are incredibly high. Rather than think about it as a disaster waiting to happen, you should proactively think about what you can do for yourself as well as what you can do for others. One of the things that saved me during my extended unemployment is that we've always tried to have at least six months' worth of expenses available in cash— that's worth it in peace of mind alone.

  Be sure to pay it forward as well. When you have friends and family who are unemployed, be proactive. Reach out to them to see how you can help and who you can connect them with. Be sure to check in with them regularly—you have no idea what it will mean to them when they really need your emotional support.

Psychological resilience is the ability to cope with a crisis mentally or emotionally or to return to pre-crisis status quickly. Based on my experience, while there are several things you can do to become more mentally resilient, there's no substitute for having to go through this at some point in your career. It's never fun, but you'll be a stronger person coming out of the other side of all this.

> **CHAPTER TEN**
> **Resilience—When the Going Gets Tough**

REFLECTIVE QUESTIONS

- What's your definition of resiliency? On a scale of 1-10, how resilient would you consider yourself?

- Do you think you are more resilient now versus this time last year? Versus five years ago? Why or why not?

- What time in your career have you had to be extra resilient? What did you learn about yourself that you could share with others?

- What are some ways in which you have tried to increase your ability to be more resilient?

- Do you think people are born resilient, or is personal resiliency something that can be taught and learned? Discuss.

LEAP INTO ACTION

Resilience begins and ends with your attitude. If you have been mentally preparing for any number of things that could go wrong, you're not being a pessimist. You are simply creating a mental game plan, which has a Plan A, Plan B, and all the way to Plan Z if necessary. Expect and prepare for setbacks—that way, when they come your way, you'll be ready and know what to do.

 ## A MOMENT OF ZEN

Never lose hope despite personal setbacks and take the time to learn from failure.

Make lots of mistakes once (not twice). Use every challenge and every setback as a learning and growth experience. The most challenging times in my life are ones that I wouldn't change. They have molded me into who I have become. But during those times, I woke up each day with optimism and a determination to discover my purpose and lead by example. To use the old adage, diamonds are formed under pressure.

Life is not going to be precisely what you envision when you are young—there are going to be some disappointments and some remarkable highs. While you can't plan for every contingency, you can be prepared. Go with the flow and believe that other doors will open.

If you are a person who wants to be in control of every aspect of your life, you're going to be stressed. You don't have control of every-thing. So, as you face each challenge, decide what matters to you and realize that what matters will evolve and change over time.

11

Patriotism – All in This Together

Patriotism: Never losing faith in your country and what it stands for

SNEAK PEEK AT MY LEAP
How I accidentally became a witness to one of the most horrible days in U.S. History (and what it taught me).

The path that led me to see patriotism in a new light was poignant and painful. That journey started in an unlikely place—at a bookstore in Santa Monica on a rainy afternoon with a random encounter.

Red, White, and Blue

Growing up, I had a sense of patriotism, as I imagine many of us do. I felt pride when the fireworks lit up the sky on the Fourth of July, reverence when I saw a uniformed soldier, and solidarity when I stood to recite the Pledge of Allegiance.

All of that is still true, but life has taught me that patriotism is much more. I have deepened my love for this nation after witnessing the tenacity of everyday people overcoming tremendous trauma and after seeing strangers extend kindness to one another during a crisis.

A Critical Random Encounter

I was standing in line to buy several books about consulting, a career pivot I was seriously considering after leaving Taco Bell. Just before I reached the cash register, I heard a man's voice behind me.

"So, you wanna be a consultant?"

I turned around. There was a tall guy with glasses, smiling at me.

"Yeah, I'm thinking about it," I replied.

"Well, good luck. I've been a consultant for years."

He then introduced himself as Stan Slap. I told him there was no way *that* was his *real* name. He gave me his business card to prove it.

I had no way of knowing it then, but meeting Stan in that bookstore would change my life.

In the months that followed that initial meeting, Stan and I stayed in touch. I learned that he ran seminars that taught business leaders how to get internal buy-in on their strategies.

I told him I'd be interested in attending one, and he kindly agreed to let me join an upcoming one in New York City. It was scheduled for September 11, 2001, in New York City's financial district. It was originally going to be at Windows on the World in the World Trade Center, but the location changed at the last minute to a building on Water Street about six blocks away.

I arrived on a particularly crisp, beautiful night in the Big Apple. Its skyline was all lit up, confirming in my mind that there's nothing else like it in the world. Even though I'm not a native New Yorker, I can recognize several buildings from a distance, such as the Chrysler Building, the Empire State Building, and the easiest one of all, the World Trade Center.

I went to sleep that night buzzing with a bit of excitement, never dreaming of just how profoundly the next day, September 11, would forever change me and our nation. What follows is what I wrote on my laptop just after midnight on 9/12/01, since I didn't want to ever forget what had happened that fateful day:

9/11/01, 7:01 a.m. I awoke to a gorgeous autumn day and headed out early, so I could have time to grab a quick breakfast.

8:17 a.m. After a quick bite and cab ride, I arrived at the training room on the 13th floor of the Water Street building with plenty of time to spare. I looked out the window and was pleased with the awesome view of the New York Harbor and the Staten Island Ferry I had from my chair.

8:25 a.m. Stan walked in and instantly recognized me. I thanked him for inviting me to the seminar, and he told me, "It's going to be a great day." Though the seminar was supposed to start at 8:30 a.m., Stan explained that we needed to wait for everyone else to show up—so, we just chatted to pass the time.

8:35 a.m. I met Holly and Paul from Boston, who had been working with Stan over the summer. We looked out the window and all commented on what a glorious day it was. Like every American, we had no idea how much our lives were about to change.

8:50 a.m. I was beginning to wonder when we were going to get started. I then noticed what looked like some paper floating past the window. I went over to take a closer look and noticed the whole sky seemed to be filled with floating papers. Some of the papers appeared to be burned along the edges. I mentioned this to Holly, and we started to wonder what in the world could be causing this.

8:55 a.m. Stan finally decided it's time to get started. I glanced outside and noticed the singed paper was *still* coming down. I thought to myself: "What in the hell was going on?"

9:05 a.m. Stan started to talk about the power of leadership. Suddenly, the lights started to flicker, and it felt like the building was shaking just slightly. Stan looked puzzled. We all went over to the window and looked outside. The sky was no longer blue. It was gray, and it was raining—no, pouring—paper. There was a flurry of fiery paper bits, coming down like snowfall. We looked down and saw a large crowd gathering on the street below. They were all looking up at the buildings and pointing to something we could not see.

9:25 a.m. We are totally baffled. Holly suggested we go outside to see what's going on. I looked outside again and decided there was no way I wanted to go into a crowd that now looked like it was easily a couple of thousand deep. I decided I'd rather take my chances inside, rather than be in a potential mob.

9:45 a.m. Someone ran into the room and said a plane had hit the World Trade Center. I immediately assumed they were talking about a small aircraft, such as a Cessna. I couldn't imagine how a pilot could have made such a mistake and hit a building as big as the World Trade Center. We talked about the time a military plane hit the Empire State Building back in the '40s.

We all assumed this was a tragic but minor aircraft accident.

Someone else came back to the room with more information. We learned that a second jetliner had hit the World Trade Center, and this was some type of terrorist act. We were also told that the Pentagon had been hit.

10:00 a.m. At this point, everyone started to stir. Stan asked the group what we wanted to do. We decided to take a 30-minute break to figure out what was going on. There was a growing sense of panic in the room, so I was happy to get out of there.

10:05 a.m. We went down to the main lobby and looked outside. Everything was completely covered with ash. It was dark as dusk. It looked like it was snowing. A janitor invited us to come back up to the third floor to join a group in the company cafeteria to see if we could learn anything more on the news.

10:10 a.m. We walked into a large room where a couple of guys were trying to get the TV reception to work. They could not get any signal. We didn't know it at the time, but all of the TV stations had gone off-air because all of the broadcast towers were at the top of the World Trade Center. They were now buried beneath tons of rubble.

There was a radio sitting on a table with a weak signal. About a dozen people were trying to listen to what had happened. The announcer said two jetliners had crashed into the World Trade Center towers. There were reports another plane had crashed into the Pentagon and another in western Pennsylvania. The radio announcer said it was the worst attack on the U.S. since Pearl Harbor. I called home on a payphone to let my family know I was OK. They had been watching the morning news and were relieved I was safe.

This was starting to feel like a disaster movie. I told Stan I felt like I was waiting to wake up from a very bad dream.

10:15 a.m. Stan and I decide to venture outside. Immediately, I was surprised by how hard it was to breathe. The air was so thick with smoke and dust. I had my camera on me and snapped a couple of pictures. We all went back inside. Back in the cafeteria, someone had put some facemasks on the tables. We all grabbed one, knowing we'd need it when we went back outside.

10:55 a.m. Stan and I went back outside with our facemasks on but weren't sure which way we should go. We could not believe how much ash had fallen. It was like Pompeii outside. Everything was covered in several inches of thick ash. All you could hear outside were sirens—a wall of sound, entirely of sirens blaring.

11:00 a.m. We walked west for a couple of blocks. We reached Wall Street. It was utterly deserted. The iconic Wall Street bronze bull was covered in ash. The visitor's tent in front of the Stock Exchange was completely buried in ash. You couldn't see beyond the Stock Exchange. It looked like a thundercloud had descended on Wall Street. It was as black as night. This remains in my memory the most surreal, haunting scene I have ever witnessed.

We walked down an alley. I looked down and saw a single sandal in the ashes. I told Stan there's just no way a shoe could have come this far. We were still four blocks away from the World Trade Center.

We continued down the alley. Stan bent over to pick up a burned piece of paper. It was a fax cover page from one of the brokerage firms inside the World Trade Center. Most of the page was burned, and the only portion we could read was the headline: ***Morning Report, September 11, 2001, 9:00 am.***

11:15 a.m. My eyes were starting to sting and tear up from all the smoke. I began to get concerned about being out in these conditions and wondered what the long-term effects might be from breathing all this ash, even with a face mask. I could not imagine how anyone could breathe at all a couple of blocks closer to the World Trade Center, even with a face mask. I could not see more than a block ahead in the black gloom. It was eerily dark, even though I kept reminding myself it had been a clear fall morning just a couple of hours ago.

We all agreed it was time to turn back even though it had only been 15 minutes since we had gone outside. It seemed like hours.

We decided we would go back to the Water Street office, find whoever was left from the seminar group, and then go back to Stan's hotel about 15 blocks to the north. When we got back to the office, only one of our fellow attendees was still there. He agreed to join us on our trek out of there.

11:20 a.m. We put our face masks back on and started walking north. Cars had been abandoned in the middle of the road, covered in ash, with their headlights still on. Cabs were abandoned with the engines running. Everyone was heading out on foot. I was amazed at how calm everyone was despite the unearthly setting.

11:30 a.m. There were thousands of people in the streets as we got away from the Wall Street area. There were no cars except for emergency vehicles. Thousands of people were crossing the Brooklyn Bridge on foot.

11:50 a.m. During the hike to Stan's hotel, I caught brief snatches of conversation. Everyone seemed to be talking on his or her cell phone, which baffled me since I couldn't get mine to work. People were on every corner offering water to anyone who needed it. One woman was sitting on a doorstep crying, but everyone else seemed calm. Or maybe we were all in a collective state of shock. Whatever it was, we were all in this together.

As we hiked out of Lower Manhattan, I couldn't help but smile as I saw young men selling small American flags for $1 on the street corners. Where did they get so many U.S. flags that quickly? No matter, it was a reassuring sign that patriotism and capitalism were alive and well in the Big Apple that day.

I asked Stan what he would do if he were the president right now. I couldn't hear his answer because there was a tremendous roar as several F-15 fighters flew overhead. We looked back to where we'd been. There was smoke pouring over all the buildings. I wondered why we couldn't see the World Trade Center towers but figured they were covered in all the thick black smoke. We hadn't heard the news yet: There were no World Trade Center towers left to see.

12:15 p.m. We finally made it back to Stan's hotel. We went up to Stan's room to finally see what was happening on TV.

12:20 p.m. We can't believe what we see on CNN. The video showed the jetliner hitting the World Trade Center and the collapse of both buildings. I couldn't get the thought out of my mind that we were initially supposed to have this seminar in the Windows of the World on the top floor of the World Trade Center. I kept that thought to myself, since I figured Stan had enough to worry about right now.

We spent the rest of the afternoon watching the news and calling our friends and families to assure them we were safe. Stan's wife was on a flight that was in the air but was ordered to land immediately. Somehow the news had reached the passengers while they were still in the air, and there was understandably a lot of tension until it landed.

Stan also learned that one of the seminar attendees had planned to take the subway, get off at the World Trade Center, and walk over to the session. When he entered the subway station that morning, he didn't realize the subway fare had increased. He missed his train while he was trying to get the right change. Not having the right change in his pocket saved his life.

6:50 p.m. It started to get dark outside, and I wanted to get back to my hotel in midtown before it got much darker. I stepped outside and looked back at the Financial District. Smoke was still billowing up into the sky. The streets were almost totally deserted, and we started walking north. A girl on rollerblades skated down the empty street. Everything was very quiet except for the nonstop sound of sirens in the distance.

7:25 p.m. I didn't think I'd be able to find a cab, and I was right. I walked north for 30 blocks and picked up some food to eat when I got back to my hotel room.

8:20 p.m. I made it back to my room in time for President Bush's address to the nation from the Oval Office. I couldn't help but wonder if the plane that crashed in western Pennsylvania was supposed to hit the White House. There were rumors it was shot down before it got to D.C.

9/12/01, 12:05 a.m. I started typing about what had happened that day on my laptop while watching the news. I switched over to the BBC, and they reported that while Osama Bin Laden denied he was responsible for any of this, he was fully supportive of it. After typing for an hour, I finally tried to get some sleep.

The Terrible Toll

When I woke up later, the official body count was just starting to come in on the news. Up to 260 people had died on the jet airliners that crashed. At least 200 firemen died in NYC. Up to 800 were rumored to be dead at the Pentagon. I couldn't even imagine how many thousands must have died that day in the two World Trade Center towers. My heart went out to all the innocent victims and their families. I was wondering how all of this was going to end.

In the days and weeks that unfolded, it was devastating to learn that 2,977 Americans were killed that day.

Before that fateful day in September, I didn't seriously perceive any threats to our American freedom and way of life. I took it all for granted. I think many of us did. I hope none of us will in the future when dealing with challenges we need to face together.

CHAPTER ELEVEN
Patriotism—All in This Together

REFLECTIVE QUESTIONS

- What is your definition of patriotism? How do you balance the need to be patriotic with the feelings and rights of citizens in other countries?
- Where were you on 9-11-01? What do you remember from that day?
- What are some ways we should remember and honor the first responders who went to the World Trade Center on 9-11-01?
- What should we teach our children about 9-11-01?

LEAP INTO ACTION

Patriotism is a word often misused to divide people. On that fateful day in NYC, I saw what true patriotism was all about: all kinds of people coming together to help each other after a tragedy. That spirit didn't last very long in the U.S, but we should all endeavor to remember what it was like and assist those who need our help regardless of their current situation in life.

A MOMENT OF ZEN

"Be here now"—do what you can to help
others while you still have the chance.

Always remember we're all going to die. Living as though this is not true is self-deception. Know yourself and choose how you will live carefully.

We live in a world that feels increasingly transactional at every turn. The importance of a "quid pro quo" for every act seems to be more and more embedded as the norm. Take time to understand the whole human being with whom you are dealing rather than just what is obvious on the surface. Please do not make your life transactional.

Savor every moment. Show up for the most important life events for family, friends, and colleagues, and be fully present. Know how to tell the truth to others and how to guide them in ways they can hear rather than reject. Extend yourself to the stranger and those in need. Love fully. Be of faithful service to others. Enjoy the journey and know that the seeds you plant along that journey will be the garden in which you end the journey. Let it be lush and inspiring, and let it remind you of the good you have done at every stop along the way.

12

Agility— Go with the Flow

Agility: The ability to learn quickly and adapt to new situations with speed and ease

> *"Learn from yesterday, live for today, hope for tomorrow. The important thing is to not stop questioning."*
> *—Albert Einstein*

SNEAK PEEK AT MY LEAP
Why and how I went "back to school" to learn about marketing.

Harry Truman noted that while all readers are not leaders, all leaders read. I agree—lifelong learning is critical if you are going to stay on top of your profession. Especially if you're in a career, such as marketing, where the only thing you can count on is it is always going to be evolving and changing.

When I joined eBay in 2002, it was one of the "hottest" companies in the world. I was coming off an 18-month unemployment period, and I was looking forward to getting back to work. The biggest personal challenge this new job posed was where our family was going to be living.

A Long Commute

My family and I lived in Orange County, over 400 miles from eBay's headquarters in Silicon Valley. My wife and I had promised our sons they would not be moving by the time they got to high school. I made the difficult decision to commute from Orange County to the Bay Area every week. It would be tough on the family, but we decided it was worth the sacrifice. As it turned out, I would be working the most extended hours of my career while at eBay, so I would not have seen my family any more than if we had moved closer to the company.

Unlike other times when I joined a company with established roles and organizational structures, I was initially given just one person to manage, and a promise more was coming. They were right: six months later, I was running six different groups. I was responsible for the team in charge of educating eBay sellers. I managed the PowerSellers team who worked with the biggest sellers on the platform as well as the Trading Assistants team who helped the folks who helped others list and sell items on eBay.

One of my favorite groups I managed was the Giving Works team, which helped nonprofits raise money from auction sales—a program that helped raise over $10 million for the victims of 9-11. I was also responsible for the Events team, which put on various meetings and conferences around the U.S. for eBay buyers and sellers, including eBay Live, a massive gathering held every summer.

Since I loved to create new business opportunities, my favorite team was the one in charge of creating new strategic partnerships for eBay with other companies. RadioShack reached out to us to see if there would be any interest, and we thought it was at least worth considering. At the time, RadioShack had a network of over 5000 stores across the U.S., which we thought might offer convenient drop-off and pickup locations for eBay buyers and sellers.

In addition to managing these teams, I quickly discovered that while I thought I knew a lot about marketing, I knew practically nothing about digital marketing and e-commerce. The frustrating part was there were no books or classes I could take since digital marketing best practices were being created in real-time. To learn e-commerce, I decided to become an eBay seller. I eventually bought and sold over 500 items on the site, including a car I drove to work every day. As far as digital marketing goes, I'm still learning even today—and so are all the other marketers in the world since it requires an ever-changing skillset.

The Shack Ain't Where It's At

We arranged for Meg Whitman, our CEO, to visit Leonard Roberts, CEO of RadioShack. When we arrived at their headquarters in Fort Worth, Texas, I was blown away by how luxurious their executive floor was. The top two floors of the twenty-story Tandy Center—named after the company's original name, Tandy Leather Company—were just for the principal executive offices. When you walked into Leonard's office, it took up *half* of the entire top floor. You didn't realize when you first walked into his office there was a whole *other office* inside this one that was just as big. Since Meg and I worked in identical size cubicles back at eBay headquarters, I couldn't help but smile at the absurdity of the size of Leonard's office(s).

After some small talk, Leonard started asking Meg what it was like to have an office where everyone including her had the same amount of space to work in. RadioShack was considering downsizing to a campus-like setting that would be like what we had at eBay. She told Leonard it suited her just fine. Leonard then declared he would trade his entire office for just a fraction of Meg's stock in eBay. Meg smiled and simply replied, "I bet you would."

We wrapped up our meeting and headed back to California, deciding that we should pass on this partnership. I wasn't at all surprised when RadioShack went out of business about a decade later.

The E-Commerce World Awaits

Since I had international experience before joining eBay, I soon shifted to working with our emerging global markets, including Latin America, Canada, Australia, and Taiwan.

The most pressing international issue I needed to address was in Taiwan. eBay was in a tough fight against Yahoo to see who the leader in e-commerce in the island nation would be. The best way to get to know the team and check out the competition was to head over there in person. There were some initial concerns over a recent SARS outbreak, but flights were still going there. I would be heading there by myself, so I could change my travel plans quickly if needed.

The first indication this was not going to be a typical trip was when I transferred from my LAX to Tokyo flight, which was packed. My flight from Tokyo to Taipei, Taiwan, had only six people on it, not including the flight crew. There were multiple temperature checks when you went through airport security, including a scanner you walked through, which showed your body's thermal image. At the hotel, I was asked, "Which floor do you want?" When I asked the front desk staff what they meant, they said there were so few hotel guests they were assigning each hotel guest *an entire floor* to help prevent the spread of the virus.

If I'd known how dire the situation was on the ground before heading to Taiwan, I would have delayed my visit. But since I was already there, we went to work. The first thing we did was divide our eBay Taiwan team in half and had them work in two different buildings in separate parts of the city. That way, if one person got sick and infected his or her team, we could still have a way of managing the business.

The pandemic eventually passed, and we continued to do business in Taiwan for several years. But the eBay model didn't survive in Asia—having purchased or started companies in Japan, China, and Taiwan, all of them were eventually either sold or shut down.

Despite our eventual failure in China, it was an eye-opening experience for me. I had been to several Chinese cities when I was with KFC International a decade before, and one of my strongest memories from that time was thousands of bikes crowding the streets. Now that I was back, there were no bikes to be seen, just an unending mass of cars and air pollution so bad that you could go an entire week without seeing the blue sky.

Other markets were more successful. eBay Australia started strong and never slowed down. eBay Canada did well and created a separate classified listings business called Kijiji, Swahili for "village." They chose that name because it captured the essence of what eBay was trying to create worldwide—a site where people can connect with others in their community.

One of the most exciting markets I was responsible for was in Latin America, where I'd previously launched KFC in several markets. Marcos Galperin was a student at the Stanford Graduate School of Business when he attended a Meg Whitman lecture in one of his classes. After she finished her presentation on how well eBay was doing in the U.S., Marcos turned to his fellow Argentinian classmates and said he knew what he wanted to do when he graduated.

Marcos headed back to Buenos Aires and started his own version of eBay—called Mercado Libre, which means "free market" in Spanish—soon after graduating in 1999. It was rapidly growing in several Latin American markets, and rather than directly competing, eBay invested in the startup with 10% equity and a right of first refusal, which was the right to buy the entire company for a negotiated price.

Before I eventually left eBay, one of my biggest regrets was not persuading our senior management team to exercise its right to buy Mercado Libre before it went public. It now has a market cap about twice as big as eBay's, powered in part by MercadoPago, the Latin American equivalent of PayPal, which has over 100 million users.

How eBay Scaled the Business

Working at eBay was one of the most exciting and challenging phases of my career. The growth at the time was mind-blowing. I was used to working on businesses in which a good year was +10% growth. In contrast, it would not be unusual for parts of the eBay business to have a compounded annual growth rate of 100% for multiple years.

For example, Simon Rothman started at eBay in an operations role and enjoyed buying various items on the website. One day, he was looking for a toy Ferrari to buy his nephew for his birthday. He was disappointed he didn't see any toy cars listed but was shocked when he discovered *actual* vehicles listed for sale.

Simon went to Meg and said he thought this might be worth pursuing as a dedicated part of the platform. She agreed and designated him as head of the business. A few years later, eBay Motors had grown into a multi-billion-dollar business and became the leading seller of used cars in the U.S.

I was able to use my international marketing experience from PepsiCo and Yum! Brands at eBay. We set up a "marketing college" for our international teams in which we all worked on a global strategy to leverage marketing in all our markets. We had quarterly meetings in various locations around the world in which we shared what worked—and just as important, what didn't work and why. We even toyed around with the idea of creating a "global marketing tax" to help pay for some of our more ambitious marketing projects. There was so much pushback from country managers we eventually decided not to pursue this funding idea.

Listening and Responding to the eBay Community

From a marketing perspective, we were doing as much as we could to stay in touch with our users. Meg created something she called "eBay Panels." This is how it worked each quarter: we would invite a mixture of buyers and sellers from across the country to come to eBay headquarters for a couple of days. This new group would meet with Meg and other senior executives with no preset schedule. She would start the meeting by asking what was on the seller's and buyer's minds, which then became the working agenda. Various functional leaders would then come by over the next several days and have an in-depth discussion on different topics.

When this initial meeting was over, these "eBayers" would join all the others who had made a similar trip to eBay HQ to form new eBay Panels. We would regularly reach out to these panels either by email or phone any time there was a significant policy decision pending, such as pricing or changes to what could and could not be sold on the site. The eBay Panel program had its drawbacks. For example, we eventually had to limit terms to one year since "old-timers" on the panel would become very vocal and opinionated. Despite this limitation, consumer-focused companies would be wise to set up a similar listening program.

We wanted to make sure we stayed in touch with various communities created from buying and selling on eBay in a broader sense. For six years, I oversaw eBay Live, an annual gathering of eBay sellers and all the vendors who were part of the eBay ecosystem. We held the most significant event in Las Vegas, where over 15,000 people showed up—many more than we had planned on.

The primary focus was educational—there were dozens of classes you could attend—but it was also a chance to thank our sellers for making it all possible. This was a considerable investment—over $10 million each time we held it—and eventually, the finance team got the company to stop having them, since we could not measure an immediate ROI. But while they lasted, it was an incredible way of seeing the myriad of ways eBay had impacted people worldwide.

Seriously Underestimating the Competition

While all this growth was going on, we kept a close watch on what Amazon was doing. Amazon started in 1994, one year before eBay, but for a while both companies were considered equals in the e-commerce space. When eBay started, Jeff Bezos launched Amazon Auctions to put some pressure on eBay. eBay, in turn, launched a new website with fixed price listings, eBay Express, to compete against Amazon.

We were shocked when Amazon announced they would be launching a new service called Amazon Prime in 2005. For $79 per year, you could have free unlimited shipping for over one million items. I did some quick back-of-the-envelope calculations and thought they were insane. There was no way they could ever break even on this kind of program—it would lose millions of dollars annually.

But in retrospect, this was a brilliant "category killer" move that helped Amazon become the dominant player in e-commerce. Today, over 140 million Amazon Prime members pay $119 a year for a wide variety of benefits, including Amazon Prime Video. What seemed an insane idea at the time demonstrated the genius of Jeff Bezos in creating a business that went from being an occasional book shopping experience to something millions of Americans—and millions more worldwide—use every day.

Growth via Acquisition

In addition to worrying about competition such as Amazon, Meg and her senior team also looked for companies to acquire, matching up what eBay needed to help accelerate our growth. Shortly after I joined eBay, Meg announced we were buying PayPal for $1.5 billion. PayPal had started three years after eBay, and buyers and sellers on eBay were the primary reason it had grown so rapidly.

Some of the initial PayPal executives, later known in the national press as the "PayPal Mafia," turned out to be some of the most powerful and influential leaders of Silicon Valley, including:

Max Levchine, a Ukranian immigrant who co-founded PayPal with Peter Thiel. Max wrote the initial code for the platform and later became a substantial Yelp shareholder.

Peter Thiel, a German American immigrant who was the first CEO at PayPal, was the first outside investor in Facebook.

Elon Musk, a South African immigrant who co-founded an online bank called X.com, merged his company with PayPal. Elon would go on to create Tesla and SpaceX and become one of the world's wealthiest persons.

Reid Hoffman, an American who was the first COO at PayPal, whom Peter Thiel nicknamed "PayPal's Chief Firefighter" since Reid oversaw handling the many crises they faced in the early days. Reid went on to be the co-founder of LinkedIn.

It would be hard to think of another startup in business history with as many executives who created such enormously successful companies. Did you notice anything these executives have in common? Three of the four executives were immigrants to America—as was the founder of eBay, Pierre Omidyar, born in Paris of Iranian parents, and Jeff Skoll, a Canadian immigrant who was eBay's first president. For any American worried about immigrants coming to the U.S., I would note eBay and PayPal would not be here today if we didn't have immigrants such as those who came here looking for a chance to create something new and worthwhile.

I would have never predicted I would have anything to do with a significant eBay acquisition, but I did. Here's what happened: we were growing very rapidly, and our expenses got ahead of our revenue projections. Our CFO at the time, Rajiv Dutta, sent around an email asking everyone to do whatever they could to find ways to save money.

During my entire time at eBay, I commuted from Orange County to San Jose Monday through Friday. Our sons were in high school, and I wanted to stay in touch with my family as much as possible during the week. One day my sons called me on my cell phone and said they had come across a new way to stay in touch. It was called Skype, which was a free service using video over the internet as well as instant messaging. My sons thought this would be a fantastic way to stay in touch. It was a lot more fun to have a Skype call with video—this was years before Zoom took over the world—and besides that, it was free! So, we started using Skype every night to catch up.

Based on my experience using Skype, I responded to Rajiv's email by writing to him to tell him how I had been using Skype for several months. I thought it could be an excellent way for the company to save money on telephone expenses, especially considering how costly international calls were at the time. In my email to Rajiv, I admitted I didn't know what we spent on international calls annually but guessed it was a significant amount.

I was disappointed I didn't hear anything back from Rajiv on my suggestion but figured he was busy with the many issues a CFO must manage. I continued to Skype my family every day and was impressed by its ease of use.

About three months after I sent my suggestion about using Skype to Rajiv, we got a memo from Meg saying there would be a mandatory meeting for all VPs and above later that afternoon. There was a lot of buzz about the reason for this meeting, but no one had a clue on what it might be.

There were about 30 of us in the conference room with Meg. All the international offices had dialed in as well, which meant it was the middle of the night for some folks. Meg stood up to start the session. Her remarks were the briefest I'd ever heard from her. She simply welcomed everyone, smiled, and said she would turn the meeting over to Rajiv for a big announcement.

Rajiv walked to the front of the room and began his remarks. "About three months ago, Kip Knight sent me a memo in which he described a company called Skype. It was a new type of way for people to communicate via video anywhere in the world. We've spent the last 90 days doing a lot of due diligence, and I'm pleased today to announce eBay is buying Skype for $2.6 billion in cash and stock."

As I sat in the front row listening to all of this, my Blackberry started buzzing nonstop. I glanced at it and saw a growing number of text messages asking me why I had done this. I was in shock. Never in my wildest dreams would I have imagined eBay buying Skype. I just thought it might be a way to save some money for the company.

Meg's rationale for the Skype purchase was that she thought it would be an excellent way for buyers and sellers to communicate with each other when discussing a potential transaction. Given the PayPal purchase's success from several years before, this seemed a logical extension of making the eBay platform more user-friendly.

Having bought and sold many items on eBay by this time, buying Skype didn't sound like a big idea to me. As a seller, the thought of having to have a video call with potential buyers to answer their questions was unappealing. It would take a lot of time, and it would be easier just to answer their questions via email or instant chat.

My gut reaction was consistent with many other sellers, and Skype never caught on with eBay sellers. Despite this, Skype continued to grow because it was a convenient and inexpensive way to stay in touch with friends and family around the world. Rajiv was enthralled with Skype and became its president shortly after it was acquired. Later, Rajiv was promoted as president of PayPal and was elected to eBay's board of directors. Sadly, a few years later, Rajiv died from colon cancer at the young age of 51. He was a terrific business leader and was always a pleasure to work with during my time at eBay.

It turns out the Skype acquisition wasn't so bad financially for eBay. Six years after buying Skype and selling off portions of it over the years, eBay sold its remaining part of the business to Microsoft. eBay doubled the money that had been initially invested, and Skype has remained a significant player in the international communication business.

Changing of the eBay Guard

As 2008 approached, Meg was getting to wrap her time as CEO and potentially make a run for governor of California. She had brought in a former head of Bain, John Donahoe, as her backfill several years before, which was personally disappointing since I was hoping my boss Bill would be the next CEO. John was looking to bring some new talent to the executive team, and the HR department made many of us a severance offer we couldn't refuse. It had been a tremendous six-year run for me, and it was a great time to move on.

Looking back on my time at eBay, it was an incredible learning experience and one in which "agility" was something I tried to practice every day. Three critical insights on how you can be more agile in your own career would include:

1. **Just because it's never been done before isn't a reason not to give something a try.** In the previous companies where I'd worked, someone usually had "been there, done that," so you could typically find someone who could show you the ropes. That was rarely the case at eBay. A lot of what we were doing was making it up as we went along. For example, Pierre gets credit as the first to develop an online rating system for e-commerce via "feedback points." He did this because he didn't have time to personally resolve a growing number of issues between buyers and sellers. And it worked! So in the spirit of agility, when in doubt, keep trying new solutions until you find something that works.

2. **Don't get cocky.** When I first joined eBay, the company's amount of positive PR was terrific. We started to believe our press releases. We seriously underestimated Alibaba and Amazon, which eventually grew to be dramatically bigger than eBay. It's hard for a company or a person to remain humble when the press and everyone else tells you how amazing you are. You can be cocky and agile for a while, but the odds are that cockiness will eventually become your weak spot and undoing.

   I've read enough history books and business case studies to know that while it's great to reach for the stars, you need to continually remind yourself to appreciate your current good fortune and not take any of it for granted.

3. **"The disruptor eventually becomes the disrupted."** This is a Meg quote, and it's spot on. The challenge for any business is to know when to pivot and reinvent itself. The status quo is a very comfortable place to stay—why mess up a good thing? If you look at a long list of once-dominant players in their category at one time—including Sears, Blockbuster, Circuit City, and RadioShack—they resisted the need to adapt to a changing environment. Like in evolution, business is "survival of the fittest." Companies that do this well are the ones to bet on in the long run. It's much better to disrupt yourself before your competition does it to you.

CHAPTER TWELVE
Agility—Go with the Flow

REFLECTIVE QUESTIONS

- What's the most challenging thing you ever attempted to do so far in your life that required agility? What was the outcome? What did you learn about yourself? Would you try it again? Why or why not?

- Do you welcome new ideas, and are you more comfortable with what's "tried and true"? Why?

- What's been the most significant change in technology during your life? How did you learn about it? How important has it been to you since it launched?

- What do you think the next big significant change will be due to technology? Why? What are some of the positives and negatives of this change?

- Which companies or categories do you think are the most vulnerable to change? If you were in charge, what would you do to become more agile?

LEAP INTO ACTION

If you study huge trees that grow in weather-intensive environments, the trees that ultimately survive multiple storm seasons are the ones that are flexible and bend in the wind. If they don't, their branches get ripped off, and the tree gets uprooted. Be a lifelong student who is willing—even eager—to learn new skills and adapt to new situations. That's what makes the journey worthwhile and will give you the agility to go the distance.

A MOMENT OF ZEN

Recognize the power of AND.

Speaking from today to my 25-year-old self, my advice would be not to view life as a choice between my "success formula" OR personal growth, continued learning, and spirituality. I would suggest unleashing the power of AND. Our capabilities are extraordinarily greater than even the most incredible visionary can imagine.

One of my all-time favorite songs is John Lennon's "Imagine." I am inspired by its spirit every time I hear it. So, 25-year-old self, imagine bold, God-inspired possibilities. Go forth and be great at creating spectacular success for your fellow humans on this planet in its great hour of need.

13

Honesty – The Freak Pit

Honesty: Sincerity, consistency, and openness
in one's words and actions

> *"Honesty is often very hard. The truth is often painful.*
> *But the freedom it can bring is worth trying."*
> *—Fred Rogers*

SNEAK PEEK AT MY LEAP
**How I learned to walk on fire and
go into business for myself.**

There are times when you find yourself in a situation in which you a.) didn't ever envision signing up for, b.) did not want to do it in the first place, and c.) wish you could get out of once you were in it. But sometimes when that is the case, things happen that create memories you cherish and would not trade for anything. This is one of those stories.

By February 2008, I had been at eBay for six years. In Silicon Valley, that's a lifetime. When I first joined eBay, we had about 2,000 employees. That number had grown to over 16,000.

First, we expanded from the original campus to a small office in a business park. Then we needed the whole building. Then we needed the entire complex consisting of about ten buildings. Then we added an even larger office park near the San Jose airport. We now had international offices in at least a dozen countries. Our startup days were gone forever.

Transition Time

While I was still enjoying my work as VP of Marketing at eBay, getting things done quickly or without spending a lot of money was getting harder. Product changes that were no big deal in 2002 seemed to take a Herculean effort to get done by 2008. A product manager explained this phenomenon to me because as more and more code was written for the eBay platform, it made even the most superficial changes riskier and more expensive.

As he explained the situation, "It's like there's a minor heart problem in the center of your body, but to get to it, we've got to cut through layers of skin, nerves, organs, and other body parts—and do it all without killing you in the process."

Meg would be stepping down as CEO soon with rumors she was considering running for governor of California. She had always promised once she hit the ten-year mark, it would be the appropriate time to turn over the reins to a new CEO, and that time was quickly approaching.

I'd been through enough organizational changes to know once the CEO changes, it was anybody's guess what the resulting "musical chairs" would be for everyone else further down the ladder.

I was starting to seriously think about what life after eBay might look like. I was toying with the idea of going into business for myself and starting a marketing consulting business but wasn't quite sure that was the best next step for my career.

"We Hear You're a Great Marketer."

As I was considering my post-eBay career options, I got a phone call at work one day from Will, who said he worked for the Tony Robbins organization.

Will explained why he was calling, "We've been asking around to determine who is a great marketer, and your name keeps coming up."

I told Will I was flattered and asked what the reason for his call was.

"Tony Robbins would like to extend a special invitation for you to attend a Personal Power Seminar as his guest. It will be held in two weeks at the Los Angeles Convention Center. Even though this event would normally cost you over $5,000, there will be no charge for you," he stated.

I was wondering where this conversation was going. My only recollection of Tony Robbins was from late-night television commercials in which a parade of "What Ever Happened To..." celebrities gushed about how Tony had changed their life.

"Why are you making me such a generous offer?" I asked.

Will continued, "Well, as I said, we would like for an expert marketer like you to come in and evaluate what you think of Tony's Personal Power Seminar. It's a fantastic program, but we haven't been nearly as successful in marketing it effectively to large corporations as Tony would like. You can give us a candid assessment of how we're doing and what we could do to promote our programs to corporations better."

I was a bit surprised that somebody I had never met thought I would give up an entire weekend to go to some event and work on an evaluation of their program for free. It would cost me more than my own time since Will mentioned I'd have to pay for my travel expenses and meals. Their cost would be zero, since I figured the incremental cost of one more person attending a session such as this would be nothing. This was an easy decision to make.

"Well, I appreciate the offer, but no thanks. Good luck," I said.

Will didn't want to take "no" for an answer. "Do you realize this program is already sold out and worth over $5,000 to you? Tony is going to be very disappointed in you, since he was looking forward to your assessment of his program."

Despite Will's efforts, I replied, "As I said, Will, I'm flattered, and I'm sorry I can't do it, but my answer is no." With that, I wished him a good day and went back to the ever-growing number of emails piling up in my inbox.

My cell rang. I noticed a call from my son, Tom, who had just started working a new job in L.A. This was an unexpected treat, since once he started working full-time, we typically only talked on the weekend.

I answered the phone. "Hi, Tom, nice to hear from you. How's it going?"

He said he just felt like calling me up to let me know his new job was off to a decent start.

I told him that was great. "Hey, Tom, you won't believe who just called me."

Tom asked who had called.

"Some guy from the Tony Robbins organization. They wanted me to spend a whole weekend with them in L.A. in a couple of weeks at what they call a Personal Power seminar. All I would have to do is evaluate what I thought of their seminar from a corporate perspective. I told them no way. Can you believe they wanted me to go?" I asked.

The phone was silent for a moment. Tom finally said, "So, you turned them down?"

I continued, "Absolutely. Tony Robbins seems to me to be a bit of a nut job. There's no way I'm going to spend a weekend with a couple thousand of his crazy converts. No thanks!"

More silence. Then, Tom finally responded, "Dad, I *like* Tony Robbins."

Now it was my turn to be quiet. "Tom, I know on occasion you like to be sarcastic, just like me. Are you serious? Do you actually *like* Tony Robbins?" I asked.

I found Tom's latest revelation about being a Tony Robbins fan to be hard to believe. I half expected Tom to burst out laughing any second.

He didn't laugh but instead had a serious tone of voice. "Yes, I do. I think he's inspirational. I've read one of his books, and he had some interesting ideas."

A thought suddenly occurred to me. "Tom, what if you and I were to go to this Personal Power seminar in L.A. together?"

"Wow, do you think that's possible?" he asked. This call was getting more and more surreal. Tom rarely got excited about going to any kind of event. He now sounded like he just won free tickets to the Super Bowl.

"Well, I can try. Let me call them back and see what I can do."

Tom enthusiastically said that would be great. I promised I'd call him back very soon with an answer.

I looked up "recent calls" on my cell phone and hit redial for Will's phone number.

"Hi, Will, this is Kip Knight. I've been thinking about your generous offer and have reconsidered. I will do it. The only condition is I'd like for my son Tom to come along with me," I said.

Will paused and replied, "No way. The offer was just for you. That's worth $5,000. If your son comes, that's worth $10,000."

I was beginning to wonder how they did business accounting at the Tony Robbins organization. I replied, "Will, actually, your cost if I come, is zero. If Tom comes with me, it's still zero. I don't know how you can even begin to think you're giving anything up. My time is worth a lot. You'd be getting a bargain if I did this for you."

Will hemmed and hawed and said he'd have to think about it and call me back. Fifteen minutes later, he called and said that Tony would allow Tom and me to attend even though this was highly unusual.

We were supposed to show up in two weeks at the L.A. Convention Center on Friday at 1:00 p.m. The Personal Power seminar would continue through the weekend and finish late Monday afternoon.

I called Tom back, and he excitedly replied, "Dad, this is going to be a great weekend!"

I told him, at a minimum, I would enjoy spending some quality time with him and was curious to see what this seminar was going to be about. While I've been to several corporate training seminars over the past 25 years, I'd never signed up for anything like this.

Excuse Me, What's a "Fire Walker"?

The time for the Personal Power seminar arrived quickly. I took that Friday off to fly down on Thursday night from San Jose to Orange County to stay at our house and then drive up on Friday morning to meet Tom. We decided we would stay at a downtown L.A. hotel, so we would not have to drive the hour-long drive back to Orange County every night. We had time to get some lunch before the seminar started at 1:00 p.m.

We found a local restaurant that looked decent. As we were sitting there with our food, I couldn't help but notice many people walking around with black t-shirts with a picture of a fire emblazoned on the front and the words "Fire Walker" printed on the back. I mentioned this to Tom.

"Oh, that's for the firewalking part of the seminar," he explained.

"The WHAT?" I asked since I thought we would listen to some lecture, not risk going to the emergency room.

Tom continued, "From what I hear, all those black shirt folks are previous seminar attendees. They come back as volunteers to help with the firewalk later today."

I mumbled something about this wasn't what I was planning on doing as I nodded for the waiter to bring us the bill. I looked at Tom and said, "I've never considered fire walking before today, but I guess there's a first time for everything."

Tom agreed. "This will be fun!" he said as we left to head down the street for the convention center.

There was a mass of people waiting to get inside. You could see various designated lines for the different levels of attendees. There was the "Bronze" line for folks who had paid $2,000 for the seminar. Those in the "Silver" line had shelled out $3,500 to attend.

The "Gold" attendees—that would have included Tom and me, except we didn't have to pay anything—forked over $5,000 each to come here. To note, there's no way I would have paid even the Bronze fee based on my going-in assumptions about what this weekend was going to be like.

I was trying to figure out just what the difference was between Bronze, Silver, and Gold. Suddenly, it became apparent to me what the value proposition was: it determined your starting position when you got to *run for your seat.* That's it—nothing more.

Since, like Southwest Airlines, this was all open seating. All the incremental money you paid for Silver or Gold got you a two-or four-minute head start on all those losers in Bronze.

Tom and I were walking at a leisurely pace to go to our seats when they let the Silver group go. We were practically run over by the stampede of the Bronze group running for their seats a few minutes later.

We found two seats about ten rows back from the stage. The rows were the longest I'd ever seen—about 100 seats wide with no breaks. I wasn't thinking very strategically when we opted for center seats. Once everyone had sat down, I concluded that I wasn't going to be able to get to the bathroom for the foreseeable future, since getting there would mean tripping over fifty pairs of legs to get the end of the row.

Tony walked on stage, and the crowd went wild. Man, this guy was a giant! He looked a bit like that James Bond movie character,

Jaws. Giant head and hands and at least seven feet tall. Tony was very relaxed and seemed to be in his element.

"Hello, L.A.!" he yelled, with blaring rock-and-roll music choreographed for his dramatic entrance, along with impressive stage lighting. "Are you ready to become your personal best?"

"*YES, TONY, WE ARE!*" the crowd roared back.

I will have to give this Tony guy his due. He was as charismatic as anyone I've listened to on stage. He told us about his humble beginnings growing up in a low-income family. He shared with us how his first job was as a janitor, and he ended up sleeping in a car.

He then went on to talk about how he had decided there was more to life than just getting by. He started reading and studying what made people successful. Years had gone into this work, and his Personal Power seminar was the result: Tony's gift to us for a mere couple of thousand bucks each.

All this was choreographed tighter than a Broadway musical. Tony would go on for about 15 minutes or so. Then the music would crank up with some high-energy song—"Eye of the Tiger," anyone? Everyone would start jumping up and down. I realized another rookie mistake I'd made: You can't jump up and down very well or very long in thin leather-soled shoes.

While everyone was jumping up and down to the music, people would start running up and down the aisles looking for someone to hug. This being L.A., there was no lack of attractive females. Every 15 minutes or so, if you were a female who fit the bill, you could count on two, three, four, even five guys giving you the biggest bear hug of your life.

Then the music would fade out, the lights would go down, and Tony would be grinning on stage as if he'd just figured out how to pick winning lottery tickets that week. Based on what he was charging for this session, I guess he didn't need to. Sometimes he would mix up his routine and get one of those giant water guns to spray the audience.

Sometimes he would throw Tony Robbins t-shirts into the crowd. He was quite the entertainer: six hours went by quickly without a break.

Finally, Tony said we were on our own for the next 90 minutes to get dinner. You would think that for the kind of money the attendees were paying, you'd at least get some sort of boxed meal. But that wasn't part of the deal. Before he let us go, he got very earnest and declared, *"Tonight, we walk on fire!"*

Tom and I headed over to a nearby diner packed with many Bronze, Silver, and Gold attendees. I had been thinking about this pending event for much of the afternoon.

"Tom," I asked, "do you think we're really going to have to walk on fire?"

Tom nodded, "Yes, I've talked to friends who have done this seminar before, and you do have to walk on fire. Sometimes people get hurt and have to go to the hospital."

I vaguely recalled hearing about a Burger King executive outing that attended a firewalking event that went horribly wrong in Miami many years ago. "Hospital?" I gasped.

Tom smiled, "Oh, I'm sure we'll be fine. This will be a lot of fun." He continued calmly eating his salad.

Cool Moss, Cool Moss, Cool Moss

As we re-entered the convention center after dinner, the stage had been transformed with about ten different size screens in the background. If you didn't know any better, you'd swear you were now attending a Burger King convention, since every one of the screens was a different version of what "flamed broiled" looks like up close and personal. Various "fire" songs were blasting away on the sound system, such as "Ring of Fire" by Johnny Cash and "Burning Love" by Elvis.

The stage went dark, and Tony walked out with a spotlight on him as he boomed, "Welcome back! Los Angeles—are you ready to WALK ... ON ... FIRE?!!!"

"*Yes, Tony, yes!!!!*" the crowd enthusiastically responded. Except for me. I'm thinking to myself, "Maybe not. Probably not. Seems like a great way to get seriously hurt."

Tony put his arms in a Jesus-nailed-to-a-cross position—something I noticed he did pretty frequently—and said, "Okay, let's do this! But before we do, I want to remind all of you that as part of this seminar, before you walked in this room, you all signed away all your legal rights in terms of walking on fire. If you get hurt, we have no responsibility. You are doing this of your own free will. We have five ambulances standing by in case they are needed, but there are no guarantees you won't get seriously injured or maybe even die from firewalking."

"*Yes, Tony!*" the crowd shouted. I thought it would have been nice if, at this time, Tony had confirmed if the typical medical insurance paid by attendees would cover skin grafts and crutches, since these were not included as part of the overall Personal Power budget.

Tony continued, "There are three fundamental rules you must *always* follow if you are going to walk on fire. Firewalking is an ancient tradition that's been practiced for thousands of years. I have carefully studied the secrets of how this is done. Tonight, I will enable you to do something most people think is impossible. Follow these rules, and you should be safe. Ignore or violate any of them, and you will burn."

Tony pointed to the ceiling with his index finger, "Fire Walker Rule Number One: you need to create a *Special Move*. This is a personal, physical motion to get your mind in the right place before you walk on fire. Once you make your Special Move, your mind will instantly be taken to a different place to prepare you to walk on fire. I will give you a moment to figure out what you want your *Special Move* to be."

I looked at Tom and asked, "Do you have any idea what he's talking about?" This concept wasn't tracking at all with me.

Tom smiled and said, "Sure, I'm going to do something like this." And he stood up, crossed his arms over each other, made two swift downward motions with each arm twice while saying, "Woosh, woosh!"

Tom's Special Move looked impressive. "I like it!" I declared. "I'll use that one, too!"

Tom looked irritated and said, "Hey, that's not fair! I came up with my Special Move all on my own just for me."

I nodded, "It's perfect. I'm going to need all the help I can get, so I hope you don't mind if I use it." And with that, I mimicked what he had shown me and made two swift downward moves with both arms while quickly exhaling through my mouth with a "woosh, woosh!"

"Still doesn't seem right," Tom grumbled as Tony asked everyone to sit back down and pay close attention.

Tony held up a "V" symbol with two fingers and continued, "Fire Walker Rule Number Two:

"NEVER look down when you are walking on fire. You must look up to the heavens. If you look down, you will see the fire, and you will burn. You must look up to the stars and chant something to, put your mind in a different place. You must chant something like cool moss... cool moss... cool moss."

The crowd started quietly chanting, *"Cool moss. Cool moss. Cool moss."*

Tony nodded in agreement and then said, "That's right! That's the idea—that's exactly what you need to do. Put your mind in a place far away from the fire. Cool moss."

The audience continued chanting, *"Cool moss. Cool moss. Cool moss."*

About this time, I was thinking to myself: it's all fine, and my mind could be transported to a place with lots of lovely, cool moss. In the meantime, however, my poor feet were going to be traveling across the same cooking element I had used on many Boy Scout campouts to cook raw meat to perfection: *red hot coals.*

Tony waved his arms up in the air and urged everyone to be quiet, and continued, "OK, now everyone listen to me very carefully. This is the most important rule of all. Fire Walker Rule Number Three."

He held up three fingers and solemnly declared, "Once you begin your Fire Walk, you must ALWAYS walk at a slow and steady pace the entire time until you reach the end of the coals. If you run, you will burn. It's as simple as that. Under NO circumstances should you run. Walk slowly. Walk lightly. Walk with lightness in your heart and mind. Otherwise, you will be going to the emergency room later this evening and may never walk again."

I continued thinking to myself: "Now that you put it that way, Tony, would it be OK if you made an exception and let me wear my shoes when it's my turn to walk over the coals? I promise I'll walk slowly."

Tony made his Christ-like gesture again and screamed, "Listen to me, my people. I have shared with you the secrets of the ancients. Now it is time for you to select your Fire Walker Companion and prepare to WALK ... ON ... FIRE!!!!!"

I looked at Tom and asked, "So you want to be my Fire Walker Companion?"

Tom was still irritated at me for stealing his Special Move and said, "No, I think not. You be sure to enjoy that Special Move of mine." And with that, Tom turned and disappeared into the crowd to seek another Fire Walker Companion.

I'm into Barbie

I spotted a couple standing a few feet away. I walked over to them.

"My name is Kip. I know three might be a crowd, but I was wondering if both of you would be willing to be my Fire Walker Companions this evening?" I asked.

They smiled at me. The man spoke first. "I'm Tim from the Royal Canadian Mounted Police. I went to Tony's Personal Power last year, and it changed my life. I loved it so much I brought my wife with me this time. This is my wife, Barbie."

"Nice to meet you, Kip. We'd be happy to be your Fire Walker Companions. Oh, Tim, it's almost time!" she squealed in delight.

The fire theme music started up again, and Tony came back into the spotlight. "OK, the time has come. It is time to WALK ... ON ... FIRE!"

With that, on cue, all the doors on the left side of the convention center opened at the same time, and the music was going full pitch as the Ohio Players sang *"FIRE!"*

I looked outside. It looked like the entire city of Los Angeles was on fire. There was a bonfire with flames shooting up about 30 feet straight up. It was without a doubt one of the most enormous bonfires I'd seen in my whole life, and that's saying a lot, considering the number of campouts I'd been on. The vast Guy Fawkes bonfires when we lived in England were massive in size. But nothing compared to this in terms of flame height and ferocity.

Holy shit. This was way more than I had bargained for. I looked around to see if I could find Tom and get the hell out of here while there was still time. No luck. I guess there was no turning back now.

We had already taken our shoes off and were told to "walk to the fire." So, we started walking across the massive parking lot. Since I typically don't walk across parking lots in my bare feet, and it was pitch dark, I thought there was a good chance I'd step on a nail or some broken glass before I even made it to the fire. Come to think of it, maybe that would be a good thing, since it would send me to the hospital with my feet cut instead of being barbequed.

Two thousand people gathered near the bonfire. As we got closer, I could see there were about thirty different "Fire Walks" that had been arranged parallel to each other. Each Fire Walk was about three feet wide and forty feet long. Even though it was dark, you could see everyone's facial expressions from the glow of the hot coals.

I walked alongside Tim and Barbie as we picked one of the Fire Walks. She just would not shut up about how excited she was. "Timmy, oh Tim, isn't this amazing!" she said in a voice that made me think that if Disney ever needed a new recording for the animated movie *Snow White*, she would have nailed it.

There were several people in line ahead of us at one of the Fire Walking stations, and they had already started their walks. I studied them carefully. They put what Tony had told them to do into practice. They made their Special Move. They chanted, *"Cool Moss. Cool Moss. Cool Moss,"* as they began their walk. Their eyes lifted unto the heavens. They walked at a steady pace.

As they made it to the other end, a Fire Walker volunteer was waiting with a bucket of water to douse their feet. They were all smiling and laughing.

OK, that's not so bad. I can do this, I thought.

Tim and Barbie held each other in their arms and looked deeply into each other's eyes. "Which of us should go first?" they asked as they turned to look at me.

"Hey, I'm in no rush. One of you can go first. Knock yourself out," I replied.

Tim looked at Barbie and smiled. "You go first, honey. You're ready."

I could sense a slight hesitation in Barbie's voice. "Oh, no, Timmy, I'm not quite ready. You go first, and we'll cheer you on."

Tim put his shoulders back and stuck his chin out. I thought all he needed now was his Canadian Royal Mounted Police hat, and he'd look just like the cartoon character Dudley Do-Right.

"Very well, then, Barbie. I will do it!" Tim replied.

He made his Special Move; he started chanting the cool moss chant and steadily walked across the coals. In total, it took him all of 20 seconds. He turned around with a huge smile.

"I love you, Barbie!" he screamed.

"I love you so much, Timmy. I am SO proud of you," Barbie beamed back.

I looked at Barbie and said it was her turn. She hesitated and said she wasn't quite ready, so I should go instead.

I figured I might as well get this over with.

I took a deep breath and made my Special Move. I looked up at the stars and made my first steps. "*Cool moss, cool moss, cool moss,*" I chanted.

I took slow and steady steps. I could feel the heat on my feet, but I was already about halfway through the firewalk when my self-confidence took a giant leap forward. *Damn, I was walking on fire!*

Then something happened. Having spent many a night sitting around and observing campfires, as best I could tell, my right foot went down on a branch of a tree that was still very hard and didn't give in to the pressure of your foot the way flaky, soft coals do.

It was as if someone had taken a hot nail and hammered it into the middle of my right foot.

My right leg started to give out. It took all my willpower not to immediately go into a 100-yard dash to try to get to the end of the coals. I gritted my teeth as I looked to the heavens and moaned, "*Cool moss, cool moss, cool moss.*"

I barely made it to the end of the firewalk before I collapsed on the wet grass. The bucket of water thrown on my feet felt better than I could ever imagine. I sat up and carefully looked at the right sole of my foot. You could see where the hot branch went into my foot. Yep, that was going to leave a mark. My foot was throbbing, but I hobbled back up on both feet so I could cheer Barbie on.

Tim and I could see Barbie was still nervous.

Tim shouted across the firewalk, "Come on, Barbie, you can do this!"

Barbie suddenly had a determined look and nodded her head vigorously, yelling, "I can do this, Timmy! I know I can!"

She started to make her Special Move as Tim and I cheered her on. She began to put her foot out to get started on her walk.

A Fire Walker volunteer quickly walked up to Barbie and held up his hand. "HALT!" he shouted.

Barbie looked very confused and asked, "Why?"

The Fire Walker volunteer looked down at the firewalk and shook his head. He looked up at Barbie and declared, "Not enough coals."

With that, he quickly clapped his hands twice, and this huge guy with a giant wheelbarrow came over with a big shovel. You could see the determined look on his face from the glow of the coals in the wheelbarrow. He dug his shovel into the glowing embers and started at one end of the fire walk with a fresh layer of coals. He finally emptied the entire wheelbarrow of glowing hot coals to the other end, then disappeared.

Barbie didn't look quite as confident as she had a few minutes ago. She looked like she'd seen a ghost or something.

Tim and I shouted, "Come on, Barbie, you can do this! Go for it!"

Barbie meekly looked up at Tim with eyes as big as saucers and pleaded, "I'm scared, Timmy, I'm so scared."

"It's all in your mind, Barbie! I believe in you. I believe in us!" he countered.

Once again, Barbie hesitantly made her Special Move. I could hear her beginning her "*cool moss*" chant. She stepped out on the coals and started walking toward us. The coals were so bright you could see her face as if we were doing this in the middle of the day.

At first, I thought Barbie was going to be just fine. Though she looked worried, she was making a good time walking across the coals. She was already halfway across and would be with us in less than 10 seconds.

And then something happened. Perhaps she stepped on the same kind of branch I'd had the misfortune to step on. Maybe she looked down at the coals instead of the heavens. Maybe she forgot to think about *cool moss* at the time she needed it most.

Whatever happened, I could tell we had a serious problem. Barbie's eyes got even bigger, and she started screaming. She broke into a sprint. As she ran for Tim, all I could hear was Barbie yelling at the top of her lungs, "*It burns! It burns, Timmy! Oh, my God, it burns!*"

And while it might have just been my imagination, I also thought I could hear the sizzling of Barbie's feet as she ran across the coals to Timmy.

She collapsed into Tim's arms, sobbing. I looked down at her feet. I have seen burnt marshmallows that didn't look as bad. Unfortunately, Barbie has violated Fire Walker Rule Number Three by running across the coals and paid the price. She would not be going out on the town dancing with Timmy anytime soon, from what I could tell.

Barbie was crying uncontrollably on the ground next to Tim. I walked up to them and made my escape. "I'm going to give you two some alone time now. Thanks for being my Fire Walker Companions."

Tim's face indicated to me they would not be coming back for another Personal Power seminar next year. Assuming Barbie didn't divorce him first for making her permanently disabled.

I looked out into the crowd, and Tom came wandering up to me.

"Tom, thank God. Are you OK?" I said with relief.

"Sure, Dad, piece of cake. How did you do?" Tom asked.

I started walking alongside him with a distinct limp and replied, "Well, I'm not going to the hospital tonight, which is more than I can say for the others in my group."

We finally made it back to the hotel. My right foot throbbed all night long, and I didn't get much sleep.

The Freak Pit

We went back on Saturday morning for Day Two. I'll summarize Saturday by saying Tony couldn't make it—he claims he had to rest his voice—but his stand-in kept saying, "If you thought Friday's Fire Walk was amazing, you're not going to believe Resurrection Sunday!"

Oh, boy, can't wait, I thought. What were they going to do now? Nail us all to a cross?

Sunday arrived, and Tony was back with a voice that didn't sound like it had benefited much from taking the day off. The basic premise of Tony's talk on that glorious Sunday morning was we are our own worst enemy. We are all programmed with negative thoughts. To achieve our full potential, we must destroy those negative thoughts and rebuild them with positive affirmations.

OK, got it: out with the bad, in with the good. All the time, I kept wondering about what the big deal was with this so-called Resurrection Sunday.

This went on for hours. Tony kept telling us all about how we "have unlimited power that we rarely use, and we are our own worst enemy in achieving our potential," whenever he came out on the stage. At one point the lights went down, and he sat down in the middle of the stage in a lotus position.

Let me mention that we'd been standing up for two hours right before this happened. I was standing about 10 feet away from Tom in the aisle. Close enough to barely see him in the near-total darkness but not close enough to reach him.

Tony told us to close our eyes and dwell on our biggest limiting thought. Hmmm, I thought to myself. Nothing immediately came to mind. I had a happy childhood. I love my wife and two boys. Great career so far. I was feeling very blessed.

Finally, one limiting negative thought popped into my head: *I can never start my own business because I have spent my whole life working for large corporations.*

Now I'll admit, on the I've-had-such-a-shitty-life scale, this is probably way down on the low end. But I thought that was the best I could do on short notice, so I dwelled on that one.

Tony was starting to rant on stage. "I want you to dwell on your negative limiting thoughts. I want to think about what a failure you've been through because of it. I want you to wallow around in it."

I started to notice a few folks around me begin to sniffle and sob very quietly. It was barely noticeable at first, but it was discernible. No biggie in terms of public displays of emotion. I've seen much worse in various budget meetings I've been in over the years.

Tony continued to jabber away about how pathetic we were for about 10 minutes. Then Tony took it up a notch and screamed, "OK, people, it's now ten years in the future. You have kept your limiting thoughts in your head for a whole decade. You've disappointed your friends, your family, but most of all, yourself. You are a total failure. You can't even look at yourself in the mirror. You're so disgusted with yourself."

Wow, that's a bit harsh. Okay, so before this weekend, I thought that going into business by myself might be a bit scary, but I wasn't feeling any self-pity about it. But as I was thinking about all this, I noticed there weren't quiet sobs and sniffles around me anymore.

Nope, we were way past that stage. I'm talking loud, sobbing, crying, moaning and the occasional scream. I looked over at Tom, but it was too dark to see what was happening.

Now Tony was in full "giddy up" mode and continued, "OK, you pathetic losers, it's now 20 years in the future, and your life has been a total waste of oxygen. What kind of a *freak pit* have you been living in? You should have never been born. And it's all because of that negative limiting thought that you have refused to let go of your whole miserable, worthless life."

I thought to myself, "Alright, that's it. I'm out of here. I'm not a loser, and I don't have to listen to this. Let me get Tom and get out of here right now."

Except there was one minor problem. I couldn't walk down the aisle to get out. That's because there were hundreds of people rolling around on the floor curled up in small bundles, screaming at the top of their lungs. Tom and I would not have made it ten feet without tripping over numerous bodies.

I hung in there. Tony eventually let us release our negative limiting thoughts and replaced them with a happy thought. Mine was a promise to me that within a year, I would start a marketing consulting company called KnightVision Marketing no matter what it took; just let me out of here, Tony!

I called it quits after Sunday since I needed to get back to work. Tom stayed for the final day, which focused on healthy eating habits and personal fitness.

Feedback Is a Gift

That Wednesday, I had promised to get on a conference call with Tony's team. They were anxious to hear about what I thought of the weekend and what tips I could give them to get more corporate clients to sign up.

I'm generally full of ideas on what you can do to improve one's marketing, but in this case, I was at a complete loss on what to share this time.

"What did you think of the Personal Power seminar, Kip?" Will asked.

"Oh, it was interesting. My son and I enjoyed it. Thanks for inviting us," I warmly replied.

"Well, do you think we could get some more corporations to send their employees to attend?" he continued.

I was trying my best to be diplomatic. I continued, "I'm not sure corporations should be your target market. It might be better to go after individuals and small business owners."

They weren't buying this logic and pushed, "That's who we've always gone after. The reason we wanted you to go was to tell us how to get more corporate employees to go."

I tried one more time to dissuade them calmly. "I just don't think that's a good idea."

They kept pressing. "Come on, we paid over $10,000 for you and your son to attend the Personal Power Seminar. You have to tell us why we can't get more Fortune 500 companies to send their employees to our seminars!"

I couldn't stand it anymore. I started yelling into the speaker-phone, "*ARE YOU ALL OUT OF YOUR FREAKING MINDS? LEGIONS OF CORPORATE LAWYERS ARE GOING TO HAVE A FIELD DAY WITH WHOEVER IS SENT TO YOUR EVENT. THEY ARE GOING TO SUE YOU FOR THEIR EMPLOYEES GETTING BURNED ON THE FIREWALK, FOR THE NONSTOP SEXUAL HARASSMENT FROM ALL THE UNWANTED HUGS, AND FOR THE YEARS OF THERAPY THEY'RE GOING TO NEED AFTER THAT UNBELIEVABLE FREAK PIT EXERCISE!*"

There was total silence on the other end for a minute, and then some-one meekly replied, "OK, Kip, thanks for your feedback," and hung up.

Oh, well, feedback is a gift, so I guess they needed to think about the candid feedback I had just given them.

While it wasn't an ideal way to deliver my honest opinion, I did feel I owed it to them. I didn't realize it then, but this was my first ethical test as a marketing consultant. I could have taken the easy, but not honest, approach and spun some BS about what a life-changing event it was for me. I probably could have even gotten some paid work out of it. But I would be operating from a place of total dishonesty. Although I didn't know at the time just how successful my future marketing consultancy would eventually become (and it turned out to be very successful), I knew I would always be honest with my clients, even when the news was not good.

Fittingly, this eruption of blunt feedback is what sparked Knight-Vision Marketing. Six months later, I left eBay and was outside the corporate world for the first time in my life. Take that, freak pit, and thank you, Tony! I figured if I could survive walking on fire, starting my own business would not be so scary after all.

CHAPTER THIRTEEN
Honesty—The Freak Pit

REFLECTIVE QUESTIONS

- What's the biggest fear holding you back from doing something you've always wanted to do in your life? What would be the upside of overcoming this fear? How much do you want to do something about it?

- Think of a stressful work situation you've had. How did you resolve that situation? If you had to do it again, would you address it the same way? Why or why not?

- How comfortable are you at giving candid feedback to others? If not, is this something you would want to get better at? What are some steps you could take to get started?

LEAP INTO ACTION

One of Shakespeare's most famous lines from his plays (from *Hamlet*) is "to thine own self be true." Honesty starts with being honest with yourself. What do you really want out of life? What is holding you back from reaching your full potential? It's only after you've been able to answer these questions that you can begin to truly honor your authentic self and be the person you want to be. You can start small by setting personal boundaries in terms of what you want and don't want which in turn will boost your self-image and confidence.

A MOMENT OF ZEN

Be true to yourself and your values.

Stay authentic and true to yourself. When I was a young man, I was told that I needed to work on adding a "mean face" to my toolbox. I'm not a mean face person and trying to be harsh and contemptible just isn't who I am. When I finally let go of trying to fit into a mold that didn't fit me and embraced my authentic style, I was able to become a strong, confident leader who is approachable and can communicate and collaborate at all levels.

Hold your values tightly and your ideas loosely. Keep your ego in check and be open to feedback. However, when a client or boss asks you to do something that violates your core values, stand your ground and be prepared to walk away. At the end of the day, if you can't look at yourself in the mirror, you'll have a hard time getting ready for work the next morning.

14

Empathy – The Road Less Traveled

Empathy: The ability to understand and share the feelings of others

> *"Could a greater miracle take place than for us to look through each other's eyes for an instant?"*
> —Henry David Thoreau

SNEAK PEEK AT MY LEAP
How I learned how to be more empathetic by going on a 500-mile bike ride in Southeast Asia.

If you keep doing the same things over and over, it's easy for your world to get narrow in the way you look at it. Sometimes it takes a radical change of scenery to get you to appreciate some key insights you might have missed up to this point in your life journey.

My younger brother Kevin and I grew up enjoying all sorts of outdoor fun together, primarily through Boy Scouts. But as Kevin and I got older and busier, our outdoor adventures became a lot rarer.

"I've Found the Perfect Trip for Us."

Over time, Kevin proved to be a lot more adventurous than I will ever be. He's climbed several intimidating mountains—such as to the base camp of Mount Everest—rafted down the Colorado River, and flies his own plane. On occasion, he would invite me on one of these thrill-seeking outings, but I never could muster the will or time to join him. After we both passed our 50th birthdays, Kevin increasingly reminded me we weren't getting any younger. He insisted we should plan one more grand adventure we would remember for the rest of our lives.

"I have found the perfect trip for us," he proclaimed one day.

"And what would that be?" I asked.

"My friend Spence and I have been looking at different trip options, and the one we both liked is a 500-mile bike ride between Bangkok and Saigon."

Five hundred miles? Going on a long bike ride made me think of a good friend and colleague at eBay, Bob Hebeler. He was about my age and had challenged me to start riding again several years earlier. Based on his encouragement, I had started to get back on a bike for short rides on local trails. But I knew I was in no shape for a ride that long without some serious preparation.

Bob was an incredible athlete. He commuted to eBay headquarters from Santa Cruz and back several times a week, a 50-mile round trip that included climbing and descending Mount Charlie. He was one of the nicest people you could ever hope to know, universally admired, and liked by everyone.

Tragically, before I left eBay, Bob died in a cycling accident while riding in the Santa Cruz mountains. Bob's death was a sober reminder that bike rides came with a certain amount of risk—and could be a lot risker in South Asia, where many roads were crowded and in poor condition.

"How long does the trip last?" I asked Kevin.

"Three weeks on the road," Kevin explained. "We'll be with twelve other cyclists from around the world, and there will be a supply truck that will follow us the entire time. We'll have some days that we won't even bike, like when we check out the temples at Angkor Wat. The roads are flat the whole way, so you can't complain about pedaling up mountains. You've got to sign up for this!"

I debated the pros and cons of this "adventure" in my mind. On the one hand, three weeks was a long time to be on a bike, especially in a part of the world that wasn't famous for having decent roads or even potable water.

On the other hand, it was true we weren't getting any younger, and, as adventures with Kevin go, this one was on the tamer side of the scale. Since I had recently left eBay and was just starting my own marketing consultancy, taking one month off—one week for travel there and back plus three weeks of biking—seemed feasible.

"Okay, I'm in. Let's do this."

The first thing I did was go out and buy a new mountain bike, which could take a lot more abuse on the road than a regular road bike. I wanted one with enhanced shock absorbers, which can make a huge difference when you're going along a route that's got more potholes in it than asphalt.

To get ready, I rode an increasing number of miles on my new bike every weekend. I started at 10 miles and increased it by 5-mile increments until I could go for a 40-mile bike ride and not be completely wiped out. I signed up and completed a 100-mile bike race in Southern California just before I left for the trip. I thought it was a good sign that I managed to finish—even though I didn't set any land speed records.

After six months of riding a bike daily, I thought I was ready for whatever waited for me in Asia.

In retrospect, while all this physical preparation was important for getting my body in shape for the bike trip, I'm not sure anything I could have done could have prepared me for this trip mentally. What I failed to consider was not only were the roads in Southeast Asia in pretty bad shape, but there was also going to be a lot more traffic on fairly narrow roads with lots of potholes and other hazards. It was probably better I didn't know that at the time, or I might have backed out. I went to my doctor and got all the required immunizations needed for the trip.

The logistics for getting started turned out to be more complicated than I originally planned. Three weeks before I was scheduled to leave for Bangkok, I got an invitation to give a speech in Amsterdam for an international marketing group as one of my first "clients" for Knight-Vision Marketing, a marketing consultancy company I'd just started.

The speech sounded like a lot of fun, but I didn't think the timing would work. Until I learned from the client they would fly me over on business class. I ended up flying twice the distance to get to the "starting line" in Bangkok but figured I would make some great contacts for KnightVision Marketing while I was in Europe.

Packing for the trip was a bit of a challenge. I needed to bring business clothing for Amsterdam along with a minimum amount of warm clothing, then land in the sweltering heat of Bangkok to ride on a bike over 500 miles through the backcountry of Cambodia. I managed to get everything I needed for the next month in a duffel bag, a messenger bag, and a small carry-on.

Before leaving, I was talking to a friend who had been to Cambodia recently. He mentioned how poor everyone was outside the cities. When I asked him if there was anything I could do to help while I was over there, he mentioned there was a chronic lack of pencils and paper for kids going to school. If I could bring school supplies with me during our rides in the country, they would be greatly appreciated. That sounded like a good idea, and I planned to do this once we arrived.

Beginning in Bangkok

After arriving in Bangkok following my speech in Amsterdam, I met Ian, our guide for the bike trip. He was from the U.K. but had lived in Asia for the past five years. Ian had led this bike trip four other times, so we would be in good hands.

I also had the chance to meet the rest of the bike team, which included 14 of us. There were three couples: Lucy and Chris, Dale and Adam, and Clive and Helen; seven males: me, Kevin, Jon, Bruce, Jeff, Vince, and Ian; and one single female, Lindsey. Since my brother Kevin was going to be rooming with his friend Jon during this trip, I would be rooming with Bruce, a banker from Texas. We visited a local Buddhist temple, where we would have our bikes blessed before we took off the next day.

Based on my friend's suggestion, I also went to a local stationery store to stock up on pencils, pens, paper, and pencil sharpeners. Some items in Thailand are a bargain, such as food. But this was not the case when it came to school suppliers. Everything was more expensive than if you went to Staples here in the U.S. That really didn't matter to me. I went ahead and stocked up before we hit the road.

We started our journey on a Sunday morning. The traffic would be just a fraction of what it was on a weekday.

Even so, it would be risky, so Ian arranged to take us outside the city by van. We boarded around 11:00 a.m. The pickup trucks were loaded with our bikes, fresh water, and food. We headed northeast about 200 kilometers to enter Khao Yai National Park. It's Thailand's first national park, which was created in 1962.

The difference in the scenery and climate once you entered the park was dramatic. The park itself was huge: 2,170 square kilometers at a high enough elevation that was noticeably cooler than in Bangkok.

We planned to spend three nights here to get acclimated to our bikes and road conditions before heading into Cambodia.

The road vehicles were unlike anything I saw before. Entire families rode on one motorcycle. My favorite vehicle was the "traveling rock and roll band" on the back of a pickup truck, followed by two truckloads of teens on a dance floor inside the trucks—all dancing to the beat.

We spent the next couple of days exploring the lush jungle trails, going on bike rides within the national park to prepare for our trek to the Cambodian border. The heat was intense. I drank water nonstop and applied sunblock at every break. At one of our rest stops, Jon noticed a bottle of squid juice sitting on the table. I'm a big fan of Tabasco sauce, but after trying squid juice, I decided I'd stick with my traditional favorite sauces.

When the time came for us to leave Khao Yai National Park, we headed out at dawn. We rode our bikes down a long hill, and it was pretty much all downhill most of the way out of the national park. We rode 70 miles on our first full day on the road. It was the second-longest bike ride I've ever done—the longest was 100 miles which I did to get ready for this trip while I was still in California. Seventy miles sounds even more impressive if you state it in kilometers—113 km.

The next day, we continued our journey to the Cambodian border. Again, we got an early start. I had been dreading the heat. But as it turned out, our biggest problem that day would be wild dogs. Let's be clear: I love dogs. But I would soon learn wild dogs are not the same as those we grew up with as kids.

Before we left for this trip, Kevin kept talking about the danger of wild dogs during this trip. He wanted to bring mace as protection. I've never been *that* afraid of dogs, wild or not. I just figured if I yelled back at them, they would leave you alone.

We cruised along, and Lindsey was in the lead when she saw the first wild dog. She headed over to the other side of the road, and the next biker up was Jon. He yelled at the dog. The third rider back was Kevin. I guess Jon did an excellent job of scaring the dog chasing him, as the dog gave up on him and went right after Kevin.

It surprised Kevin enough that he slammed on his front brakes, did a complete flip over the handlebars, and almost landed on the dog. He was fortunate he didn't break any bones. We took a break for Kevin to get some bandages and then continued.

During our rest break, I figured the best defense against wild dogs was a good offense. I found some small rocks that would fit in the cracks of my helmet and loaded up. We rode along, and I soon got the chance to test my new anti-dog defense system. I could see a pack of wild dogs tracking me at a good pace on the other side of a picket fence. I saw an open fence gate coming up fast that would in effect "let the dogs out."

I reached up to my helmet and got a rock ready as I passed by the gate. As soon as the first dog came running out of the gate, it headed straight toward me, with a nasty snarl. I started screaming and threw the rock over his head. The dog made a sudden stop and ran off in the other direction.

Score one for the bike riders.

After biking for six hours, we arrived in Aranyaprathet, Thailand. We were making good time and planned to take the next day off to rest. Ian briefed the group that the next part of the trip was going to be the most challenging part due to several reasons: a.) the road was going to go from paved asphalt to dirt, b.) distances were going to be longer, and c.) there would be no more convenience stores or food huts, which we'd come to rely upon for something cool to drink.

Ian had one other warning for us. He warned us that the road ahead would be very dusty because it was the dry season. We all needed to buy some masks soon if we didn't want to eat a lot of dust over the next week or so.

We all went to dinner that night. Afterward, I walked over to the local night market. It looked like the equivalent of the county fair in the U.S.—except for the crickets being cooked in woks. There was also a Buddhist temple that looked serene in the moonlight.

I walked back over to the hotel where Ian sat out in front enjoying a beer. He was nice enough to give me one as well.

As we sat in front of our hotel, I commented to Ian, "Wow, the Third World is really something."

Ian took a long swig of his beer and smiled. "Kip, this ain't the Third World. That's waiting for us across the Cambodian border. Compared to over there, this is like staying at the Conrad Hilton."

Crossing into Cambodia

We got up before sunrise to begin our 35-mile stretch to get to the Cambodian border, but we were not sure how much would be paved versus dirt.

Getting across the Cambodian border was a tribute to bureaucracy. First, you had to get your luggage loaded up from the van into push-carts. Then, you had to get in line on the Thailand side and get your card filled out and your passport stamped.

Next, you had to go outside and bike for about a half-mile on the Cambodian side. Then, you had to get in another line, where you got your Cambodian visa stamped.

Finally, you had to get your luggage loaded from the cart to the van.

When we were finally finished with all the challenges of getting across the border, we switched from riding on the opposite side of the road we rode on in Thailand, where they drive on the left side of the road. There were several roundabouts on the road with several hundred bikes, motorcycles, cars, trucks, vans, tuk-tuks, and pushcarts moving all at once.

Everyone seemed to be always headed in a different direction from us. But what made it challenging for us, as well as dangerous, were the motorcycles that carried wide loads on their backseats—such as five giant hogs laying on the back of a motorcycle.

Once we got out of town, it wasn't bad at all. The road stands were few and far between, but the local kids couldn't be more excited to see us on our bikes. They would all run out to the road and yell "Hello!" and "What's your name?" To me, this was proof positive money and happiness aren't directly correlated. I don't think I've seen happier humans anywhere on the planet, despite a lack of most of the physical things and comforts we take for granted in our daily lives.

I learned from Ian we were on the longest bike ride his travel company offered. They had been doing this bike trip from Bangkok to Saigon for about four years. In total, there were about 150 riders who had completed the trek. Of that, maybe a third were Americans. He concluded we were either a prestigious cycling group or an insane posse. My vote was for the latter.

We ate a lot of dust the next day. The weather wasn't too bad in the early part of the day, but by 10:00 a.m., it was stifling. We covered about 50 miles that day. Ian reminded us to save our strength, since we still needed to cover about 85 miles the next day to get to our next stop in Siem Reap on schedule. As I fell asleep thinking about the ride the following day, I kept pondering the age-old wisdom of Yoda when Luke declared he would not be afraid. Yoda's response was curt: "You will be."

The following morning, to get as much mileage behind us before the day got too hot, we decided to leave before the sun came up so we could eat breakfast on the road. We weren't sure how much of the 85 miles would be paved and how much would be dirt.

We soon found out.

We made excellent time for the first 20 miles. The sunrise was incredible. We made it to an old temple where we stopped for breakfast. The meal included baguettes—a relic from the French when Cambodia was called French Indochina. If you didn't believe the food was from Cambodia, all you needed to do was check the label: "Made in Cambodia" was stamped on the outside of the baguette—not the bag, but the bread itself. Ian was able to buy about 50 baguettes for $7 USD.

By the time we finished breakfast, the sun was up, and we were in the middle of the Cambodian countryside. The local kids were up with the sun. Imagine riding down a road on your bike in Cambodia and seeing dozens of kids, mile after mile, running up to the side of the road and acting as if you were the most prominent celebrity they ever dreamed of meeting one day. They yelled out no matter how far they were from the road. Ian said practically everyone took a car or bus through this part of Cambodia, so we were some of the few Westerners they had ever seen.

The paved road gave out at about the 30-mile mark. The dirt road wasn't so bad at first. Then it got bad, worse, and then much worse.

Since dirt roads are such a foreign concept to most of us, I thought it would be helpful to share a dirt road rating system I invented based on my experience that day. There were five levels in my road rating system, which I have termed "rut levels":

Rut 0: This is a level, paved road. This is what you drive on every day in the U.S. When you're riding your bike on this type of road, you can dwell on anything you like without a care in the world.

Rut 1: This is your preferred kind of dirt road. Pretty smooth, maybe a chunk of rock or gravel here and there, but overall, smooth sailing.

Rut 2: This class of dirt road has a couple of grooves, and you must be a bit careful not to hit them or you might crash. You can still daydream a bit while pedaling without putting yourself in much danger.

Rut 3: This type of dirt road has a lot of potholes. They have a particular machine over in Cambodia that punches holes in the dirt by some sick engineer with no sense of humor. Your helmet will seriously rattle, and your wheels are going to go tat-tat-tat-tat. You don't have much time to think about anything—perhaps a casual thought about how much you can jostle your kidneys before you lose all bladder control.

Rut 4: This is the worst class of dirt road—it's just a collection of potholes, one right after another. It feels like you've gone down to the Home Depot and strapped you and your bike into a paint mixer machine. You can't think about anything other than staying upright on your bike. If someone were to ask you your name at this stage, you would need to get back to him or her.

I was determined to finish this part of the ride even though it rated at least a Rut 3 classification. Like Churchill said, "When you're in hell, keep going." I pressed on another seven miles until it was time for a break. We stopped at a hut in the middle of the countryside.

We bought some semi-cool drinks in a small hut. Ian saw some local kids and told me this would be a good time to get out the boxes of pencils and sharpeners I bought in Bangkok to give away. The kids couldn't have been more grateful. You would have thought you were giving them bars of gold. They wanted to make sure all the other kids at least had a box of pencils before they would accept a pencil sharpener that I also brought for them.

It made you want to cry. They were so grateful. These are the same kind of kids who were so excited to see us along the road. These were some of the most extraordinary children I'd ever been around.

At that moment, I was overwhelmed with a feeling of empathy. Of course, I could not know the struggles they faced daily. But I could imagine it, almost feeling what it must have been like—deeply. Years have passed, and the human connection I felt in that moment remains. Even after many years, I can still see their faces, lit with joy.

Unfortunately, it was time to get back on the dirt road. Ian mentioned the last time he went through this part of Cambodia, the entire road we were on was dirt. He had no idea when the paved road would start again before we reached town. Well, at least he was honest, but I could have used a good lie from him right about then, such as: "Sure, right down the road, it's paved and smooth as a baby's butt."

But it was not to be. **Rut 3** soon became **Rut 4** road conditions.

I was truly amazed a road could be this bad. Then I remembered Ian mentioned the reason this road took so long to pave. It seemed the brother-in-law of Cambodia's prime minister owned an airline that flew into Siem Reap for tours of Angkor Wat. He deliberately wanted to keep this road in such lousy shape that tourists would want to fly to Siem Reap instead of driving. I mentally reserved a special place in hell for this guy. I guessed he never biked this road, unlike the thousands of his countrymen who did it every day—and had for decades.

I made it to a bridge, and the dirt road became something the X Games should seriously consider as a new event. I kept thinking, "You have got to be kidding!" before slamming down on the next hole. I was grateful for my bike's shock absorbers but wondered how in the world those ahead of me on road bikes got through this obstacle course. The road bikers in our crew were getting the worst of it.

Then the road started to improve ever so slightly. I felt optimistic—maybe there was a paved road that was only a couple of kilometers ahead! Down the road, I could see a water truck approaching from the opposite direction. It was hosing the road with plenty of water to keep the dust down. A cool shower right about now sounded mighty nice.

As the water truck came past me, it reminded me of being under the waterfalls at the national park, where we stayed at the start of this trip, which seemed a long time ago. The road underneath me instantly changed to mud.

All I could think of at this stage was: "Houston, we've got a problem." The bike instantly went out from under me. The good news: landing on hard mud wasn't too bad. The bad news: my rearview mirror, rear light, camera, bike, and butt were now all on the road with heavy traffic going around me.

As I laid in the middle of the road, I thought, "To hell with this. I'm done biking on this road."

I stood up and flagged down a large empty wagon being towed by a motorcycle. I got some money out of my wallet and started waving some dollar bills. He put my bike in the wagon, and I climbed aboard. After another 15 minutes, we finally made it back to a paved road, and I was able to put all my bike gear back together again. I paid and thanked the driver and rode with Bruce for the next mile, where the rest of the crew was already eating lunch.

I didn't have any shame at all in giving up. If discretion is the better part of valor, sometimes you just admit defeat and accept that you can beat the road on most bike rides, but some days the road will beat you. Today the road won.

We made it to Siem Reap around 2:00 p.m. after eight hours of riding for a total of 85 miles with 40 of that on horrific dirt roads. We checked into our hotel and had a nice team dinner at a restaurant by the river. The locals were very friendly, and the sunset was amazing.

Up until this point on our trip, we'd seen plenty of interesting sites and some amazing people in Cambodia, especially the children. Although they didn't have much in terms of material possessions, they were some of the happiest people I met in my life. In the next couple of days, we were going to be wondering why they weren't the saddest people on the planet.

The Tough Keep Going ... And Going ... And Going

By day 17, our crew was exhausted, and muscles we didn't even know we had were sore. As we neared the Vietnam border, we battled heat, humidity, and wind. The miles were long and hard. We stopped every 14 miles but kept having to slow down due to the relentless headwind.

We stopped in front of a local farmer's stand for some blessed shade, which was in very short supply. The locals brought us some mats to sit on; in return, we gave them some food, for which they were very grateful. It was hard to eat much in this heat, but since you knew you would need the fuel, you ate—and drank more water than you ever drank in your life—and made sure it was flavored with electrolytes to replace all the salt your body was losing.

The only irritating folks on the road were the drivers of these enormous Land Cruisers. I was especially irritated with three United Nations vehicles as they whizzed by our bikes, stirring up a dust storm. They were single drivers in huge, brand-new vehicles going about 80 miles per hour. I could only imagine the impression it gave to all these poor people. No wonder the U.N.'s nickname out here was "Useless Nations." I'd make all those bureaucrats ride bikes for at least part of the time as a job requirement if I were running the joint.

We finally made it into the town where we were staying for the night around 5:00 p.m. We had done 11 hours of cycling that day with very few breaks. We staggered to our room, showered, and went to a local restaurant, where I had some fried noodles and vegetables. We all fell asleep around 9:00 p.m. and planned to leave for the next town at 7:00 a.m. We were scheduled to do another around 75 miles the next day.

I woke up and tried to move; it wasn't easy. We managed to all get our sore bodies out of bed to get ready for the long ride ahead of us. We had a quick breakfast, where I invented a new sandwich: PB&T— sandwich, peanut butter, and tomato. Delicious!

The weather was marginally better for biking that day, and the roads were decent by Cambodian standards.

Throughout this entire stretch, I continued to give away school supplies to children at each stop. You can't get a bigger "bang for your charity buck" than giving away school supplies to kids in Cambodia.

They don't have any money to spare, and they are very grateful for anything you contribute.

So, the next time you might be feeling a bit sorry for yourself for whatever reason or think the world might be out to get you, here is a potential solution for all that ails you: buy a ticket to Cambodia, get on a bike, and start pedaling to the rural areas with some school supplies to give away. Your fan club will be waiting. They will literally be jumping up and down. They are so excited you decided to grace them with your kindness. This will put your own problems into perspective.

We stayed in the town of Skuon the night before our last full day on the road in Cambodia. It was the first time Ian had stayed there. It might very well be the last. The hotel was the worst. For the rest of my life, if anyone says the hotel or motel they stayed in recently was terrible, I will always confidently reply, "Well, at least it's not as bad as Skuon."

Where did this confidence come from? I'll let you be the judge.

This was the only hotel I ever stayed in that had nothing in the room—no soap, shampoo, toilet paper—nada. The sink didn't drain; it just dumped right out on the floor into a hole that went God knows where.

The one item Skuon is famous for is its fried tarantulas. A couple of folks from our group went to the local market in the afternoon to check them out. I didn't get a chance to eat them, since I was catching up on my blog entries. The spider lady came around that night at dinner to sell us some more, but everyone said they were full enough with rice and vegetables.

Jon joked that the local parents promised fried spiders to their kids as a special treat if they ate all their vegetables, then changed his mind after eating one. He decided they could use it as a threat.

About 1:00 a.m., my roommate Bruce got violently ill. We'll never know if it was the fried tarantula or something else he ate. If we had taped the sounds in the room that night, it would've been an excellent soundtrack for *The Exorcist*. Bruce said later that after he threw up five times, he thought he was done. No such luck. He lost count. At 5:00 a.m., I suggested we take him to the hospital, but he told me he'd rather take a bullet to the head than go to the local hospital in Skuon.

We got up at 6:00 a.m. to get ready for our ride into Phnom Penh.

I was a bit concerned about this final phase of our bike ride. It wasn't the next 200 miles that concerned me, since this would be the shortest leg of our trip. It was that Ian kept talking about it the way Eisenhower spoke about the Normandy landing. He indicated the roads would get progressively worse, and we had to cross a bridge that was scary as hell.

I was determined to finish this part of the ride on my bike despite a lack of sleep and tired muscles. I helped get Bruce in the supply van with the driver, as there was no way he would be able to ride today, and the rest of us reluctantly got back on our bikes.

The day heated up fast. Jon promised to convert to Buddhism if Buddha could make a Coke truck collide with an ice truck and form a giant Slurpee. We didn't see nearly as many kids either.

The rice fields got greener, and, just as Ian promised, the roads got progressively worse. In some places, the road was only about as wide as my driveway back home. And in some areas, the road simply disappeared; it was as if someone needed the asphalt and just took it somewhere else.

I was able to stay in my favorite "guarded" position in front of our supply van as we rode our bikes down the road. I told the driver to stay close to me, so I wouldn't get run over—or at least improve my chances of not getting run over.

The motto for Cambodian drivers should be: "We categorically reject the laws of physics." I cannot believe what these folks carried on a motorcycle. One guy had an entire bedroom dresser on his bike. It made circus acts I've seen look like amateur hour.

We finally stopped right before the bridge going into Phnom Penh. I found it hard to believe we would ride our bikes over this bridge with that much traffic. It looked about as crazy an idea as if we wanted to head straight into the Lincoln Tunnel in NYC at the peak of rush hour on our bikes heading in the wrong direction.

Vince volunteered to watch my back. We started up the bridge into the city. There was a narrow lane for pedestrians and one for motorcycles and bikes. The lampposts on the bridge were one more thing to look out for because if you weren't paying attention, you would hit one of those and go falling off the bridge into the water about 100 feet below.

About halfway up, a motorcycle ahead of me blew out its back tire that scared the hell out of me; it sounded like a gunshot at first. We went around the disabled motorcycle and finally made it to the other side of the bridge.

Lindsey was on my left backside, and Vince was on my right as I followed the supply van into the city with hundreds of cars and trucks flying in all directions around us. We finally got to the hotel and were relieved to be there without any injuries.

The team had a great lunch at a local Chinese restaurant. After relaxing in the afternoon, we went over to the Foreign Correspondents Club for drinks. There was a fantastic view of the river and the city. The most impressive thing about that day could be summed up in four simple words: we all arrived safely. That was something worth celebrating.

The Killing Fields

I love history because I believe those who don't learn from history are doomed to repeat it. One of the most important lessons from history is simple: all it takes for evil men to succeed is for good men to do nothing.

And in the case of Cambodia, even good men couldn't save millions of victims. We started the next day in Phnom Penh by going to the National Palace and National Museum, where the king lived. Before this trip, I didn't know much about the history of Cambodia; if this country's history were a play, it would have more twists and turns than a Shakespearean tragedy.

Phnom Penh was founded in the 1300s. In 1863, Cambodia became part of French Indochina. In 1941, Prince Sihanouk, just 19 years old, became king, and in 1953, Cambodia was granted its independence from France. The Vietnam War started, at least the U.S. part of it, in the early 1960s, and from what I can tell, that's when it went from bad to worse in Cambodia.

The Khmer Rouge, an extreme form of the Communist Party led by Pol Pot, used the U.S. bombings to rally peasants against the General Nol regime, a former Cambodian general who had U.S. support. King Sihanouk initially supported the Khmer Rouge, who the Chinese also supported. By 1975, the Khmer Rouge defeated the Nol government and marched into Phnom Penh on April 17th, 1975.

Starting in 1969 and continuing until 1973, President Nixon authorized bombings in Cambodia, claiming it was "a pure Nixon doctrine— Cambodians helping Cambodians." After the Khmer Rouge took over Phnom Penh, under the pretense of evacuating the city because the U.S. was about to bomb it, they had everyone go to the countryside. They promised everyone they would be back in their homes in three days.

Despite Nixon's acclaim for being great at international relations, such as opening U.S. relations with China, he really screwed this one up. Nixon was trying to stop the North Vietnamese from using the Ho Chi Minh Trail that went through Cambodia to supply the Viet Cong in South Vietnam. That strategy was ineffective and just made it easier for Pol Pot to take over Cambodia.

The population of Phnom Penh went from 1 million down to about 40,000 in just three days and stayed that way for the next four years. Imagine evacuating Manhattan and making everyone work in the swamps of New Jersey growing vegetables, and you start to get the idea. Many died in the transition.

Pol Pot wanted to outdo the Chinese in terms of the true communist lifestyle, so he tried to eliminate all traces of modern life and have everyone work on a farm. He created something called "The Angkar," a mysterious group of officials who represented the government. Pol Pot also wanted to triple rice production; it was a fiasco. Rice production dropped, and what rice was produced got shipped to China to pay for all the weapons they bought, as they had no foreign currency or tax revenue.

Pol Pot eventually went mad and killed his government leaders while many of the Cambodian people starved. The Khmer Rouge set up dozens of "security centers," (which were designated with names such as "S-21") that were schools converted to torture chambers. First, you were tortured and then killed. And if you mentioned anyone you knew during your "confession," they were tortured and killed as well. That was what we visited that afternoon at one of the many killing fields near the city.

If you were in Cambodia while all this was happening and were a businessperson, educator, or any type of professional, you were given a death sentence. You might die now or a bit later, but there was no doubt you were going to be killed. That included Europeans and Australians who happened to be in the country at the wrong time. At the killing fields located on the outskirts of Phnom Penh, you could still see clothing and bones sticking out of the mass graves scattered around the grounds—despite it being over three decades ago.

Our tour guide's neighbor, Vann Nath, was a prisoner of S-21 and was one of seven survivors of 14,000 tortured there. Everyone else died in the killing field; to save bullets, they just hit them over the head or buried them alive. Vann Nath wrote a book called *A Cambodian Prisoner Portrait* I highly recommend—along with *First They Killed*

My Father by Loung Ung, who writes about her family's hell on earth during the reign of the Khmer Rouge.

All things considered, it's amazing Cambodians are willing to smile at all. But as they say there, "The egret forgets, but the snail always remembers." They might be willing to forgive their enemies and torturers, but they will never forget what they did to them. It was an emotionally exhausting day. I don't think most Americans have a clue of what happened over here, but they should. We certainly played a part in creating this mess.

I would miss Cambodia. They deserve better. I hope they get to have a brighter future.

Enjoying the Vietnam Vibe

When the time finally came for us to cross into Vietnam, we packed up all the gear and braved the Phnom Phen traffic one last time.

We were going to cross by boat and made it down to the dock on the Mekong River. We were on the boat for about three hours; it was an enjoyable ride.

We went through Cambodian Border Control and got back on the boat to head down the river to go through the Vietnamese Border Control, which was a lot more modern-looking and efficient than our experience coming into the Cambodian border ten days earlier. Once we got through, we met our guide, who would be with us for the remaining portion of our trip. Ian informed us Mr. Foo was famous for guiding trips, so Ian always tried to get him for his tours.

We got on our bikes and started biking in Vietnam.

I was surprised by how different Vietnam was compared to Cambodia. It was the greenest place that I ever saw. Due to the Mekong River, they could irrigate and grow crops all year long. There were neat, tidy villages made up of tiny houses all along the road with substantial rice fields beyond the road. The road was narrow but well paved. Best of all, there were very few cars. There were lots of bikes and motorcycles.

The kids were just as excited to see us as the Cambodian kids were. This was my favorite stretch of biking so far.

We made a brief stop, where we had some squeezed cane sugar—as you can imagine, it was incredibly sweet—and we kept going. Dusk set in when we reached the second ferry, and I was glad my bike light still worked despite several crashes it had endured.

After another 15 minutes, it was completely dark, and we made it to the hotel that was located right on the bank of the Mekong River. We checked in and went down to the dock, where they had a terrific restaurant with plenty of the local fare.

We were going to spend the next 24 hours on a boat traveling 150 miles down the Mekong River. I've always loved boats and the water, so, for me, this was definitely a great way to travel. It was very relaxing compared to the stress of riding a bike and looking out for the next motorcycle or truck that might hit me.

Around 3:00 p.m., we docked the boat for the day. Ian asked if we'd like to do a 20-mile round-trip bike ride to a bird sanctuary. I thought it sounded like fun, and 10 of us decided to go for it. The bird sanctuary was cool, with hundreds of egrets gathering there as day turned into dusk.

On the way back to the boat dock, Ian casually mentioned we were a bit behind schedule, so we might need to pick up the pace to get back to the hotel before it got completely dark. I had now been with Ian long enough to know he was the master of understatement. What he meant to say was we were going to have to pedal as if the Devil himself was after us. We did about 21 miles per hour on the way back to the hotel; that was a personal best for me on this trip.

Kevin and Spence elected to sleep outside on the roof of the boat that night and asked me if I wanted to join them. I declined since I had made it this far without getting malaria, so I decided to stay inside the cabin.

It was a rough night on the boat. Lucy was ill, and the folks who elected to sleep on the roof of the boat had a rough time, since several nearby boats decided to party until 1:00 a.m. Despite not getting enough sleep, we all got up at 6:00 a.m. to take off for the floating market. This was where all the sellers in the local markets go to get their produce delivered via the various canals that weave all over the Mekong River Valley. There was an amazing variety of fruit and vegetables. These merchants lived on the water their whole lives along with their families.

We headed back to the boat and pulled up the anchor to head downstream. We stopped after about an hour to get on the bikes for one last ride of about 25 miles. It was pretty much a dirt path all the way and some of it was awful. You really had to concentrate, especially when going over the bridges, which went up in the air and had no guard rails. If you had a motorcycle heading at you from the other direction, it was the ultimate game of "chicken." A couple of times I thought I was going to get pushed out of the way and end up in the river.

When I was on my bike the first week of this trip, I was a nervous wreck with all the traffic and horrible road conditions. The second week was better despite the dirt roads and sweltering and muggy weather. By the time we got to this point in the trip, nothing could freak me out.

For instance, in the middle of heavy traffic, a motorcycle came roaring up from behind me; the passenger reached over and reached out to touch my stomach, and then yelled out, "Coochee, coochee, coo!" He laughed as the motorcycle roared off ahead of me. If that had happened in the first week on the road, it would have caused me to crash. I was a veteran of the road by Week 3, and that incident didn't even make me cringe.

We made it to the final school we would be visiting to give away the last of our school supplies to the kids. When I asked the headmaster if they had any foreign visitors visit the school before, he said yes—30 years ago! We had tea with the headmaster and got back on the bikes to continue biking down the river path.

Of all the many pleasant surprises on this trip, the kids we met were the best part. I'll never forget them. They were always thrilled to see us and seemed to be the happiest people, despite having practically nothing in terms of physical possessions or financial security.

These little guys and gals couldn't care less what the stock market did today (it was crashing in the U.S. as we were getting ready to return) since they had nothing to begin with. They never stopped smiling at us in every village we passed.

We finally made it to the end of the bike ride part of our trip. Ian suggested that since we started our ride getting our bikes blessed by Buddhist monks, we should finish it by going to a local religious ceremony. He indicated we were fortunate to be able to stop and see a Cao Dai church service. A monotheistic religion started in Tay Ninh, Vietnam, in 1926, it now has over two million followers. As a combination of Christianity, Buddhism, Islam, and Confucianism, they believe all religions have value. If everyone could agree that was indeed true, this world would be a much better place.

There was no way we could bike to the center of Saigon and survive, so we had a van pick us and our equipment up on the outskirts of town that night and take us to our hotel. The bike-riding part of the trip, all 510 miles, was finally over, and it was time to start to get ready to head back to the U.S.

The Winners Write the History Books

The following day, Ian gave us a guided tour of downtown Saigon, also known as Ho Chi Minh City. We passed by the Opera House, the headquarters of the local Communist Party, first-class hotels, and the main post office. It might seem weird to check out a post office, but this was one of the architecturally interesting buildings in town. We checked out a Hindu temple, the first one we had seen on this trip. It featured Ganesh, the elephant-head god with a man's body, who was the god of prosperity and wealth.

A group of us headed over to the Reunification Palace, where the North Vietnamese Army rammed through the gates on April 30, 1975. This is also the black-and-white photo of the helicopter leaving the roof during the final evacuation of Americans leaving the city.

By this time of the day, it was hot and humid, so we headed back to the hotel to take a break. Our next challenge was to get the bikes ready to ship back home. We didn't have enough boxes for all the bikes, so Lucy, Ian, and I headed over to a bike shop.

After we finished packing up all our bikes, we went back out to visit the War Remnants Museum. It was sobering. It's said that the winners get to write the history books. That was clear at this museum: the U.S. was portrayed as the "evil aggressor" and the Vietnamese as innocent victims.

We left the museum after a couple of hours for the walk back to the hotel. Crossing the street in Saigon was like playing a live version of Frogger. Ian taught us to walk at a steady rate as the motorcycles and cars whizzed by. It worked but it took some getting used to. God help you if you changed your pace or stopped; you'd likely get run over and probably never get up. All I knew was the traffic was always moving. I never saw anyone stop for a pedestrian. You just had to go for it if you wanted to get to the other side of the street.

During dinner, Ian briefed us on the tunnels we were going to be visiting on our last day in Vietnam. They were used by North Vietnamese during the war to survive the bombings.

We headed out to the tunnels of Cu Chi early in the day to avoid the crowds. The tunnels were built in the 1950s during the war against the French and are located just outside Saigon—or Ho Chi Minh City as it is now referred to by the locals. The tunnels were part of a larger network throughout the entire country and served as the Tet Offensive base in 1968.

We crawled through a short section of the tunnels that were about 200 meters long. The width of the tunnels has been doubled to accommodate the Western visitors. It's hard to imagine what it would have been like to have lived down there for weeks at a time.

We stopped to look at a rubber forest on the way home. Thirty years ago, this area was carpet-bombed and didn't have any foliage. It's come a long way since then, but you could still see the bomb craters.

Goodnight, Saigon (aka Ho Chi Minh City)

On our final day in Vietnam, our team gathered for a farewell dinner in Saigon. We had all gone through a lot together the previous three weeks. Frankly, we had to endure a lot more than I thought we would, both physically and mentally. During the first week of bike riding, I wasn't even sure I would physically be able to make it.

By the second week, I got my "second wind," and now that the third and final week was over, I was sorry to see it coming to an end. It was amazing how well this team stuck together no matter how tough it got. Everyone did a great job of looking after each other and helping each other out when they needed it. If a team was only as strong as its weakest link, this was an incredibly strong team.

We headed for the airport at 3:00 a.m. for a 6:00 a.m. flight to Hong Kong that would get us back to San Francisco at 8:00 a.m. on Saturday, four weeks to the day I left California. It felt more like four months, but in a good way.

Nirvana Isn't Just a Grunge Band

I picked up a book on Buddhism at the beginning of our trip that talked about a Buddhist principle called "compounding." The idea is simple enough: compounding asserts that most people spend way too much of their lives being distracted by things that don't matter in the long run, such as money, prestige, food, drugs, etc. It is called "compounding" because you need more and more of whatever it is you crave to get the same effect you got when you first started.

The past three weeks on our bike trip were all about "anti-compounding"; we carried only what was needed, and our "souvenirs" were going to be the memories we carried home from this trip. Seeing kids with few physical possessions, who were some of the happiest kids I ever met, was proof enough to me that "compounding" had a lot of merit to it.

We flew out of the Tan Son Nhat International Airport in Vietnam and landed in Hong Kong to change planes for the final leg of our journey to Los Angeles. As we waited in the Hong Kong airport, there was a group of Americans who were a living example of compounding. They evidently had just finished a long cruise, and one older woman wouldn't stop complaining. She whined about the cruise staff for 15 minutes. I left to get something to eat with Jon and she was still at it when I returned 30 minutes later, complaining about the quality of the food, and not getting enough of it.

This woman was not going to reach "nirvana" in her current lifetime. Maybe during her next time on Earth, she can come back as a rice farmer in Skuon, where the quality of the cruise waitstaff wasn't going to be on her "Top 10" list of concerns.

Sadly, most Westerners never get the chance to meet or understand people who live in different countries or cultures. That's hard to do when you're traveling on a bus at 70 mph. The best way to get to know another country or culture is to open your mind and see the world from their perspective.

Walk a mile in their shoes—bike a mile or 500 on their roads. Understand their world and appreciate their human experience. Study their ways and history before you go to their country. Then get to know them as individuals while you are there. Show them you care and respect them, and you will be well on your way to being an enlightened traveler. This level of empathy can make you a wiser, kinder person who deeply appreciates the amazing diversity of all people.

To my way of thinking, there's no better way to do this than on a bike. There's a poem by T.S. Elliot called "Little Gidding" that comes to mind:

We shall not cease from exploration
And the end of all our exploring
Will be to arrive at where we started
And know the place for the first time.

We boarded our plane at the Hong Kong airport. As we headed back to the U.S., I reflected on how much I appreciated where and how I lived, but with a new respect for the different cultures and values in other parts of the world we all share.

This adventure of a lifetime had instilled in me an empathy I never knew possible. I was soon sound asleep on the plane heading east, ready to reenter the world of daily compounding, but at least I now had a place in my mind I could retreat to if it got too crazy.

Achieving nirvana might have to wait a while for me, but the vivid memories of this incredible bike ride and the empathy I learned along the way will suit me just fine for the time being.

CHAPTER FOURTEEN
Empathy—The Road Less Traveled

REFLECTIVE QUESTIONS

- How empathetic are you? Do you wish you were more empathetic? Why or why not?

- Have you ever spent time in a part of the country or world that was radically different from what you were used to? What did you learn about yourself?

- What are some ways in which we can teach our children to be more empathetic?

- How are you doing good in the world? How do you feel about the level of impact you are making?

- How well do you think we're doing as a country in terms of showing empathy? Is this something we should be working on? In what ways?

LEAP INTO ACTION

One way to become more empathetic is to support organizations that try to help those in need. One group I've supported for a number of years is Plan International USA (www.planusa.org) in which you can sponsor a young girl, or several, in developing countries to help her reach her full potential. In addition to providing financial support, sponsors send and receive letters with the girls they support. It's a wonderful charity. I would recommend that you seriously consider helping.

A MOMENT OF ZEN

Start with empathy, listen more, talk less, and recognize your good fortune.

Since empathy and awareness are two essential elements of wisdom, my spouse introduced me to a concept some years ago that helped me deal with difficult people. It's called "observing ego" usually manifested as the inability to understand how one's actions might be affecting those around them. We can all easily list our least favorite bosses who suffered from this deficit. Some might also call this the essence of EQ vs. IQ. You and I have also met many people in the business world with high IQ but low EQ.

Everyone is shaped by their unique life experiences, which form their perspective. In so many situations, we just can't understand where someone else is coming from. When I was younger, I cared less because I had my perspective and knew it was the "right" one.

Now, I listen more, talk less, and use empathy to fill in the gaps. This mindset has led to personal and professional growth.

Ask more questions, listen more. I thought I had to know all the answers. Now I know that to be untrue. We never have all the answers. And sometimes, having the right questions is much more valuable.

Everyone is raised differently. Every person brings to the workplace their behaviors and personality long in the making. Respect and celebrate those with varying backgrounds. This is part of the diversity discussion that often gets limited to age, race, or sex. Understanding and capitalizing on everyone's life experience can be a catalyst for growth and a continuous source of inspiration for the entire organization.

I would encourage those at the start of their careers to just appreciate what they have and look around them, seeking out the greatness in their midst.

15

Helpfulness – A Marketer Goes to the White House

Helpfulness: Being of service to others by doing thoughtful things that make a difference in the lives of others (as well as our own)

> *"If you are not willing to learn, no one can help you. If you are determined to learn, no one can stop you."*
> *—Zig Ziglar*

SNEAK PEEK AT MY LEAP
How we taught others to become better strategic communicators around the world.

You might have seen a movie with a dramatic scene where the phone rings and the voice on the phone tells the recipient to come to the White House and help government officials face a looming crisis. That's essentially what happened to me when I got a call one day from someone representing the National Security Council (NSC).

It was near the end of the G.W. Bush administration in 2008. Islamic terrorism was a growing threat in Iraq and other countries in the Middle East. The international image of the country had taken a beating during the so-called "War on Terror" that followed the September 11th attacks in the U.S. The global reputation of the United States had significantly declined, mainly due to widely publicized incidents such as horrific prisoner abuse by U.S. soldiers at Abu Ghraib prison.

Could You Please Come to Washington D.C.?

According to the person on the phone who reached me at home, senior officials in the NSC thought it might be helpful to have some folks outside of Washington D.C. with marketing expertise come to advise them on what the U.S. could do to win "The War of Ideas" against Islamic terrorists. Would I be interested in coming to Washington to meet with the NSC and some other marketers to discuss this topic at the White House?

My initial reaction to this unexpected proposal was a mixture of curiosity, skepticism, and excitement. It's not very often a marketer is asked to do something to help our nation. Besides, I'd always wanted to learn more about how the federal government worked. On the other hand, what could come out of a meeting like this that would have any real impact?

I figured it would be better to go to the meeting and see what happened rather than assume it would be all for naught.

One month later, several other marketers and I were seated in the Cabinet Room of the White House with representatives of the National Security Council. It's a bit surreal to be sitting in a room right across the hall from the Oval Office. The meeting was scheduled to last for one hour.

We started our discussion by sharing some observations about the current challenges the U.S. was facing from a marketing and public relations perspective. We noted the irony that the United States, home to many of the best marketing teams in the world, couldn't take all that collective marketing experience and talent and apply it to improve the country's image abroad.

There was consensus that the State Department, the federal agency primarily responsible for maintaining and enhancing the U.S. brand, lagged compared to what most U.S. corporations were currently doing, especially in social media. At many embassies worldwide, holding a press conference and distributing a press release was still the primary means of communication, just like it had been done the past half-century.

As the White House meeting was starting to wind down, a thought occurred to me. I raised my hand to be recognized. "What we've been talking about is an ongoing marketing challenge that is going to require professional teams with marketing training. The U.S. already has some of the greatest marketers in the world in the private sector. What if we had some of these marketing experts in the private sector teach federal government officials how to think more like professional marketers in tackling these communication issues?"

There was a moment of silence. One of the NSC officials finally commented that vetting an outside vendor for the kind of marketing training I was proposing would be complicated and time-consuming, especially if the vendor had never done it before. It probably would not be worth the effort, especially since there wasn't a budget for doing this.

I thought about all the marketing training we had created over the years for KFC and eBay. I responded, "What if we did it pro bono? I'm pretty sure I could pull together a pretty amazing team of marketers who would be happy to share their expertise at no cost if it might help the country."

Some in the room voiced skepticism that marketing professionals would be willing to give up their time without compensation for what I was proposing. Still, there was also agreement that if we could put it together, it might be helpful to federal agencies such as the State Department. And no one could not argue about the price tag. I knew based on previous experience we could figure out a way to get everyone to help out despite the lack of a budget once we got underway.

Creating a Marketing College for the U.S. State Department

When I returned to California, I remember standing in front of a whiteboard with several other marketers and asking the question, "How do you even begin to organize something like this? How do we create a framework for U.S. government employees to start thinking about marketing and communication strategy?" We spent several weeks coming up with several ideas for the curriculum and formats.

We finally decided the only way to validate this concept would be to hold what we would call "The U.S. Marketing Communication College" (USMCC), which is a glorious title for what we envisioned as a one-week seminar. But we also thought this could be the start of an ongoing network of knowledge sharing for anyone in the federal government who attended. We knew we would probably get some of it, maybe even a lot of it, wrong as we got underway. But we were willing to give it a try. We developed some initial guiding principles we wanted to leverage in creating and delivering this marketing training:

- **Pragmatism**—We would focus on practical applications rather than academic or theoretical. If you want to read about marketing, there are plenty of great books out there already. We wanted to make sure what we taught could be applied as soon as participants got back to their post anywhere in the world.

- **Real-World Examples**—This would be a considerable challenge since the only case studies we could cite would be based on the private sector rather than anything from the military or government. But we knew we'd need to have these "proof points" if our material would be meaningful and relevant to our "students."

- **Networking**—Given how rapidly the marketing world was changing, we wanted to ensure anyone who went through our initial training could stay in touch and learn from each other and from our faculty to solve some of the marketing challenges they were facing. We would create a private website to share all the materials we developed and use it as a place to showcase case studies and allow students to ask faculty members for help on a communication issue they were trying to solve.

Having created marketing training seminars at KFC and eBay, I knew something this ambitious would require a team effort, especially since we were working without a budget to hire any vendors to assist us. It was gratifying to have the marketing professionals I knew all volunteer to help without any compensation. There are numerous marketers who made significant contributions to teaching at USMCC over the years—some who joined from the beginning and some who joined later. But I wanted to take the opportunity to thank and recognize some of them:

Jim Nyce, one of the marketers at the initial White House meeting, volunteered to teach marketing research. Jim was a recognized leader in his field and had a 200+ person research team working for him at Kraft.

Norm Levy, the "godfather" of the internal consultants at P&G who created and taught the copy seminars I attended while I worked there. Norm was one of the country's leading experts in developing powerful communication strategies.

Gary Briggs, who was the head of marketing at Google, then Facebook, was happy to teach about marketing to youth, a critical target audience for the State Department.

Klon Kitchens, a former Special Ops member of the military and intelligence expert, and **Dale Cassidy,** an in-depth intelligence expert, stepped up to teach ways to better understand violent extremists and ways to counter their messaging.

Victoria Romero, practicing clinical psychologist, is an expert on child development and was a fantastic lecturer on various aspects of applying psychology to various marketing issues.

Nancy Zwiers, who I worked with at P&G and who went on to be the head of marketing at Mattel, was an expert in creativity and the value of play in educating youth.

Bob Pearson, a communications expert who worked for Michael Dell and created several successful marketing agencies, taught several USMCC courses on how technology was dramatically changing how marketing campaigns were developed, deployed, and evaluated.

Ed Tazzia, who was on the interview panel that hired me at P&G, deserves the most kudos for nurturing the USMCC program for almost an entire decade on a pure volunteer basis.

We held our first USMCC session in August of 2008 at the Foreign Service Institute (FSI) in Arlington, Virginia. The FSI is the main campus of the U.S. State Department. It offers a wide variety of courses, including an incredible number of language immersion courses—to note, you must learn the local language of your next post before going there if you work for the State Department.

We had about 40 students in our initial class. They came from various agencies in the federal government, including the State Department, U.S. AID—which is in charge of international development and disaster assistance to global markets—the National Counterterrorism Center, Department of Defense, and other US government agencies. They had extensive international experience, and many of them had flown back from their posts worldwide to attend this event.

In addition to our classroom exercises, we created some networking opportunities during the week to get to know the faculty better and meet other students. I was lucky enough to know some senior officials such as Betty Hudson at National Geographic. They were willing to host a reception for us, along with some private sector companies who helped pick up the tab for the catering. It might have been easier to do a lot of what we did if we had a budget, but if you don't have one, you learn to get creative and get others to pitch in for a good cause.

"Good But Not Great": Back to the Drawing Board

Our first attempt at creating the USMCC program was considered an overall success, but we knew we had a lot of room for improvement. Like I'd done with my other training programs, we had students fill out extensive evaluations at the end of every day on what they liked and what still needed work. We came away from that week with an incredible amount of student feedback and quickly realized this training program was even more challenging and complicated to implement than we originally thought.

Why? Here were the main concerns we had based on the student evaluations:

First, we didn't have a proven communication strategy model we could utilize. We knew a lot about marketing in the private sector. Still, none of us had any experience in dealing with the kind of issues the U.S. government, especially the State Department, was having to deal with every day.

A bad day for a marketer in the private sector is when your new marketing campaign doesn't deliver the sales you promised your boss. A bad day in the State Department is when one country threatens to go to war with another, or a terrorist group releases a horrific video on what they've done with captives, or a mob is rioting just outside your embassy.

Second, we didn't have any "real-world" examples our students could relate to. Most of them had spent their entire career in government. Share a case study about how Tide detergent utilized Facebook to reach homemakers, and then trying to connect it to countering Twitter campaigns from Al-Qaeda just didn't work. It was like trying to teach English to French students by speaking Mandarin—we got a lot of blank stares from students during our classes. They could not make the connection to the points we were trying to make without examples they could relate to—and it's easy now to see why they couldn't.

Third, we made a mistake in our first class sessions of getting sucked into policy discussion and debates, which went nowhere and confused and alienated some students. In other words, some of our students wanted to talk about the policies they thought were needed for "Brand USA." We stressed we were there to share marketing principles and strategies that could work for them, regardless of a particular U.S. policy. But we kept getting distracted by policy debates that erupted during class discussions.

Finally, we needed more senior management "air cover." By that, I mean there was a lot of feedback from our students that unless and until their boss believed in the importance of what we were teaching them, they would not be able to put it into action. Most of our students were in mid-level management positions—they had plenty of "on the ground" experience but hadn't reached a top role in government yet. They intuitively agreed with what we were teaching them but were skeptical it would make much of a difference unless they had support from their superiors.

Having worked on training programs before, we were somewhat discouraged with what we were dealing with, but based on the overall enthusiasm of our students and the faculty, we knew we could somehow figure this out. With our first attempt at creating USMCC, our faculty didn't appreciate just how dramatically different the private sector and federal agencies were. But now that we knew, we were determined to get to work and make our training program better based on all the valuable feedback we had received.

Eureka: A Communication Model as Simple as A-B-C-D-E

The most significant improvement we made was something Ed Tazzia eventually came up with. We were trying to figure out a model we could use to organize all our marketing principles. In class, we talked about audiences, goals, content, delivery channels, and how to evaluate it all. But how do you make all this simple enough to remember and use on an everyday basis?

When we shared this challenge with our students, one of them asked: "Why not try something straightforward to remember, like the first five letters of the alphabet?" Ed took that idea and ran with it. He came up with what we now call the "ABCDE Communication Model," and it's what's called a "strategic filter." All great learning models allow you to reflect on what you are doing, identify critical missing pieces, and show you how to get to where you want to go.

Here's the ABCDE Communication Model we used, based on what we had learned about creating communication strategies at Procter and Gamble:

Audience — Who is your message aimed at?

Behavioral objective — What do you want them to do?

Content — What is your communication strategy, including the benefits, the reason to believe, tone, and character?

Delivery — How do you plan to deliver your intended communication strategy—both the message itself and the communication channels you use?

Evaluation — How will you assess your campaign's impact?

We were enthusiastic about this model because it provided a robust process to ensure you think through all the critical elements of an effective communication strategy. At the same time, it is simple to explain and remember.

Best of all, it helped us bring to life the mantra we emphasized to all our students: *Strategy before execution.* Most marketing campaign creators, including those from State, confuse activity with intent. Ensure your strategy is developed first, then—and only then—should you focus on executing it well.

Now that we had a communication model we could base our teachings on, we went to work on the other problems we knew we had to solve.

Keeping It Real

Getting more "real-world" examples was fixable. We asked incoming new students to bring in some of the most challenging communication problems they were dealing with right now.

We turned these into "case studies," which teams of students would work on during the week and present to all of us on the last day of class. We also created a private website only accessible to students. They could use the private site to post their best practices and case studies worldwide and ask faculty members for help.

The policy discussion issue was the most manageable problem to fix. We just didn't allow it to happen after that first class. Before they arrived for the class, we told everyone that we were there to teach them how to become better professional communicators. We would leave the policy decisions to elected officials and others in government. We were there to teach how to do a better job in communicating new policies. We would leave the rest up to the policymakers. Policy debates never happened after that, at least not in our USMCC classroom.

The biggest challenge we faced was getting senior support for the program. This was especially challenging since priorities would change every time there was a change in the administration—starting with the President but extending to the Secretary of State and Under Secretary. We would begin to make inroads with critical leaders at the upper levels of State, and then "musical chairs" would happen, so we'd have to start all over again. We figured this would require equal parts of patience and persistence—and we were right.

A Long and Impactful Run

The good news is the USMCC program lasted eight years, which frankly was seven years longer than I initially thought it would. The pro bono USMCC program lasted for two administrations: G.W. Bush and Obama; three Secretaries of State: Rice, Clinton, and Kerry; and seven Under Secretaries of State for Public Diplomacy: Glassman, McHale, Stephens, Sonenshine, Stengel, Wharton, and Goldstein.

When the Trump administration took over in 2017, there were some dramatic changes at the State Department and Foreign Service Institute. We suddenly lost the critical support we'd had over the years to continue our training. So USMCC officially ended.

Looking back, we had an impressive run while it lasted, and we had trained enough people around the world that we hope what we shared will continue to work in U.S. embassies around the world for years to come.

As we wrapped up our pro bono public service initiative, we were proud of what we had accomplished. We had held a total of 13 one-week sessions over eight years, including two outside of Virginia: one in Hawaii and one in Brussels—where we had the U.S. Ambassador to Belgium as one of our students. We taught almost 900 diplomats and State Department personnel. The USMCC program got better every year, since we had more real-world case studies and became better at understanding our students and what they needed.

We received numerous emails over the years from our students who told us USMCC was some of the best training they had during their entire career—that was rewarding enough for our faculty. We developed an impressive number of case studies that were made accessible online that showed how the ABCDE communication model could make a real difference in the planning and execution of numerous programs worldwide. It was amazing how much time and effort our faculty was willing to contribute without any compensation other than our students' appreciation.

In addition, it's encouraging to note the State Department has come a long way in how they manage its communications programs. In 2016, they created a "Global Engagement Center" (GEC), which does an admirable job in coordinating efforts to recognize and counter disinformation campaigns by "bad actors." State has gotten much more sophisticated in how they develop, implement, and evaluate social media campaigns. These efforts take time and require considerable resources, but they are paying off in the field along with the efforts of our allies—and in coordinated opposition to countries that wish us ill.

Our admiration for the various teams at the State Department and other federal agencies has grown over the years. They work incredibly hard, many times in a challenging and sometimes dangerous work environment in countries other Americans are not even allowed to visit. They don't make anything close to the kind of money you can make in the private sector and must deal with a complex bureaucracy every day that would drive most of us in the private sector nuts in a short amount of time. They rarely get any public recognition—and when they do, it's probably more about their ambassador and not them.

The State Department is frequently accused of "wasting taxpayer dollars" on foreign aid and programs that are critical to helping our allies and keeping our enemies at bay. Most Americans claim they would rather spend money on the military and not diplomacy. But based on what the USMCC faculty have experienced by working with the State Department, it's the combination of diplomacy *and* military strength that makes a real difference in keeping the peace.

A personal outcome that came out of all my work with USMCC is I'd always wanted to write a book but wasn't quite sure what it should be about. As we were holding our final USMCC session, it occurred to me there was more than enough meaningful content to create a book based on all our work at USMCC. Bob Pearson, Ed Tazzia, and I then got together and wrote: *Crafting Persuasion: A Leader's Handbook to Change Minds and Influence Behavior.* We also created an interactive website to go along with it at www.craftingpersuasion.com.

Our book was published in 2019 and is available on Amazon and other leading book sites. We're pleased this book is now being used at a growing number of colleges, universities, and government agencies to train non-marketers on how to create and implement an effective communication strategy.

Valuable Lessons Learned

What are some ways to use it to advance the causes you believe in when it comes to education? Here are some ideas for you to consider:

- **Is there a process worth teaching?** If you reflect on everything you've ever learned in your life, it usually involves understanding and mastering a process that yields the desired result. For example, with a new language, you start with vocabulary, then grammar rules, then sentences, then move on to practicing dialogue. If you are learning to play golf, you start by learning the rules of golf, swinging different clubs, and then practicing on the range and golf course. If there is an existing process you can teach on something you're passionate about, then get going! If not, you might need to develop your process first. With USMCC, we created the ABCDE Communication Model and used it to teach non-marketers how to start thinking more strategically about their communication strategies and campaigns. Without this as a foundation, we would not have been successful.

- **Can you create a network of teachers?** If you want to educate a group on a particular topic or skill, there's very likely a group of individuals who would be delighted to join your cause. Think about all the problems and causes that could use your help, such as homelessness, drug abuse, and human trafficking. If you're passionate about doing something about issues such as this and other causes you care about, one of the best ways to make a difference is to find others who also want to contribute. If just one of us had wanted to help the State Department get better at teaching communication strategy and execution, it would not have worked. With a dozen communications experts teaching students, we were able to make a significant impact addressing this critical need over time.

- **Can you share examples with others to demonstrate your efforts are making a difference?** Once you have a proven process and a network of teachers willing to share their experience and expertise, the final and most critical action is for you to make sure your "target audience"—the people you want to reach—are shown it's worth the effort.

  That's easier to do today than ever before—your website and social media can be used for testimonials, case studies, shout-outs, and "real-world" examples to bring your efforts to life. Referring current students to former students who successfully used the ABCDE Communication Model to solve communication problems made a big difference in getting our ABCDE Communication process utilized as a "best practice" in embassies worldwide.

There's no lack of huge issues threatening all of us today—just watch the news to be reminded. While many of these challenges seem overwhelming, that's no excuse for not trying to make this world a better place. Don't wait around until you get an official title or permission—that's probably never going to happen—so get going and act!

It's amazing what you can achieve with a small, dedicated team like the one we had at the U.S. Marketing Communication College.

As Margaret Mead observed, "Never doubt that a small group of thoughtful committed citizens can change the world; indeed, it's the only thing that ever has."

> **CHAPTER FIFTEEN**
> **Helpfulness—A Marketer Goes to the White House**

REFLECTIVE QUESTIONS

- Who have been some of the influential teachers in your life? What did they do that made such an impact?

- What's the most challenging subject you ever had to learn? Did you eventually figure it out? What did you learn about yourself in the process?

- What are some of the most effective ways you like to teach someone? How do you like to learn?

- What causes or issues are you most concerned about? What are you doing to try to make a difference regarding this cause or issue? If you haven't done anything yet, what small steps could you undertake to get started?

LEAP INTO ACTION

We all have "teachable moments" in which we can help someone understand an issue better, solve a problem, or open their mind to new possibilities. When you get this opportunity, make the most of it. You never know just how consequential your teachings might be for that person—or for an entire country.

A MOMENT OF ZEN

Follow your passion and become a lifelong learner.

Do what you enjoy. I was so driven to get into leadership roles that I didn't get to have as many years doing the things that I enjoyed myself. I only coded for a small amount of time. I didn't lose my understanding of coding when I became a manager, but I missed what I left behind. I really liked it and sometimes think about what I could have created in the world if I had hacked more myself.

Read broadly and read deeply. Books are how you steal other people's wisdom and experiences. Go for what lights you up inside **AND** give everything you've got to make it work. Be open-minded with a keen sense of intellectual curiosity as each learning opportunity helps build the foundation of knowledge and confidence, which will make you more experienced and provide knowledge-based wisdom based on real-life learnings that you have accumulated and can lean on to guide you over time.

Pick learning opportunities over money when it comes to a new job. You should be willing to switch categories if the learning opportunity is greater.

How Great Managers Help Their People Leap

> *"Train people well enough so they can leave,*
> *treat them well enough so they don't want to."*
> —*Richard Branson*

A theme throughout this book has been the significant impact my managers had on me in positive and negative ways. My best managers gave me the courage and support to do what I would have initially thought would be extremely difficult or perhaps even impossible. My worst managers made me realize that the sooner I could get away from their negative energy and influence, the better.

So, for this final chapter of *Learn to Leap: How Leaders Turn Risk Into Opportunities*, I wanted to focus on what great managers do to help their people "leap" to reach their true potential.

Everyone Deserves a Coach

I love coaching marketing executives. It's what led me in 2018 to start a new business called CMO Coaches (www.cmocoaches.com). Our team of executive coaches is focused on helping marketing leaders get to the top of their profession. One of my motivations for starting CMO Coaches and writing this book is that it is the kind of support I needed when I was CMO at Taco Bell but wasn't readily available.

For many companies, their most valuable company asset goes home every night—and hopefully comes back the next day. Developing these employees to "be the best they can be" for many companies might seem to be a "nice when we have time to do this" kind of goal. That kind of thinking is flawed and short-sighted. If your employees are your most valuable assets, why in the world would you not invest in them on a regular basis?

Creating a robust process and culture that values serious reflection and continuous improvement for *all* employees is one of the most critical competitive advantages your company can develop.

Why aren't more companies investing in coaching and training their employees? My theory is they have lost sight of what this could mean for their company and their employees if they did this well. In a perfect world, companies would recognize the value coaches and mentors have in bringing out the best in all levels of employees. Here's why companies need to significantly increase their investments and efforts in training and coaching *all* their employees.

The Value of Training and Coaching Employees

I was lucky enough to start the first half of my career at two of the best companies on the planet, P&G and PepsiCo. What they sometimes lacked in agility they offset with other core capabilities. One of those areas of competitive advantage honed over the years was helping their employees figure out their career development plans and who should be responsible for what when. Then they made sure you had the resources and support to turn your development plan into a reality.

These companies helped me develop my game plan to grow as a business leader and execute it. They made sure I knew my success and growth were important to them. In short, they invested in me and put their money on what they said was most valuable to them—their employees.

P&G has a simple philosophy in how you become a strong business leader. You just have to worry about two things—*your results and your people.* The tricky bit was getting them both right *at the same time.* If you crushed your numbers but crushed your team at the same time to get your results, you were a short-term leader—and likely a soon-to-be former employee. If your team loves you, but your business results sucked, you were also going to be shown the door.

Getting the results needed to grow the business while growing the capability of your team *at the same time* was a constant challenge—as it is for any start-up, but even more so. So how can a company achieve this critical balance in today's ever-changing business environment?

My "Ah-Ha" Moment

As I progressed in my career, I had the privilege of working in various companies in several categories in different countries and cultures around the world. I've enjoyed managing a number of leaders and teams over the years—ranging from a team of one to managing over 80,000 employees when I was president of H&R Block Retail in the U.S. I wanted them to remember me as one of their managers they were delighted to have as a boss and know that a high personal priority for me was to help them grow professionally.

As I look back over my 40-year career on what it was like to manage so many people and reflecting on what I was taught about managing people, I've come to realize there are just five insightful questions all employers—especially start-ups—should discuss with their employees regularly.

These questions should be positioned in a way that enables the employee to learn something insightful and valuable about themself, rather than just telling them what they should think or do. Here are the five questions worth asking regularly:

1. **APPRECIATION:** *What do we appreciate about you?*

   This question might sound either a bit obvious or perhaps even unnecessary. But it's critical to regularly ask and answer this question with each of your direct reports. Think about it: you or someone hired them because they would contribute something unique and valuable to your business. Perhaps it was his or her attention to detail. Or knowledge of a particular topic. Or the way he or she collaborates with others.

   Whatever it was and hopefully still is, a manager should ask and answer this question to give their employees positive feedback on what the company appreciates about them as part of their ongoing development plan. It costs you nothing and reminds them of what makes them valuable to your team. Trust me—your employees won't get tired of hearing this kind of positive feedback —chances are they are starving for it.

2. **SELF-IMPROVEMENT:** *What have you done to improve yourself, and what have you learned about yourself over the past year?*

   School isn't out for the summer, or any other time of the year, when it comes to someone's personal career development. As their fearless leader, you should be challenging your employees to continually "raise the bar" on their performance and reflect upon what they have learned about their capabilities and potential over the past year.

3. **OPPORTUNITY:** *What could you have done better in the past year? Why?*

It doesn't matter how great a year they had—or lousy, for that matter. There is always the opportunity to learn from successes and failures. In my experience, failures seem to be a lot more instructive, so encourage them to seriously examine what they learned from their mistakes. You should also encourage your employees to be comfortable and vulnerable enough with you to recognize their own missed opportunities and what they would do differently next time if given a chance—as well as being able to explain why.

4. **VISUALIZATION:** *Where do you see yourself in 12 months and in five years? Why?*

Asking this question can yield some very valuable insights with your employee, such as: Is there alignment between what you *think* they are capable of compared to what they *want* to achieve? Are they being appropriately ambitious, or perhaps too ambitious, with their career goals? Does what they are doing now compared to what they want to be doing in the future make sense in terms of their planned career progression?

5. **ASSISTANCE:** *What can I do to help you develop yourself to your full potential?*

If an employee fails, it is not just the fault of the employee. Some, if not a lot of the blame, falls squarely on their manager. As their manager, you must let your employees know you believe in them and want them to succeed. You should be their "North Star" and continue to believe in them, even at times when they don't believe in themselves. If you're not willing to do this, ask yourself if you want to be in the people development business at all.

Well, What Are You Waiting For?

That's it. Five simple questions to help your direct reports grow in their business career and personal development—fundamental questions about appreciation, self-improvement, opportunity, visualization, and assistance. Don't take my word for it that this process works—prove it to yourself.

Ask these five questions to a single employee at their next annual review. Better yet, don't even wait for that—*schedule this conversation with one of your direct reports before the end of this month.* Give them the five questions to think about in advance and be sure to set up enough time to have a meaningful conversation with them on each question. If you are an "individual contributor" with no direct reports, share these questions with your manager in advance and set up a time to have an in-depth discussion with her or him.

This initial conversation will show you why this is a critical conversation ALL your managers need to have with ALL employees on a regular basis. These conversations open up all kinds of future possibilities for your employees to grow in ways never imagined.

This should lead to a thoughtful conversation about the employee's career development plan. Maybe they want to sign up for a training course. Or a new assignment to stretch them. Maybe it's time to consider getting them a coach or mentor.

Whatever it is, the manager should understand what their direct reports are asking for and why it will help them advance their career. By listening and responding to what their employees need for their own career development, a company can decrease employee turnover, enhance their management bench, and create a significant competitive edge over their competition.

Today Is Your Time to Leap

I hope you've enjoyed my stories and trust there are some nuggets of wisdom that can help you in your life and career now and in the future. If you take just one thought away from this book, recognize the importance of taking a chance on opportunities that come your way.

One of my favorite passages from great speeches are the closing lines of John F. Kennedy's inaugural address: "With a good conscience our only sure reward, with history the final judge of our deeds, let us go forth to lead the land we love, with His blessing and His help, but knowing that here on earth, God's work must truly be our own."

Life is short; careers are even shorter. It's time for you to take that leap into the great unknown with the confidence of knowing that doing so will make you a better person and perhaps maybe even make this world a better place. Your willingness to turn that risk into a fantastic opportunity can make a huge difference in your life and the lives of so many others.

As you've read in this book, taking a "leap of faith" has worked for me on numerous occasions. I know it can for you as well. Here's wishing you exceptional and satisfying "leaps" throughout your career and life.

Acknowledgments

This book has been a tremendous collaborative effort. Many of my friends and colleagues made many significant contributions in so many ways, which I greatly appreciate. I'd like to thank them for all their generous help and suggestions.

I've been fortunate to have had some incredible bosses during my career—some mentioned in this book—who I've learned a great deal from. I've tried to include some of their wisdom in this book, including Mike Lanning, Margo Ross, Rob Malcolm, Ross Love, Vandy Van Wagener, Mark Upson, Bill Encherman, John Lilly, Colin Moore, Peter Hearl, Peter Waller, Dwight Riskey, Jeff Jordan, Don Butler, and especially Bill Cobb. Bill was my boss for two decades (at Yum! Brands, eBay, and H&R Block) and an incredible leader and coach.

I've got a fantastic group of fellow coaches I'm working with at CMO Coaches, who significantly helped contribute to my thinking, including Alan Gellman, Carilu Dietrich, Susan Wayne, Nancy Zwiers, Bob Pearson, Mike Linton, Gary Briggs, and Jennifer Leuer.

Many of my friends contributed to the "Moment of Zen" at the end of each chapter and provided plenty of helpful feedback on my drafts. I could have written an entire book on the wisdom they offered. A big thank you to Peter Hearl, Dave Wallinga, Dana Robert, Bob Lustig, Lynette Christensen, John Lilly, Gary Briggs, Richard Haasnoot,

Nancy Zwiers, Westley Koenen, Tom Gerke, Vance Caesar, Maynard Webb, Alan Gellman, Francisco Morales, Rob Malcolm, Betsy McLaughlin, Cliff Marks, Sandy Climan, Tim Scott, Harry Kangis, Mike Ribero, Jennifer Leuer, Jeff Burrill, Ed Tazzia, Bill Cobb, Susan Wayne, Rob Chesnut, Mike Linton, John Pain, Kari McNamara, Peter Waller, Mike Lanning, Klon Kitchen, Paul Fletcher, Ash Iyer, Stephen Parkford and Guy Kawasaki.

I'd like to especially thank Marlena Medford for her tireless work on editing this book with me and giving me the right creative nudges when I needed them—and a shout-out to Dan O'Brien, who did a great job organizing the initial content. I'd also like to thank several of my friends who provided detailed feedback on my initial chapters, including Richard Haasnoot and Karl-Eric Briere.

A manuscript doesn't become a book unless you've got a great team to do their magic. I'd like to thank the team at 1845 Publishing for all their hard work, including Bob Pearson, Tamara Dever, Monica Thomas and Misti Moyer. Kudos to Katie Rhead as well for her initial creative artwork.

My biggest thanks go to my family for making many contributions to this book, including my wife Peggy, my sons Tom and Chris, my parents Margaret and Delos, and my siblings Kevin, Anne, and Tim— with a big shoutout to my Dad and Tim for great initial edits.

About the Author Kip Knight

Kip Knight is Operating Partner at Thomvest Ventures, a venture capital firm based in San Francisco. He's also the founder of CMO Coaches (www.cmocoaches.com), a coaching network that works with current and emerging marketing leaders. He co-authored his first book—*Crafting Persuasion: The Leader's Handbook to Change Minds and Influence Behavior*—with Ed Tazzia and Bob Pearson.

Kip has served in a variety of marketing and senior management roles at Procter & Gamble, PepsiCo, Yum! Brands, eBay, and H&R Block. He is the founder of the U.S. Marketing Communication College (USMCC), a pro bono organization which has trained hundreds of diplomats from the U.S. State Department in communication strategy. His work has enabled him to work in over 60 countries around the world.

Kip splits his time between Orange County and the Bay Area in California with his wife, Peggy. They have two sons, Tom and Chris, and are the proud grandparents of two grandchildren.

If you would like to learn more about working with
CMO Coaches, visit our website at
www.cmocoaches.com.